DUE

**WITHDRAWN
UTSA Libraries**

Small Cities in Transition: The Dynamics of Growth and Decline

Small Cities in Transition: The Dynamics of Growth and Decline

Edited by

Herrington J. Bryce
Vice President, Academy for Contemporary
Problems, formerly Director of
Research, Joint Center for
Political Studies

A Joint Center for Political Studies book
published by
Ballinger Publishing Company • Cambridge, Massachusetts
A Subsidiary of J.B. Lippincott Company

 This book is printed on recycled paper.

Copyright © 1977 by Joint Center for Political Studies. All rights reserved. No part of this publication may be reproduced, stored in a retrieval system, or transmitted in any form or by any means, electronic mechanical photocopy, recording or otherwise, without the prior written consent of the publisher.

International Standard Book Number: 0-88410-473-7

Library of Congress Catalog Card Number: 77-9629

Printed in the United States of America

Library of Congress Cataloging in Publication Data

Forum on Problems of Small Cities, Washington, D.C., 1976.
   Small cities in transition.

   Conference was sponsored by the Joint Center for Political Studies.
   1. Cities and towns—United States—Congresses. I. Bryce, Herrington J. II. Joint Center for Political Studies. III. Title.
HT123.F7   1976   301.36'3'0973   77-9629
ISBN 0-88410-473-7

Contents

List of Figures	xiii
List of Tables	xv
Foreword	xxi
Preface	xxiii
Introduction: Statement of the Problem *William Alonso, Howard Lee, A.J. Cooper,* *Doris Davis,* and *Jessie Rattley*	1
Part I *Population Growth, Decline and Policies*	11
Chapter One **Recent Trends in City Population Growth** **and Distribution** *Glenn Fuguitt* and *Calvin Beale*	13
Number and Population Size of Incorporated Cities	14
The Growth of Cities	16
City Growth and Annexation	19
Implications of Post-1970 Trends	24

Chapter Two
Characteristics of Growing and Declining Cities
Herrington J. Bryce   29

Methodology	30
Rates of Population Growth, Region, and Relative Size	30
Race and Population Growth	37
Housing and the Age of Cities	41
Per Capita Income	41
A Paradigm of Decline	43

Part II
Migration and Population Policies   49

Chapter Three
Government's Role in Population Movement: Policy by Indirection
Norman Beckman   51

How Does Government Influence Population Movement?	51
State Efforts to Protect or Support Their Communities	57
Legal Questions and the Courts	61
New Policy Options for Dealing with Community Growth and Decline	64

Chapter Four
Black Residential Clusters in the Suburban Ring
Harold Rose   73

Targets of Black Population Growth in Non-Central City Locations	74
The Rush to Suburbia	75
A Comparison of the Older and Newer Black Suburban Ring Communities	78
Black Ring Movers—Where Do They Originate?	79
Racial Dispersion in Suburban Ring Environments	80
Differences in Rate of Suburbanization	81
Social Rank and the Housing Environment	83
Economic Security and the Suburban Environment	86

Psychological Security and Black Suburbanization	89
Emerging Residential Patterns and the Quality of Life	92

Part III
Economic Growth and Decline   93

Chapter Five
The Urban Development Process
Wilbur Thompson   95

Current Trends	95
Growth Industries Make Growth Areas	96
From Multipliers to Migration	99
City Size and Innovation	102
Disequilibrating Growth: Rapid Change Induces More Change	104
Equilibrating Growth: Rapid Change Restrains Further Change	106
City Size as a Restraining Force: Households and the Quality of the Environment	107
City Size as a Restraining Force: Falling Skills, Rising Costs, and "Industrial Filtering"	109
The Process of City Building Is Alive and Well	111

Chapter Six
Changes in Manufacturing and Retailing Employment in Medium-Size Cities
Seymour Sacks   113

The Medium-Size City Defined	113
The Influence of World War II	115
Economic Activity—Population Growth	117
The Regional Pattern	131
Manufacturing and Retailing	144
Conclusions	150

Part IV
Economic Characteristics of Small Cities   153

Chapter Seven
The Relevance of City Size
David Puryear   155

Diversification and Urban Size 155
Efficiency and Urban Size 158
The Costs of Urban Size 161
An Open Question Still 166

Chapter Eight
Fiscal Problems of Smaller Growing and Declining Cities
Thomas Muller 167

General Characteristics of Growing and Declining Cities 167
Fiscal Characteristics of Growing and Declining Cities 169
Density and Costs 172
Why Do Some Cities Grow, Others Decline? 175
Coping with Growth and Decline 178
Findings 184

Part V
Federal Impact on Cities 187

Chapter Nine
Cities: Their Increasing Dependence on State and Federal Aid
John Shannon and *John Ross* 189

Municipal Dependency and Its Growth Within the State-Local Fiscal System 190
Municipal Dependency and Its Growth by City Size Class 194
Municipal Dependency and Its Growth Among the Various States 196
Policy Implications 206
A New Approach Is Necessary 208

Chapter Ten
The Urban Impact of Federal Policies: Their Direct and Indirect Effects on the Local Public Sector
Stephen Barro 213

Federal Urban Policy—An Overview 213
Examining the Effects of Federal Action 215

The Urban Economy as a Three-Sector System	216
The Federal Government and the Local Public Sector	223
Federal Policy Impacts	238
Implications for Federal Policy Development	241

Chapter Eleven
Federal Aid for Cities: A Multiple Strategy
Richard P. Nathan and *Paul R. Dommel* — 245

Framework for Analysis	245
Urban Aid and Political Imperatives	247
Defining Urban Need	252
Aid to Neediest Cities	256
Targeting Urban Aid: Transfer Payments	258
A Multiple Strategy	262

Part VI
The Metropolitan Setting and the Future of Small Cities — 265

Chapter Twelve
The Coming Age of the Polynucleated Metropolis
Werner Z. Hirsch — 267

The Suburban Framework	267
Industrial Location Patterns	269
Residential Settlement Patterns	270
Demographic Considerations	270
Housing and Transportation Costs	273
Government Activities	275
The Emerging Pattern: Polynucleated Urban Areas	277
Some Concluding Thoughts	281

Chapter Thirteen
Transformation of the Nation's Urban System: Small City Growth as a Zero-Sum Game
Brian Berry — 283

A National Society	283
The Nation's Urban System: Classical Patterns	287
Urban-Regional Growth and Decline: New Directions	290

Theories of the Growth Transition	295
Solvents for Metropolitan Glue	298

Chapter Fourteen
The Future of Suburban Cities and Their Black Populations
Phillip Clay — 301

The Shape of Metropolitan Areas	301
The Suburban Crisis	305
Demographic Trends	305

Part VII
Conclusions: Planning for the Future — 313

Chapter Fifteen
Planning the Needs of Small Cities
Herrington J. Bryce, Gloria Cousar, and Stephanie Fain — 315

Planning Background	315
Definition of Planning and Planning Needs	317
Methodology	318
Findings	319
Priorities	324

Chapter Sixteen
Summing Up: Adjustment to Growth and Decline, Population Size and Production Diversification
Herrington J. Bryce — 331

Local Control	332
Geographic Region and Policy	333
Size and Diversification	333
The Model and Data	334
The Results	335

Epilogue — 337

1: A Note on Variations in Leading Streams of Migration to the Washington, D.C. Metropolitan Area
Vera J. Banks — 339

2: City Employment and Economic Development
Carolyn Shaw Bell   343

3: A Fourth Stage in Our National Development?
Ralph R. Widner   347

4: The Urban Fiscal Dilemma
Ransford W. Palmer   351

5: Urban Governments and Economic Policies
Selma J. Mushkin   353

6: Federal Programs to Assist the Cities
George E. Peterson   359

7: The Borrowing Costs of Small City Borrowers
John E. Petersen   365

8: The Metropolitan Future: Accidental or Designed?
James L. Sundquist   369

9: Local Economic Development Policy
Benjamin Chinitz   373

10: The Future of Small Communities
Ann C. Macaluso   377

Notes   381

Index   397

About the Authors   413

List of Figures

2-1	Percentage of Population Distribution, by Regions	33
4-1	Older Black Suburban Ring Colonies	75
5-1	Synthesis of Disequilibrating Expansionary and Equilibrating Dampening Forces	100
6-1	Year of Maximum Manufacturing Employment	146
6-2	Manufacturing Employment by City: Changes in Employment, Successive Censuses	148
6-3	Retailing Employment by City: Changes in Employment, Successive Censuses	149
9-1	Growth in Dependency by City Size Class, 1962-1975	197
10-1	Schematic Diagram of the Three-Sector Approach to Urban Impact Analysis	218
10-2	Federal Policy Impacts on the Local Public Sector	239
11-1	The Three Equity Concepts	246
11-2	Formula for Indexing Community Hardship	258
12-1	Factors Affecting Spatial Settlement Patterns	268
12-2	Labor Force Participation over a Working Life of Cohorts of Women Born in Selected Time Intervals, 1886-1955	273

List of Tables

1-1	Number and Population of Incorporated Cities, by Size, U.S., 1950-1970	15
1-2	Percent Change of Incorporated Cities, by Initial Size, Metropolitan and Nonmetropolitan, 1950-60 and 1960-70	16
1-3	Ratio of Category Change with Total Population Change, Metropolitan and Nonmetropolitan Incorporated Cities, by Initial Size, U.S., 1950-60 and 1960-70	17
1-4	Percent Change of Incorporated Cities, by Initial Size and Metropolitan and Nonmetropolitan Groupings, U.S., 1950-60 and 1960-70	18
1-5	Percent Change of Incoporated Cities, by Initial Size and Region, U.S., 1950-60 and 1960-70	20
1-6	Percent of Places Annexing, by Initial Size, Metropolitan Status, Region, and Decade, U.S., 1950-60 and 1960-70	22
1-7	Number of People per Annexing Place, by Initial Size, Metropolitan Status, Region, and Decade, U.S., 1950-60 and 1960-70	23
1-8	Annual Rates of Population Change and Net Migration, by County Location Groups, U.S., 1950-60, 1960-70, and 1970-75	25

List of Tables

1-9	Percent Change and Distribution of Total Population, by Metropolitan and Nonmetropolitan Location Groups, 1950-70, with Projection to 1980	26
2-1	Percent Change in Population (1960-70) for Fastest Growing and Declining Cities	31
2-2	Growth Rates of Cities and Counties, and City Population as Percent of County's (1970)	34
2-3	Percent Employed Outside County of Residence for Fastest Growing and Declining Cities, 1970	36
2-4	Percentage of Population Attaining Four Years of High School or More for Fastest Growing and Declining Cities, 1970	38
2-5	Percent Black Population for Fastest Growing and Declining Cities, 1970	40
2-6	Percent Employed in Manufacturing (1970) for Fastest Growing and Declining Cities	42
2-7	Percent of 1970 Housing Units Built Prior to 1950 for Fastest Growing and Declining Cities	44
2-8	Per Capita Income for Fastest Growing and Declining Cities	45
4-1	Primary Suburban Ring Destinations of Black Migrants, 1960-70	76
4-2	Secondary Suburban Ring Destinations of Black Mirgrants, 1960-70	76
4-3	New Construction and Vacancies as a Percent of Total Housing Stock	85
4-4	A Comparison of the Economic Security Ranking and Socioeconomic Status Ranking of Black Populations in 15 Suburban Communities of Recent Entry	88
6-1	City Population Characteristics	118
6-2	Manufacturing and Retailing Employment, 1939 and 1947	122
6-3	Employment Characteristics, 1947	124
6-4	Manufacturing Employment, 1947	128
6-5	Manufacturing Employment Growth Rates	131
6-6	Employment Characteristics, 1972	132
6-7	Manufacturing Employment, 1972	134
6-8	Manufacturing and Retailing Employment as a Percent of Population, 1947 and 1972	137
6-9	Changes in City Employment, Population, and Area, 1947-1972	139

6-10	Percent Change in City Employment, Population, and Area, 1947-1972	141
8-1	Growing and Declining Cities, by Size and Region, 1970-71	168
8-2	Service Outlays, Municipal Wages, Employment, and Income as a Function of City Size	170
8-3	Characteristics of Selected Cities	171
8-4	Growing and Declining Cities with 50-200,000 Population	172
8-5	Growing and Declining Cities with 200,000 to 500,000 Population, 1970	173
9-1	Per Capita Expenditures, Per Capita Aid, and Dependency, by Jurisdictional Type—1962, 1975, and Growth, 1962-75	191
9-2	General Purpose Local Government Dependent on State and Federal Aid—1962, 1975, and Growth, 1962-75	193
9-3	Per Capita Expenditure, Per Capita Aid, and Dependency, by City Population Size Class—1962, 1975, and Growth, 1962-75	195
9-4	Municipal Dependency on State and Federal Aid—1962, 1975, and Growth, 1962-75, by City Size Class	196
9-5	Municipal Dependency, by Size Class, on General Revenue Sharing, 1975	198
9-6	Municipal Dependency on State and Federal Aid, by State, 1975	199
9-7	Growth in Municipal Dependency on State and Federal Aid, by State, 1962-75	202
9-8	The Correlation of Municipal Dependency on State Aid with Municipal Dependency on Federal Aid	205
9-9	Municipal Hardship Index, Dependency on Federal Aid, and Dependency on General Revenue Sharing, 1975	207
9-10	Municipal Hardship and Municipal Dependency on Federal Aid, 1975	209
9-11	Public Welfare Circuit-Breaker Plan	210
10-1	Major Determinants of Outcomes in the Three Sectors of the Urban Economy	220
11-1	Folded-in Grant Distributions Compared with Projected 1980 Allocation of CDBG Funds Within Metropolitan Areas	250

xviii List of Tables

11-2	Folded-in Grant Distributions Compared with Projected 1980 Allocation of CDBG Funds Among Central Cities, by Region	251
11-3	Indices of Overcrowded Housing, Poverty, and Extent of Pre-1939 Housing, by Region and Community Type	253
11-4	Comparison of Projected CDBG Grants to Metropolitan Areas for Fiscal 1980 with Allocations Under an Alternative Formula Equally Weighting Population, Poverty, and Pre-1939 Housing	254
11-5	Comparison of Formula Allocations to Metropolitan Areas Under the CDBG Formula and the Dual Formula Alternatives	255
11-6	Growing and Declining Cities in the CDBG Program During the Period 1960-70, Showing Black Population, Per Capita Income, and Median Housing Values and Rates of Change	257
11-7	Percent of Persons in Poverty Status, 1974	259
11-8	Percent Central County Population Receiving Welfare Payments, Selected Cities and Central City Hardship Rankings	260
11-9	Welfare Burden, by State, NA=.76	261
12-1	Median Family Income, With and Without Working Wives	274
12-2	Proportion of New Dwelling Units Outside Six Central Cities, 1960-70	275
14-1	1960 and 1970 Black Suburban Population and Concentration of Blacks in Major Suburban Cities of Selected SMSAs	306
14-2	Trends in Relative Value of Owner-Occupied Homes Among Selected Suburban Cities in Selected SMSAs, 1960-1970	307
14-3	General Characteristics of Metropolitan Population, by Race and Place, 1960-70	309
14-4	Comparison of Selected Housing Variables, by Race, in Areas Outside the South, 1970	310
14-5	Comparison of Housing Units Occupied by Blacks in the Central City vs. the Suburbs, Outside the South, 1970	311
15-1	Distribution of Common Planning Needs in Small Cities, by Size	320
15-2	Distribution of Common Planning Needs in	

	Small Cities, by Region and Metropolitan Status	321
15-3	Distribution of Common Planning Needs in Small Cities, by Percentage 1960-70 Population Change and Metropolitan Status	323
15-4	Distribution of Common Planning Needs in Small Cities, by Percentage Housing Built Prior to 1950 and Metropolitan Status	325
15-5	Distribution of Common Planning Needs in Small Cities, by Percentage of Persons Below 1970 Poverty Income Level and Metropolitan Status	327
15-6	First Priority Planning Needs in Small Cities, by Size	328
15-7	First Priority Planning Needs in Small Cities, by Region	329
15-8	First Priority Planning Needs in Small Cities, by Percentage 1960-70 Population Change	329
16-1	The Impact of the Current Economic Crisis on Small and Medium-Size Cities	333

Foreword

The problems of America's cities have been, especially in recent years, a focal point of concern by the public and by policy analysts. Contrary to the assertions of former President Richard Nixon, the urban crisis continues, and although we have been aided by extensive recent social science research in understanding the dimensions of that crisis, several important issues remain inadequately examined. It is clear, for example, that the specific problems of cities vary widely and that efforts at all levels of government to deal with these problems must be more sensitive to these differences.

It is also becoming increasingly apparent that size is an important factor in determining the kinds of problems cities face. The large older cities of the Northeast and North Central regions, for example, have a vastly different array of problems from those of the small southern and midwestern cities. Furthermore, the capacity of small cities for service delivery and for utilization of some federal assistance programs is extremely limited. Often the needs and limitations of these smaller cities are overlooked in the development of federal assistance programs for cities. These are among the considerations that prompted the Joint Center for Political Studies to conduct a special review and analysis of the problems of small cities.

Our study took the form of a forum in our ongoing Public Policy Program. Smaller cities, especially those in the South and Midwest, contain a large percentage of the nation's black population and black elected public officials. Thus, the Forum on Problems of Small Cities was designed to uncover the special needs of these jurisdictions while at the same time focusing greater attention on the problems faced by blacks outside the metropolis.

The papers presented in this volume were prepared originally for JCPS and were discussed in detail at the Forum. They reflect our hope for the development of long range and timely measures for balancing the consequences of urban growth and for reversing patterns of decline. Both identifying and responding to the needs of small cities represent a major challenge to our vast technology of urban management.

We are grateful to the scholars and public officials who shared their knowledge with us, and to Herrington J. Bryce, formerly Joint Center Research Director, and his staff, who planned and coordinated the Forum on Problems of Small Cities.

Eddie N. Williams, *President*
Joint Center for Political Studies

Preface

While we focused on the plight of large cities, smaller cities, as a rule, have grown by leaps and bounds. Aside from this general picture, however, numerous small cities remain stagnant and many continue to decline. Hence, among smaller cities, there are also problems of growth, decline, and stagnation. What is the future of the smaller city? What are the problems attendant to their growth and decline? What are the solutions? What is the role of small cities in the system of cities? If there is a fundamental assumption of this book it is that we cannot look at small cities in isolation from large cities. We cannot understand one without understanding the other.

On December 20, 1976, the Joint Center for Political Studies, through a grant from the Ford Foundation and research aid of the National Science Foundation, held a conference that addressed the problems of growth and decline of smaller cities. The conference also dealt with such issues as the future of the smaller city in our system of cities, the planning needs of smaller cities, and the role of federal and state aid in meeting the financial necessities of these cities. This volume is the product of the conference.

The introduction is based on a panel discussion among a leading regional economist (William Alonso from Harvard), two mayors of declining small cities (A.J. Cooper and Doris Davis), and a former mayor and a council member of two rapidly growing cities (Howard Lee and Jesse Rattley). They outline some of the major problems of smaller cities.

In Part I, Calvin Beale and Glen Fuguitt look at growth trends.

They compare the growth rates of places with populations of 2500 and over for two decades. They also project growth rates for these places for the next decade and look at the roles of annexation and metropolitan status in determining differential growth rates. They find that cities with populations of 25 to 50 thousand grew at a much faster pace than the nation as a whole. The socioeconomic differences of growing and declining cities within this size class are then examined by Herrington J. Bryce: How do growth cities differ from declining cities?

In Part II, Norman Beckman looks at the roles of federal and state governments in determining the differing growth rates among cities. He closes with a discussion of some court cases that affect population growth and distribution. One item of that policy relates specifically to exclusionary zoning. To what extent are blacks represented in the flow to suburbia? Many blacks who live in suburbia live in black enclaves or clusters, some of which are in transition. Harold Rose examines the quality and process of development of these clusters.

Turning from population to economic change in Part III, Wilbur Thompson discusses the process of economic growth and decline as related to industrial location, changes in employment, and technological diffusion. He addresses the issue of the economic future of small cities. The future of cities is frequently defined in terms of changes in employment in the manufacturing and retailing sectors. The second paper in Part III, written by Seymour Sacks, analyzes changes in employment in these sectors since World War II and concludes that region and age are more important in determining growth than size.

In Part IV, David Puryear looks at the importance of city size and concludes from an analysis of the literature that size is important in determining industrial diversification and efficiency. Thomas Muller analyzes the economic adjustment problems that growing smaller and medium size cities have and their fiscal capacity to make these adjustments.

One of the ways in which cities have adjusted to change and, indeed, one of the major causes of the regional disparities in growth rates is believed to be federal expenditure policies. John Shannon and John Ross, in Part V, demonstrate that small cities are not exempt from this growing dependence on federal and state aid. This is followed by an assessment by Stephen Barro of various federal policies and the way they affect local economic growth. The Community Development Block Grant is a major source of federal assistance to small as well as large cities for the purpose of development. Richard Nathan and Paul Dommel show the inequities associated with region, city size, and economic status, and suggest an alternative formula for dealing with this problem.

The distribution of federal funds as noted by Nathan and Dommel are factors that determine the gestalt of our metropolitan systems. In Part VI, Werner Hirsch looks at the future of our metropolitan system and the role of the smaller city in that system, given the trends alluded to earlier. This is followed by Brian Berry's suggestion that because of numerous developments, the economic interaction among cities will change. He discusses the role of smaller cities in this new system of cities. Phillip Clay discusses the components of the metropolitan setting and compares the process of central city decline with developments in older suburban cities.

As smaller cities adjust to change, use more federal funds, and prepare for their futures, planning will play an important role. Part VII is based on an original questionnaire sent to 500 small cities. Herrington J. Bryce, Gloria Cousar and Stephanie Fain assess the planning needs and distinguish between the needs of growing and declining small cities.

I want to thank a number of individuals for their contributions to this effort. First, I wish to thank my family for its patience and counsel. Dolores Wainwright had the major administrative responsibilities for the conference. Ellen Scudder assisted in the conference and pulled together Chapter One, based upon the luncheon discussion. Kenneth Dobson, Louis Blair, Yvonne Perry, Robert Weaver, Emmet Moten, Melvin Mister, Joel Bergsman, and Nampeo McKinney were discussants of various papers at the symposium. Robertino Bryce-LaPorte, Elvira Bright, Shanti Duncan, Barbara Taylor, Amelia Walker, Lorenzo Merritt, and Yvonne Wooten were extremely helpful at the conference. Aura Rapton and Barbara Buhl helped in the final stages of this book.

I would also like to thank the Academy for Contemporary Problems for permitting me the time to complete this volume.

Herrington J. Bryce
(1977)

Introduction

Introduction: Statement of the Problem

William Alonso, Howard Lee, A.J. Cooper,
Doris Davis, and Jessie Rattley

Editor's Note: This is the record of a discussion among a leading regional economist (William Alonso), two mayors of declining cities (A.J. Cooper and Doris Davis), a former mayor of a rapidly growing city (Howard Lee), and a city council member (Jesse Rattley). Many of the problems they discuss are the focus of this book.

Lee: Why has attention suddenly turned to the problems of small cities? I think four reasons stand out. First, there has been a sudden shift in migration trends. In the past, people moved out of the small town and into the big city. Now, it appears that exactly the opposite is the case. Since 1970, the smaller cities have seen rapid growth, at the expense of larger ones. The second reason is that there is, increasingly, an awareness of a need to anticipate the problems that spin off from growth. Third, I think, is the increasing numbers of black mayors of small cities and the attention they have called to the problems of small cities. Finally, the problems of big cities have encouraged many people to consider the option of small city development as a way to relieve the pressure on the urban metropolis.

Davis: In my opinion, one of the major problems, in terms of public policy, is the absence in most federal aid legislation, of a formula which accounts for proportionate need. Programs such as General Revenue Sharing do not take this need factor into full consideration.

Rattley: The problems of Newport News may not seem as dire as the problems of Detroit, because Newport News is comprised of only 140,000 people. The fact is, however, the problems are a very serious concern to those of us who live there. While it is the big city mayor who commands the attention of high level administration officials, the fact is that most people in this country live in the cities with population under 500,000. Small city mayors seldom get to bring their problems directly to the administration; we have to do it in conjunction with the National League of Cities.

Cooper: I think we must first agree on the definition of a small city. I find it difficult to accept cities with population of 150,000, 250,000, or 500,000 as small cities. Small cities are just that: small, with populations of 500, 1000, 15,000, 25,000 or 50,000 people. We ought to talk about what differentiates small cities from big ones.

What do small cities need? First, they need planning (comprehensive planning). Second, they need the hardware to get things done, and they need technicians. But that requires money. Small cities can't afford to buy the pipes for a sewage system, nor can they afford to pay the salary of the civil engineer who designs and builds it. We lack professionals to attract an industrial tax base.

Small cities have a difficult time lobbying effectively because they are victims of a political bias that operates against them. Small cities are underrepresented—if represented at all—within the leading organizations which represent locally elected officials. To qualify for Comprehensive Employment and Training Act (CETA) funds, smaller cities must become part of a consortium revolving around a large one—primarily to lessen the paperwork for Washington bureaucrats.

In order to become eligible for counter-cyclical assistance under the Public Works Assistance Act, small cities must submit labor statistics based on the CETA consortium. We have found that our statistics have often been reported inaccurately and they can't be corrected. The Law Enforcement Assistance Administration renders cities smaller than 100,000 ineligible for aid. These are some of the things I think we have to change for small towns. We are going to have to do it through the trade associations, state municipal associations, or county organizations.

Large cities must become more responsive to the needs of the small ones. As small cities continue to organize and structure their interests (witness the Southern Conference of Black Mayors, representing 103 mayors in sixteen southern states), we may be placed in adversary positions. On Capitol Hill, the result could be devastating, as congressmen are torn between the competing interests of large and small cities.

Alonso: I guess I am the only person here who has not been elected to anything. But I have been looking at the question of cities, big and small. One thing that is very striking is that being small does not define a city. There is a range of very different small cities: cities that are booming, cities in decline, cities that are being transformed from market towns to industrial centers.

I wonder to what extent it will be possible for smaller cities to pool their political efforts on the basis of being small, and to what extent they will have to form into different coalitions. For instance, the small cities in the plains states, which are now experiencing a tremendous boom because of the resource base development, are sure to shoot up, and then shoot down, once the basic period of construction is over. Similarly, many of the southern small cities are being transformed into modern cities in the sense of industrialized and post-industrialized cities.

I think there may be some common themes aside from changing formulas of revenue sharing which, indeed, are important. Let me give you an example. There has been a great deal of talk, by both political parties, of the deregulation of transport and communications industries. Now, should that happen, it would change the economy of getting things—products, services, ideas, information—in and out of the small cities. It would put them at a much greater comparative disadvantage than they are today, because, for example, it does not pay for an airline to service a small city; it doesn't pay to make a computer linkage, and so forth.

For the past 200 years people have been leaving the small cities, and for the past six years, or so, that process has reversed. Indeed, if you look at the statistics nationally, whereas before there was talk of the disappearance of small cities, now they are growing, as a whole, far faster than the metropolitan areas. The net movement of population and industry is in their direction. So, to make my two points more concisely: first, there are all kinds of small cities and it may not be easy to group their interests; and second, something—nobody quite knows what—has happened to the American society in the last half dozen years which has transformed the process by which most of us form our preferences for places.

Rattley: I would like to share with you a thought I have in reference to the layers of government. It seems to me that we have to make it very clear to the people who serve at the federal, state, and local level, that there must be a partnership in delivering services to all citizens. It has been my experience, many times, that the federal people say, "These are federal dollars. You always come, hat in hand, begging for federal money." The state government says basically the same thing. We must get the message across that we are serving the same people. If we develop a partnership, communication would be much easier.

There are many pieces of legislation passed daily in the Congress of the United States, and in the state houses, which set certain criteria that the local governments must meet. These laws and programs have a financial impact on localities. I think all federal aid and state legislation should have an accompanying financial impact statement. Many programs require the local government to foot the bill. The heavy reliance of local governments on real estate taxes limits the amount of revenue local governments have at their disposal.

When local officials complain to legislatures about their lack of funds, we are often accused of mismanagement. In the first place, many small communities cannot, by law, operate through deficit financing. We are required to maintain a balanced budget. We have to justify our expenditures in order to get money from Washington—money that belongs to us in the first place.

Lee: The central theme of this discussion so far, leads me to think that the prospects for solving small city problems are pretty dismal. Would it make sense for the federal government to embark on a program of block grants, or give the responsibility for addressing city problems back to state governments? Should the federal government pass revenues directly to cities? Should there be more technical assistance? Should assistance be more in the form of services than of dollars?

Cooper: I'd like to respond to Professor Alonso's statement about the dissimilarity of cities. While cities may be different, it seems to me that a systematic approach could be relevant to cities of varying sizes and situations. We need a commitment from legislatures not to adopt legislation requiring expenditures from cities and local governments unless there is an accompanying appropriation to cover that expenditure, or, at the very least, an authorization for direct taxation of the people—an authority that many of us do not have, or have only on a limited basis.

Davis: I think you raised a good point. We are the ones on the firing line. We are the ones our citizens look to for direct services. A Congress representative need never appear to answer why the Labor Department exaggerated the number of Title VII jobs coming into our cities. Further, I think there is an assumption that because cities are small, they lack the capacity to administer funds competently; hence, there is fear about direct allocation. I think that revenue sharing has shown that this assumption is not true.

Question (from floor): What reasonable prospects for solutions to small city problems do we have without a national urban policy? It seems to me that most of the problems (housing, unemployment, etc.) are not indigenous to the city, and do require policies specifying the role and functions of city, state, and federal governments in responding to these problems.

Cooper: President Carter's speech to the U.S. Conference of Mayors in Milwaukee this past summer was the first statement we have had approaching an endorsement of a national urban policy. A comprehensive national policy will help every type of city.

Question: To say that the problems of New York City, especially the fiscal problem of near bankruptcy, are exactly the same as a small city is stretching the truth a little bit. Don't you think the unique fiscal problems of big cities ought to be viewed more sympathetically?

Cooper: Many small as well as large cities are on the brink of bankruptcy. Smaller cities are having terrible cash flow problems because of heavy dependence on federal funds, which only come at certain specified times. When a grant is two or three months late, we are two or three months late in paying our bills. We also have the problem of access to bond markets, unrated issues, things of that nature. Let's face it, small cities haven't had the benefit of many of the social programs, either. People who live in small cities have every bit as much right to basic services as those who live in large cities. We have to spread our resources around.

Davis: The proportionate need and fiscal dilemmas of small cities are very comparable to those of large cities. In many small cities we have had to undertake the same kinds of fiscal cutbacks in terms of labor and services. A sizeable percent of our budget goes to salaries and wages. Even suburban cities find that industry is opting to move farther and farther out. We have to have a national policy that will shift the burden of welfare and education away from the property tax base. The financial burden in these two areas alone is crippling our ability to provide other needed services.

Rattley: I think the point ought to be made that we cannot separate ourselves from the problems experienced by New York City. Those problems had a very definite impact on cities of all sizes, especially in the bond market.

Alonso: It seems to me that there are two ways of using the word "city." And we are concentrating on one. The city is a municipal corporation, and, as near as I can tell, with few exceptions (such as Palo Alto, California) all cities are in money troubles. But there is another meaning to the word city, which is the combination of people, of institutions, of businesses, of buildings that constitute the real city: the social city. To focus exclusively on the municipal corporation and its problems may in fact blind us for the long term changes that are taking place, in terms of the composition of the population, and in terms of what people want.

It's quite different, say, in Wilkes Barre, where, I believe, there are more deaths than births because the young people have left, than in a city in the South, where young people are still coming in, where they are learning city ways, where there are a lot of kids and a great deal of turnover. It's different in the plains states, where a city as part of an extended agriculture is being invaded by, say, the coal industry, and so on. In that sense, it seems to me that the problems of these cities are quite different.

Now, I'm sure we all share the need for more and simpler money from the feds. I wouldn't dispute that. But, a city that is stable or declining in population, as many small cities are, has a problem maintaining its housing stock. This is quite different from a rapidly growing city, where additions to housing stock must be made; and to the water system, and so on. The French operate almost all their local government by what we would call revenue sharing. They have an interesting idea, at least with respect to some designated growth towns. Their formula is based not on the present, but on the mix of the present population and the estimated future population. Having to anticipate growth is different from a static situation.

Question (from floor): In defining the unique needs of small cities, you alluded to the need for a structured relationship in order to get attention. I would like to get your reaction to the concept of using both your political constituency and the media to focus attention on the problems of small cities. I think that this has to be done at the local level, and perhaps expanded to include a national strategy.

Davis: We were used by the media in Compton. The media made quite a to-do over the fact that our city had been rated third highest in crime per capita for a city its size. This had quite a negative effect. It frightened away many citizens, and we lost a great deal of industry and many commercial businesses. I think the media can be used, if they are willing to cooperate in a positive way. We cannot get the media out when there are positive things happening in our community. It is very important to get the media to focus on our problems, and possibly on some solutions, but not in a sensational way. We need information.

Cooper: In the Southern Conference of Black Mayors, we work through our state groups: the Alabama Conference of Black Mayors, the Mississippi Conference of Black Mayors. By having meetings of these organizations in the respective cities where we have black mayors, we have been able to give the local media news. Rather than "use" the media, we give them things that they find they can use, which will also have a positive impact. Through our local organizations, we have been able to have an impact on the governors of various states. For example, in Mississippi, our local organization is administering a $200,000 grant, through the state of Mississippi and a major foundation. We've been able to get the attention of federal economic development agencies regarding the problem small towns have in applying for local public works projects.

Lee: I believe that the future of the small city must include close cooperation with state government, primarily because we do lack political clout, as well as trained technicians. The state must assume a supportive role. We must maintain a partnership with larger cities, but we would be remiss if we did not recognize the very special problems that small cities face (1).

 *Part One*

Population Growth, Decline, and Policies

 Chapter One

Recent Trends in City Population Growth and Distribution

Glenn V. Fuguitt and Calvin L. Beale

All of us are aware that urbanization and metropolitan decentralization are major dimensions of population redistribution in the United States, and indeed throughout the world. Since the inception of this country, incorporated cities have captured a greater and greater share of the population and have multiplied in number following the classic pattern of urbanization.

As time has gone on, most of the population growth has taken place in metropolitan area development, so even as population has concentrated into places, it has decentralized to those places and unincorporated territory found peripheral to large cities. These patterns, moreover, must be seen in terms of regional population shifts, which are resulting in notable buildup of people in the western and southern parts of the nation.

The objective of this chapter is to examine the patterns of population change in incorporated places having over 2,500 people within the United States, over the past two Census decades (1950-1970). We have included all sizes of cities differentiated into several classes, so trends can be seen in the total urban context. The locational aspects of city population change have been assessed in terms of the metropolitan-nonmetropolitan distinction, and in more

---

This work has been supported by the Economic Development Division, Economic Research Service, U.S. Department of Agriculture, and by the College of Agricultural and Life Sciences, University of Wisconsin-Madison, through a Cooperative Agreement. Analysis was aided by a "Center for Population Research" grant, No. HD05876, to the Center for Demography and Ecology, University of Wisconsin-Madison, from the Center for Population Research of the National Institute of Child Health and Human Development.

detail by size of SMSA for metro places, and by metropolitan adjacency and size of largest place in the county for nonmetropolitan places. We have also considered regional differences and the effects of annexation on population growth.

In looking at growth, urban centers are classed by size at the beginning of a decade, and are followed over the interval. Thus places incorporated during a decade are not included in the city growth for that decade, and the few places disincorporating over a decade are excluded. The constant metropolitan definition employed is as of 1973, which is the situation in 1970 updated to reflect the results of the 1970 census. County equivalents for metropolitan areas are used in New England. The size of largest place classification for nonmetropolitan counties is as of 1970.

By considering incorporated centers over 2,500, we are using the traditional census demarcation between urban and rural. Census, however, recognizes other territory as being urban, specifically unincorporated places over 2500 and thickly settled territory around metropolitan centers. Thus our cities do not include the entire urban population identified according to census definitions.

This is, of course, not an exhaustive demographic review of the situation regarding cities. We are not dealing with the characteristics of the populations involved, with the economic functions of cities as reflected by occupational and industrial composition, with the differentials in work and residence patterns, or with the recent trends in number and distribution of various race and ethnic groups. Within the scope of this chapter, it is necessary to be concerned simply with how these cities have grown or have failed to grow in population size.

NUMBER AND POPULATION SIZE OF INCORPORATED CITIES

There has been a continuing increase in the number and total population of people living in incorporated cities. Table 1-1 shows the number of places increased from 3,877 to 5,284 over the 1950-1970 period, and the population residing in such centers grew from 87 million to 122 million. This is also an increasing proportion of the nation's population, showing a continuing urbanization trend.

Today about six out of ten people live in incorporated cities, and more than half of these are in places of 10,000 to 500,000 in size. Comparing the size groups, the percent of the population in very large centers is decreasing, and this is also true to a slight extent for centers under 10,000, whereas the proportion of the total U.S. population residing in middle sized cities increased from 31 to 36 percent between 1950 and 1970.

Table 1-1. Number and Population of Incorporated Cities, by Size, United States, 1950-1970

City Size	1950			1960			1970		
	No. of Places	Population	Percent Distrib.	No. of Places	Population	Percent Distrib.	No. of Places	Population	Percent Distrib.
500,000+	18	26,591,395	17.6	21	28,595,050	15.9	26	31,761,468	15.6
250T-500T	23	8,241,560	5.5	30	10,764,878	6.0	30	10,465,030	5.2
100T-250T	66	9,726,696	6.4	79	11,376,832	6.3	97	13,887,989	6.8
50T-100T	126	8,930,823	5.9	180	12,511,961	7.0	230	16,079,089	7.9
25T-50T	250	8,738,065	5.8	367	12,754,065	7.1	456	15,768,325	7.7
10T-25T	752	11,514,028	7.6	972	14,983,607	8.4	1129	17,592,055	8.7
2500-10T	2642	13,061,552	8.6	3032	15,210,592	8.5	3303	16,562,674	8.2
All 2500+	3877	86,804,119	57.4	4681	106,196,985	59.2	5284	122,116,630	60.1
Other population		64,517,944	42.6		73,108,084	40.8		81,176,914	39.9
Total population		151,322,063	100.0		179,305,069	100.0		203,293,544	100.00

The addition of numbers of places over the twenty-year period comes through both new incorporations and the growth of smaller places across the 2,500 threshold. Most of the new places consequently are in the smaller size groups, but at the same time, there has been a shift of places between groups, mostly to the larger size categories, making for an increase in the number of places within groups at each successive census.

THE GROWTH OF CITIES

When cities of common size are considered together, some growth characterizes all classes. Table 1-2 shows the aggregate growth over the 1950-60 decade of the 3,877 places classed by size (as in Table 1-1) in 1950, and the same over 1960-70 for the 4,681 places classed by size in 1960. If one considers all incorporated cities together, then overall population growth has been less than that of the remaining population both in 1950-60 and in 1960-70. This is because of rapid growth of unincorporated territory and small village population in metropolitan areas (compare the last three lines of Table 1-2). A considerable proportion of this remainder population also was in places newly incorporated over each decade considered, and much was no doubt designated as urban by the Census, at least at the end of each period.

Table 1-2. Percent Change of Incorporated Cities by Initial Size, Metropolitan and Nonmetropolitan, United States, 1950-60 and 1960-70

Initial City Size	1950-60			1960-70		
	Total	Metro	Nonmetro	Total	Metro	Nonmetro
500,000+	.3	.3		.1	.1	
250T-500T	17.6	17.6		8.2	8.2	
100T-250T	15.7	15.7		13.8	13.8	
50T-100T	16.4	16.4		11.7	11.7	
25T-50T	23.5	29.0	10.0	17.4	22.8	4.6
10T-25T	32.0	46.7	15.7	19.5	28.2	7.5
2500-10T	32.0	54.4	14.2	21.5	35.8	8.1
All 2500+	16.6	17.2	14.1	11.6	12.5	7.1
Other population	21.0	48.3	−1.8	15.9	27.3	2.9
Total population	18.5	26.3	3.0	13.4	17.1	4.3

A decentralization pattern is evident in the sense that there is an inverse association between place size and growth in both metropolitan and nonmetropolitan areas. A major difference of the table, however, is the lower growth level of nonmetropolitan places as compared to metropolitan places of comparable size. The latter cities, of course, are generally closely tied to metropolitan centers as suburbs or satellites.

Another major distinction in the table is between the two decades, with generally low growth levels in the latter period. This was a time of lessened population growth levels nationally, and widespread decline in fertility levels. In order to take this national shift into account, we calculated ratios of city growth in each size class to overall national growth percentage change for each decade (see Table 1-3). This table shows that overall growth of metropolitan urban places paralleled that for the United States as a whole. For both 1950-60 and 1960-70, metropolitan growth was 93 percent of total growth.

Metropolitan places under 25,000, however, do appear to be growing less rapidly relative to total growth in 1960-70 than in 1950-60. There is an even more striking decline in the relative growth of nonmetropolitan cities of all sizes. At the same time, however, there was a shift from decline to growth in the nonmetropolitan

Table 1-3. Ratio of Category Change with Total Population Change, Metropolitan and Nonmetropolitan Incorporated Cities, by Initial Size, United States, 1950-60 and 1960-70

Initial City Size	1950-60			1960-70		
	Total	Metro	Nonmetro	Total	Metro	Nonmetro
500,000+	.02	.02		.01	.01	
250T-500T	.95	.95		.61	.61	
100T-250T	.85	.85		1.03	1.03	
50T-100T	.89	.89		.87	.87	
25T-50T	1.27	1.57	.54	1.30	1.70	.34
10T-25T	1.73	2.52	.85	1.46	2.10	.56
2000-10T	1.73	2.94	.77	1.60	2.67	.60
All 2500+	.90	.93	.76	.87	.93	.53
Other population	1.14	2.61	(−)[a]	1.19	2.03	.22
Total population	1.00	1.42	.16	1.00	1.28	.32

[a](−) Segment change negative, so no ratio computed.

population outside incorporated cities, as shown in the next to last line of Tables 1-2 and 1-3. Thus the relative decline in city growth and corresponding increase in the remaining population indicates a definite trend of increasing population decentralization in nonmetropolitan America.

Table 1-4 presents an elaboration of the metropolitan and nonmetropolitan categories considered previously. Standard Metropolitan Statistical Areas (SMSAs) have been differentiated by total size

Table 1-4. Percent Change of Incorporated Cities by Initial Size and Metropolitan and Nonmetropolitan Groupings, United States, 1950-60 and 1960-70

Initial City Size	In SMSA by Size				Not in SMSA by Size Largest Place in County				
					Adjacent to SMSA		Not adjacent to SMSA		
	GT1 Mill.	500T- 1Mill.	250T- 500T	LT 250T	2500- 10000+	LT 10000 2500		2500- 10000+	LT 10000 2500
1950-1960									
500,000+	.3								
250T-500T	20.7	12.2							
100T-250T	12.1	16.6	15.6	25.4					
50T-100T	13.0	11.3	21.6	18.2					
25T-50T	27.0	22.4	50.5	26.6	9.3		10.8		
10T-25T	55.9	21.7	44.7	38.1	15.3		17.5		
2500-10T	71.4	31.2	39.0	41.3	19.9	10.5	30.9	8.7	
All 2500+	14.3	17.0	25.8	26.4	15.1	10.1	18.5	8.0	
Other population	73.1	42.0	27.9	19.7	9.0	-2.7 -3.8	4.2	-8.8	-9.4
Total population	26.8	25.5	26.7	24.3	11.7	.2 -3.8	10.9	-4.3	-9.4
1960-1970									
500,000+	-.1	11.3							
250T-500T	7.6	8.4	12.7						
100T-250T	22.3	16.7	9.6	3.6					
50T-100T	15.6	8.2	9.2	9.4					
25T-50T	26.0	19.2	20.3	18.2	6.8		2.4		
10T-25T	30.4	29.2	21.7	22.6	8.1		7.8		
2500-10T	41.3	43.3	21.3	22.7	17.1	6.0	14.5	4.6	
All 2500+	11.2	16.5	13.1	13.8	9.6	5.3	7.0	4.3	
Other population	36.6	17.9	23.0	19.2	12.0	3.0 2.3	6.1	-4.6	-3.6
Total population	17.4	17.0	17.1	15.2	10.9	3.6 2.3	6.6	1.0	-3.6

as of 1970; nonmetropolitan counties have been grouped by size of their largest city in 1970, and by whether or not they are adjacent to a metropolitan area. The bottom line of each panel shows for both decades that the different-sized metropolitan areas were growing at about the same level, whereas both adjacency and size of largest place in the county appeared to have a positive impact on growth in nonmetropolitan areas.

In the 1950s, incorporated cities were growing more rapidly in smaller than in larger sized SMSAs, whereas the reverse was true for the balance of the population. There was not a similar pattern for 1960-70, however. Considering all size groups, the inverse relation between place size and growth is found for both time periods within all these location categories. Finally, the nonmetropolitan decentralization process is more clearly evident within counties having larger centers of 10,000 and over than was shown in the preceding two tables for all nonmetropolitan counties together.

As might be expected, there are important regional differences in the growth patterns of incorporated cities. These differences, moreover, conform with overall regional trends of population redistribution, according to Table 1-5. Within most size classes, places grew the most rapidly in the West, followed by the South. Places grew least rapidly in the Northeast and North Central regions. A number of size classes in the Northeast had overall population declines, a phenomenon that will be considered further in our discussion of annexation.

The growth rate of places over 250,000 in every region is clearly below the level that would have occurred in the absence of net out migration. In the West and South all other size classes were growing at such rates as to require either substantial inmovement of people or annexation.

Within each of the regions the negative association between size and growth holds up in the metropolitan sector. The pattern in the nonmetro sector is mixed, however. In the North Central states there is a positive association between place size and growth among nonmetropolitan cities. This is the traditional pattern found in many studies of smaller rural trade centers, particularly for those located in the Middle West.

CITY GROWTH AND ANNEXATION

Cities grow in population not only by filling their territory but also by adding to their corporate limits through annexation. This adds to the complexity of the study of growth, for annexation is a legal process, and cities differ in the extent to which they are able to

Table 1-5. Percent Change of Incorporated Cities by Initial Size and Region, United States, 1950-60 and 1960-70

	Northeast		North Central		South		West	
	1950-60	1960-70	1950-60	1960-70	1950-60	1960-70	1950-60	1960-70
All Places 2500+	1.1	0.3	13.8	9.4	28.3	16.9	39.2	25.5
Metropolitan								
500,000+	-3.4	-1.3	-3.7	-8.2	12.0	9.9	17.2	9.3
250T-500T	-6.6	-6.1	10.3	11.4	31.3	8.3	21.6	8.8
100T-250T	-3.8	-6.8	12.2	5.7	28.9	26.9	39.5	27.5
50T-100T	.2	-1.4	16.9	12.4	27.3	13.8	34.8	26.2
25T-50T	7.2	5.1	12.2	16.4	41.2	29.3	65.3	48.2
10T-25T	13.6	6.6	50.0	29.1	37.3	25.9	97.4	65.6
2500-10T	20.8	11.0	71.7	40.7	64.2	55.8	99.8	65.2
All 2500+	1.1	.5	14.5	10.2	32.1	19.7	41.7	25.6
Nonmetropolitan								
25T-50T	3.0	-8.1	13.3	7.2	9.1	3.9	12.2	10.9
10T-25T	-2.0	-2.3	12.6	7.2	24.0	7.7	24.4	16.5
2500-10T	2.1	1.0	9.5	5.3	16.9	11.1	28.1	11.4
All 2500+	.6	-2.4	11.4	6.3	18.1	8.7	24.7	25.6

annex because of variations in state law and opportunity. As a consequence, there is not always a close correspondence between the thickly settled territory of a city (in the geographic sense) and the territory the municipal limits encompass.

This does not mean growth due to annexation is "spurious" and should be eliminated from consideration. It usually reflects genuine growth, with real consequences for the functioning community. But it is important to know the extent to which observed growth is due to annexation, and to identify areas where annexation is either highly prevalent or very infrequent. Decentralization, measured by comparing growth in and out of incorporated centers, also is affected by annexation possibilities and accomplishments.

A majority of all urban incorporated places typically annex some population in the course of a decade. In both the 1950s and 1960s, about two-thirds of the nonmetro incorporated places and one-half the metro incorporated places have done so. These national averages, however, conceal wide regional differences. Appreciation of these differences (shown in Table 1-6) is particularly important to the understanding of regional variation in growth of incorporated cities.

On the one hand, in the western region, over 80 percent of both metropolitan and nonmetropolitan places have annexed in each recent decade. But on the other hand, in the northeastern region, a comparatively small proportion of places annex, or are able to engage in annexation. In the 1960s, only 12 percent of metropolitan cities and 27 percent of nonmetropolitan cities had annexed population in that section of the country. There are no extreme differences in the propensity to annex by place size, but in general, the larger the place, up to a half-million in size, the more likely annexation has been.

Despite the fact urban and national population growth rates were lower in the 1960s than in the 1950s, there was no overall lessening in the propensity of places to annex. There was a noticeable decline, however, in amount of population acquired per annexing places, especially in metropolitan areas. The "Total" section of Table 1-7 shows that metropolitan places with annexations had an average of 4.1 thousand persons living in the annexed territory in 1970, compared with an average of 7.3 thousand in 1960. Similar declines prevail among all size classes for the U.S. as a whole, and in general across the regions. The average proportion in annexed territory in nonmetropolitan areas also dropped in the nation, and in all regions except the North Central.

The very small amount of population cities acquired in the Northeast region, even when they did annex, is particularly noticeable in Table 1-7. For example, metropolitan places in the Northeast

Table 1-6. Percent of Places Annexing, by Initial Size, Metropolitan Status, Region, and Decade, United States, 1950-60 and 1960-70

	Total		Northeast		North Central		South		West	
	1950-60	1960-70	1950-60	1960-70	1950-60	1960-70	1950-60	1960-70	1950-60	1960-70
All Places 2500+	59	58	20	16	63	62	72	72	83	82
Metropolitan										
500,000+	33	38	20	0	43	50	25	50	50	50
250T-500T	83	67	33	0	86	60	100	82	83	83
100T-250T	56	62	13	10	79	79	81	76	75	93
50T-100T	63	57	23	6	75	63	91	84	86	83
25T-50T	59	54	4	3	73	55	87	87	96	82
10T-25T	54	49	18	11	61	52	82	71	83	82
2500-10T	49	48	19	15	59	55	65	67	88	82
All 2500+	53	50	18	12	62	55	73	71	86	82
Nonmetropolitan										
25T-50T	78	82	36	14	97	98	83	90	50	82
10T-25T	79	77	31	28	81	79	93	85	92	93
2500-10T	60	65	22	28	57	66	66	68	78	80
All 2500+	64	68	25	27	64	70	71	72	80	83

Table 1-7. Number of People per Annexing Place (in Thousands), by Initial Size, Metropolitan Status, Region, and Decade, United States, 1950-60 and 1960-70

	Total		Northeast		North Central		South		West	
	1950-60	1960-70	1950-60	1960-70	1950-60	1960-70	1950-60	1960-70	1950-60	1960-70
All Places 2500+	3.9	2.2	.6	.5	2.3	1.9	4.9	2.5	6.0	3.7
Metropolitan										
500,000+	66.1	11.8	.1	a	46.1	4.2	251.2	20.4	7.6	10.1
250T-500T	62.6	36.1	0	a	37.5	49.2	100.6	31.4	52.1	29.0
100T-250T	38.7	18.4	.4	.7	19.1	16.6	48.5	21.8	66.3	18.1
50T-100T	13.2	8.3	.8	.3	10.5	6.5	16.7	9.9	20.9	9.0
25T-50T	10.4	6.4	.2	.4	5.5	3.8	11.6	7.1	16.7	8.0
10T-25T	5.1	3.1	1.0	2.2	1.9	2.1	6.2	2.2	8.8	5.7
2500-10T	2.1	1.3	.7	.4	1.4	1.4	2.8	1.3	3.2	1.8
All 2500+	7.3	4.1	.8	.7	4.3	3.3	11.0	4.6	10.0	5.8
Nonmetropolitan										
25T-50T	2.8	2.9	.8	.2	2.6	3.1	3.2	3.1	5.7	4.1
10T-25T	2.2	1.5	.3	.4	1.4	1.7	3.1	1.7	2.7	1.8
2500-10T	.7	.5	.3	.2	.3	.7	.8	.7	1.1	.6
All 2500+	1.1	.9	.3	.3	.8	1.1	1.4	1.1	1.6	1.1

aNo places annexed in this category.

that did annex, only acquired an average of 800 persons each in the 1960s, and 700 persons in the 1970s. In contrast, in the West, annexing metropolitan places added an average of 10.0 thousand and 5.8 thousand people in the two time periods respectively. The regional differences are particularly noticeable for places over 100,000. The minimum average number annexed outside the Northeast was 16.6 thousand for centers 100,000 to 250,000, while the corresponding figure for the Northeast was only 700.

The absence of much annexation in the Northeast helps explain the low city growth rates and the strong indication of decentralization in that region. Many of the northeastern towns are simply full and the state laws make annexation extremely difficult. Their growth can only occur outside the corporate limits. In the remainder of the country, annexation is widely prevalent and most (up to 90 percent) of the population growth of places is in territory newly acquired during the decade.

Prevailing laws and regulations seem to doom small and medium sized cities of the Northeast to demographic stagnation and decline. Under these circumstances, their populations increasingly consist of lower and middle income people, unable to participate in the suburban settlement occurring beyond their boundaries. By contrast, in the West and the South, many cities are able to recover, within their municipal limits, much of the middle and upper class suburban development.

IMPLICATIONS OF POST-1970 TRENDS

Reliable population figures on incorporated places are obtained only every ten years in the Census of Population. Since 1970, however, in cooperation with state officials, the Bureau of the Census has prepared annual estimates of county populations. These have revealed some remarkable, unpredicted shifts in the pattern of population change (1, 2, 3).

Table 1-8 compares 1950-60, 1960-70, and 1970-75 annual rates of population change and net migration for the total populations of the ten groups of metropolitan and nonmetropolitan areas considered earlier.[a] There has been a recent slowing of growth and net

[a]Altogether 3,100 counties and county equivalents were used in this tabulation. Alaska is represented by 24 election districts for which comparable census data could be obtained over the time period. The Independent Cities of Virginia were combined with adjacent counties. Net migration for 1950-60 and 1960-70 was calculated by the residual method, with birth and death data from the Bureau of the Census. The 1975 estimates and 1970-75 net migration figures are found in U.S. Census, *Current Population Reports*, Series P-25 and P-26, for individual states published in 1976.

Table 1-8. Annual Rates of Population Change and Net Migration, by County Location Groups, United States, 1950-60, 1960-70, and 1970-75

County Groups	Annual Rate of Population Change			Annual Rate of Net Migration		
	1950-1960	1960-1970	1970-1975	1950-1960	1960-1970	1970-1975
SMSAs	2.32	1.57	.77	.78	.44	.08
GT 1 Million	2.36	1.60	.42	.94	.52	−.20
500T-1 Million	2.26	1.57	1.06	.66	.42	.32
250T-500T	2.36	1.58	1.27	.63	.35	.47
LT 250T	2.17	1.41	1.45	.43	.15	.62
Nonmetro	.30	.43	1.22	−1.23	−.54	.62
Adj. 10,000+	1.11	1.03	1.34	−.40	.01	.67
2500-10,000	.02	.36	1.27	−1.39	−.50	.76
LT 2500	−.39	.22	1.60	−1.81	−.62	1.12
Not Adj. 10,000+	1.04	.63	1.18	−.65	−.53	.44
2500-10,000	−.45	−.18	−.88	−1.98	−1.05	.37
LT 2500	−.99	−.37	1.31	−2.45	−1.17	.89
United States	1.69	1.25	.89	.16	.17	.23

migration for the SMSAs of greater than 500 thousand population, and a corresponding increase for smaller sized SMSAs. At the same time, the nonmetro sector has also increased in population and net migration.

This has been particularly true of the more rural nonmetro counties. Notice that in both the 1950s and the 1960s, there was a consistently positive association between SMSA size and the rate of net in-migration. Since 1970, this relationship has completely reversed and is now consistent on a negative basis. There is a similar shift within the nonmetropolitan population.

The possible short term consequences of these trends for population distribution are illustrated in Table 1-9. We have projected the 1970-75 annual rates of population change through the remainder of the decade to obtain 1980 population estimates, under the assumption that these 1970-75 rates will continue unchanged. In the left side of the table, actual percent change figures for 1950-60 and 1960-70 are compared with those for 1970-80 based on estimated populations. In looking at these percentages, one must keep in mind that the overall United States population growth rate would only be about three-fourths that of the 1960s, according to these projections, and this may well be expected, unless the birth rate takes a substantial upturn very soon.

Table 1-9. Percent Change and Percent Distribution of the Total Population, by Metropolitan and Nonmetropolitan Location Groups, 1950-1970, with a Projection to 1980 of the 1970-75 Annual Rate of Growth, United States

	Percent Change			Percent Distribution			
Location	1950-60	1960-70	Projected[a] 1970-80	1950	1960	1970	Projected[a] 1980
SMSAs	26.3	17.1	8.0	66.6	70.9	73.2	72.4
GT 1 Million	26.8	17.4	4.3	37.8	40.5	41.9	40.0
500T-1 Million	25.5	17.0	11.1	11.6	12.3	12.6	12.9
250T-500T	26.7	17.1	13.4	9.3	9.9	10.3	10.6
LT 250T	24.3	15.2	15.3	7.9	8.2	8.4	8.9
Nonmetro	3.0	4.3	12.9	33.4	29.1	26.8	27.6
Adj. 10,000+	11.7	10.9	14.2	8.2	7.8	7.6	7.9
2500-10,000+	.2	3.6	13.5	6.3	5.4	4.9	5.1
LT 2500	−3.8	2.3	17.2	1.8	1.4	1.3	1.4
Not Adj. 10,000+	10.9	6.6	12.4	6.6	6.2	5.8	6.0
2500-10,000	−4.3	1.0	9.1	7.0	5.6	4.9	4.9
LT 2500	−9.4	−3.6	13.9	3.5	2.7	2.3	2.3
Total	18.5	13.4	9.3	100.0	100.0	100.0	100.0

[a]The 1980 population was projected by applying the compound interest formula to the annual rate of growth over 1970-75. Thus it shows what the 1970-80 growth rates and the 1980 distribution would be *if* the apparent 1970-75 trends continue for the remainder of this decade.

With such declining overall growth, a continuation of 1970-75 trends would mean lower growth in the 1970s than the 1960s for all but the smallest sized SMSAs, though the other groups of SMSAs, except the largest, would still be growing faster than the nation as a whole. All six nonmetro groups of counties, however, would register a more rapid growth during this decade than previously, and the growth contrast—particularly for the smaller, more rural nonmetro counties—is striking.

The consequences of a continuation of 1970-75 growth in terms of relative distribution are seen in the last four columns of Table 1-9. In part because of the marked growth decline of metropolitan areas of more than one-half million, smaller metropolitan areas and nonmetro counties containing cities of 10,000 or more people all show some increase in the proportion of United States population living in them.

We can conclude, therefore, that U.S. population currently is concentrating in areas where small and medium sized cities (10,000 to 500,000) are the major centers. It is quite possible, however, consistent with the pattern of increasing decentralization revealed in the preceding analysis of the 1950s and 1960s, that most small and medium sized cities themselves will have little increase and together even show a decline in the proportion of national population living within their corporate limits.

Indeed, we expect there may be an increase in the proportion of cities sustaining absolute population loss, although their hinterlands may be simultaneously growing. Our studies of the trends of nonmetropolitan population lead us to think that the current preference for having a residence in the open country is making it increasingly difficult for much population concentration to occur within corporate limits, even where annexation policies are fairly permissive.

Chapter Two

Characteristics of Growing and Declining Cities

Herrington J. Bryce

Fuguitt and Beale (Chapter One) found that cities 25,000 to 50,000 in population grew faster than the national rate.

All cities of a larger size either grew slower or at the same rate as the nation as a whole. These authors also found that there was a sharp difference among cities in this 25,000 to 50,000 size class. Precisely, they found that between 1960 and 1970 only those cities which were in a metropolitan area grew faster than the nation as a whole; nonmetropolitan cities grew slower.

In an earlier study, these authors discovered that among nonmetropolitan cities, the rate of growth was greatest among those 25,000 to 50,000 in population (1). Thus, the growth rate of these cities stands out whether we look at them strictly in terms of their metropolitan status or as a composite group.

The central question of the present paper is: what factors, in addition to metropolitan status, distinguish rates of growth among cities of this size? Specifically, do the most rapidly growing cities differ significantly from the most rapidly declining? The purpose of this chapter is not to test a model of growth and decline, rather it is to highlight the role of some variables which reoccur in the various chapters of this book. For a further discussion of differences between growing and declining cities, see Chapter Eight of this book (2).

This material is based upon research supported by the National Science Foundation under Grant No. ERS74-21286 to the Joint Center for Political Studies—Howard University. Any opinions, findings, and conclusions expressed in this publication are those of the author(s) and do not necessarily reflect the views of the National Science Foundation. Assisted by William McCoy and Ellen Scudder, only the writer is responsible for errors which appear.

The data used in this study are taken from the *County and City Data Book, 1972*, and the rankings are derived from a special computer run. Cities are compared along several indicators. These include rates of population growth 1960-70, the size of the city population relative to the county, the percent of residents employed in manufacturing, the percent which commutes and per capita income. All cities in this study are incorporated, and population data refer to the 1970 decennial census; hence, we are referring to cities which were in the population size class of 25,000 to 50,000 in 1970.

METHODOLOGY

The data in the tables presented in this chapter are based on the ranking of all 455 cities that were in the population size class 25,000 to 50,000 in 1970. The chi-squares (χ^2) are derived by testing the hypotheses that growing cities ranked above (below) the median in terms of the specific indicator.

RATES OF POPULATION GROWTH, REGION, AND RELATIVE SIZE

Table 2-1 shows the 50 cities that grew fastest and the ones that declined most rapidly between 1960 and 1970. The rates of population change among the more rapidly growing cities ranged between 3167.5 percent (Bowie, Maryland) to 72.7 percent (Visalia, California). In contrast, the rates of population change in the more rapidly declining cities ranged from a high of —33.3 percent (Anderson, South Carolina) to a low of —6.3 percent (Anniston, Alabama and Hoboken, New Jersey).

The causes of growth and decline varied. Bowie's growth was due to a fill-in process: a subdivision was built within the city limits. Fountain Valley and Cyprus, California benefited from the spillover from the Los Angeles area. Mentor, Ohio grew mostly because of annexation. Virtually all of Titusville's growth in Florida was due to annexation. Anderson's decline was due to deannexation. In 1959, Anderson annexed an area which was subsequently declared an unconstitutional act by a state level court. In the early 1960s, a major military installation was closed down in Harlington, Texas, and this represented a $50 to $60 million loss to the economy and contributed to its rapid decline.

The 1960 census counted the crews on vessels stationed in Newport. In the 1970 census, the vessels were in the Mediterranean, and consequently the crews were not counted. While Newport did

Table 2-1. Percent Change in Population (1960-70) for Fastest Growing and Declining Cities (Population Size Class 25-50 Thousand).

Fastest Growing Cities			Fastest Declining Cities		
City, State	Percent	City Size Class Rank	City, State	Percent	City Size Class Rank
Bowie Town, MD	3167.5	1	Anderson, SC	−33.3	449
Cypress, CA	1700.9	2	Newport, RI	−26.5	448
Fountain Valley, CA	1441.9	3	Johnstown, PA	−21.3	447
Mentor, OH	747.8	4	Hamtramck, MI	−20.2	446
Titusville, FL	376.1	5	Atlantic City, NJ	−19.6	445
Milpitas, CA	313.1	6	Harlingen, TX	−18.7	444
Boca Raton, FL	309.5	7	East Chicago, IN	−18.5	443
Walnut Creek, CA	302.3	8	Portsmouth, OH	−17.8	442
Melbourne, FL	235.8	9	McKeesport, PA	−16.5	441
Fairfield, CA	194.9	10	Poughkeepsie, NY	−16.4	440
Richardson, TX	189.0	11	Zanesville, OH	−15.4	438
Newark, CA	174.7	12	Bangor, ME	−14.8	437
Hurst, TX	167.7	13	Roswell, NM	−14.4	436
Rosemead, CA	164.7	14	Elmira, NY	−14.1	435
Brookland Park, MN	157.2	15	New Castle, PA	−13.9	434
Arvada, CO	155.1	16	Key West, FL	−13.7	433
Pompano Beach, FL	141.3	17	Newport, KY	−13.5	432
Brook Park, OH	139.4	18	Salina, KA	−12.7	430
Livermore, CA	134.8	19	Vicksburg, MS	−12.6	428
Northbrook, IL	134.6	20	Prichard, AL	−12.2	427
Glendale, AZ	127.9	21	Norwood, OH	−12.0	426
Palatine, IL	126.4	22	Battle Creek, MI	−11.9	425
Escondido, CA	124.7	23	Amsterdam, NY	−11.3	424
North Olmsted, OH	114.0	24	Cumberland, MD	−11.0	423
Del City, OK	109.8	25	Williamsburg, PA	−10.9	422
Kaneohe, HA	107.5	26	Jackson, MI	−10.3	421
Corona, CA	106.4	27	Austin, MN	−10.2	420
North Chicago, IL	106.1	28	Wheeling, WV	−9.8	419
Lewiston, ID	105.4	29	Williamsport, PA	−9.6	418
Farmer's Branch, TX	104.5	30	Chelsea, MA	−9.3	417
Upland, CA	104.5	30	Orange, NJ	−9.0	416
Coon Rapids, MN	104.3	32	Ithaca, NY	−8.9	415
Troy, MI	103.2	33	Meridian, MS	−8.7	414
Chapel Hill, NC	103.1	34	Phenix City, AL	−8.5	413
Normal, IL	97.6	35	Paducah, KY	−8.3	412
N. Las Vegas, NE	96.6	36	Big Springs, TX	−8.0	411
Raytown, MO	95.0	37	Alton, IL	−7.8	408

	Fastest Growing Cities			Fastest Declining Cities		
City, State		Percent	City Size Class Rank	City, State	Percent	City Size Class Rank
Littleton, CO		93.6	38	Easton, PA	−7.8	408
Frindley, MN		92.7	39	Watertown, NY	−7.6	407
San Rafael, CA		90.5	40	York, PA	−7.6	407
Newport Beach, CA		86.0	41	New London, CN	−7.5	406
Mt. Prospect, IL		85.1	43	University City, MO	−7.3	405
Warner-Robbins, GA		79.7	45	Goldsboro, NC	−7.1	404
DeKalb, IL		78.4	46	Highland Pk., MI	−6.9	403
Lompac, CA		75.4	47	Troy, NY	−6.8	403
Kenner, LA		75.3	48	Kokomo, IN	−6.7	402
Menomonee Falls, WI		73.4	49	Ashland, KY	−6.5	401
Novato, CA		73.4	49	Alliance, OH	−6.4	400
Fort Collins, CO		73.2	51	Anniston, AL	−6.3	398
Visalia, CA		72.7	52	Hoboken, NJ	−6.3	398

Source: Calculations in this and other tables in this chapter are based on data taken from Department of Commerce, Bureau of the Census, *County and City Data Book, 1972*, (U.S. Government Printing Office, 1973). William Lindamood wrote the computer program for all calculations.

$X^2 = 100$ df $= 1$ p $< .01$

experience decline, it may not be as dramatic as the census figures indicate. Johnstown, Pennsylvania has experienced dynamic decline due to net out-migration. The process has continued unabated into the 1970s. The county as a whole is declining as well. Johnstown's economy is entirely dependent on the coal and steel industries; when production declined, job prospects diminished and out-migration ensued.

Regional Distribution of Growth and Decline

As Figure 2-1 shows, the most rapidly growing small cities are concentrated in the West; sixteen of these cities are in California. The greatest concentration of the rapidly declining small cities is in the Northeast; there are no Northeast cities listed among the top 50 in terms of growth. Clearly, there is a high correlation between growth and region, even among small cities. But the most intriguing aspect of the regional distribution of growth is that the South is almost equally represented among the fastest growing and fastest declining small cities.

Growing Cities and Their Counties

In general, growing cities tend to be small relative to their

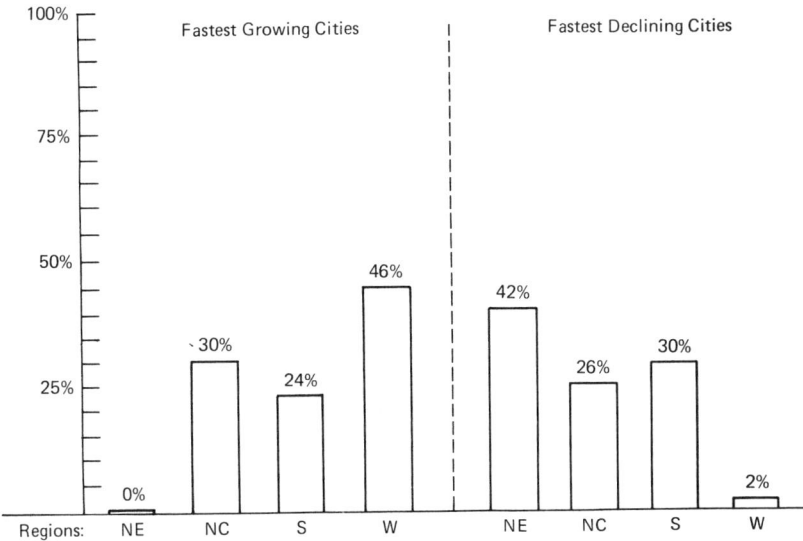

Figure 2-1. Percentage of Population Distribution, by Regions.

counties. The data in Table 2-2 show that 60 percent of the most rapidly growing cities represented less than 10 percent of their county's total population. Only 22 percent of the declining cities accounted for such a percentage of their county's population. Another important finding in Table 2-2 is that, by and large, rapidly growing small cities tend to be located in rapidly growing counties (3). Moreover, the rate of growth of these cities exceeds the rate of growth of their counties. On the other hand, declining cities are more likely than not to be part of a growing rather than a declining county.

York, Pennsylvania, for example, is an old, densely populated city which is fully developed. The growth areas of the county are the areas that surround York and that benefit from out-migration from York. This process redistributes the county's population at the

Table 2-2. Growth Rates of Cities and Counties (1960-70), and City Population as Percent of County's (1970), for Cities of 25,000-50,000 Population.

Fastest Growing Cities				Fastest Declining Cities			
City, State	Percent	Growth Rate of City	Growth Rate of County	City, State	Percent	Growth Rate of City	Growth Rate of County
Bowie Town, MD	5.3	3167.5	85.0	Anderson, SC	26.1	−33.3	7.1
Cypress, CA	2.2	1700.9	101.8	Newport, RI	36.6	−26.5	15.1
Fountain Valley, CA	2.2	1441.9	101.8	Johnstown, PA	22.7	−21.3	−8.1
Mentor, OH	18.7	747.8	32.6	Hamtramck, MI	1.0	−20.2	0.2
Titusville, FL	13.3	376.1	106.4	Atlantic City, NJ	27.3	−19.6	8.8
Milpitas, CA	2.6	313.1	66.1	Harlingen, TX	23.9	−18.7	−7.1
Boca Raton, FL	8.2	309.5	53.0	East Chicago, IN	8.6		
Walnut Creek, CA	7.1	302.3	35.9	Portsmouth, OH	35.9	−17.8	−8.6
Melbourne, FL	17.5	235.8	106.4	McKeesport, PA	2.4	−16.5	−1.4
Fairfield, CA	26.0	194.9	27.8	Poughkeepsie, NY	14.4		
Richardson, TX	3.5	189.0	52.3	Zanesville, OH	42.5	−15.4	−1.7
Newark, CA	2.5	174.7	18.2	Bangor, ME	26.5		
Hurst, TX	3.8	167.7	33.0	Roswell, NM	78.3		
Rosemead, CA	0.6	167.7	16.6	Elmira, NY	39.3	−14.1	2.9
Brookland Park, MN	2.7	157.2	13.9	New Castle, PA	35.9	−13.9	−4.9
Arvada, CO	79.0	155.1	69.5	Key West, FL	55.7	−13.7	4.7
Pompano Beach, FL	6.2	141.3	85.7	Newport, KY	29.4	−13.5	2.2
Brook Park, OH	1.8	139.4	4.4	Salina, KA	81.0	−12.7	−14.8
Livermore, CA	3.5	134.8	18.2	Vicksburg, MS	56.6	−12.6	6.6
Northbrook, IL	0.5	134.6	7.1	Prichard, AL	13.1	−12.2	1.0
Glendale, AZ	3.7	127.9	46.0	Norwood, OH	3.3	−12.0	6.8
Palatine, IL	0.5	126.4	7.1	Battle Creek, MI	27.4	−11.9	2.2
Escondido, CA	2.7	124.7	31.4	Amsterdam, NY	45.7	−11.3	−2.4
North Olmsted, OH	2.0	114.0	4.4	Cumberland, MD	35.4	−11.0	−0.1
Del City, OK	5.2	109.8	20.1	Wilkinsburg, PA	1.7	−10.9	−1.4
Kaneohe, HA	4.8			Jackson, MI	31.8	−10.3	8.5
Corona, CA	6.0	106.4	49.9	Austin, MN	57.3	−10.2	−9.7
North Chicago, IL	12.4			Wheeling, WV	75.1	−9.6	3.6
Lewiston, ID	85.8	105.4	12.2	Williamsport, PA	33.5		
Farmer's Branch, TX	2.1	104.5	39.5	Chelsea, MA	4.2	−9.3	−7.1
Upland, CA	4.8	104.5	35.5	Orange, NJ	3.5	−9.0	1.0
Coon Rapids, MN	19.7	104.3	79.7	Ithaca, NY	34.1	−8.9	16.5
Troy, MI	4.3	103.2	31.5	Meridian, MS	67.2	−8.7	Z
Chapel Hill, NC	13.4	103.1	26.4	Phenix City, AL	55.7	−8.5	−2.1
Normal, IL	25.3	97.6	24.5	Paducah, KY	54.3	−8.3	1.7
N. Las Vegas, NV	13.3			Big Springs, TX	76.0	−8.0	−5.8

	Fastest Growing Cities			Fastest Declining Cities			
City, State	Percent	Growth Rate of City	Growth Rate of County	City, State	Percent	Growth Rate of City	Growth Rate of County
Raytown, MO	5.1	95.0	5.0	Alton, IL	15.8	−7.8	11.7
Littleton, CO	16.3	93.6	42.9	Easton, PA	13.7	−7.8	6.5
Frindley, MN	18.9	92.7	79.7	Watertown, NY	34.8	−7.6	0.8
San Rafael, CA	18.9	90.5	40.8	York, PA	18.5	−7.6	14.4
Newport Beach, CA	3.5	86.0	101.8	New London, CN	13.7	−7.5	24.2
Mt. Prospect, IL	0.6	85.1	7.1	University City, MO	5.0	−7.3	35.3
Warner-Robbins, GA	53.2	79.7	60.7	Goldsboro, NC	31.4	−7.1	4.1
DeKalb, IL	46.0	78.2	38.6	Highland Pk., MI	1.3	−6.9	0.2
Lompac, CA	9.6	75.4	56.4	Troy, NY	41.3	−6.8	7.0
Kenner, LA	8.9	75.3	62.0	Kokomo, IN	52.9	−6.7	19.7
Menomonee Falls, WI	13.7	73.4	46.2	Ashland, KY	55.8	−6.5	0.4
Novato, CA	15.1	73.3	40.8	Alliance, OH	8.8	−6.4	1.4
Fort Collins, CO	48.2	73.2	52.8	Anniston, AL	30.6	−6.3	7.5
Visalia, CA	14.5	72.7	11.8	Hoboken, NJ	7.5	−6.3	−0.5

Source: See Table 2-1.
Z Less than 0.5%

expense of York. A second growth area is in the south of the county; this area benefits from the present no-growth policy that prevails in Maryland County, which abuts York County. A third growth area is Fairview Township, which is influenced by the Harrisburg market. Thus the county gains from spillovers from other counties. Elmira, New York offers another variation of the phenomenon. This city, primarily blue collar, has suffered out-migration in part because of the closing of a television tube plant that was only partly offset by the opening of a food processing plant. But Jefferson County benefits from the employment opportunities that were created by the opening of Corning Glassware.

Another variation is represented by Webster Groves, Missouri, an old city, fully developed, with little turnover in housing and thus little opportunity for changing land use patterns. Part of the decline, however, was due to a shift of land use from residences to a highway. A substantial part of the county's growth occurs in unincorporated areas. A higher proportion of the residents in this area work in St. Louis.

Table 2-3 shows another perspective of the relationship between counties and declining cities. A small percentage of the workers in declining cities work outside their counties. On the other hand, in many growing cities a very large percentage of the workers work

Table 2-3. Percent Employed Outside County of Residence for Fastest Growing and Declining Cities (Population Size Class 25-50 Thousand) 1970

Fastest Growing Cities			Fastest Declining Cities		
City, State	Percent	City Size Class Rank	City, State	Percent	City Size Class Rank
Bowie Town, MD	56.5	13	Anderson, SC	6.0	271
Cypress, CA	59.6	10	Newport, RI	5.0	297
Fountain Valley, CA	30.0	84	Johnstown, PA	3.2	385
Mentor, OH	46.8	32	Hamtramck, MI	16.7	137
Titusville, FL	4.0	344	Atlantic City, NJ	5.2	291
Milpitas, CA	19.2	125	Harlingen, TX	4.0	344
Boca Raton, FL	17.9	130	East Chicago, IN	8.0	228
Walnut Creek, CA	41.8	45	Portsmouth, OH	6.3	264
Melbourne, FL	2.4	420	McKeesport, PA	2.9	401
Fairfield, CA	8.1	225	Poughkeepsie, NY	N/A	N/A
Richardson, TX	9.1	213	Zanesville, OH	7.0	251
Newark, CA	27.8	91	Bangor, ME	4.6	307
Hurst, TX	16.4	140	Roswell, NM	3.1	392
Rosemead, CA	1.4	224	Elmira, NY	4.0	344
Brookland Park, MN	15.5	142	New Castle, PA	12.5	168
Arvada, CO	56.1	14	Key West, FL	0.8	455
Pompano Beach, FL	8.1	225	Newport, KY	60.0	8
Brook Park, OH	4.4	319	Salina, KA	5.1	294
Livermore, CA	8.8	214	Vicksburg, MS	2.7	408
Northbrook, IL	13.1	165	Prichard, AL	4.3	325
Glendale, AZ	1.8	435	Norwood, OH	3.4	373
Palatine, IL	8.1	225	Battle Creek, MI	6.1	267
Escondido, CA	1.5	440	Amsterdam, NY	28.1	89
North Olmsted, OH	6.0	271	Cumberland, MD	3.9	349
Del City, OK	3.2	385	Williamsburg, PA	4.1	335
Kaneohe, HA	0.9	454	Jackson, MI	4.6	307
Corona, CA	26.7	93	Austin, MN	4.3	325
North Chicago, IL	2.0	433	Wheeling, WV	17.2	135
Lewiston, ID	8.7	215	Williamsport, PA	3.0	397
Farmer's Branch, TX	3.3	378	Chelsea, MA	20.4	123
Upland, CA	33.9	67	Orange, NJ	20.7	122
Coon Rapids, MN	59.6	10	Ithaca, NY	2.5	419
Troy, MI	38.1	59	Meridian, MS	3.3	378
Chapel Hill, NC	21.4	115	Phenix City, AL	59.8	9
Normal, IL	5.9	277	Paducah, KY	10.0	203
N. Las Vegas, NE	4.3	325	Big Springs, TX	4.4	319

Fastest Growing Cities			Fastest Declining Cities		
City, State	Percent	City Size Class Rank	City, State	Percent	City Size Class Rank
Raytown, MO	10.5	198	Alton, IL	17.3	134
Littleton, CO	41.1	48	Easton, PA	22.5	108
Frindley, MN	68.8	2	Watertown, NY	2.9	401
San Rafael, CA	39.7	52	York, PA	3.8	165
Newport Beach, CA	18.9	127	New London, CN	4.1	335
Mt. Prospect, IL	4.8	302	University City, MO	47.9	28
Warner-Robbins, GA	9.3	208	Goldsboro, NC	3.5	365
DeKalb, IL	8.0	228	Highland Pk., MI	15.3	144
Lompac, CA	2.9	401	Troy, NY	40.7	17
Kenner, LA	38.4	58	Kokomo, IN	4.3	325
Menomonee Falls, WI	63.8	4	Ashland, KY	14.3	154
Novato, CA	30.2	183	Alliance, OH	11.6	184
Fort Collins, CO	5.4	284	Anniston, AL	2.7	408
Visalia, CA	4.0	344	Hoboken, NJ	24.7	98

Source: See Table 2-1.
$X^2 = 9.76$ df = 1 p < .01

outside the city and the county. Thus, these cities benefit not only from the economic health of their respective counties, but from surrounding counties as well.

This is not true of declining cities, most are nearly totally dependent upon the economic health of their own counties. The commuting field and labor markets of growing cities are larger, and they benefit by exporting labor. In a sense, their economic base is a high quality of human resources. This is shown in Table 2-4, which compares the educational attainment of the population in growing and declining cities.

RACE AND POPULATION GROWTH

The fastest growing cities as a rule are lily white. Almost 68 percent of them had virtually no nonwhites. In contrast, only in 10 percent of the declining cities was the nonwhite population that miniscule. Indeed, in many of these cities, the black population was above the national average (see Table 2-5).

The explanation for this phenomenon is not simple. Cities that have experienced rapid growth may have imposed exclusionary barriers against blacks and the poor. But what appears to be also the case, is that many of these cities do not have the type of employ-

Table 2-4. Percentage of Population Attaining Four Years of High School or More for Fastest Growing and Declining Cities (Population Size Class 25-50 Thousand) 1970

Fastest Growing Cities			Fastest Declining Cities		
City, State	Percent	City Size Class Rank	City, State	Percent	City Size Class Rank
Bowie Town, MD	86.4	9	Anderson, SC	39.6	433
Cypress, CA	74.8	66	Newport, RI	58.5	219
Fountain Valley, CA	78.0	41	Johnstown, PA	40.1	429
Mentor, OH	68.0	119	Hamtramck, MI	30.9	450
Titusville, FL	72.2	84	Atlantic City, NJ	35.4	443
Milpitas, CA	61.7	183	Harlingen, TX	42.5	409
Boca Raton, FL	73.2	75	East Chicago, IN	34.8	444
Walnut Creek, CA	82.1	18	Portsmouth, OH	44.2	399
Melbourne, FL	65.5	142	McKeesport, PA	40.2	428
Fairfield, CA	73.4	71	Poughkeepsie, NY	47.8	355
Richardson, TX	85.1	13	Zanesville, OH	43.8	401
Newark, CA	60.2	199	Bangor, ME	63.2	157
Hurst, TX	67.5	123	Roswell, NM	57.3	235
Rosemead, CA	47.9	354	Elmira, NY	52.1	297
Brookland Park, MN	76.8	52	New Castle, PA	45.6	388
Arvada, CO	76.8	52	Key West, FL	51.1	312
Pompano Beach, FL	60.3	197	Newport, KY	25.0	456
Brook Park, OH	60.4	203	Salina, KA	66.3	132
Livermore, CA	75.5	61	Vicksburg, MS	47.5	362
Northbrook, IL	85.7	11	Prichard, AL	25.2	455
Glendale, AZ	55.6	251	Norwood, OH	36.0	440
Palatine, IL	79.3	31	Battle Creek, MI	47.1	369
Escondido, CA	62.7	167	Amsterdam, NY	43.9	400
North Olmsted, OH	75.3	63	Cumberland, MD	46.9	418
Del City, OK	65.0	145	Williamsburg, PA	57.4	231
Kaneohe, HA	72.2	84	Jackson, MI	49.4	336
Corona, CA	58.7	217	Austin, MN	61.1	188
North Chicago, IL	53.7	277	Wheeling, WV	47.1	369
Lewiston, ID	61.4	185	Williamsport, PA	53.4	280
Farmer's Branch, TX	69.5	105	Chelsea, MA	41.3	421
Upland, CA	67.9	120	Orange, NJ	45.4	390
Coon Rapids, MN	68.9	108	Ithaca, NY	73.3	73
Troy, MI	70.2	103	Meridian, MS	49.4	336
Chapel Hill, NC	85.8	10	Phenix City, AL	29.4	452
Normal, IL	78.7	32	Paducah, KY	45.9	383
N. Las Vegas, NE	54.5	269	Big Springs, TX	54.2	270
Raytown, MO	68.8	112	Alton, IL	45.8	387

Fastest Growing Cities			Fastest Declining Cities		
City, State	Percent	City Size Class Rank	City, State	Percent	City Size Class Rank
Littleton, CO	77.2	48	Easton, PA	42.1	415
Frindley, MN	71.9	88	Watertown, NY	56.7	244
San Rafael, CA	77.9	43	York, PA	37.8	216
Newport Beach, CA	86.6	8	New London, CN	51.0	314
Mt. Prospect, IL	78.0	41	University City, MO	60.9	191
Warner-Robbins, GA	66.5	131	Goldsboro, NC	40.1	429
DeKalb, IL	68.9	108	Highland Pk., MI	43.0	407
Lompac, CA	70.6	101	Troy, NY	45.5	199
Kenner, LA	46.4	380	Kokomo, IN	49.3	339
Menomonee Falls, WI	68.6	114	Ashland, KY	53.1	285
Novato, CA	77.7	45	Alliance, OH	49.6	333
Fort Collins, CO	73.4	71	Anniston, AL	42.5	409
Visalia, CA	60.2	199	Hoboken, NJ	26.6	454
Pacifica, CA	71.8	90	Cheyenne, WY	67.4	125
Corvallis, OR	82.1	18	Wyandotte, MI	42.1	415
Fairborn, OH	61.4	185	Webster Groves, MO	73.3	73
Seaside, CA	62.8	163	Steubenville, OH	47.0	372
Saratoga, CA	84.4	16			
New Berlin, WI	71.6	93			

Source: See Table 2-1.
$X^2 = 39.10$ df = 1 p = < .01

ment that would attract the unskilled in great numbers. They are not manufacturing centers (see Table 2-6). At the same time, it is possible that the high percent of blacks in declining cities is partly a function of the greater opportunities these cities offer for employment in manufacturing in spite of their high unemployment rates. It is also related to the fact that for a variety of reasons blacks are less mobile than whites. (As mentioned above, nearly 10 percent of the rapidly declining cities had virtually no nonwhites.)

We might be witnessing a rather interesting turn of events. During past decades the declining counties of the South were principally black (4). These counties declined as a result of the black exodus to the North. Today, declining cities have larger black populations than growing cities. This fact might be related to immobility. Blacks left the South partly because of the decline of agriculture and the rise of manufacturing, thus influencing the decline of some counties. Now, it might very well be that they are tied to these manufacturing cities which are on the decline as new nonmanufacturing cities emerge.

40 Population Growth, Decline, and Policies

Table 2-5. Percent Black Population for Fastest Growing and Declining Cities (Population Size Class 25-50 Thousand) 1970

Fastest Growing Cities			Fastest Declining Cities		
City, State	Percent	City Size Class Rank	City, State	Percent	City Size Class Rank
Bowie Town, MD	2.5	214	Anderson, SC	25.7	41
Cypress, CA	0.0	0	Newport, RI	7.2	136
Fountain Valley, CA	0.0	0	Johnstown, PA	6.3	146
Mentor, OH	0.0	0	Hamtramck, MI	11.9	100
Titusville, FL	9.0	118	Atlantic City, NJ	43.9	12
Milpitas, CA	5.3	155	Harlingen, TX	1.3	248
Boca Raton, FL	2.6	211	East Chicago, IN	27.4	39
Walnut Creek, CA	0.0	0	Portsmouth, OH	4.7	165
Melbourne, FL	12.0	99	McKeesport, PA	10.3	108
Fairfield, CA	7.5	133	Poughkeepsie, NY	18.5	64
Richardson, TX	0.0	0	Zanesville, OH	8.7	121
Newark, CA	0.0	0	Bangor, ME	0.0	0
Hurst, TX	0.0	0	Roswell, NM	4.0	178
Rosemead, CA	0.0	0	Elmira, NY	7.6	132
Brookland Park, MN	0.0	0	New Castle, PA	6.1	148
Arvada, CO	0.0	0	Key West, FL	11.8	101
Pompano Beach, FL	20.6	53	Newport, KY	3.0	198
Brook Park, OH	0.0	0	Salina, KA	3.1	195
Livermore, CA	0.0	0	Vicksburg, MS	49.3	8
Northbrook, IL	0.0	0	Prichard, AL	50.4	6
Glendale, AZ	0.0	0	Norwood, OH	0.0	0
Palatine, IL	0.0	0	Battle Creek, MI	20.1	55
Escondido, CA	0.0	0	Amsterdam, NY	0.0	0
North Olmsted, OH	0.0	0	Cumberland, MD	2.9	201
Del City, OK	0.0	0	Williamsburg, PA	20.0	57
Kaneohe, HA	0.0	0	Jackson, MI	13.0	91
Corona, CA	0.0	0	Austin, MN	0.0	0
North Chicago, IL	16.6	73	Wheeling, WV	3.7	185
Lewiston, ID	0.0	0	Williamsport, PA	3.0	198
Farmer's Branch, TX	0.0	0	Chelsea, MA	1.9	225
Upland, CA	0.0	0	Orange, NJ	35.9	19
Coon Rapids, MN	0.0	0	Ithaca, NY	5.1	157
Troy, MI	0.0	0	Meridian, MS	33.5	26
Chapel Hill, NC	10.2	109	Phenix City, AL	37.2	18
Normal, IL	1.6	239	Paducah, KY	17.4	69
N. Las Vegas, NE	24.3	44	Big Springs, TX	5.2	67
Raytown, MO	0.0	0	Alton, IL	16.1	77
Littleton, CO	0.0	0	Easton, PA	6.3	146

Fastest Growing Cities			Fastest Declining Cities		
City, State	Percent	City Size Class Rank	City, State	Percent	City Size Class Rank
Frindley, MN	0.0	0	Watertown, NY	0.0	0
San Rafael, CA	0.0	0	York, PA	12.9	48
Newport Beach, CA	0.0	0	New London, CN	11.3	103
Mt. Prospect, IL	0.0	0	University City, MO	20.0	57
Warner-Robbins, GA	8.5	122	Goldsboro, NC	48.0	10
DeKalb, IL	1.8	227	Highland Pk., MI	55.3	2
Lompac, CA	4.2	174	Troy, NY	4.6	93
Kenner, LA	20.1	55	Kokomo, IN	7.8	130
Menomonee Falls, WI	0.0	0	Ashland, KY	2.4	219
Novato, CA	3.4	187	Alliance, OH	10.6	107
Fort Collins, CO	0.0	0	Anniston, AL	34.6	21
Visalia, CA	0.0	0	Hoboken, NJ	4.1	176

Source: See Table 2-1.
$X^2 = 38.48$ df = 1 $p < .01$

HOUSING AND THE AGE OF CITIES

One would expect that the more rapidly growing cities would have a housing stock of more recent vintage—that is, they will be younger cities. A chi-square of 77.6, significant at the point of 0.01 level, indicates that growing and declining cities are significantly different in terms of age.

Few of the rapidly growing cities have over 30 percent of their housing stock built prior to 1950. On the other hand, many of the declining cities, such as Hamtramck, Michigan; Chelsea, Massachusetts; and Highland Park, Michigan; have cities with over 80 percent of their housing built prior to that year. Declining cities are distinctly older (see Table 2-7).

PER CAPITA INCOME

The existing literature on migration patterns provides sufficient evidence that people tend to gravitate towards higher income areas and that higher income individuals tend to be the most mobile. Indeed, the literature suggests a backwash effect. Those who are left behind in declining cities are the unskilled and many who are outside of the labor force partly because of age.

Although some cities have experienced relatively fast rates of

42 Population Growth, Decline, and Policies

Table 2-6. Percent Employed in Manufacturing (1970) for Fastest Growing and Declining Cities (Population Size Class 25-50 Thousand)

Fastest Growing Cities			Fastest Declining Cities		
City, State	Percent	City Size Class Rank	City, State	Percent	City Size Class Rank
Bowie Town, MD	8.3	416	Anderson, SC	35.3	119
Cypress, CA	34.0	129	Newport, RI	8.5	413
Fountain Valley, CA	33.8	134	Johnstown, PA	40.2	64
Mentor, OH	44.1	33	Hamtramck, MI	44.9	30
Titusville, FL	26.7	219	Atlantic City, NJ	10.1	392
Milpitas, CA	40.8	59	Harlingen, TX	10.9	382
Boca Raton, FL	18.5	316	East Chicago, IN	55.9	1
Walnut Creek, CA	21.5	211	Portsmouth, OH	24.7	238
Melbourne, FL	21.9	272	McKeesport, PA	38.2	78
Fairfield, CA	9.6	402	Poughkeepsie, NY	27.7	206
Richardson, TX	32.0	152	Zanesville, OH	32.1	150
Newark, CA	38.9	74	Bangor, ME	13.6	364
Hurst, TX	32.4	147	Roswell, NM	9.1	406
Rosemead, CA	29.2	184	Elmira, NY	30.9	168
Brookland Park, MN	26.5	221	New Castle, PA	35.6	114
Arvada, CO	19.3	303	Key West, FL	4.2	450
Pompano Beach, FL	10.9	382	Newport, KY	33.9	132
Brook Park, OH	37.9	80	Salina, KA	12.5	371
Livermore, CA	10.8	384	Vicksburg, MS	16.0	345
Northbrook, IL	26.5	221	Prichard, AL	28.9	189
Glendale, AZ	21.8	274	Norwood, OH	48.6	9
Palatine, IL	30.9	168	Battle Creek, MI	30.8	171
Escondido, CA	18.5	316	Amsterdam, NY	42.9	42
North Olmsted, OH	27.7	206	Cumberland, MD	24.7	238
Del City, OK	12.6	370	Williamsburg, PA	24.0	248
Kaneohe, HA	9.7	400	Jackson, MI	33.3	138
Corona, CA	30.7	172	Austin, MN	39.9	66
North Chicago, IL	35.7	110	Wheeling, WV	22.8	262
Lewiston, ID	21.6	279	Williamsport, PA	38.8	75
Farmer's Branch, TX	27.4	209	Chelsea, MA	28.1	203
Upland, CA	27.2	212	Orange, NJ	24.4	243
Coon Rapids, MN	35.5	115	Ithaca, NY	11.4	379
Troy, MI	35.7	110	Meridian, MS	17.5	327
Chapel Hill, NC	3.9	453	Phenix City, AL	34.8	122
Normal, IL	10.4	389	Paducah, KY	16.3	342
N. Las Vegas, NE	4.9	448	Big Springs, TX	10.4	389
Raytown, MO	24.1	247	Alton, IL	37.6	82
Littleton, CO	22.2	269	Easton, PA	42.7	43

Fastest Growing Cities			Fastest Declining Cities		
City, State	Percent	City Size Class Rank	City, State	Percent	City Size Class Rank
Frindley, MN	33.5	137	Watertown, NY	22.9	259
San Rafael, CA	10.7	386	York, PA	43.3	23
Newport Beach, CA	19.5	299	New London, CN	26.2	228
Mt. Prospect, IL	30.7	172	University City, MO	16.6	337
Warner-Robbins, GA	5.3	446	Goldsboro, NC	21.8	274
DeKalb, IL	16.8	335	Highland Pk., MI	33.7	135
Lompac, CA	9.9	396	Troy, NY	23.9	137
Kenner, LA	14.1	362	Kokomo, IN	49.4	5
Menomonee Falls, WI	35.1	120	Ashland, KY	28.2	200
Novato, CA	8.0	420	Alliance, OH	45.4	28
Fort Collins, CO	9.2	405	Anniston, AL	27.8	205
Visalia, CA	11.8	376	Hoboken, NJ	37.5	84

Source: See Table 2-1.
$X^2 = 12.24$ df = 1 $p < .01$

decline, they have nevertheless remained relatively high in terms of per capita income. University City, maintains a high level of income because of the existence of Washington University and the kinds of firms that agglomerate around universities. Similarly, Poughkeepsie, New York, while losing population, remains the regional center of government and the location of a high paying employer, IBM. On the other extreme, some rapidly growing cities have ranked very low in terms of per capita income. Kenner, Louisiana, for example, ranks low in per capita income. It is a residential community, with little industrial base, and a high percentage of blacks. Its growth is in part a spillover of population from the New Orleans-Baton Rouge area. A similar situation holds in North Chicago, which is a rapidly growing blue collar city.

According to the data in Table 2-8, growing cities have higher per capita incomes than do declining cities. Indeed, while only 20 percent of the growing cities have per capita incomes of less than $3,000, almost 58 percent of the declining cities have per capita incomes below this level. Indeed, the chi-square statistic of 16, which is significant at the 0.01 level, emphasizes the difference between these two groups of cities.

A PARADIGM OF DECLINE

Small cities are not a homogeneous group. Although the growth rate for small cities is faster than that for the nation as a whole,

Table 2-7. Percent of 1970 Housing Units Built Prior to 1950 for Fastest Growing and Declining Cities (Population Size Class 25-50 Thousand)

Fastest Growing Cities			Fastest Declining Cities		
City, State	Percent	City Size Class Rank	City, State	Percent	City Size Class Rank
Bowie Town, MD	2.9	451	Anderson, SC	63.0	144
Cypress, CA	3.5	447	Newport, RI	83.9	29
Fountain Valley, CA	1.5	454	Johnstown, PA	90.8	6
Mentor, OH	20.6	387	Hamtramck, MI	97.8	1
Titusville, FL	7.8	438	Atlantic City, NJ	79.6	48
Milpitas, CA	2.6	452	Harlingen, TX	43.3	274
Boca Raton, FL	6.6	444	East Chicago, IN	83.4	34
Walnut Creek, CA	10.5	431	Portsmouth, OH	84.7	27
Melbourne, FL	12.4	424	McKeesport, PA	85.3	25
Fairfield, CA	11.4	428	Poughkeepsie, NY	87.5	16
Richardson, TX	3.2	450	Zanesville, OH	86.2	21
Newark, CA	8.9	434	Bangor, ME	75.3	71
Hurst, TX	1.6	453	Roswell, NM	40.2	295
Rosemead, CA	49.7	234	Elmira, NY	93.8	3
Brookland Park, MN	7.4	441	New Castle, PA	86.4	20
Arvada, CO	7.8	438	Key West, FL	60.7	159
Pompano Beach, FL	6.8	443	Newport, KY	85.9	22
Brook Park, OH	3.4	448	Salina, KA	54.0	201
Livermore, CA	13.5	419	Vicksburg, MS	70.1	101
Northbrook, IL	16.3	403	Prichard, AL	59.6	167
Glendale, AZ	20.5	388	Norwood, OH	89.9	7
Palatine, IL	17.8	397	Battle Creek, MI	82.3	40
Escondido, CA	17.3	399	Amsterdam, NY	89.8	8
North Olmsted, OH	15.7	407	Cumberland, MD	85.2	26
Del City, OK	17.7	398	Williamsburg, PA	80.8	45
Kaneohe, HA	9.6	433	Jackson, MI	88.5	10
Corona, CA	27.2	364	Austin, MN	66.4	124
North Chicago, IL	55.3	194	Wheeling, WV	83.5	32
Lewiston, ID	53.5	205	Williamsport, PA	92.2	4
Farmer's Branch, TX	4.1	446	Chelsea, MA	91.2	5
Upland, CA	22.2	382	Orange, NJ	77.8	57
Coon Rapids, MN	8.7	436	Ithaca, NY	85.4	23
Troy, MI	17.0	401	Meridian, MS	61.2	155
Chapel Hill, NC	33.4	332	Phenix City, AL	50.6	231
Normal, IL	31.7	342	Paducah, KY	61.9	151

Characteristics of Growing and Declining Cities 45

Fastest Growing Cities			Fastest Declining Cities		
City, State	Percent	City Size Class Rank	City, State	Percent	City Size Class Rank
N. Las Vegas, NE	7.0	442	Big Springs, TX	41.4	287
Raytown, MO	14.5	413	Alton, IL	75.7	66
Littleton, CO	14.9	411	Easton, PA	88.4	12
Frindley, MN	8.8	435	Watertown, NY	86.8	18
San Rafael, CA	30.5	350	York, PA	88.9	7
Newport Beach, CA	28.4	360	New London, CN	72.1	86
Mt. Prospect, IL	11.8	426	University City, MO	62.9	145
Warner-Robbins, GA	13.8	418	Goldsboro, NC	48.8	238
DeKalb, IL	48.0	247	Highland Pk., MI	96.0	2
Lompac, CA	15.1	409	Troy, NY	86.3	11
Kenner, LA	16.7	402	Kokomo, IN	72.4	83
Menomonee Falls, WI	18.5	394	Ashland, KY	68.4	115
Novato, CA	15.9	406	Alliance, OH	78.0	55
Fort Collins, CO	37.8	313	Anniston, AL	64.0	139
Visalia, CA	36.9	321	Hoboken, NJ	89.4	9

Source: See Table 2-1.
$X^2 = 77.6$ df = 1 $p < .01$

Table 2-8. Per Capita Income for Fastest Growing and Declining Cities (Population Size Class 25-50 Thousand) 1970

Fastest Growing Cities			Fastest Declining Cities		
City, State	Per Capita Income	City Size Class Rank	City, State	Per Capita Income	City Size Class Rank
Bowie Town, MD	$3868	76	Anderson, SC	$2788	353
Cypress, CA	$3725	94	Newport, RI	$2907	312
Fountain Valley, CA	$3601	116	Johnstown, PA	$2443	424
Mentor, OH	$3672	100	Hamtramck, MI	$3232	203
Titusville, FL	$3306	186	Atlantic City, NJ	$2554	405
Milpitas, CA	$2938	303	Harlingen, TX	$1909	455
Boca Raton, FL	$5772	13	East Chicago, IN	$2822	341
Walnut Creek, CA	$5040	26	Portsmouth, OH	$2672	382
Melbourne, FL	$2921	308	McKeesport, PA	$2798	346
Fairfield, CA	$2737	363	Poughkeepsie, NY	$3451	140
Richardson, TX	$4167	53	Zanesville, OH	$2404	430
Newark, CA	$3007	278	Bangor, ME	$2553	406

Fastest Growing Cities			Fastest Declining Cities		
City, State	Per Capita Income	City Size Class Rank	City, State	Per Capita Income	City Size Class Rank
Hurst, TX	$3569	121	Roswell, NM	$2568	402
Rosemead, CA	$2873	324	Elmira, NY	$2549	407
Brookland Park, MN	$3329	179	New Castle, PA	$2469	420
Arvada, CO	$3232	203	Key West, FL	$2567	403
Pompano Beach, FL	$4051	60	Newport KY	$2308	441
Brook Park, OH	$3259	199	Salina, KA	$2930	306
Livermore, CA	$3592	118	Vicksburg, MS	$2299	442
Northbrook, IL	$5672	14	Prichard, AL	$1796	456
Glendale, AZ	$2684	380	Norwood, OH	$3148	228
Palatine, IL	$4148	54	Battle Creek, MI	$3138	230
Escondido, CA	$3125	234	Amsterdam, NY	$2910	311
North Olmsted, OH	$3929	70	Cumberland, MD	$2680	381
Del City, OK	$3079	249	Williamsburg, PA	$3347	173
Kaneohe, HA	$3413	152	Jackson, MI	$3125	234
Corona, CA	$3075	250	Austin, MN	$3167	224
North Chicago, IL	$2432	426	Wheeling, WV	$2964	295
Lewiston, ID	$2877	322	Williamsport, PA	$2605	393
Farmer's Branch, TX	$3925	71	Chelsea, MA	$2844	334
Upland, CA	$3825	80	Orange, NJ	$3393	159
Coon Rapids, MN	$2750	360	Ithaca, NY	$2940	302
Troy, MI	$4757	31	Meridian, MS	$2396	431
Chapel Hill, NC	$3311	184	Phenix City, AL	$2100	451
Normal, IL	$3003	281	Paducah, KY	$2779	355
N. Las Vegas, NE	$2537	411	Big Springs, TX	$2658	385
Raytown, MO	$3792	85	Alton, IL	$2993	287
Littleton, CO	$3713	95	Easton, PA	$2764	358
Frindley, MN	$3519	129	Watertown, NY	$2892	315
San Rafael, CA	$4914	28	York, PA	$2862	180
Newport Beach, CA	$6735	5	New London, CN	$3375	168
Mt. Prospect, IL	$4576	34	University City, MO	$4410	41
Warner-Robbins, GA	$3049	260	Goldsboro, NC	$2125	450
DeKalb, IL	$2900	314	Highland Pk., MI	$3011	277
Lompac, CA	$2839	336	Troy, NY	$2812	196
Kenner, LA	$2392	432	Kokomo, IN	$3116	236
Menomonee Falls, WI	$3351	172	Ashland, KY	$2994	286
Novato, CA	$3427	149	Alliance, OH	$3063	255
Fort Collins, CO	$2796	347	Anniston, AL	$2411	429
Visalia, CA	$3242	202	Hoboken, NJ	$2592	396

Source: See Table 2-1.
$X^2 = 16$ df $= 1$ $p < .01$

substantial numbers of these cities are declining—some dramatically. The South is almost equally represented among the fastest growing and declining cities—a fact that should modify our view of the South as a growth area.

The data show that growing and declining cities are significantly different in key socioeconomic characteristics. Many of these characteristics are the consequences or even the causes of decline. The overdependence on manufacturing is an example. The decline of the steel mill in New Castle, Pennsylvania, and the automobile plant in Highland Park, Michigan certainly contributed to the secular decline in these cities; the age of the city and its inability to utilize the fill-in process of growth also restrain growth. This appears to be the case of Williamsport, Pennsylvania. Growth is especially hindered where annexation is ruled out.

It seems to be possible to isolate a series of indicators of a declining city or a city that might be viewed as a primary candidate for decline. The following characteristics are most relevant:

- Annexation is rendered impossible either by state law, political resistance, or because the city is land locked.
- The city is a heavy manufacturing center with little room for the reorganization of plants.
- The city is fully developed.
- The city is old in terms of construction, both residential and commercial.
- The city is heavily dependent upon itself and its county for employment.

As we can see very clearly from the findings of this study, knowing that the city is located in the South or in the so-called sunbelt is not enough to define its growth status. Moreover, knowing the growth status of the county is not enough. Many rapidly declining cities sit in the midst of rapidly growing counties.

Part Two

Migration and Population Policies

 *Chapter Three*

Government's Role in Population Movement: Policy by Indirection

Norman Beckman

The future of small and medium sized cities in the United States will depend upon the population distribution policies of the federal, state, and local governments, and on the courts. The need for public policy concerning population distribution arises from the equity, economic, social, political, and environmental impact of human settlement patterns.

HOW DOES GOVERNMENT INFLUENCE POPULATION MOVEMENT?

Public activities impact on the location of development, inducing employment and population resettlement, through a myriad of programs and plans often designed for other purposes but frequently having an unintended effect on the location of people. The *President's 1974 Report on National Growth and Development* identifies seven types of federal activities which have major growth influences. These are: grants and loans to state and local governments; location and employment levels of federal installation; procurement of goods and services; direct and indirect federal construction of public works; taxation; credit management; and regulatory activities.

Taking a more historical view, James Sundquist has observed that population distribution in the past has been a matter of federal policy:

> In the first hundred years of the nation, the government pursued a deliberate policy of dispensing population westward. Motivated in part by

desire to confirm its title to the empty continent, the government subsidized turnpikes, railroads, and river navigation, herded Indians onto reservations, and opened public lands to settlement.

Once the continent was spanned, governmental programs continued to encourage a balanced regional development—reclamation, navigation, and electric power projects traditionally, and more recently the sophisticated and broader efforts authorized in the Appalachian Regional Development Act and the "depressed areas" legislation of the 1960's... there is apparently no clear sense of national purpose like that which motivated the early policies for western development. The present regional and rural development programs essentially are the product of legislative log-rolling—the chance balancing of political forces analogous to economic laissez-faire (1).

States are enacting environment, land use, and development legislation, promoting economic growth, and modifying areawide and local powers to deal with growth. The evolution of substate planning and districting, including federal and state use of these new multi-county planning districts is one way of affecting the distribution of growth and population.

At the local level a variety of strategies, many of which are currently testing the bounds of judicial acceptability, are being employed to control population movement and density. Three approaches in particular have been identified (2) in regulating population growth at the local level. One is the "traditional" approach—the reliance is on conventional methods of land use control such as large lot zoning, subdivision regulation, prescriptions on multiple unit dwellings, trailer parks, etc., in order to regulate community growth.

Another is the "timing" or "when" approach. This technique, employed in Ramapo, is designed to control the timing, not the fact, of growth. It requires private development to proceed at a predetermined pace of development, as opposed to a "natural" or unconstrained growth approach.

And a third is the "how much" approach. This approach, used in Petaluma, stresses the amount of growth that is acceptable, fixing annual building quotas to accomplish that end. The same end may be achieved by limiting municipal services, either directly or through the imposition of a moratorium on construction until services are provided.

Actually there is a host of federal government programs aimed at rural or small city development. A mere enumeration of federal laws and programs designed to promote economic development in rural areas and limited to those aimed directly at state and local government agencies would include the following:

Rural development research
Agricultural and rural economic research
Rural housing site loans
Rural rental housing loans
Very low income housing repair loans
Community facility loans
Water and waste disposal systems for rural communities
Business and industrial development loans
Resource conservation and development loans
Cooperative Extension Service
Rural electrification loans
Rural telephone loans
Rural telephone bank loans
Great Plains Conservation
Resource Conservation and Development
Soil and Water Conservation
Grants and loans for public works and development facilities
Loans for businesses and development companies
Planning Assistance Community Economic Adjustment
Appalachian Regional Development.

In contemporary times the most novel and experimental approaches to migration policy making were formulated during the depression. The Resettlement Administration, created in 1935, undertook a wide range of housing and resettlement projects across the country, in part to remove submarginal farms from cultivation and to experiment with different types of agricultural settlements. This was also in part a demonstration program for new community development initiatives, including the Greenbelt Towns, but war priorities intervened before broader efforts could be undertaken. One regional development approach that did have positive impacts on growth and development was the Tennessee Valley Authority (TVA). The TVA was controversial during the 1930s as a public corporation operating in a heretofore private realm; in practice, however, it quickened the pace of economic development for a whole region.

By the early 1960s the decline in population and economic activities in smaller jurisdictions throughout the country led to the enactment of a new series of economic development programs aimed at nonmetropolitan parts of the United States:

> Typified by the Area Re-development Administration, they were designed to provide public works assistance to poor communities and to supplement state and local financial incentives for attracting industry by providing low interest industrial loans.

But these programs proved ineffective for two reasons: (1) the funds available for them were far too few and spread too thinly to reverse the strong rural-urban shift in the nation's economic geography; and (2) the concepts upon which the programs were based were rooted more in nostalgia than in national economic realities (3).

In 1965 the Appalachian Regional Development Act and the Public Works and Economic Development Act established federal-interstate regional commissions assigned the task of developing plans for large segments of the nation bypassed by the mainstream of national growth. By their nature they were expected to coordinate the actions of federal and state governments in the geographic areas assigned to them. These same statutes encouraged multicounty, areawide planning for public facilities and economic development.

The Public Works and Economic Development Act of 1965 has since been amended and expanded to include provisions for economic adjustment assistance to areas that have been adversely affected by the loss of a major economic unit in their locality and a job opportunities program designed to "stimulate, maintain or expand job creating activities in areas . . . which are suffering from unusually high levels of unemployment."

The Rural Development Act of 1972, consisting of six titles, deals with most of the high priority needs of nonmetropolitan America, such as loan and grant assistance, planning, fire protection, conservation, education, and research. Of particular concern are the elements of the Act that provide for community facilities, rural housing, economic development, and environmental improvement. To assist rural areas in providing essential community facilities, the Act expands the existing loan programs for rural water, sewer, and solid waste disposal to include all other essential community facilities.

To encourage the economic development of rural areas, the Act provides loans and grants to public bodies for the development, construction, or acquisition of land, buildings, plants, equipment, access streets and roads, and other facilities involved in measures designed to facilitate development of private business and industrial enterprises.

Titles IX and X, both added in 1974, provide money for special economic development and adjustment assistance, and for a job opportunities program. The special economic development and adjustment assistance is to be used when an area is threatened or is experiencing severe unemployment arising from economic dislocation, caused by either private or government action or regulation. The job opportunities program allows the Secretary of Commerce to make grants, and to stimulate, maintain, or expand job creating activities in areas suffering from unusually high levels of unemployment. Both urban and rural areas are eligible for participation in these programs.

In the Housing and New Community Development Act of 1970, Congress explicitly declared that the federal government must assume responsibility for the development of a national urban growth policy that would foster the continued economic strength of all parts of the United States, including central cities, suburbs, smaller communities, local neighborhoods, and rural areas. Further, the policy should help reverse trends of migration and physical growth that reinforce disparities among states, regions, and cities. To assist in the development of the policy, the President was directed to submit to Congress a report in the February of each even-numbered year.

The Agricultural Act of 1970 and the Rural Development Act of 1972 also bear directly on national growth policy. The Agriculture Act declared a congressional policy of achieving "a sound balance between rural and urban America." It directs executive agencies to locate and maintain insofar as practicable new federal offices and facilities in areas or communities of lower population density.

The Rural Development Act of 1972 directs the Secretary of Agriculture to establish—and report on progress toward attaining—goals for rural areas. New rural categorical aid programs were authorized, and the Secretary of Agriculture was directed to give preference to "rural" communities. The thrust of these goals is to provide job and income generating economic conditions in rural areas and small towns, as well as in large urban areas, so that the people of the United States will have a greater choice in deciding where to live. Access to jobs, income, and services in nonmetropolitan areas is seen as a necessary precondition to halting the migration to overcrowded and overburdened metropolitan areas.

Pursuant to the 1972 Act, the Second Annual Report of the Secretary of Agriculture spelled out current rural development goals that the Department believes impact on nonmetropolitan areas. These goals are as follows:

> Assist in the creation of a climate conducive to growth in the employment base of rural America, thereby providing a range of job opportunities for those who wish to live in rural areas.
>
> Contribute to the development of job opportunities in rural areas which generate incomes equal in terms of effective purchasing power to those in metropolitan areas.
>
> Support a "balance" between rural and metropolitan populations compatible with the overall national quality of life and economic health.

Facilitate the attainment of access to standard quality housing in rural areas equal to that of metropolitan areas.

Aid local governments to provide equal access to community facilities and services for nonmetropolitan residents (4).

The Regional Development Act of 1975 (P.L. 94-188) had two major provisions: one extended the Appalachian Development Act of 1965 and the other extended and amended Title V of the Public Works and Economic Development Act of 1965. Title V created the Regional Action Planning Commissions in 1965 and the new law has extended their existence for two more fiscal years, until the end of September 1977. In addition, the new law has expanded the mission of the regional commissions. They are now required to conduct demonstration projects in the fields of energy, health, nutrition, and education in addition to conducting joint regional transportation studies with the Secretary of Transportation.

The Housing and Community Development Act of 1974, Title I, provides for:

> ... a modified form of special revenue sharing. The community development block grant program replaces a series of categorical programs ... including: water and sewer and neighborhood facilities, urban renewal and neighborhood development program grants, public facilities, urban renewal and neighborhood development program grants, public facility loans, open space, urban beautification and historical preservation grants, Model Cities grant and rehabilitation loans ... 20%-25% of the funds are earmarked for nonmetropolitan areas (5).

Studies of federal outlays of money indicate no particular bias against small and medium size communities. An analysis of 1970 expenditures for construction indicate that in large metropolitan areas (those over one million) federal investment in new construction averaged about 40 percent less per capita than in metropolitan areas with fewer than 250,000 inhabitants. Similarly, in metropolitan areas with gross densities over 3,000 people per square mile, federal investment in new construction consistently averaged about 60 percent less per capita than in less dense metropolitan areas. Defense spending is substantially above average in the smallest metropolitan areas. The pattern for the sample year 1970 does, on the whole, tend to favor smaller metropolitan areas and areas with lower densities at the expense of large areas and areas of high density across most federal expenditure categories, particularly those with explicit urban development objectives.

The President's 1974 national growth and development report concluded that:

Federal outlays in the aggregate flow to metropolitan and nonmetropolitan areas roughly in proportion to their respective population. The metropolitan areas, as defined in April 1973, with about 73 percent of the national population, received about 75 percent of these selected FY 1973 outlays.... On a per capita basis, community development outlays were higher in nonmetropolitan counties than in metropolitan counties and highest of all in totally rural nonmetropolitan counties not adjacent to metropolitan areas. These differences in community development outlays were largely a function of extensive interstate highway construction in sparsely settled counties.... Across the urban to-rural continuum, per capita outlays for human resource development were largest in the most rural of nonmetropolitan counties and smallest in the fringe counties of the large metropolitan areas (6).

A *National Journal* survey of financial relationships between the states and the federal government has found that federal tax and spending policies are causing a massive flow of wealth from the Northeast and Midwest to the fast growing southern and western regions of the nation:

The flow of federal funds from the Northeast and Midwest to the South and West followed patterns in fiscal 1976 almost identical to those of the previous year... The Northeast sent $12.6 billion more to Washington in the form of taxes than it received in federal spending, compared with $10.8 billion the year before. The 'balance-of-payments' deficit for the five Great Lakes states, $18.6 billion in 1975, increased to $20.1 billion the following year.

While the losers kept losing, the winners kept winning. The surplus for the South advanced from $11.5 billion in 1975, to $12.6 billion in 1976, while the favorable balance of payments in the West dropped only slightly, from $10.6 billion to $10.4 billion.

Finally, a study of the so-called sunbelt and the Northeast-Midwest regions (7) examined the impact of federal expenditures in two regions. The southern states are among the poorest in the nation and the northern states among the richest. It concluded that while per capita federal spending is higher in the South than in the Northeast, both regions receive less in federal spending than the national average.

STATE EFFORTS TO PROTECT OR SUPPORT THEIR COMMUNITIES

One of the challenges in the development of a population distribution policy lies in devising a workable approach to critical growth activities of fifty diverse state governments and with coordinating these individual policies and programs of the many federal agencies.

A Council of State Governments study (8), prepared as a support document for the *President's 1974 Report on National Growth and Development*, documents a range of approaches adopted by state governments in attempting to manage growth. Emphasis is placed on recent and innovative approaches appraised as being successful. Legislators, citizens groups, and commissions in states throughout the nation are attempting to define growth and population distribution policies for their states. While for each state there are special concerns and points of emphasis (reflecting the great diversity among the states), there are strong common threads that have the potential for forming a national policy. Six basic approaches are identified in the Council of State Governments survey.

Economic Diversity

The desire for the diversified economy is contained in a number of the state growth plans. In Colorado it is recommended that the state encourage a diverse and stable economic base tailored to the state's needs by attracting and providing incentives for a variety of industries that are environmentally desirable, relatively insensitive to the national economy and other external influences, and with a sound future potential.

The states have attempted to promote economic development in various ways over the years:

> The methods range from establishing overseas offices to attract foreign industry (15 States) to industrial development programs which provide services such as leasing buildings and providing loans or guarantees (30 States). Twenty States utilize revenue or general obligation bonds to finance industrial development and 43 have authorized cities and counties to do so. All 50 States use tax incentives in one form or another, and many States are developing manpower training programs that are geared to the needs of newly arrived industries.
>
> Generally, the States have remained neutral as to the specific location of new industries in the State, although in recent years several States have acted to encourage industrial development in specific areas so as to achieve a better balance of jobs and services. For example, in 1974 the State of Missouri implemented a new Interim Investment Plan designed to provide concentrated doses of State assistance to certain intermediate size growth centers in order to develop their potential as regional centers of employment opportunity and commercial services (9).

Population Dispersal

A companion goal is dispersal of economic activity to support a dispersed pattern of settlement. Colorado seeks balanced population distribution with growth directed away from its congested Front

Range and environmentally fragile mountain areas. Rhode Island has chosen a policy of centralization to achieve service efficiencies and maintain its open space and rural landscape. Its programs encourage compact development, in-fill, and anti-sprawl.

Innovative state legislation in 1975 affecting population distribution included the following:

> One state required certain state activities to comply with local land use plans and requirements. Three enactments provided increased state assistance to local governments to fulfill their part of state planning. Twelve states mandated some form of local planning, ranging from specific zoning ordinance requirements to comprehensive plans. Seven enactments dealt with increasing the capacity of local governments to meet environmental and land use needs, usually by permitting localities to issue revenue bonds to finance pollution control facilities. Three states moved toward the development of a comprehensive statewide land use plan, while 14 enactments around the nation grappled with the ever-important issue of strip mining regulation, control, and reclamation.
>
> One new area of action emerged in 1975—the protection of the family farm... Four states enacted legislation designed to restrict, and in some cases outlaw, corporate and foreign investment in farming operations (10).

Guiding Development

A Massachusetts statewide growth policy proposal, released in draft by the Office of State Planning in October 1975, concludes that the State itself is a major contributor to costly and inefficient development. Its proposals would bring state investment policy in line with a growth policy strengthening existing population centers. Vermont's Capability and Development Plan, adopted by the General Assembly in 1973, is explicit in favoring a settlement pattern based on cluster planning and new community planning to economize on the costs of roads, utilities, and land usage.

Conserving Energy

The Florida Legislature's growth policy suggests that in the state the growth of energy consumption should be controlled by the long range availability of energy. The energy conservation criteria of the Vermont state plan are applied under the state's development permit system.

Environmental Impact

The Vermont Capability and Development Plan calls for selective economic development based on "maximum economic benefit with minimal environmental impact."

Strengthened Local Government

Local governments and regional councils of local governments are regarded by most states as the first line of growth policy implementation, with many states recognizing that their own state development and capital investment policies have to reinforce, not undermine, local efforts to achieve state goals.

In Oregon, state goals have the force of regulations to be carried out by local units of government. States also differ in the degree to which local plans must conform to areawide plans. One state required certain state activities to comply with local land use plans and requirements.

Other Directives

The President's 1976 Report identified still other innovative directives from the state designed to facilitate economic development in stagnated communities and those with growth potentials (11). The new instruments adopted by the states over the past five years also broaden the range of state incentives for financing the expansion of plant and equipment and of municipal infrastructure that may be a prerequisite for development.

For example, to provide venture capital, the state of Connecticut has created a product development corporation which enters into 50-50 joint financing arrangements with private businesses. To increase the willingness of banks to make expansion loans for small firms, the Kansas Development Credit Corporation, a privately funded but public purpose financial intermediary, began in the late 1960s to purchase the guarantee portion of these loans for resale to the state pension fund.

Pooling of Small Business Debt Issues

To help make capital available, Connecticut has created an "umbrella" revenue bond program for the state redevelopment authority. As a result, the market for securities of small companies is effectively broadened and the high costs of borrowing reduced.

Municipal bond banks for financing infrastructure such as schools, sewer systems, and feeder roads, have generally been viewed as a prerequisite for directly productive investment. State consolidation of financing permits an increase in the ratio of borrowing to capital expenditures for small cities with less than prime ratings.

Finally, there may be a need for some states to increase the authority of local communities to perform key community development functions. The President's 1976 Growth Report gave the findings of a Community Development Capability Study conducted by the National League of Cities and the U.S. Conference of Mayors. The specific limitations on municipal authority most frequently identified included·

Timing and sequential control powers and flood plain control powers.
Renewal powers such as the ability to write down land costs, clear privately owned land, lease land to private developers, or sell or donate property to individuals.
Authority to pay requisite costs for relocation assistance and provision of replacement housing.
Direct legal authority to provide various types of housing subsidies, such as cash rental subsidies. In many instances, however, these functions can be performed by an independent authority or district.

The limitations that constitutions or home-rule charters in 20 states place on the ability of localities to extend credit to individuals, corporations or other organizations inhibit the ability to leverage Federal funds by establishing revolving funds for rehabilitation, land development, and business development loans or certain types of special purpose land banking. However, removing these limitations must be weighed against the need to insure local fiscal soundness and managerial capability, which is a responsibility of the states (12).

LEGAL QUESTIONS AND THE COURTS

Population policies are made more complicated by the problem of reconciling the goal of equal access to public services and a host of other constitutional objectives with community desires to institute no growth or slow growth policies. Before turning to specific current court cases, we can identify the constitutional grounds for challenging a range of growth management techniques (13).

Due Process

The Fourteenth Amendment to the United States Constitution says that no state shall deprive any person of property without due process of law. This provision has never been considered a limitation on the police power of the state to pass and enforce laws for the health, safety, morals, and general welfare of the people. Recent cases indicate that the courts recognize the importance and scope of the growth problems and are willing to give governments some leeway.

Equal Protection and Right to Travel

Legislative provisions concerned with population distribution necessarily discriminate. Unless a plaintiff can show that the public action discriminates on racial grounds, or that no rational basis exists for the classification created, his suit will likely fail.

Eminent Domain

The use of eminent domain as a growth control tool has received increasing emphasis of late. Police power regulation is simply not pervasive enough by itself to control growth effectively in areas of rapid urbanization. Problems arise in the expense involved in actually acquiring property as a means of implementing the goals of growth management.

State Constitutional Provisions

As creatures of the state, municipalities have no inherent power to legislate. Only with a specific delegation of legislative authority can a municipal government exercise the police power.

The courts in 1975 were especially active in trying to resolve the conflicts caused by the goals of equity and growth management (14). In a major decision, the Court of Appeals for the Ninth Circuit reversed a lower court's decision and held that the City of Petaluma, California, has the right to limit its expansion to preserve its "small town" character, open space, and low population density (*Construction Industry Association of Sonoma County* v. *City of Petaluma*).

The court distinguished the Petaluma plan from other ordinances that have been struck down by courts as being impermissibly exclusionary: "The Petaluma Plan does not have the undesirable effect of walling out any particular income class nor any racial minority group."

The Supreme Court of New Jersey made a significant decision in *Southern Burlington County NAACP* v. *Township of Mount Laurel* where the question was whether a developing municipality like Mount Laurel has any obligation to make possible a variety of types of housing within its boundaries, including low and moderate income housing, to reflect the needs of citizens in the area as a whole.

In 1976 the Supreme Court moved to clarify the extent to which suburbs have an affirmative legal obligation to help alleviate discriminatory housing patterns in adjacent cities. The Supreme Court's decision in *Hills* v. *Gautreaux* involved a suit against the Department of Housing and Urban Development for providing financial assistance to racially segregated public housing projects in the Chicago area.

That ruling marked the culmination of a protracted course of litigation, spanning more than a decade, stemming from actions taken by the Chicago Housing Authority, assisted by HUD, in the construction of low and moderate income housing in Chicago. CHA was found to have maintained site selection and tenant placement policies which had the effect of confining public housing to racially impacted areas of the city.

HUD was also found to have abetted the process by "knowingly sanctioning and assisting CHA's racially discriminatory public housing program" through its financing and support in violation of the 1964 Civil Rights Act and the Fifth Amendment to the Constitution. Consequently, HUD was directed to develop and implement a "comprehensive metropolitan area plan" of housing subsidization to ameliorate the effects of its past actions. This latter order was affirmed by the Supreme Court. In doing so, the Supreme Court cited the case of *City of Hartford* v. *Hills* in which that city and two of its residents brought action against Secretary of Housing and Urban Development and seven suburban communities.

The Federal District Court held that approval of applications which did not contain any estimate of the number of low and moderate income persons expected to reside within the city was contrary to law; that approval of application of one city without consideration of generally available information concerning the number of low and moderate income persons expected to reside within the city was arbitrary and capricious; and that expenditure of any of the funds under the grants would be enjoined.

On January 11, 1977, the Supreme Court handed down a decision in *Village of Arlington Heights* v. *Metropolitan Housing Development Corp.* The case was the latest in a recent series of lower federal court decisions involving a challenge, under the Equal Protection Clause and federal civil rights laws, to local zoning and land use policies which, by restricting development of low and moderate income housing, are alleged to deprive blacks and other racial minorities of their right to equal housing opportunity. The court upheld the villagers' right to take zoning actions so long as those actions were not overtly discriminatory.

In 1975 the same issue was before the Court in *Warth* v. *Seldin* (1975) but it there refused to rule on the merits, finding the plaintiffs in that action lacked standing to attack the local exclusionary policy. The Supreme Court in 1976 did uphold City of *Eastlake* v. *Forest City Enterprises, Inc.*, a municipal ordinance that required that any land use changes agreed to by the city council be approved by a 55 percent vote in a referendum.

The court found that local land use regulations must promote the "general welfare" to be valid, and that municipalities must consider the general welfare of persons living outside the boundaries of the municipality. Thus, the court imposed upon the township of Mount Laurel an affirmative legal obligation to provide for its "fair share" of the housing needs of the region around it, especially in the low and moderate cost categories.

In a similar ruling in Pennsylvania (*Township of Williston* v. *Chesterdale Farms, Inc.*), the Pennsylvania Supreme Court held that "suburban municipalities within the area of urban outpour must meet the problems of population expansion into its (sic) borders by increasing municipal services, and not by the practice of exclusionary zoning."

In *Berenson* v. *Town of New Castle*, the New York Court of Appeals ruled that the town of New Castle, whose zoning ordinance excluded multifamily residential housing must defend the reasonableness of its ordinance in terms of its impact on regional housing needs: "there must be a balancing of the local desire to maintain the status quo within the community and the greater public interest that regional needs be met."

NEW POLICY OPTIONS FOR DEALING WITH COMMUNITY GROWTH AND DECLINE

Advocates of new national migration policy initiatives fall into two major groupings: those who would improve the performance of market and government processes, and those who would more directly rearrange the settlement pattern itself through such measures as the creation of new communities, restricting the growth of major metropolitan areas, managing the volume and direction of internal migration, and more stringently regulating industrial location.

Various strategies have been proposed both in terms of program and institutional reform to deal with the problem of decline in small and medium size cities. The Governors' Conference has called for a national population and growth distribution policy. The policy approaches described here include a national public works investment policy proposed to the House Committee on Public Works, a strategy for balanced rural-urban growth by the Department of Agriculture, a tax incentives policy growing out of a review of European experience, and a program of assisted migration for unemployed and low income workers.

The Advisory Commission on Intergovernmental Relations has spelled out criteria for local assignment of governmental functions as a guide to the channeling of federal and state support. Also examined are proposed new institutional reforms and a series of current policy issues with respect to growth and development facing the 95th Congress, the new Administration, and the states.

A National Public Works Investment Policy

A science advisory panel to the House Public Works Committee (15) has identified some five basic alternatives for achieving more effective patterns of population distribution and growth as follows: (a) leave decisions solely to states and localities; (b) establish federal standards, but without direct federal involvement in implementation; (c) provide federal incentives and rewards for regional cooperation at the interstate or substate level; (d) keep experimenting as at present with new federal interstate substate organizations created as the need arises; or (e) establish a national system of interstate and substate organization.

The panel went on to make the following recommendations, among others:

The United States should have an explicit national population distribution policy, covering both inter-regional and intra-regional patterns of settlement.... One objective of the national population distribution policy should therefore be to help the smaller metropolitan areas and those nonmetropolitan areas that have substantial growth potential attract a larger share of the country's employment expansion—and hence of its population increase—than they have been able to attract in the past. The national population distribution policy would provide a necessary guide for planning at multistate regional, state, substate regional, and local levels. Such a policy would help to modify unrealistic expectations at the local level, especially ones that cannot be mutually reconciled at the regional or national level.

The federal government should assist state and local public works only when they are embodied in comprehensive state, substate regional, and/or local land-use infrastructure plans. It should encourage comprehensive substate regional planning by appropriating funds authorized for the purpose.

To influence private investors to locate jobs in areas designated for development by the national population distribution policy, a system of incentives, or a combination of incentives and charges, should be instituted.

Incentives for relocation of individuals to areas designated for assistance under the population distribution policy should also be offered.

The Congress should recognize the potential of new communities in locations relatively distant from presently urbanized areas. Further experimentation by both public and private enterprise in the development of outlying new communities should be encouraged.

Population distribution measures are no substitute for policies and programs that will help to bring an end to the country's aggregate population growth within the space of five to seven decades (16).

Multifaceted Strategy for Growth

A recent study (17) spelled out seven different strategies or policy options for encouraging balanced growth and small community development. The seven strategies include the following: stop outmigration, reduce natural increase of population, expand capital stock, and expand markets.

The author has proposed an overall strategy for nonmetropolitan community stabilization and growth, as follows:

> Rural development requires a multifaceted approach which relies heavily on creating added jobs in rural areas as well as on expanding the labor force to fill these jobs. This strategy needs to be coupled with some improvement in the productivity of resources and in the rate of accumulation of capital to offset possible undesirable side effects. Expanding capital in rural areas was a useful adjunct to a balanced rural development strategy but was not an adequate basis for a single strategy. Capital enhancement depending on a tax and transfer tended to benefit one sector at the expense of the other. Strategies to extend markets for local products were found to make positive but minor contributions for which the gains in one sector were at the direct expense of the other sector unless exports were directly coupled with the creation of new jobs. Strategies to directly inhibit outmigration from a lower-income sector were found to further depress the average level of income in that sector (18).

Tax Subsidy for Plant Location

A recent examination to identify what European experience in population distribution policy might be applicable in the United States concluded:

> It is hard to foresee any general acceptance of a system of controls on land use that operated out of Washington, and yet if the states were to endeavor to control growth within their boundaries, they would immediately run into the same problems that are now appearing in Europe on the international scale.
>
> Nevertheless, one feature of the European approach could be adopted here—the incentive system. We would probably have to use an indirect tax subsidy, but that that would be feasible is indicated by the fact that such a measure has passed the Senate twice, both times being lost in conference. That measure would have applied a higher rate of investment credit to plants located in depressed areas, as defined under current law, than is granted to plants elsewhere (19).

Individual Relocation Assistance

Studies by Peter Morrison of the RAND Corporation (20) indicated that an important element of national growth policy should include strengthening of the effectiveness of migration on individuals.

Assisted migration would match an unemployed worker who cannot find work locally with a job elsewhere for which he is, or could be, qualified; and enable him to relocate, if he so desired, with a minimum of disruption and risk. This procedure would strengthen the private and collective functions of migration, both by increasing the *amount* of migration and by rationalizing its *direction*. For would-be migrants, the need to reduce the indecisiveness and uncertainty that may block migration. Those who do move can be helped to migrate more effectively by choosing destinations based on economic judgment, not hit-or-miss information from friends and relatives living elsewhere (20A).

Evidence supports both the rationale and feasibility of relocation assistance when it is augmented with human resource development. Recent demonstration programs have shown that, by redirecting migration, unemployed persons with widely varying backgrounds and skill levels can be helped to find jobs and increase their earnings. By underwriting the risks that prevent workers from moving, relocation assistance can help achieve a more efficient allocation of the labor force. At the same time, it promotes fulfillment of the American principle that a person's material well-being and social status should rest on his achievements (20B).

Criteria for Community Assignment of Responsibilities

The Advisory Commission on Intergovernmental Relations has tried to identify the criteria for national assignment of municipal functions to communities. These criteria can be useful in identifying the particular kinds of small and medium size communities that should be assisted by the federal and state governments with a view to stabilizing their economies or controlling their growth.

Economic Efficiency. Functions should be assigned to jurisdictions (a) that are large enough to realize economies of scale and small enough not to incur diseconomies of scale; (b) that are willing to provide alternative service offerings to their citizens and specific services within a price range and level of effectiveness acceptable to local citizenry; and (c) that adopt pricing policies for their functions whenever possible.

Fiscal Equity. Appropriate functions should be assigned to jurisdictions (a) that are large enough to encompass the cost and benefits of a function or that are willing to compensate other jurisdictions for the service costs imposed or for benefits received by them, and (b) that have adequate fiscal capacity to finance their public service responsibilities and that are willing to implement measures that insure interjurisdictional fiscal equity in the performance of a function.

Political Accountability. Functions should be assigned to jurisdictions (a) that are controllable by, accessible to, and accountable to their residents in the performance of their public service responsibilities; and (b) that maximize the conditions and opportunities for active and productive citizen participation in the performance of a function.

Administrative Effectiveness. Functions should be assigned to jurisdictions (a) that are responsible for a wide variety of functions and that can balance competing functional interests; (b) that encompass a geographic area adequate for effective performance of a function; (c) that explicitly determine the goals of and means of discharging public service responsibilities and that periodically reassess program goals in light of performance standards; (d) that are willing to pursue intergovernmental policies for promoting interlocal functional cooperation and reducing interlocal functional conflict; and (e) that have adequate legal authority to perform a function and rely on it in administering the function.

Remaining Substantive Policy Issues

A recent study by the Congressional Research Service on rural development goals prepared at the request of the Congressional Rural Caucus (21) identified a host of policy questions relevant to policy for dealing with growth and decline in small and medium size cities.

Manpower training. What has been the impact of federally funded manpower development and training programs on rural areas?

Credit requirements. Are many rural areas or rural-based businesses chronically credit short? If so, is this because yields for comparable risk investments are lower in rural areas? Or is it due to an underdeveloped system for harnessing savings or steering outside funds into rural communities.

Transportation. An efficient transportation network is a key factor in the economic growth of a regional or local economy. Are many rural areas failing to grow because of curtailment of rail services or the inadequacy of highways?

Sewer and water facilities. What is the range of need in small and medium size communities for sewer and water facilities and other community facilities over the next five to ten years?

Health. What are the particular health programs of smaller urban areas and how are they to be met? With 672 counties and service areas designated as critical health shortage areas and nonmetropolitan populations generally underprovided with medical care, what can be done to induce an adequate number of doctors and related health personnel to locate in rural areas?

Pending Legislative Issues

Legislation to establish new national population and growth institutions did not make much progress in 1974, 1975, or 1976. The increasing new national awareness of the results of nonpolicies or conflicting, unorchestrated policies may well lead to support for the creation of such national machinery. Some of the specifications that would be needed have been proposed to the Congress. Furthermore, some elements are already in place, and need only to be fully implemented (22).

Congressional attempts in recent years to develop national policies relating to environmental protection, forest resources, economic planning, science and technology, oceans, food, materials, energy, and land use all have implications for population and growth policy. All of them are unresolved. Nowhere in the federal government is there an institutional capacity for examining the relationships of these developing policy areas with one another, or the implications of each individual policy area for population growth and decline in any given community.

These relationships need to be identified and addressed before national policies are determined, not afterward. Yet, neither Congress nor the Executive branch has any institutional mechanism for recognizing and reconciling these frequently conflicting relationships. Most recently, in the 94th Congress, the Balanced Growth and Economic Planning Act (S. 1795) served as a focus for a national debate over the role of the federal government in national economic planning, and represented the primary legislative vehicle for considering national growth and development institutions.

A national economic plan would establish long term economic objectives, paying particular attention to the attainment of the goals of full employment, price stability, balanced economic growth, an equitable distribution of income, efficient utilization of private and public resources, balanced regional and urban development, stable international relations, and meeting essential national needs in various sectors of the economy. Such proposals, as well as the report of the U.S. Advisory Committee on National Growth Policy Processes, which was released in early 1977, will undoubtedly keep the issue of national growth policy before the nation.

In addition to proposals for federal institutional reform, growth related issues in 1977 and beyond (23) will include continued experimentation as state and local policy makers try to develop tools for providing adequate services and managing growth at the areawide level, not only in metropolitan areas but also in sparsely settled multicounty rural areas. The executive branch, Congress, and even the courts are also likely to play a role in determining whether there will be a proliferation of single purpose areawide agencies or the creation of a single, comprehensive regional agency.

The unforeseen and unanticipated surge of growth in certain rural areas will pose new problems both for the in-migrants to these areas and those already there. At the same time, the recently documented rise of certain regions of the nation—especially the sunbelt states—at the expense of the older Northeast and Midwest industrial regions will pose a host of questions for policymakers. These growth patterns have been affected to some extent by federal activities ranging from the location of defense installations to the national highway program. Should the federal government, therefore, take action to deal with these regional shifts of power, such as directing federal expenditures on the basis of regional needs?

The Advisory Committee on National Growth Processes (24) was set up in 1976 to develop recommendations for establishing a national policy making process and structure for developing a "program of balanced national growth and development, and as a system for coordinating these efforts with appropriate multistate, regional and state governmental jurisdictions." The Committee has concluded that the federal government, through its regulatory decisions, its leasing of public lands, procurement policies, subsidies, tax policies, and establishment of performance and quality standards has increasingly affected each region's abilities to cope with its problems.

The Committee recommends a special study of regional mechanisms. These selected or newly established regional mechanisms should provide for shared decisions on a regional basis between federal, state and local governments, and should provide analyses of the impact of future and present national policies.

A recent analysis of the state role in small and medium size urban areas (25) identified five key areas for state action. The first is assuring coherence of state policy by resolving contradictions in the policies of the various state agencies. The second is to develop local government institutions that are capable of overcoming the problems of smallness. One method of doing this is the establishment of substate planning and development districts which can provide circuit-riding "city managers," and can provide assistance to local governments in dealing with the federal and state programs. The remaining areas of state concern should be the provision of education, health, and transportation services.

Business Week, in reviewing national and regional patterns of growth and development in recent years showed none of the timidity that characterizes recent Federal policy statements in appraising the impact that new national policies and programs have had, both hidden and overt, on national growth and development.

Business Week recommendations went far beyond the actual policy initiative initiated by the national government in 1975 with recommendations along the following lines:

Federal government policy's uneven impact on the various regions must be revised and redirected toward slow-growth areas.

The North and Far West must cut back selected services and slim their fiscal profile.

The entire fabric of State-local relationships may have to be altered.

Renewed emphasis will have to be placed on equalization of economic opportunity.

Federalization and greater standardization of welfare should be pressed.

The tax code should be changed to provide a better balance of incentives between home ownership and renting and between new and existing structures.

Environmental constraints in the Northeast must be selectively eased and the pressures to do this should not be resisted (26).

All in all, in the last few years no final answers to the issues related to population distribution and its impacts were discovered, but basic questions were raised. First we must recognize, define and understand the problems. In the last few years, we may have paved the way for the development of population growth and distribution policies and the institutions to monitor and implement these policies.

Chapter Four

Black Residential Clusters in the Suburban Ring

Harold M. Rose

The American population is constantly in the process of changing places of residence. The sum total of both intra and interurban moves during the most recent decade has resulted in more Americans concentrated in the suburban rings of metropolitan areas than in central cities or non-metropolitan areas.

Paradoxically, however, as this new development is being ushered in there is evidence that still another settlement pattern is gathering momentum. During the early years of this decade the movement to exurbia was known to be increasing, thus allowing a more affluent segment of the population to acquire access to an environment of ultimate choice.

Both popular and policy oriented descriptions of the suburbanization process have emphasized the emergence of a growing white noose surrounding an increasingly black central city. As cities become the modal place of residence of blacks and other minorities, the aged, and the poor, it is evident that it becomes more difficult for them to provide that battery of services we have come to think of as the standard set. The increasing level of disamenities in the nation's larger central cities has recently stimulated a growing number of blacks to seek residence in the suburban ring of a select set of metropolitan areas.

The primary objective of this chapter is thus to evaluate the black suburbanization experience as a means of ascertaining how it varies from place to place, and the extent to which residence in these new environments enhances people's life chances.

TARGETS OF BLACK POPULATION GROWTH IN NON-CENTRAL CITY LOCATIONS

Black populations have been present in selected suburban locations in the nation's largest metropolitan areas since before World War II. These historic black enclaves, which seldom constituted growth zones, went essentially unnoticed by scholars studying the process of suburbanization. This no doubt occurred because these residential environments seldom appeared congruent with the suburban ideal. Irene Taeuber was one of the earliest scholars to take note of the presence of blacks in the suburban ring. But she was cautious not to identify these enclaves as suburban. While she noted that at least 25 percent of the black metropolitan population was to be found outside of the central city in 1950, she also indicated that "the growth of Negro populations outside of central cities of the SMSAs cannot be identified with a movement to the quiet lanes of suburbia" (1).

These historic enclaves, while failing to be identified as suburban because of their lack of amenities, affluence, and social status, have played a significant role in providing access to more recent generations whose goal is to escape the increasingly oppressive environments in some central city locations. The early black residential enclaves were identified by this writer more than a decade ago as "All-Negro towns" (2). These were communities which were 95 percent or more black and had attained a minimum size of at least 1000 persons.

Carter Woodson recognized a number of these communities even prior to 1930. He saw them as places of residence of people characterized by higher strivings who were seeking refuge from a hostile world (3). He did not view these communities as suburban places, but rural places where hope prevailed. The early black suburban ring communities predated the rush to the suburbs, and thus permitted those of rural southern background to practice rural life styles in the shadow of some of the nation's largest central cities.

The original group of All-Negro towns previously identified included ten communities, none of which exceeded 10,000 people in 1960 (see Figure 4-1). Six of these communities were located in northern metropolitan areas, while another four were to be found in southern metropolitan areas. This group, plus that group of black enclaves situated in larger majority white communities, represent the initial black presence in the suburban ring. (Black agricultural communities in southern locations were excluded from this universe.)

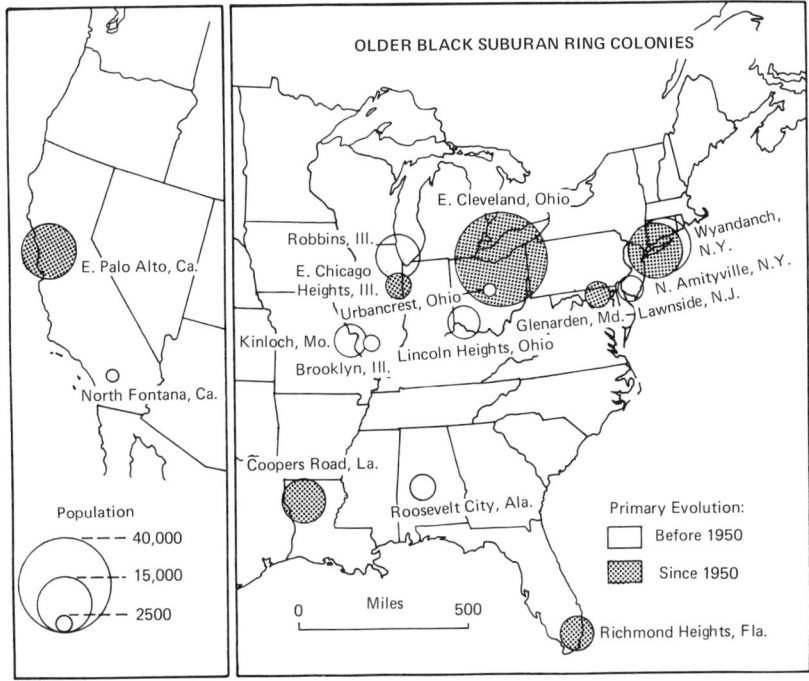

Figure 4-1.

This pioneer set of communities were in some ways prototypes for future black settlement in the suburban ring. They constitute what is being identified here as black colonies to distinguish them from other forms of black suburban ring settlement.

THE RUSH TO SUBURBIA

The largest black movement ever to the suburban ring got underway during the previous decade. But most of that movement was destined for those rings where there already existed sizeable black populations, although a few exceptions do show themselves. Ten metropolitan areas were the principal targets of the approximately one-half million blacks who chose these new environments. The major destinations included outlying zones in the SMSAs of Los Angeles, New York, Washington, Chicago, Cleveland, Miami, St. Louis, San Francisco, Philadelphia, Detroit, and Newark (see Table 4-1).

While the primary movement was confined to those places iden-

Table 4-1. Primary Suburban Ring Destinations of Black Migrants, 1960-70

Ring Identification	Total Black in-migrant population	Total in-migrant population
Los Angeles-Long Beach, CA	100,000	192,000
Washington, D.C., Md., Va.	71,175	516,654
New York, NY	46,842	432,398
Newark, NJ	40,163	84,941
Cleveland, OH	36,119	164,176
Chicago, IL	34,811	595,571
St. Louis, MO, IL	29,765	199,469
Detroit, MI	10,826	241,647
San Francisco-Oakland, CA	27,705	270,600
Miami, FL	25,139	250,596

Source: General Demographic Trends for Metropolitan Areas, 1960-1970, Final Report PHC 2–Selected States, U.S. Bureau of the Census, Census of Population and Housing.

tified in Table 4-1, there is evidence of a secondary movement pattern in another nine metropolitan rings which were not previously the place of residence of large numbers of blacks (see Table 4-2). It was not until this most recent period that both social scientists and social commentators began to take notice of the presence of blacks in non-central city locations within metropolitan systems.

Table 4-2. Secondary Suburban Ring Destinations of Black Migrants, 1960-70

Ring Identification	Total Black in-migrant population	Total in-migrant population
Cincinnati, OH	5,170	78,473
Dayton, OH	3,894	58,850
Atlanta, GA	3,887	249,816
Flint, MI	3,662	42,815
Jersey City, NJ	3,300	−6,491
San Diego, CA	3,113	124,236
Baton Rouge, LA	3,093	24,336
Pittsburgh, PA	2,786	−61,704
Baltimore, MD	2,719	170,382

Source: General Demographic Trends for Metropolitan Areas, 1960-70, Final Report PHC 2–Selected States, U.S. Bureau of the Census, Census of Population and Housing.

This was probably an outgrowth of the uniqueness of the phenomenon and a need on the part of some to demonstrate that black progress was indeed occurring, as the last bastion of segregation was being penetrated. Farley was one of the earliest to identify what has now become recognized as patterns of black suburbanization (4). He has been followed by a succession of social scientists whose interest in the phenomenon is growing and includes the work of Connolly (5), Pendelton (6), Schnore (7), and, more recently, Berry and others (8).

Improvements in black income levels and increased job security have made it possible for blacks to expand the range of their search for alternative residential environments. But most of these improvements have been slow in coming and did not really begin to show themselves until the middle sixties. This is congruent in timing with the movement pattern of blacks to new non-central city locations.

The precise way in which black residential zones have emerged has been conditioned by the status of the black mover, the response of white neighbors, and the influence and attitudes of realtors. The most recent movement patterns have led to the development of an alternative mechanism, which has fostered the greater presence of blacks in the suburbs. The latter process might be described as the spillover process, to distinguish it from the colonization process that accounted for the initial black presence in the ring. At the present both processes are at work, although in some instances there tends to be a fusion of the two.

The largest number of recent suburban movers have been involved in the spillover process. The latter process is more fully developed in the largest central cities in the country. It is in those communities where we more often find central city ghettos that have expanded to the edge of the city. Where this has occurred, additional residential increments become available on the suburban side of the political boundary. These new zones frequently represent the tip of the ghetto, which is now no longer confined to the city.

Where this pattern prevails one is more likely to find higher status blacks representing the modal population than is true in colonizing residential configurations. In those central cities where spillover development is not yet possible because of the small size and recency of the black presence, the number of blacks in the suburban ring is relatively small. It is in those metropolitan areas where black ghettos are described as third generation centers that we find the number of blacks in the suburban ring small. Thus first and second generation ghetto centers—those in which blacks have been present in large numbers since before World War II—are the principal source areas for much of the present movement to the metropolitan ring.

The largest share of black movers to the ring of any of the principal target zones are confined to a limited number of communities. It has been previously shown that only three or four communities, even in the principal metropolitan rings, serve as the target of black movement (9).

About 20 communities were the targets of black suburban movement during the sixties. Another sixty communities within the ten primary metropolitan target zones represented secondary destinations. The modal size communities in which black movers were destined was 25,000.

A COMPARISON OF THE OLDER AND NEWER BLACK SUBURBAN RING COMMUNITIES

A number of differences distinguish the newer suburban residential developments from the old. Among the most obvious is size of place. The earlier black movers often settled in smaller places. This partially reflects the character of the outlying zone that was available to black movers during the two different time periods. During the earlier period, when blacks were seeking residential environments compatible with those of previous rural residence, the move took place on undeveloped land.

On these isolated parcels they could practice a rural lifestyle without undue pressure or influence by urban governments. These isolated enclaves, which evolved as black residential sanctuaries with few physical amenities, were often eventually incorporated as All-Negro towns. These small communities were frequently politically independent even though they represented communities of economic marginality. These pioneer communities did indeed provide protection from a hostile world, but seldom integrated blacks into the emerging life style sometimes described as the myth of suburbia.

It is true that there were some blacks in older, upper middle income white communities, but they were confined to the black quarter or represented live-in service personnel. Connolly describes the latter situation in connection with the early status of blacks in the communities of Pasadena, California, and New Rochelle, New York. Between 1910 and 1930 the latter two communities were the third ranking black communities in their respective states (10). Thus urban oriented blacks were situated in close proximity to their places of employment, whereas rural oriented blacks were developing independent communities with few modern amenities, but removed from the congestion of central city environments.

The newer communities of occupancy possess more of the attributes that we normally associate with suburban life than was true of the communities of initial occupancy. Prior to the most recent decade, blacks occupying these outlying locations were less well off on both economic and residential quality attributes than were central city blacks.

In some of the original colonies, however, a modern residential environment has been superimposed upon an old pre-modern environment. This practice has been fairly commonplace in those communities where raw land was available for development and the communities themselves were situated favorably in terms of proximity to the central city. Pent up demand for suburban single family residences on the part of a black population that had previously been unable to participate in this market made residence in these new communities indeed attractive. In some instances the character of the original community was vastly changed, whereas in others these new developments simply served as islands in an environment of general despair. The range of residential amenities within a single community might span the environmental spectrum in some of these older colonies as an outgrowth of post-1960 residential development.

BLACK RING MOVERS—WHERE DO THEY ORIGINATE?

Now that we have developed some understanding of the forces that have led to the emerging pattern of black suburban ring development, we are in a position to investigate the residential origin of this mover population. The current movers to the suburban ring were most recently residents of the central city in the same metropolitan area. The buildup of pressure on central city housing markets growing out of three decades of large scale migration from southern rural and small towns has provided the impetus for the development of alternative markets.

While most movers are of central city origin, there are variations in place of origin related to the developmental character of the target communities. Spillover or ghettoizing suburban development is almost totally fueled by movers of central city origin. These communities are frequently the place of residence of upwardly mobile blacks whose current income is sufficient to provide them with options previously not available to them. Often movers to the new black colonies were persons who previously lived elsewhere in the suburban ring. In such cases the original colonies, whatever their character, served as ports of entry to suburbia.

Second generation families of the original colonies mature and seek places of residence in nearby communities. This pattern is probably best illustrated in the case of Pasadena, and its nearest neighbor Altadena. Blacks have long been present in Pasadena, but only began to settle in Altadena on a large scale during the sixties. Altadena residence represents an upward move and the bulk of movers originate elsewhere in the SMSA. The latter pattern currently represents the modal pattern of white settlement in the suburbs.

The inverse of this situation exists in the case of Inglewood, California, which abuts the western edge of the Los Angeles central city black community. The mover population destined for Inglewood principally originates in the city of Los Angeles. Thus the location of a given target community within the metropolitan ring will basically influence the origins of its newcomer population.

In those instances where the central city black community has not yet proceeded to the edge of the city, central city contributions to the development of black colonies is not strong. In such instances older colonies tend to generate a good deal of the incremental demand, as well as movers from nonmetropolitan areas. It appears that some nonmetropolitan movers are bypassing the central city altogether and moving directly to a suburban colony. Examples of the latter development are in evidence in both the Chicago and New York metropolitan rings.

Prior to the most recent decade, blacks growing up in these outlying colonies were destined for the central city at some critical point in the life cycle. Now it appears that some are exercising the option to live elsewhere in the SMSA. Only in Detroit, among our primary metropolitan areas, is there still more movement from the ring to the central city than is to be found in the opposite direction. This no doubt partially reflects the status of blacks in a given colony, and the environmental attributes in nearby communities where black entry is not constrained by artificial barriers.

RACIAL DISPERSION IN SUBURBAN RING ENVIRONMENTS

Employing data from five of the major target rings, the variations in patterns of residential segregation can be highlighted. The most intensely segregated rings among this group of metropolitan areas are found in Miami and St. Louis. In 1970, 96 and 90 percent of black ring residents respectively were found in neighborhoods with at least 400 blacks. This is a crude index of an absence of dispersion.

Generally when blacks are found in neighborhoods where their numbers exceed 400, the area is already majority black or in the throes of racial transition. Among these five metropolitan rings only Los Angeles shows signs of a major departure between suburban residential patterns and central city residential patterns, but this may be misleading. Rabinovitz's recent assessment of the Los Angeles pattern shows that most blacks are concentrated in a limited number of communities (11).

Some commentators might attribute this emerging pattern to the income characteristics of the black mover population, and subsequently the income characteristics of the previous population occupying the present spaces. It is true that most black movers can be described as working class, and the households they displaced are also often working class. However, there is evidence that blacks at the upper end of the income spectrum are more dispersed than is the average black suburban mover. Those black households earning more than $25,000 per year were often found destined for communities in which blacks constituted a very small percentage of the population.

Given the small size of this group in 1969, and their demonstrated directional bias in selecting a place of residence, one might expect this category of black mover to reside within a less racially segregated environment. But seldom does this group account for more than 3 percent of all black suburban movers. Thus their propensity to reside in less segregated environments will hardly influence the overall pattern.

No doubt Weaver was only partially correct when he stated "For middle class blacks greater dispersion seems probable. In the first place, in moving to the suburbs they are seldom interested in transfer from one racial ghetto to another, and few cities have enough black upper income families to support a separate suburb" (12). Yet we find enclaves of black middle income movers in a number of suburban communities throughout the nation.

It becomes fairly obvious that income alone does not determine the racial makeup of a given neighborhood. Age, one's prior residential experiences, and one's occupational status are likely to represent important secondary determinants.

DIFFERENCES IN RATE OF SUBURBANIZATION

As was previously indicated, the extent to which the central city black community was approaching the city's edge is probably the best indicator of the number and rate of black movers across the city line. Los Angeles, Cleveland, and Washington are prime examples of this thesis. Cleveland suburbs were almost devoid of blacks prior to the sixties. But during the latter decade the rapid expansion of the central city ghetto led to rapid black entry into several communities situated along the eastern edge of the city. In the Washington case a shallow corridor became the primary zone of black entry within a short period of time. But most of these places were only a short distance from the northeastern edge of the city.

Slow suburban development seems to occur where the previously described condition does not exist. In New York, Chicago, and Detroit, with their teeming black populations, the rate of suburbanization was slower than in the previous cases. In Detroit more blacks left the outlying ring for the central city than was true of those who left the city for the ring. In both Chicago and Detroit there was evidence of rapid abandonment of the central city by whites during this period. This movement no doubt created a surplus of satisfactory residential spaces within the city, thus delaying movement to the suburbs on the part of blacks. In 1970 there were only 4,000 more blacks in the Chicago ring than in the St. Louis ring, although the former had almost five times as many blacks in its total population.

Brian Berry, in describing the Chicago case, notes that most of the housing built in the Chicago suburbs during the decade was for a white population. He states, "In contrast to the net increase of 287,000 white families in suburban Chicago, only 13,261 new black families were able to obtain residence in suburbia, and many of these residences were in or contiguous to suburban mini-ghettos" (13). This indicates that blacks seldom participate in the market for new housing unless it is constructed in locations perceived to represent black social space. Thus blacks and whites seldom compete for housing in a racially undefined market.

The greatest contrast in rate and level of suburbanization among this set of metropolitan communities is that which distinguishes Los Angeles and Detroit. Both central cities had more than a half-million blacks in their population by the end of the decade, but Detroit had far fewer blacks residing in its ring. A combination of forces were no doubt at work here, but clearly the more rapid expansion of the Los Angeles ghetto toward the city's edge was a contributing factor. Another important factor might have been the attitude of the white population in the potential target communities.

There is some evidence that white attitudes in several close-in Detroit suburbs were at least moderately anti-black, and thus there existed a social climate in a number of logical target communities which might have resulted in black avoidance. This, coupled with the large number of housing units that became available as a result of central city white abandonment, made the trek to the suburbs unnecessary in the short run.

There are presently more blacks residing in the suburban ring in Los Angeles than anywhere else in the nation. There was approximately a 100 percent increase in its black ring population over a ten-year period. But as was true in Washington and St. Louis, most of that movement was concentrated in several edge communities or those located only a short distance from the city's edge. The nature of the occupational status and area of mover origin might have influenced the choice of a suburban or nonsuburban location in the latter instance. While both Los Angeles and Detroit were leading migrant destinations during the sixties, the former included far fewer persons of rural origin among its migrants.

Pettigrew and Vanneman point out that white attitudes in Los Angeles can be construed to be less racist than those prevailing in some eastern and midwestern cities (14). How important attitudes are in this equation is still somewhat incompletely understood, but supposedly these differences are among the contributing factors in the Detroit and Los Angeles examples.

SOCIAL RANK AND THE HOUSING ENVIRONMENT

In the past blacks have frequently indicated a high level of dissatisfaction with available housing. The housing issue has usually been one of those around which legislative relief has been sought. Housing legislation enacted during the late sixties was designed to aid in the amelioration of the housing problem.

Since blacks of lower status have encountered the most serious housing problems, one might expect that any improvement in the economic status of this group would lead to a search for a more satisfactory housing environment. Currently the largest number of black ring residents are to be found among blue collar workers. Only in Washington, D.C. among the primary ring destinations do we find more black white collar workers than blue collar workers. But in those rings which have only recently become the target of black entry we find that status difference between central city and ring populations has become more exaggerated.

It has been noted that the incidence of poverty in the rings of Detroit, Miami, and St. Louis shows only a slight difference from that prevailing in the central city. On the other hand, in those rings where new housing markets have become available to segments of the black population the incidence of ring poverty is much lower than that prevailing in the central city.

Black participation in suburban housing markets represents a relatively new experience. Yet as was previously noted it has not led to significant differences in the racial composition of residential areas. This stems in part from the belief on the part of some whites that they have the right to keep blacks out of their neighborhoods. Blacks themselves have exhibited a counter set of attitudes indicating a lack of enthusiasm for sharing social space with whites. Pettigrew recently demonstrated that although the majority of blacks were still willing to reside in interracial areas, "there is no widespread desire among black Americans to live in 'mostly' or overwhelmingly white areas" (15). The hesitancy of the two groups to share social space has done much to slow the process of racial residential deconcentration.

Blacks previously participating in suburban housing markets did so within the context of established black colonies. It is these housing environments with which we have the greatest familiarity. An examination of these environments, employing 1960 data, show that they seldom differed from central city environments in terms of housing quality. Only one community among the previously mentioned all-black towns bore any resemblance to suburban housing environments when an index of substandardness was employed as a surrogate for suburbanness.

Nevertheless the demand for housing in suburban black colonies continues strong in those communities in which the housing environment is in the process of being transformed. Table 4-3 indicates the extent to which a change in the residential environment in fifteen black colonies took place during the previous decade. These fifteen communities include nine of the original all-black towns and six additional communities which possess a basic similarity to this original group in terms of racial composition and spatial isolation. The index of change in the residential environment employed here is percent housing built since 1960.

There was a wide variation in the percent new construction from community to community. But, as is shown in Table 4-3, Hollydale, Ohio, Glenarden, Maryland, East Chicago Heights, Illinois, and Wyandanch, New York underwent major change, as all but the latter community more than doubled its housing stock during the decade. In those communities where the housing supply was increased through new construction, vacancy rates were generally low. High vacancy rates occurred in those communities which were characterized by relatively severe isolation from the central city.

New construction led to a reduction in the level of substandardness in communities which prior to 1960 might best have been described as rural slums. By 1972 two of the original all-black towns had made major headway in eliminating the incidence of substandardness within their domain. The extent to which these environmental transformations can be expected to continue is a function of

Table 4-3. New Construction and Vacancies as a Percent of the Total Housing Stock

Community	Percent Housing Built Since 1960	Percent Vacant in 1970
Urbancrest, Ohio	7.9	17.1
Glenarden, Md.	79.6	5.8
Brooklyn, Ill.	36.1	1.8
Richmond Heights, Fla.	31.0	1.7
Lawnside, N.J.	36.8	1.7
North Fontana, Cal.	16.0	9.2
Hollydale, Ohio	91.0	2.1
East Chicago Heights, Ill.	65.2	7.3
East Palo Alto, Cal.	15.7	4.2
Roosevelt City, Ala.	22.0	3.6
Copper Road, La.	18.2	8.5
Kinloch, Missouri	25.9	5.5
Lincoln Heights, Ohio	9.1	4.9
Robbins, Ill.	26.4	3.2
Wyandanch, N.Y.	42.0	3.2

Source: Census of Population and Housing: 1970, Census Tracts, Final Report PHC (1)–Individual SMSAs.

the ability of developers to accurately appraise housing demand that could be satisfied by constructing new units within this established universe of black colonies.

However, a number of elements work against the alterations of these environments, the chief among them being limited land area (seldom exceeding a square mile), few parcels large enough to allow the development of the minimum number of units which might represent commercial success, and the unwillingness of middle status blacks to purchase housing in areas where most residents are likely to possess lower status. In several instances new construction was initiated as a result of developers taking advantage of the provisions of new federal housing programs.

In a number of nonisolated working class communities there was evidence of housing being built under the provisions of the government's 235 housing program. Some public officials expressed a negative reaction to the presence of low income housing in their communities, but felt that failure to cooperate with the federal bureaucracy could possibly lead to their being penalized. The absence of political power in their communities made it impossible for them to reject low income housing, while politically more powerful white ring communities were able to keep low income housing out. For the low income resident wishing to escape difficult environments in the central city, his only prospect lay in resettling either in one of these established black colonies or in one of the newly emerging black colonies.

ECONOMIC SECURITY AND THE SUBURBAN ENVIRONMENT

To this point most of our emphasis has been on that set of small black colonies which served as the original suburban locations of most black ring residents. However, while a number of these communities were considered growth communities during the previous decade, it was the spillover communities and a set of new colonies which were the major suburban black growth centers. The question of the economic well-being of the rapidly growing ring population permits comparison between the original colonies and the communities of recent entry.

We will focus attention on those aspects of life that usually receive the greatest attention from social scientists.

Life Style, Class, and Culture

Black social class distinctions were once thought of as essentially nonexistent. This can be partially attributed to the low incomes received by most blacks, such that income was an inadequate measure of social status. During the early years of the century, whatever distinctions were made were based on subjective rather than objective characteristics of the population. Thus life style, rather than class, emerged as the primary distinguishing characteristic of the group.

Even as recently as the 1940s, Drake and Cayton used such terms as "respectables" and "shadies" to differentiate segments of Bronzeville's population (16). Others have employed more explicitly culturally oriented distinctions in view of the widespread economic deprivation that made economic differentiation difficult. One such distinction was between the acculturated and the externally adapted (17). Somehow these distinctions were designed to differentiate between the practitioners of a normative culture and those who might loosely be described as deviant.

The residents of the original all-black towns were most often persons of low social status as measured by income. These were likewise persons who had been born in the South and were seeking a nonurban environment in an urban setting. While the social status of a number of these communities is in the process of change as a result of the improved social class position of their recent entrants, it appears safe to suggest that the social position of these new residents is likely to differ from that of black movers to other places.

Measures of Economic Security

We have combined the level of unemployment, extent of poverty, and extent of welfare dependency to derive an index of economic security. Among the all-black towns only two can be viewed as being economically secure, while another six are described as marginally secure. The secure communities include Glenarden, Maryland and Hollydale, Ohio, both of which are strongly middle class when income is used as the single measure of status.

The extremely insecure communities in this group are those whose populations are aging, whose level of educational attainment is low, and who were not targets of growth during the previous decade. Poverty is endemic in the economically insecure communities. The well-being of the economically secure communities generally exceeded that of its nearest neighbor community, while the security of places farther down the security continuum were worse off than their nearest neighbor. However, the greatest discrepancy between the all-black town and its nearest neighbor was likely to be related to the racial characteristics of the latter.

Economic Security in Communities of Recent Entry

That set of communities in which there was minimal or no black presence prior to the sixties were more economically secure than were the previously described communities. Among this group less than one-fifth could be described as insecure, while more than one-fifth were extremely secure (see Table 4-4). The communities which constitute the most economically secure include Warrensville Heights, Ohio, Takoma Park, Silver Spring and Suitland, Maryland and Shaker Heights, Ohio. Thus the most economically secure communities were situated in the Cleveland and Washington metropolitan rings.

By employing three measures of economic security rather than a single direct measure based on income, we evolve an array that differs somewhat from that of a ranking on income alone or that derived through the use of factor analysis. The community which ranks highest in income status alone—Carson, California—is identified as being marginally secure, but is found among the highest ranking communities when status is derived using a factor analysis format.

Table 4-4. A Comparison of the Economic Security Ranking and Socioeconomic Status Ranking of Black Populations in 15 Suburban Communities of Recent Entry

	Security Ranking		Socioeconomic Status Ranking
Secure	Warrensville Heights, Ohio Takoma Park, Md. Shaker Heights, Ohio Suitland, MD Carol City, Fla. Spring Valley, N.Y.	High Status	Silver Spring, Md. Suitland, Md. Carson, Cal. Takoma Park, Md. Hayward, Cal. Warrensville Heights, Ohio Carol City, Fla.
Relatively Secure	Hayward, Cal. Roosevelt, N.Y. University City, Mo. Markham, Ill.		Daley City, Cal. Shaker Heights, Ohio Spring Valley, N.Y. University City, Mo. Pomona, Cal.
Marginally Secure	Carson, Cal. East Orange, N.J. Maywood, Ill. Hempstead, N.Y.	High Middle Status	Westmont, Cal. Altadena, Cal. Seat Pleasant, Md.

Source: Harold M. Rose, *Black Suburbanization*, Ballinger Publishing Co., Cambridge, Mass., 1976.

Only four of the all-black towns possess status levels akin to those of the fifteen ranking communities of recent entry; they are Glenarden, Maryland, Hollydale, Ohio, East Palo Alto, California, and Wyandanch, New York. Technically, the latter two communities are also communities of recent entry, but because of their racial composition they were previously identified as all-black towns. The most economically insecure of the communities of recent entry are Wellston, Missouri, and Richmond, Willowbrook, and Florence-Graham, California. The economically insecure communities tend either to be marginally working or lower class. But even so, poverty is far less extensive in the communities of recent entry than in the colonies of original settlement.

Contributors to Economic Security

As stated previously, some of the all-black towns are relic communities. Their occupational structure is more nearly akin to what may be described as the traditional black occupational structure.

There are some vestiges of the traditional occupational structure in a selected number of the newly suburbanizing communities. The private household worker category is probably the best indicator of vestiges of an older occupational structure. The percent of private household workers exceeded the national average in Freeport, New York and maintains relatively high levels in nine other communities. The highest levels as a rule tended to show themselves in the colony-like developments as opposed to the spillover developments.

Among the higher status communities, working wives were a common feature. Middle class status appears to be strongly related to the presence of a working wife. Communities in which black women are often described as clerical employees are distinguished from communities in which private household employment is a significant employment category. This also serves to indicate the median age differences in the population within the two community groups.

Connolly has previously shown that in those communities where the median family income exceeds $12,000 the labor force participation rate of working wives is extremely high (18). In four communities the participation rate for working wives surpassed 65 percent. These communities included University City, Missouri, Warrensville Heights, Ohio, Takoma Park, Maryland, and Markham, Illinois. Working wives are far less often found in the labor force in the all-black towns. In East Palo Alto, only one-third of the wives were in the labor force. The differential role of the participation of wives in the labor force in the two sets of communities probably represents differences in cultural orientation, growing primarily out of differences in the age structure and level of educational attainment of the two female groups.

In attempting to assess the economic consequences of such moves on the job situation of the mover population we find the picture somewhat muddled. Most of the movers to the suburban ring however have settled in a cluster of communities along the city's edge and commute to the central city where they are employed. It is therefore apparent that higher status black suburban residents exhibit journey to work patterns that largely parallel those of their white counterparts.

PSYCHOLOGICAL SECURITY AND BLACK SUBURBANIZATION

It can be assumed that an expressed preference for residence in a community with a specific racial makeup is also related to feelings of psychological security. Our ability to partition the psychological security dimension in the way that was done for economic security leaves much to be desired. We will, however, briefly mention two elements that are thought to bear at least peripherally on the question.

Measures of Psychological Security

The psychological dimension is inextricably tied to a given black cultural orientation. Thus we would expect some differences among communities in terms of their expressed concerns to represent different cultural orientations and therefore differences in prevailing levels of psychological security. Two components of the psychological security dimension currently receiving some attention are that of unwanted pregnancy and community safety.

The issue of unwanted pregnancy and family size preference are directly related. It has been stated that black women have not usually had the control over their fertility behavior that was desired, and thus had seldom been able to bring preferred family size and actual family size into congruence. Likewise blacks have frequently expressed dissatisfaction with police services because of the inability of the police to insure that the environments in which they reside will be at least minimally safe. Thus the issue of crime and safety is one of some importance to blacks and is often expressed through a search for safer environments.

Fertility. It is extremely difficult to evaluate the extent to which black metropolitan ring families have control over their fertility behavior, since no direct information is available that specifies desired family size or timing or spacing of pregnancies. Information is available that illustrates current fertility levels in these communities, however. Thus it is possible to observe how current fertility behavior correlates with expected fertility behavior given the socioeconomic status of these communities, and prior indications of unwanted pregnancies among black women possessing different levels of educational attainment. From data illustrating 1970 fertility levels, where the child/woman ratio was utilized as a measure of fertility, it appears that residents in many of these communities have been unable to exert effective control over fertility. However, it must be realized some of these differences possibly reflect differences in fertility norms and practices.

The highest observed levels of fertility were associated with low status and working class communities, with few differences showing themselves in terms of time of ring entry. For instance, Pontiac, Michigan and Brooklyn, Illinois, new entry and old entry communities respectively, but both possessing low status, were characterized by similar fertility behavior. In most instances fertility levels in suburban ring communities were found to be higher than was true of levels prevailing within black central city locations. This finding might simply reflect a more favorable age structure.

It is clear that most of the communities have not been able to get their fertility down to the expected level if previously reported levels of unwanted pregnancies are to be believed. Among the communities of recent entry, only four are within 10 percent of the expected level and another six had fertility levels below the expected level based on a 20 percent deflation of national black fertility. The latter communities included Daley City and Pomona, California, Silver Spring and Takoma Park, Maryland, Shaker Heights, Ohio, and East Orange, New Jersey. Two of the all-black towns were within 10 percent of the expected level, while another three were below the expected level. The age structure in the latter, however, no doubt strongly influenced the prevailing low fertility levels.

Safety. As was true of the previous attempt to evaluate a psychological dimension of security, safety is also difficult to evaluate because of our dependence on aggregate data. Our understanding of conditions of safety in the all-black towns is superior to that of the communities of recent entry. In the former communities we were able to derive citizen perceptions of the safety characteristics of their communities. In those communities where youth constituted a small percentage of the population, and the population hovered around 2,000, a safe environment was perceived to prevail. Those communities characterized by rapid growth were perceived as becoming increasingly unsafe.

Burglary was the most frequently identified element of an increasingly insecure environment. Other problems such as drug use on the part of youth were beginning to appear in some of these communities. Many of the families who had recently moved to these communities were beginning to indicate that the problems they thought they had left behind had followed them to the new environment. Burglary was also the most serious problem in communities of recent entry. The absence of survey data makes it impossible to tap the perception of the residents of these communities. Data from FBI annual reports indicate that in some communities other crimes of violence were growing in importance.

Safety seems to be an increasing concern in working class communities, although middle income communities are not devoid of these concerns. Communities in which violent crime was most frequent included Maywood and Harvey, Illinois, East Cleveland, Ohio, and

Pontiac, Michigan. The movement to selected working class communities, it appears, does not necessarily guarantee the availability of a safe environment.

EMERGING RESIDENTIAL PATTERNS AND THE QUALITY OF LIFE

New information has recently emerged identifying the character and size of place preference expressed by segments of the American population. As was expected a majority of white residents expressed a preference for residence in small places. There is evidence that white residents generally are acquiring access to environments for which they indicate a preference.

Surprisingly, the largest number of black residents expressed a desire to reside in small urban environments (19). While small urban environments should not be interpreted as being synonymous with small town environments, it is clear that blacks have been unable to acquire access to the preferred environments.

Part Three

Economic Growth and Decline

Chapter Five

The Urban Development Process

Wilbur R. Thompson

Students of current population trends believe that they have detected, in the county population *estimates* since 1970, early but convincing evidence of a major reversal in migration flows and urban growth patterns (1). They see a clear swing away from the larger metropolitan areas and toward smaller ones and toward nonmetropolitan areas. This author has two caveats to offer in interpreting this data, besides the obvious limitation that the figures are estimates and span only a very brief time period.

CURRENT TRENDS

First, population change since 1970 appears to be more closely correlated with the degree of local specialization in manufacturing than with the population size of an urban area, at least among metropolitan areas. With better data and a longer time period in hand, we may find that it is the older urban areas that grew up around manufacturing—large or small places—that have slipped below the national average rate of population growth. This would hardly be surprising since social scientists have been heralding for some time now the twilight of manufacturing and the advent of the "post-industrial age." Thus a major national industrial transformation is reshaping the national system of cities, and is not necessarily related to city size.

Second, even if the rate of growth of very large metropolitan areas does slow to a standstill, it does not follow that we as a nation will come to live more in smaller places. Public opinion polls may report that a majority of the population would prefer to live in a small city, and even if this is not a day dream and they act on this preference, the line of argument above holds that they are likely to get caught up in this powerful urban growth process and add their weight to the building of a new metropolitan area.

It is hard to believe that we are moving away from being a "nation of cities" when we watch Colorado Springs and Tucson growing at five times the national average rate and approaching a half-million population, with Boise following behind, matching that rate. Colorado, Arizona, Utah, and Nevada, four of the fastest growing states in the nation, have assembled over 70 percent of their state population in metropolitan areas and have concentrated over 55 percent in the single largest one. These four Mountain States rank with the East in population concentration and are more "citified" than any state in the Midwest, except Illinois (which contains a national city, Chicago).

The main body of this chapter attempts to bring together a large number of more or less conventional ideas that are loosely bound by the general term "urban growth theory," and to rearrange them into a systematic framework that emphasizes two broad sets of forces: disequilibrating forces that amplify change and create major transformations in the urban system, and equilibrating forces that dampen change and stabilize the system.

The complex mechanics and dynamics of the analysis below should not be allowed to obscure the central thesis, which is simple, direct, and—if correct—is of very considerable policy importance. The urban growth process has a direction and power not easily denied, and, while we may as a nation be trying to move away from our largest metropolitan areas, we will probably in the end come to find that we have merely created a new set of large places.

GROWTH INDUSTRIES MAKE GROWTH AREAS

One would be surprised if an economist did not begin a description of urban growth by placing the local industry mix at the very center of the growth process. Other things equal, growth industries produce growing places. We will learn below that other things are not equal.

The local economy is, in a most profound and pervasive way, a distinctive bundle of industries in space. And the urban-regional economist is in fair way to make good on the boast: "Tell me your industries and I will tell your fortune." We begin here by drawing out of the local industry mix a first approximation of the expected local growth rate and then turn later to the impact of local industrial specialization on its income pattern—the level, distribution, and stability of local income.

We would, for example, expect a rapidly rising trend both in local output and in the derived demand for labor—and ultimately a rapid growth in local population—in those areas specializing in new products. New industries are virtually unbounded in their potential growth in the early stage of the exploitation of a new market. Mature industries tend, however, to find growth limited to replacement purchases plus the slow increase in population. Centers of innovation tend, therefore, to be fast growing places.

Still, even areas specializing in well established products may attain average and even above average rates of growth if the demands for these products are income elastic—that is, if a given increase in per capita income leads to a more than proportionate increase in their consumption. Few dimensions of the future have, at least up until very recently, seemed to be as foreseeable as the seemingly inexorable rise in per capita income. We have, therefore, had few qualms about projecting a steady growth of population at an average rate or better in state capitals and medical centers, to mention two of the more obvious old but vigorous (income sensitive) activities. The median ratio of state capital to total state population growth for the period 1970-75 is 1.66—two-thirds higher.[a]

We saw in the Detroit area through the first half of the twentieth century, for example, an economy that boomed on the basis of a product—automobiles—that was both a new product and one for which there was an income elastic demand. The Detroit economy then grew for two decades of the postwar period at an above average rate on the strength of the income elasticity of demand characteristic alone, long after the newness of its product had worn off. Whether this automobile economy can continue to grow at an average rate depends on whether we expect real income per capita to continue rising for the last quarter of the twentieth century (and on whether the automobile can be "domesticated" to live in a highly urbanized, energy conserving, environment regarding society).

In contrast, we saw in the pre-war and postwar Boston area the struggle to shift from specialization in an old, income inelastic product (textiles), to a new growth industry—electronics. This great industrial transformation has kept the local rate of growth in

---

[a]State capitals in smaller cities, where government employment is a large proportion of total employment, have in general been growing at about twice their state rates since 1970. In only about one-quarter of the states did the population growth rate of the state capital slip below the state rate, and in about one-half these the capital had over one-half the total state population (e.g., Boston, Minneapolis, Salt Lake City, and Denver).

employment and population in that area from dipping below the low but positive rate to which it slipped: about one-half the national rate since 1950.

A third major cause of a change in the demand for the principal exports of a local economy, and one that is likely to grow in importance and perhaps gain dominance, is a change in relative prices. With growing scarcities of energy critical raw materials, the cost of production of goods will tend to rise relative to services, and so will the costs and prices of some goods relative to others.

Again, to the extent that manufacturing operations generate more harmful or unpleasant wastes than does service work, and to the extent that we levy pollution charges on this effluent or these processes, consumption spending patterns will be turned (by changing relative prices) away from the heavy effluent goods and toward other goods and services.

Thus, in addition to changing tastes (often induced by the innovation of new products) and differing income elasticities of demand for local versus competing goods and services, our forecasts of local trends in output and employment will need to draw on projections of raw material and energy costs more than ever before.

Finally, it has become conventional wisdom in economics that productivity in the goods producing industries has been rising significantly faster than in service industries, and nothing in sight is likely to change this. Assuming wage increases in service industries similar to those in manufacturing, service prices will tend to rise faster than goods prices, quite the reverse of the argument above. These two theses would seem to have an important corollary. With scarcities and effluent hobbling manufacturing, and the secular shift to services dampening normal productivity growth, the traditional rising trend in productivity and per capita income may become a fond memory. Can we, that is, still assume a rising per capita income?

Bringing all this together, we arrive at the tentative hypothesis that the growth places of the near future will be less those that face an income elastic demand for their export goods and services and more those that face favorable relative price changes and productivity trends. In general, those select industries producing manufactured goods less exposed to critical material and energy scarcities, and less burdened with noxious wastes, and those select services that are experiencing average or better productivity gains, are the next round of growth industries; and their sites will be the next round of growth places.

To these one must of course add places of invention and

innovation, as always. But for our purposes here, we need not predict which places will be favored with the new growth industries but only that some will, and the local growth process will begin. Nor need we assume that the new growth centers created these new growth industries. They may have, by their superior amenities, attracted these new activities, as is more often than not the case across the Sunbelt. We turn now to the momentum of local growth, and to a discussion of the "disequilibrating expansionary forces" shown on the left side of Figure 5-1.

FROM MULTIPLIERS TO MIGRATION

Urban-regional economists feel most comfortable in the familiar work of translating an increase in demand for local exports into an increase in total employment and income—perhaps too comfortable. The transfer of the Keynesian (or more precisely, the international trade) multiplier from a national to a regional context was relatively obvious and easy, and was accomplished very early in the development of local growth theory. The direct effect of an increase in export sales, production, employment, and payrolls on local income, the indirect effect of this increased income on spending for local goods and services (e.g. rent, retail services, doctors), and then on to a second round of local income generation and spending, and additional diminishing rounds—all this is the staple of local economic analysis.

While the local multiplier has been well worked (perhaps overworked), very little attention has been paid to the many critical junctions at which slippage can occur in this not so mechanistic mechanism. Increased sales and production can often be squeezed out of increased productivity (output per manhour) in local plants and offices, especially if they have been running at less than full capacity.

Again, when more labor input is required for more product output, it is often cheaper to go into overtime (or from part time to full time), rather than hire new employees for a surge that may not last. Local income rises but not the number employed. Or, if the new, higher level of sales and production do persist, employment may rise due to increased labor force participation rates, as wives, teenagers, older workers, and the handicapped seek and find jobs. Thus, income and employment may rise but not local population. This is much too rich a mosaic, with far too many complex impacts and policy implications, to be casually subsumed and blurred under "the local multiplier."

100 Economic Growth and Decline

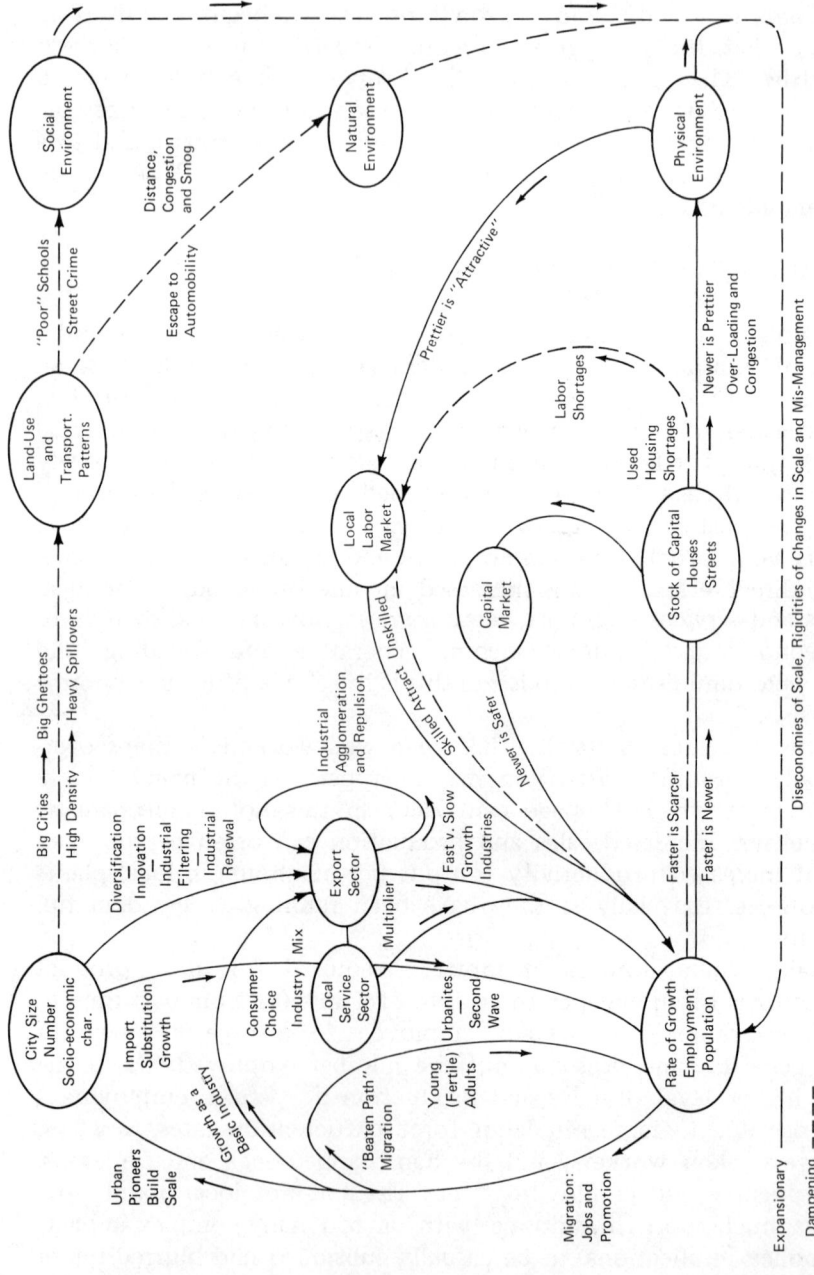

Figure 5-1. Thesis of Disequilibrating Expansionary and Equilibrating Dampening Forces.

But if the increase in local exports sales and production is large enough and lasts long enough to strain local plant capacity and labor supplies, in-migrants will be attracted in response to the rising local wage rates or higher earnings through longer work weeks or simply the new job openings, including opportunities for promotion through migration. Net in-migration of workers to fill new jobs, whether created by the expansion of existing firms or the entry of new businesses, and whether through the actions of local entrepreneurs or outsiders, generates another kind of local multiplier.

This "migration multiplier" differs significantly from the Keynesian multiplier in that the latter assumed (implicitly) a rise (or fall) in per capita income in response to changing volumes of spending, in that the population base was implicitly assumed to be constant. In sharp constrast to this business cycle multiplier, the migration multiplier assumes an increase in the local labor force (and population) and in effect a larger total local income without any necessary change in per capita income. Just more money and more people. Again, a difference with social and policy implications much too great to be swept under the rug of "total local income."

The migration multiplier could also be dubbed the planners' multiplier because it ties an increase in local exports to new households and houses, more kids and school desks, and new stores, as well as more consumption spending. This planners' multiplier is explicitly concerned with capital programming and land use planning, although it jumps a couple of steps in getting there. These two very different and distinct multipliers are almost always confused, or at least are collapsed into a single, undifferentiated impact.

In sum, the friction in the system may cause a small change in demand for local exports to change only local profits (absentee-owned ?), a moderate change to be reflected largely in per capita income, and only a large or sustained increase in exports is surely linked to the growth in local population. But the pressure builds, and later if not sooner, some new people come to town.

Net in-migration, together with natural increase in population, builds larger city size and opens up the economic feasibility of producing, locally, goods and services that were formerly imported from outside the local economy. This is descriptively called import substitution growth, and may be either a catching up or filling in operation. The local service sector both lags behind the growth of the export sector and broadens in range and variety with larger city size.

But import substitution growth is double-edged: it not only responds to basic (export) growth and larger city size, it acts in turn to cause further growth and larger size. Thriving export industries, various local multipliers, and net in-migration expand the local market and pull one new local service after another over the threshold of minimum efficient scale (over the break-even point). The rapidly enlarging range of consumer choice—from one movie house to a few and then to legitimate theatre—attracts new in-migrants looking for greater urbanity—not the least of which might be the wives of the corporate executives who make major business locational decisions.

Import substitution growth is not fully appreciated by urban growth analysts; a powerful cumulative process is at work here. The first wave of in-migrants make it much easier for the second wave to come and stay. The new library in town more than makes up for the need to share the local fishing hole or hiking trail, at least to the newcomers. If the first wave, the "pioneers," feel a net loss of well-being, they are fewer in number and are more often than not now locked in by friends, homes, and businesses—and by age. Each new wave of in-migrants build scale for and activate the next more urbane group. The "old timers" may not suffer growth in silence but they do tend to suffer it in place.

CITY SIZE AND INNOVATION

With growth to metropolitan area size comes a structural transformation in the local economy that virtually ensures, for a while, further growth at a near national average rate. The simplest and certainly the most widely appreciated structural change accompanying large size is industrial diversification. Big cities, with populations of a million or more and with perhaps a dozen or more important current "exports," can hardly avoid having a rich age mix of industries: young and fast growing, mature and slow growing; and even a few dying industries. So large a sample would, moreover, ordinarily blend an industry mix of income elastic and income inelastic products. We would not, then, expect the large diversified urban area to exhibit either very rapid or very slow growth. We would, in fact, expect urban areas to regress toward the national average growth rate with larger size.

But the long view of urban history teaches us that no competitive "open economy" can stand pat. All industries begin the process of dying from the moment of birth. In the past, large urban areas have ensured average growth and their economic future only by continually reaching for new industries. And who would not project an unending rise and fall of individual industries? Five-year projections of a local economy may be drawn from the prospects of its current industry mix, but probably ten-year and certainly twenty-year forecasts would seem to call for a theory of local industrial evolution.

Consider the folly of trying to anticipate the Los Angeles economy of the fifties and sixties by projecting over decades the cinema and citrus growth trends of the twenties and thirties, or projecting Detroit of 1900 to 1930 by extrapolating the growth curve of horseless carriages, circa 1900. How does one then make the admittedly difficult transition from, say, a five-year projection of a given industry mix to, say, a twenty-year projection of changes in the composition of that mix?

Again, great scale would seem to simplify the problem. Suppose stable growth over decades is traceable more to local capability to invent and innovate and otherwise acquire new export bases, decade after decade, than it is to the sheer number of different exports amassed at any point. Can we not establish that the large place is more than proportionately a center of invention and innovation and more able thereby to protect itself in the competition between cities? Further, does not the metropolis adapt better to change originating elsewhere?

The true economic base of the great city-region is, then, the creativity of its universities and research parks, the sophistication of its engineering firms and financial institutions, the persuasiveness of its public relations and advertising agencies, the flexibility of its transportation networks and utility systems, and all the other dimensions of infrastructure that facilitate the quick and orderly transfer from old dying bases to new growing ones.

A diversified set of current exports ("breadth") softens the immediate shock of exogenous change, while a rich infrastructure ("depth") supports the complex adjustment to change by providing the socioeconomic institutions and physical facilities needed to initiate new enterprises, convert capital from old into new forms, and retrain labor.

Large places are also better based to adapt to innovations originating elsewhere. With a wider assortment of educational institutions and more professional counselling, local workers may be more quickly retrained from declining to expanding occupations. Reemployment can often be achieved within the same local labor market, eliminating the burden of moving to keep working, so characteristic of smaller places. Finally, in the most general way, urban scale extends the range of consumer and occupational choice, consistent with high and rising levels of income and education, luring and holding the more creative and urbane individuals—that is, the very people who invent, innovate, and organize new economic bases.

With larger city size comes a richer base of research, finance, design, production, and marketing capability, to the point where industrial transitions tend to come in continuous and smooth flow. Industrial obituaries and birth notices go unheralded. At the other extreme, the remote mining town has no reason for being after the vein of ore is depleted. But in between are places that can and will make the necessary adjustment, slowly and laboriously, or could make it more surely and more easily with a little timely help, or with a little longer grace period.

It is easy to see why significant basic productive power of a local economy could remain long after its contemporary economic role has been shattered. Local economies tend to develop significant depth, including efficient utilities, responsive bankers, pluralistic transportation connections, facilities for technical or at least good vocational education, at an earlier stage and much smaller population size than that stage and size at which industrial diversification occurs (breadth).

Casual observation does indeed tend to support the impression that a local economy achieves the power to adapt, eventually, to losing a major industry at a much smaller size (100,000 population?) than that at which the diversification of local industry is so great that only weak shocks are felt (over a million population?). Viability would then precede stability.

DISEQUILIBRATING GROWTH: RAPID CHANGE INDUCES MORE CHANGE

Just as larger city size serves first to stimulate and later retard urban growth, so too the *rate* of local growth in population sets in motion forces that both feed back and reinforce that rate and act as a countervailing force. Direct and strong lines of linkage run from the rate of population growth to the standing stock of capital, both public and private, ranging from houses to schools and street capacity, as shown by the solid horizontal line near the bottom of the diagram in Figure 5-1.

Rapid growth has a favorable effect on the average age of capital: faster is newer. Simply put, if a town doubles in size in a decade, half the houses in town will be less than ten years old. And, to most people, newer is prettier. The faster growing, newer and prettier places tend then to attract new migrants, especially the affluent, who can most afford to live in them. But the affluent are most often the educated and skilled who create the new jobs that draw, in time, most others—for work or welfare.

To keep half its housing less than ten years old, a town will have to keep doubling every decade. The Phoenix area has been doing just that since 1950 and if it continues to grow at this pace until the year 2000 it would be as large then as Chicago is now, and rival New York around 2010. To reject this projection as ridiculous is to accept the aging of Phoenix as natural and inevitable. This is not necessarily an admissible thought locally.

Fast growth induces more growth in another way. Present trends tend to be extrapolated into the future, therefore rapid local growth tends to generate expectations of further increases in property values, especially in land prices. If this optimism spreads from land speculators to speculative builders, a self-fulfilling prophecy is generated, at least for a while. To the extent that heavy investors in land and buildings wield significant political power, supporting public actions and investments will also be induced.

One can hypothesize another link in this chain of local growth by reasoning from overoptimism to excessive speculative new building to lower than normal costs of doing business in the near future, as, for example, when too much new office space leads to rents below full cost. The capital losses of the landlords become the attractive and attracting rent bargains of business.

We have been made painfully aware of the reluctance of bankers to make mortgage loans in older, declining neighborhoods ("redlining"), further depressing these neighborhoods. And new buildings tend to ensure the safety of loans made to build again nearby. Perhaps the national counterpart to this neighborhood lending pattern is the interregional flow of capital from the older and shabbier industrial Northeast and Midwest to the bright, new Sunbelt. Recent events in municipal finance have caused some to wonder whether the whole Northeast is not in danger of being red-lined—or at least many of their local governments.

Rapid growth interacts with larger city size to produce a very favorable climate for professional advancement. Even in smaller places, rapid growth offers almost a sure shot at regular promotions, whether fully deserved or not. Large places, even if not growing, offer the lure of the top positions, even if they are long shots. Large, growing places would seem to be especially difficult to resist.

Local growth is attractive also in that it brings change and adds an element of excitement, or at least anticipation. One year the new library is opened; the next year it gets some books. Besides change brings a more open attitude toward further change, and thereby induces more change (growth). Growing corporations, reportedly, prefer places growing at double the national average rate. Growth, for a while, feeds on itself.

EQUILIBRATING GROWTH: RAPID CHANGE RESTRAINS FURTHER CHANGE

Change can also be equilibrating by slowing further change in a number of ways. Rapid local growth has, for example, an adverse impact on housing standards, as a sharply rising number of low and middle income households which cannot afford new houses compete ever more intensely for the fixed supply of used housing. The dashed line leading from the growth rate to the capital stock, horizontally along the bottom of the diagram in Figure 5-1, sums up this relationship simply: faster is scarcer. Beyond this physical linkage, housing shortages can lead to labor shortages severe enough to slow industrial growth.[b]

Carrying this line of reasoning a step further, labor shortages (tight labor markets) tend to reduce labor productivity, as workers change jobs more frequently and as the bargaining advantage tilts away from management and toward labor. While rising labor costs are probably more than offset by falling fixed costs per unit with the rapid growth in output of the local growth industries, the tightening of housing and labor markets begins to weigh more heavily in the balance.

Local growth can also run ahead of the capacity of public facilities, overload sanitary and storm sewers, and stall traffic on overloaded, two-lane, "mile roads" in the suburbs, wasting time, causing accidents, and increasing pollution. Again, heavy in-migration forces schools into half-day sessions, crowds court dockets ("justice delayed is justice denied"), and creates other social disorganization. It is worth noting in this regard that migrants are much more than proportionately young adults, persons in the crime prone ages.

In addition, rapid local growth and heavy in-migration crowds and overloads the fixed stock of used housing, and tends further to defer normal maintenance in this sellers' market (time of landlord advantage). Thus "urban blight" spreads and tends to offset the "faster is newer is prettier" effect discussed above. All this then feeds back and

---

[b]While this author cannot cite any careful accounts in the literature of this constraint, conversations with businessmen and community leaders in Rochester, New York support the notion that growth there in the 1950s outran the local housing supply and served to slow it; informed observers in the Piedmont area reinforce this impression on the basis of the experience there in the 1960s. Further, in the planned economy of Estonia, the housing supply of Tallinn is managed as the principal lever with which to control population growth.

serves to countervail the cumulative expansionary forces emanating from rapid growth. Faster is prettier, but faster is scarcer and more congested too.

How much of our dissatisfaction with city life throughout the postwar period has been due to larger city size and how much has been due to rapid growth is not at all clear. Nor are we sure whether the no-growth movement that has spread to so many towns and small cities across the country expresses a reluctance to get bigger or a reaction against too much, too soon. Certainly, some of the more notable strategies here have been couched in terms that imply only a desire to slow an "unmanageable" rate of current growth, such as Ramapo, New York's plan to stage or spread out its growth over two decades. Even if slowing growth is often a façade of respectability behind which to hide the desire to exclude the poor, or everyone, indefinitely, the courts have shown much more sympathy for slowing than for stopping growth.

Thus a rapid rate of growth in one period may act to slow the rate of growth in the next period, and come to be more of a restraining force on growth and ultimate city size than city size itself—that is, the diseconomies of great size. If, moreover, the rate of natural increase hovers near zero, large city size would become a passing problem, while great structural changes in the national economy could still be a strong force causing rapidly changing rates of local growth to be a perennial "urban" problem.

CITY SIZE AS A RESTRAINING FORCE: HOUSEHOLDS AND THE QUALITY OF THE ENVIRONMENT

The process of vigorous growth to very large city size comes also to be reflected in the land use pattern and transportation system of the great city, and ordinarily not favorably. Without laboring here ideas to be discussed at considerable length in later chapters, some of the more obvious diseconomies of great size are suggested by the dashed line across the top of Figure 5-1. Big cities build big ghettoes that lead in turn to segregation at great distance and "separate and unequal schools."

It is not necessary to understand the precise lines of causation that run from great ghettoes and segregated schools and neighborhoods to alienation and street crime to accept a general line of argument that the physical environment of the city becomes as much a casualty of mismanaged bigness as does the social environment. In general, *large pockets of poor* are seen by advocates of urban-rural balance as being one of the worst sins of big cities in that rural poverty is not as bad as big city because it is not as reinforcing.

Large urban population also forces higher densities and this causes heavier spillovers: if you burn refuse, I get the smell; if I choose to drive, your driving is slowed, and we both breathe the polluted air. Large cities are charged with posing a greater pollution problem because: (1) they generate more effluent per square mile (due to higher population densities), (2) the "damage cost" of pollution rises faster than its physical level (that is, a small amount is harmless but twice as much is harmful and four times as much is deadly), and (3) by definition, more people are subjected to the higher levels and costs in big city concentrations.

Without attempting to balance all this with the counterarguments that big cities permit economies of scale in waste treatment processes, can support transit as an alternative to the automobile, and help preserve unpolluted wilderness and recreational areas, let us assume for argument that the natural environment is the third casualty of urban growth to very large size.

Big city crime may be more often mentioned and racial antagonism more often left unsaid, as reasons for preferring small cities, but one should not underestimate the importance of the increasing cost and difficulty of moving by automobile through large cities. One suspects that the middle income motorist will, when pressed, choose his automobile above all else. The ardent motorist may not have to choose among the big city triad of the high cost of driving (in time if not tolls), or riding buses, or moving back in closer to his work. He may simply pack up and move to a smaller city.

To look ahead, the middle income motorist is the most vulnerable to various strategies designed to "improve" city life by disciplining "excessive" driving with rush hour tolls and/or exclusive lanes for buses. We speak of technological progress in transportation and communication as operating to decentralize population and economic activity, employing exotic illustrations of new devices such as desk terminals in the home tied into central computers. But the easy, inexpensive use of an old familiar device, the automobile, may already be more critical in locational decisions.

As cities grow larger and face harder problems in land use planning, spillover effects, and the management of movement through the city, the effectiveness of local government becomes more important. But at the same time that the public sector should be getting stronger it is getting weaker due to political fragmentation. In general, the larger the metropolitan area, the greater the number of separate and contesting governments. Time and growth and sprawl have combined to undercut even some of our more heralded achievements in metropolitan area government. The Nashville City-

Davidson County consolidation, heralded by students of urban government as a breakthrough in metropolitan area government, seems to be running behind events: almost all the area's new growth is already outside the central county.[c]

Diseconomies of very great scale, expressed in the household sector as higher (money) costs of living and the deterioration of the urban environment—social, physical, and natural environments—may lag behind the many economies of scale enjoyed by business, but sooner or later they begin to feed back and repress the overall urban growth process.

The early exhilarating effect of larger and larger population size on the business environment and the delayed but seemingly inexorable deterioration of the living environment is a point and counterpoint sequence that is becoming well appreciated by even casual observers of city life. Less well appreciated and barely understood even by professional city watchers, is the increasing drag of city size on the business sector. As population and business activity increases, so too does the cost of doing business. We turn now to explore briefly the way in which business growth and larger city size combine to drive out the simpler work, and slow further growth: "industrial filtering."

CITY SIZE AS A RESTRAINING FORCE: FALLING SKILLS, RISING COSTS, AND "INDUSTRIAL FILTERING"

If the larger urban areas are more than proportionately places of innovation and if new products tend to exhibit higher than average rates of growth in output and employment, why then have larger places tended to grow at only an average rate throughout the postwar period? And there was a very clear and strong tendency for metropolitan areas to approach the national average change in population (regress toward the mean) as they became larger. The resolution of this seeming paradox may be remarkably simple: fast

---

[c]The Nashville metropolitan area is now defined as encompassing not one but eight counties. From 1970 to 1975 the metropolitan area is estimated to have increased in population by about 7.7 percent but Davidson County registered a gain of only 0.7 percent, and accounted for only 2,900 of the 53,800 new residents. With 93 percent of the new growth, the seven ring counties have apparently added almost all of the new residential capital. Unless an unusual amount of housing replacement has occurred in the central city-county, this "metropolitan government" would seem to be aging significantly and, from a distance, seems on the way to becoming just another central city. And in the comparable Indianapolis City-Marion County consolidation, Marion County registered a population loss in the 1970-75 period estimated at 0.6 percent while the surrounding seven counties of its metropolitan area grew at about the national rate.

growing industry mixes may go hand in hand with a steady loss of competitive share in these industries.

The higher a place stands in the hierarchy of industrial skills generally, the younger its industries and the more likely it is to generate an average rate of growth out of a set of fast growing industries, dampened by declining shares of that work—the innovation of new work and the spinning off of established lines as they become routine. The lower a place stands in the skill and wage hierarchy, the older an industry tends to be when it arrives in town and the slower its nationwide growth rate.

Intermediate-size places, of, say, two hundred thousand population, tend to fashion a more or less average growth rate out of growing shares of slow growing industries. But below this size the positive change in share weakens and erodes to zero, producing slower than average growth (net out-migration) at about 25,000 population and absolute decline in employment and population, more often than not, below 2,500 population. At least, this was the broad picture up until about 1970, the last census of population.

In broad outline, the filtering down of industry through the national system of cities has seemed to progress roughly as follows. With a new process to be mastered, new industries are most often launched in the older and larger (more sophisticated) industrial centers, where the work skills are the highest, risk capital easiest to find, and where diverse and even esoteric technical supports (specialized laboratories and professional specialists) are most accessible.

The question in the early days is "who can do the job?" But in time the question changes to "where can the job be done most cheaply?" With time and production experience comes the rationalization and routinization of the maturing industrial process, and as the aging industry slides down its "learning curve" toward ever lower skill requirements, it seeks out (is competitively forced to find) cheaper labor markets.

Languishing farm service centers, with seriously underemployed rural hinterlands, searching desperately for new economic bases, stand out as pools of cheap labor. Raw farm labor can rise to the very modest demands of the now very simplified production process. And not only the high wages but also the congestion and high taxes of big cities are an unnecessary cost for simple operations that do not need either big city skills or facilities.

A filtering down theory of industrial location goes a long way toward explaining the common lament of the isolated small town: why do we always attract the slow growing and poorly paid industries? Small places find that they must run to stand still, as their industrial catches seem to come to these out-of-the-way places only to die. These industrial backwaters also struggle in vain to raise per capita income, hobbled by industries that pay at or near minimum wage rates.

Simple operations, low wage rates, and slow growth are the hallmarks of the aging industry. Both the larger industrial centers from which, and the smaller places to which, industries filter down must, it would seem, run to stand still (at the national average rate of growth in employment and population). The larger places do, however, run for higher stakes—higher wage work. Still, the larger but aging industrial centers of the Northeast and Midwest are running ever slower, saddled by their high cost structure.

THE PROCESS OF CITY BUILDING IS ALIVE AND WELL

Synthesizing the local growth process out of two expansionary and two restraining forces, one of each activated by city size and one of each activated by the local growth rate, is largely a deductive exercise supported by substantial observation but only fragmentary empirical work. It is a vast understatement to say that relative magnitudes and timing of these four lines of force cannot be specified with even reasonable precision. A good guess would be that the city size expansionary loop, circling through the business sector is set in motion much earlier—that is, at smaller city size—than the restraining loop running from city size into land use patterns and the environment.

In other words, the expansionary forces of the business sector (economies of scale and "industrial agglomeration") probably dominate up to some medium-size population (say, one-half million or so), at which point the dampening effect (diseconomies of scale or "problems of bigness") in the household sector begins to overtake the former.

Both growth rate loops, expansionary and restraining, are by definition tied to the current rate of growth, and are therefore activated almost immediately. But the impact of rapid growth on the adequacy of the fixed stock of capital ("faster is scarcer") would seem to be deactivated more readily as supply responds to demand. The impact of rapid growth on the average age of capital ("faster is newer is prettier") would seem to build to a peak more slowly and last longer. Thus the two rate of growth forces probably sum to produce a slower but longer (more stretched out) expansionary momentum than city size alone would generate.

Synthesizing the four forces would seem to generate strong, steady local growth up to a population of perhaps one-half to one million, followed by a slowing of growth to perhaps a static state at a couple of million population. One would of course expect a wide variation about these rough approximations to reflect, on the upper side, the great push from a powerful hinterland (e.g., Chicago) or the flood tide of a gargantuan industry (e.g., Detroit).

The policy importance of this conceptual formulation of the urban growth process is, in part, that it can be used to rationalize that which we are now observing: the slowing down and topping out of population growth in our older and larger metropolitan areas, notably those in the East and Midwest. But more important, this conceptual model warns us that there may be an almost unstoppable growth power in the early stages of local development, once the "takeoff point" is passed.

We may not intend to build a new set of large cities, but the powerful growth forces described above have not been suspended merely because we have mismanaged bigness in our older metropolises. At the present time, little evidence can be found or little reason adduced to believe that we will solve our urban problems by population dispersal into nonmetropolitan areas—at least not without a comprehensive and powerful national policy on the distribution of population. Whether we do or do not like our cities, the process of city building is alive and well—and now living down South and out West.

 *Chapter Six*

Changes in Manufacturing and Retailing Employment in Medium-Size Cities

Seymour Sacks

The economic growth of the medium-size city has not been systematically studied. Hidden between the large city and the smaller town are the particular problems of the medium-size city, which have not been subject to the same type of scrutiny as the two polar cases.

The very large city is easy to identify, but it is much more difficult to determine the point of differentiation between a large city and a medium sized city, and a medium-size city and a small city. If one chooses figures such as 500,000 and 150,000 the question emerges, to what years do the populations refer? As noted in Chapter One of this book, places shift from one size category to another over time. But perhaps even more important is the question whether there are systematic differences based on size.

A number of observers have distinguished cities in terms of age rather than in terms of size, and as will be indicated in this analysis, the related distinction as to region is so much more powerful than that involving size that it completely obliterates any meaning associated with size. As a result, it appears that the distinction between the large and medium-size city is far more a function of region, which in turn is a function of initial urban form and density.

THE MEDIUM-SIZE CITY DEFINED

Because there appears to be no real cutoff point between the medium and the large cities, all central cities with populations over 150,000 (with some minor exceptions) will be considered. The economic trends under consideration will focus on two of the principal characteristics that, individually and collectively, have operated to define the nature of the city: manufacturing and retailing.

Three points stand out from the analysis. First, many of the present economic problems have a considerable longevity; second, regional rather than size characteristics are of critical importance in distinguishing and understanding the nature of the current status of the city; and finally, the city can not be described in terms of average behavior.

The world of cities has no meaningful average or central tendency. Two classes of cities have emerged since World War II, those which are declining and those which show economic growth. What are the reasons?

The analysis focuses on the "daytime" city. This city might or might not be related to the "nighttime" city described in the conventional census and sociological documents. Comprehensive systematic information on the "daytime" city is very hard to come by if one deals with Roderick McKenzie (1) in the early 1930s, Creamer (2), Kain (3) and more recently Bennett Harrison (4). Attempts were made to conform the major information sources, but the results were mainly piecemeal, and only with the availability of the *Journey to Work* information for 1960 and 1970, has it been possible to put the entire picture together. Nevertheless, these earlier analyses are of great interest because of the information and the perspectives that they provide.

As in the various earlier studies, the principal focus is on manufacturing and retailing. That this should be the case is of course associated with the dominance of manufacturing activity in the total economic process, but it is perhaps more important in this analysis because of the extent to which it provided employment in the political unit called the city. The great importance of manufacturing in our economic history is again visible now that manufacturing is declining in relative terms and in many areas in absolute terms. The "industrial" city implies the manufacturing city. The "post-industrial" city implies the nonmanufacturing city.

The fact that the political unit and the economic unit are not the same poses problems. These problems have been raised and understood by most of the analysts of the location of economic activity. But in one way, they were less important because of the extent to which the city area represented a greater proportion of the population than the economic area. In *The Metropolitan Community*, Roderick McKenzie and Calvin Smith have a detailed discussion on the nature of annexations as well as an understanding of the problem of suburbanization (5).

The analysis of manufacturing and retailing employment covers all central cities with populations of 150,000 or more in 1970, with a few exceptions. Most of these cities would qualify as medium-size cities if there is a concept of the large city. Using a cutoff point of 500,000 as the big city, 66 of the 84 would have been medium-sized in 1947, and 58 (not necessarily the same) would have been medium-sized in 1973. The data reflect employment in the cities, not the employment of the residents of the city.

Because of the complete dominance of regional characteristics, the cities are shown in state order by region, rather than in the more conventional size order. The choice of 1947 (1948 in the case of retailing) is not only due to the fact that Censuses are available for these years, but because of the basic assumption of this analysis— namely, that World War II provided a deflection of underlying trends in the older, more built-up cities and unparalleled opportunities for the newer cities of the South and the West.

By looking at 1947 as a base year, it can be demonstrated that the rapid decline of the eastern cities and the great growth of the western cities had their origins at this time, and that some of them were intensified by some very unique characteristics which were not fully appreciated by earlier observers.

THE INFLUENCE OF WORLD WAR II

World War II transformed the American economy in a number of ways. In fact, each of the major American wars has had a positive employment effect on the American city. The enormous increase in manufacturing employment of the 1939-1947 era clearly occurred, to a considerable extent, in the American City. The extent to which this was the case was considered by both Coleman Woodbury (6) and John Kain (7), but it was not fully understood in terms of its consequences. Some of the difficulties were hidden by changes in definition, but others simply were not appreciated.

One of the reasons for the inadequacy of the measurement of cities by population size is that it fails to distinguish between large and "big" cities. This issue has been considered by a number of analysts, principally in terms of density gradients, but those gradients are based on "nighttime" populations and assumptions about "daytime" activities. Thus, there are some cities which are large but not "big" in terms of their downtown activity. They probably would be better modelled as suburban type cities.

On the other hand, there are some cities—in fact, an increasing number of medium-size cities—whose population characteristics are more closely akin to the "big" cities than to *many* cities of a larger size. It appears that in the foreseeable future, with only a few exceptions, the newly emerging large cities will have suburban (growth) characteristics. The ability to distinguish problem cities on the basis of size will become increasingly difficult.

The increases caused by World War II represented a deflection from the more fundamental set of declines which were the subject of Roderick McKenzie's 1933 analysis (8). For just as World War I had raised employment to new levels, followed by declines (except in the automobile dominated Midwest and in the South), so World War II appeared to deflect the earlier trends. The reasons were twofold, as has been recognized by many observers: the expansion of production, where the capital was in place and where there was a considerable labor force; and the fact that when Johnny came marching home and was demobilized, 10 million or so veterans landed in the cities in a year and a half, with a disproportionate number of them as workers and students and even unemployed.

As will be indicated, it is hard not to make these assumptions in the light of the enormous concentrations of economic activity observed in the large cities of the time. But for many cities these levels represented historic highs which were never again to be approached. For other cities, which had very little manufacturing activity, the decline of the older more built-up city was to give them new and unparalleled opportunities. Of course, two forces were to operate. The same forces mentioned by McKenzie in 1933—suburbanization and "nucleation" of retailing activity—and deconcentration and "considerable interregional shifting" (9).

Before evaluating the nature of employment in manufacturing and retailing in the cities as of 1947, a first step in the analysis has been to estimate the levels of population as of 1947. Estimates made during the war indicated declines in civilian population on a county level, except in military centers. The use of interpolations based on 1940 and 1950 data to estimate the populations as of 1947 suffers from a serious deficiency in that it fails to recognize the effects of demobilization on city population.

An alternative approach is to use the population changes that occurred between 1950 and 1960 in the 1950 boundaries and to extrapolate backwards to 1947. In those cities which showed a traditional growth pattern, interpolations gave virtually the same answers as the backward extrapolations. The results are also consistent with other data, most notably, the retailing employment in the cities.

The resulting pattern indicates upward changes in almost all cities between 1940 and 1947, as shown in Table 6-1, which are consistent with the demobilization and observed employment characteristics. More substantial changes took place in the South and West than in the Northeast and Midwest. But, unlike the Northeast and Midwest, the South and West continued to move upward. However, in the Northeast and Midwest an important differential pattern of population decline (with exceptions caused by annexations) emerged.

If this model is appropriate, then the period around 1947 represented not only historic highs in population, but also historic highs in employment, in manufacturing, and in retailing as well. This was to be the case in the cities which were to peak.

The growth between 1940 and 1947 is even more important than in the prior or subsequent periods, because it was in the context of relatively constant governmental boundaries. In the period afterward, as well as in the prior periods, a great deal of the growth in population was accounted for by annexation. Unlike all other periods, 1940-47 was almost entirely a period of increased concentration of population.

ECONOMIC ACTIVITY—POPULATION GROWTH

There was also an extraordinary growth in city economic activity that also occurred during this same period which probably triggered the population growth. The overall increase in manufacturing activity was concentrated in city areas (10). This is indicated by the fact that while there was a 50 percent increase in total manufacturing employment throughout the United States, many large cities had increases far in excess of that rate, and this was true of virtually all cities in the East and Midwest. (This, by the way, is contrary to the usual assumptions concerning the changes as occurring primarily in the West and South.)

The reasons for the concentration of manufacturing employment in the East and Midwest were in part due to the presence of a capital plant, a skilled labor force, and the existence of a preoccupying European War. The presence of so many manufacturing jobs, in turn, operated to attract a very sizeable labor force, which remained after World War II ended. This was partly responsible for the estimated growth in the central cities.

The population growth of central cities is much more clearly understood in the context of retailing employment. The increases in manufacturing were both larger and at higher rates than the increases in retailing, but there were substantial increases in retailing employment. Unlike the case of manufacturing, there were many cities in

118 Economic Growth and Decline

Table 6-1. Population Characteristics

City	City Population (Thousands)					Population Growth	Area Growth
	1940	1947	1950	1960	1973	73/47	73/50
East							
01 Bridgeport	147.1	159.2	158.7	156.7	145.0	−8.9%	0.0%
02 Hartford	166.2	181.8	177.3	162.1	148.0	−18.6	0.0
03 Washington	663.0	813.8	802.1	763.9	733.0	−9.9	0.0
04 Baltimore	859.1	952.9	949.2	939.0	877.0	−8.0	0.0
05 Boston	770.8	832.7	801.4	697.1	618.0	−25.8	0.0
06 Worcester	193.6	208.5	203.4	186.5	170.0	−18.5	0.0
07 Jersey City	301.1	305.8	299.0	276.1	255.0	−16.6	0.0
08 Newark	429.7	448.8	438.7	405.2	367.0	−18.2	0.0
09 Buffalo	575.9	594.3	580.1	532.7	425.0	−28.5	0.0
10 New York	7454.9	7924.9	7891.9	7781.9	7646.0	−3.5	0.0
11 Rochester	324.9	336.6	332.4	318.5	276.0	−18.0	0.0
12 Syracuse	205.9	222.0	220.5	215.8	184.0	−17.1	0.0
13 Philadelphia	1931.3	2092.3	2071.6	2002.5	1948.0	−6.9	0.0
14 Pittsburgh	671.6	698.5	676.8	604.2	520.0	−25.6	0.0
15 Albany	130.5	134.5	134.9	129.7	111.0	−17.5	9.8
16 Providence	253.5	260.9	248.6	207.4	170.0	−34.8	0.0
Regional Mean	942.4	1010.5	999.2	961.2	912.2	−17.8	0.6
Midwest							
17 Chicago	3396.8	3644.2	3620.9	3543.4	3172.0	−13.0	7.4
18 Fort Wayne	118.4	133.2	133.6	134.8	185.0	38.9	196.7
19 Indianapolis	386.9	426.6	427.1	428.8	728.0	70.7	587.8
20 Des Moines	159.8	174.3	177.9	190.0	199.0	14.2	17.1
21 Wichita	114.9	167.4	168.2	171.2	261.0	55.9	265.2
22 Detroit	1623.4	1903.3	1849.5	1670.1	1386.0	−27.2	0.0
23 Flint	151.5	159.6	163.1	196.9	181.0	13.4	16.7
24 Grand Rapids	164.2	176.4	176.5	176.6	190.0	7.7	91.3
25 Kansas City	399.1	463.5	456.6	433.5	487.0	5.1	292.2
26 St. Louis	816.0	888.6	856.7	750.0	558.0	−37.2	0.0
27 Omaha	234.8	248.0	251.1	261.3	372.0	50.0	98.5
28 Akron	244.7	270.0	274.6	289.8	261.0	−3.3	0.8
29 Cincinnati	455.6	506.6	503.9	495.1	426.0	−15.9	4.0
30 Cleveland	878.3	926.4	914.8	876.0	678.0	−26.8	0.0
31 Columbus, OH	306.0	369.9	375.9	395.6	540.0	46.0	299.6
32 Dayton	210.7	248.1	243.8	229.5	214.0	−13.7	53.8
33 Toledo	282.3	305.0	303.6	298.5	377.0	23.6	112.2
34 Madison	67.4	95.2	96.0	198.8	169.0	77.5	235.4

Table 6-1. (cont.)

City	City Population (Thousands)					Population Growth	Area Growth
	1940	1947	1950	1960	1973	73/47	73/50
35 Milwaukee	587.4	643.3	637.3	617.4	690.0	7.3	90.0
36 Gary	111.7	127.2	133.9	177.5	177.0	39.2	1.1
37 Minneapolis	492.3	533.3	521.7	482.8	382.0	−28.4	0.0
38 St. Paul	287.7	310.8	311.4	313.4	287.0	−7.7	0.0
Regional Mean	522.3	578.2	572.6	560.5	541.8	12.6	107.7
South							
39 Birmingham	267.5	325.3	326.0	378.1	295.0	−9.3	25.4
40 Mobile	78.7	125.5	129.0	140.4	185.0	47.4	357.6
41 Jacksonville	173.0	205.5	204.5	201.0	547.0	166.2	2439.5
42 Miami	172.1	236.5	249.2	291.6	363.0	53.5	0.0
43 Atlanta	302.2	335.9	331.3	318.9	451.0	34.3	256.7
44 Columbus, GA	53.2	61.4	79.6	73.3	160.0	160.6	1728.7
45 Louisville	319.0	381.3	369.1	328.4	335.0	−12.1	50.5
46 Baton Rouge	84.7	98.3	125.6	148.2	289.0	194.0	56.0
47 New Orleans	494.5	553.3	570.4	627.5	573.0	3.6	0.0
48 Shreveport	98.1	127.2	127.2	129.1	184.0	44.7	177.9
49 Jackson	62.1	94.5	98.2	110.7	163.0	72.5	137.5
50 Charlotte	100.8	130.7	134.0	144.8	284.0	117.3	153.6
51 Oklahoma City	204.4	240.3	243.5	254.0	373.0	55.2	1152.0
52 Tulsa	142.1	189.4	182.7	160.3	335.0	76.9	557.3
53 Knoxville	111.5	128.6	124.7	111.8	182.0	41.5	203.1
54 Memphis	292.9	386.2	396.0	428.4	658.0	70.4	150.0
55 Nashville	167.4	177.5	174.3	163.5	427.0	140.6	2221.4
56 Austin	87.9	127.4	132.4	149.1	289.0	126.8	183.9
57 Corpus Christi	57.3	93.1	108.2	124.0	212.0	127.7	699.3
58 Dallas	294.7	418.9	434.6	486.9	815.0	94.6	142.0
59 El Paso	96.8	123.9	130.4	152.5	353.0	184.9	512.8
60 Fort Worth	177.7	272.5	278.7	299.4	359.0	31.7	145.2
61 Houston	384.5	568.9	596.1	687.0	1296.0	127.8	211.5
62 San Antonio	253.8	396.5	408.4	448.2	756.0	90.7	264.9
63 Richmond	193.0	233.3	230.3	219.9	238.0	2.0	62.9
64 Tampa	108.3	121.6	124.6	134.6	276.0	127.0	194.3
65 St. Petersburg	60.8	85.9	96.7	180.8	234.0	172.4	62.1
66 Norfolk	144.3	212.2	213.5	217.7	283.0	33.4	57.2
Regional Mean	176.2	231.1	236.4	253.8	349.5	79.8	436.9
West							
67 Phoenix	65.4	106.8	106.8	106.7	631.0	490.8	1376.1

120 Economic Growth and Decline

Table 6-1. (cont.)

City	City Population (Thousands)					Population Growth	Area Growth
	1940	1947	1950	1960	1973	73/47	73/50
68 Tucson	35.5	45.3	45.4	45.7	302.0	566.7	845.1
69 Fresno	60.6	92.3	91.6	89.3	173.0	87.4	209.4
70 Sacramento	105.9	137.1	137.5	138.9	267.0	94.7	455.5
71 San Diego	203.3	295.0	334.3	507.3	575.0	94.9	225.0
72 San Jose	68.5	92.4	96.2	104.5	523.0	466.0	758.7
73 Denver	322.4	403.8	415.7	155.6	515.0	27.5	68.7
74 Honolulu	179.3	234.1	248.0	294.1	334.0	42.7	0.0
75 Albuquerque	35.4	78.4	96.8	177.5	273.0	248.2	82.8
76 Portland	305.3	377.2	373.6	301.6	375.0	−0.6	43.7
77 Salt Lake City	149.9	180.9	182.1	185.9	169.0	−6.6	10.1
78 Spokane	122.0	156.4	161.7	179.4	173.0	10.6	22.2
79 Tacoma	109.4	142.3	143.6	147.9	149.0	4.7	0.0
80 Los Angeles	1574.2	1830.5	1970.3	2471.4	2747.0	50.1	2.9
81 Long Beach	164.2	240.4	250.7	285.0	334.0	38.9	44.6
82 San Francisco	664.5	785.8	775.3	740.3	687.0	−12.6	0.0
83 Oakland	302.1	389.6	384.7	367.5	346.0	−11.2	0.0
84 Seattle	378.3	466.5	467.5	471.0	503.0	7.8	19.2
Regional Mean	263.1	336.4	348.9	392.4	514.8	102.0	231.3
National Mean	431.4	493.0	498.9	498.7	555.8	48.3	223.5

the Northeast in which retailing employment grew at a slower rate than for the United States as a whole. But the direction of growth was positive and more rapid than the increase in population, without exception, for all cities during this period.

This pattern of changes repeats an earlier pattern, at least in the case of manufacturing, for which there is data, that occurred as a result of World War I—namely the very rapid growth of manufacturing employment in the large cities. However, after World War I there were substantial declines in most cities except those associated with the automobile industry.

Most large cities showed substantially lower levels of employment even though the amount of total manufacturing employment was virtually unchanged at the census years of 1919, 1929 and 1939. World War II reversed this pattern and brought the levels of employment in cities with constant boundaries to levels which they were never again to approach. On the other hand, World War II did provide the momentum, and the changed pattern of transportation provided the opportunities, for most of the smaller and a few of the larger cities outside of the East and Midwest, to show substantial employment growth.

The employment characteristics of cities in 1947 are summarized in Tables 6-2 and 6-3. As was noted earlier, the cities are put in their respective regions. Not only did the cities of the East and Midwest have higher levels of manufacturing employment than in the South and West (because of the existence of larger cities in those areas), but the level of manufacturing employment relative to population was clearly higher in those regions than in the remainder of the nation. In fact, there were very few cities outside of the East and Midwest which reached the average employment/population levels of those regions. In the East and Midwest it was the exceptional city (Washington and Albany) that did not have a very substantial manufacturing economic base, while in the West, and to a lesser extent in the South, it was the exceptional city that did have a substantial base.

The situation can, however, be misinterpreted. The long term direction was a decline in the relative importance of manufacturing employment. This was evident in the Warren Thompson tables supported by Roderick McKenzie on the nature of employment by large city (11). This cross-sectional data hides a major change that had occurred in manufacturing industry, but which was not reported. In fact, the failure to recognize this problem lead John Kain to show the wrong numbers while saying the right thing because of some changes in definitions to be noted later (12). But two worlds of cities had emerged.

Cities whose employment patterns appear to be out of line, in the traditional economic base type of analysis, appear to be much more in line when measured against population. In both 1947 and 1974 the coefficients of variation for the proportion of the population engaged in retailing employment are about the same orders of magnitude for both years, with very restricted variations regardless of the nature of the cities or special circumstances. Thus, for the United States, retailing employment equalled 4.71 percent of the total population in 1947.

In the 84 cities the unweighted average was 7.59 percent with a standard deviation of 1.30 percent. The weighted average was slightly lower at 6.96 percent. That the cities were the retailing centers of the United States at the time is indicated by the fact that retailing employment was only 3.96 percent of the population in the remainder of the United States, or 183 percent more employment

Table 6-2. Manufacturing and Retailing Employment 1939 and 1947 (Thousands)

		Manufacturing			Retailing		
		1939	1947	1947/ 1939	1939	1948	1948/ 1939
	East						
01	Bridgeport	33.7	55.0	1.6%	7.6	11.0	1.4%
02	Hartford	23.9	34.5	1.4	12.6	17.5	1.4
03	Washington	11.1	17.8	1.6	48.1	72.5	1.5
04	Baltimore	86.2	120.9	1.4	46.2	67.7	1.5
05	Boston	66.7	101.7	1.5	64.5	74.3	1.2
06	Worcester	30.8	46.8	1.5	10.6	13.7	1.3
07	Jersey City	28.8	37.3	1.3	8.7	10.0	1.1
08	Newark	64.8	92.3	1.4	28.5	32.8	1.2
09	Buffalo	53.1	87.3	1.6	29.1	40.9	1.4
10	New York	572.8	940.2	1.6	335.8	433.6	1.3
11	Rochester	50.2	99.9	2.0	19.3	25.0	1.3
12	Syracuse	21.1	35.3	1.7	12.3	18.1	1.5
13	Philadelphia	220.7	328.6	1.5	90.7	125.8	1.4
14	Pittsburgh	49.8	81.4	1.6	43.9	63.2	1.4
15	Albany	5.6	10.5	1.9	8.7	10.6	1.2
16	Providence	46.0	61.2	1.3	15.8	19.6	1.2
	Regional Mean	85.7	134.4	1.6	48.9	64.8	1.3
	Midwest						
17	Chicago	393.2	667.4	1.7	184.5	248.7	1.3
18	Fort Wayne	13.3	30.9	2.3	7.2	10.5	1.5
19	Indianapolis	40.8	79.8	2.0	25.6	30.8	1.2
20	Des Moines	8.3	14.1	1.7	10.7	14.4	1.3
21	Wichita	3.7	9.6	2.6	7.5	12.9	1.7
22	Detroit	208.0	338.4	1.6	79.8	114.0	1.4
23	Flint	36.4	53.8	1.5	7.6	10.6	1.4
24	Grand Rapids	21.9	44.2	2.0	9.7	14.1	1.5
25	Kansas City	27.9	46.7	1.7	30.8	46.2	1.5
26	St. Louis	100.1	172.9	1.7	45.2	63.0	1.4
27	Omaha	12.1	25.4	2.1	13.8	17.7	1.3
28	Akron	39.1	76.8	2.0	12.4	18.3	1.5
29	Cincinnati	59.8	97.5	1.6	28.6	38.6	1.3
30	Cleveland	128.4	223.6	1.7	50.1	68.8	1.4
31	Columbus, OH	24.8	41.4	1.7	20.6	28.9	1.4
32	Dayton	36.5	75.8	2.1	13.2	21.7	1.6
33	Toledo	31.8	59.5	1.9	15.6	22.3	1.4
34	Madison	3.4	9.2	2.7	5.4	7.6	1.4

Changes in Manufacturing/Retailing Employment in Medium-Size Cities 123

Table 6-2. (cont.)

		Manufacturing			Retailing		
		1939	1947	1947/ 1939	1939	1948	1948/ 1939
35	Milwaukee	71.0	132.1	1.9	32.3	47.9	1.5
36	Gary	28.8	35.6	1.2	4.9	7.5	1.5
37	Minneapolis	29.5	61.9	2.1	33.0	46.5	1.4
38	St. Paul	18.5	40.6	2.2	20.0	25.3	1.3
	Regional Mean	60.8	105.4	1.8	29.9	41.7	1.4
	South						
39	Birmingham	13.7	26.5	1.9	14.3	22.2	1.6
40	Mobile	3.4	8.3	2.4	4.4	8.4	1.9
41	Jacksonville	8.3	12.2	1.5	9.9	15.0	1.5
42	Miami	3.3	7.1	2.2	12.8	22.4	1.7
43	Atlanta	23.3	36.2	1.6	23.8	35.3	1.5
44	Columbus, GA	NA	15.1	NC	3.1	4.7	1.5
45	Louisville	32.9	55.6	1.7	16.6	24.4	1.5
46	Baton Rouge	NA	4.5	NC	NA	7.8	NC
47	New Orleans	21.7	35.3	1.6	23.5	34.1	1.5
48	Shreveport	2.4	4.5	1.9	6.3	8.7	1.4
49	Jackson	2.5	4.8	1.9	4.2	6.6	1.6
50	Charlotte	9.7	13.5	1.4	7.0	10.5	1.5
51	Oklahoma City	4.8	8.6	1.8	12.2	17.4	1.4
52	Tulsa	3.6	7.9	2.2	9.9	13.4	1.4
53	Knoxville	15.4	19.3	1.3	7.3	11.4	1.6
54	Memphis	15.3	33.2	2.2	17.2	27.6	1.6
55	Nashville	13.9	21.7	1.6	10.4	14.2	1.4
56	Austin	NA	2.2	NC	5.2	8.5	1.6
57	Corpus Christi	NA	2.8	NC	3.9	7.1	1.8
58	Dallas	15.4	34.2	2.2	21.3	37.0	1.7
59	El Paso	2.2	5.0	2.3	5.3	9.1	1.7
60	Fort Worth	8.0	30.5	3.8	11.4	22.1	1.9
61	Houston	18.2	40.6	2.2	23.1	39.8	1.7
62	San Antonio	6.6	14.4	2.2	15.0	23.9	1.6
63	Richmond	20.2	28.1	1.4	14.7	21.0	1.4
64	Tampa	18.1	14.4	0.8	6.0	10.0	1.7
65	St. Petersburg	NA	1.2	NC	4.0	7.2	1.8
66	Norfolk	5.7	10.3	1.8	8.9	14.6	1.6
	Regional Mean	11.7	17.8	1.9	11.1	17.3	1.6
	West						
67	Phoenix	1.1	3.0	2.7	5.5	10.6	1.9
68	Tucson	NA	1.0	NC	NA	5.8	NC

Table 6-2. (cont.)

		Manufacturing			Retailing		
		1939	1947	1947/1939	1939	1948	1948/1939
69	Fresno	3.2	3.3	1.0	5.7	8.9	1.6
70	Sacramento	4.1	5.7	1.4	7.9	12.1	1.5
71	San Diego	5.6	18.6	3.3	10.4	18.8	1.8
72	San Jose	5.9	8.7	1.5	NA	7.5	NC
73	Denver	13.4	30.9	2.3	21.6	30.7	1.4
74	Honolulu	11.2	NA	NC	NA	3.7	NC
75	Albuquerque	NA	1.5	NC	NA	6.3	NC
76	Portland	17.9	33.8	1.9	19.8	30.4	1.5
77	Salt Lake City	3.3	7.9	2.4	10.2	14.2	1.4
78	Spokane	5.0	6.5	1.3	7.5	10.5	1.4
79	Tacoma	9.3	13.0	1.4	5.6	8.6	1.5
80	Los Angeles	80.2	161.2	2.0	92.9	131.7	1.4
81	Long Beach	3.3	8.1	2.5	7.2	15.3	2.1
82	San Francisco	37.4	61.6	1.6	44.8	55.8	1.2
83	Oakland	16.3	32.0	2.0	19.5	28.5	1.5
84	Seattle	23.5	50.2	2.1	24.1	34.1	1.4
	Regional Mean	15.0	24.8	2.0	17.8	23.9	1.5
	National Mean	41.8	64.9	1.8	25.2	34.2	1.5

NA = Not available   NC = Not computed

Table 6-3. Employment Characteristics, 1947 (Thousands)

		Total		% of Population		Retailing City as % of SMSA
		Manufacturing	Retailing	Manufacturing	Retailing	
	East					
01	Bridgeport	55.0	11.0	34.5%	6.9%	43.7%
02	Hartford	34.5	17.5	19.0	9.6	56.1
03	Washington	17.8	72.5	2.2	8.9	85.9
04	Baltimore	120.9	67.7	12.7	7.1	92.0
05	Boston	101.7	74.3	12.2	8.9	44.8
06	Worcester	46.8	13.7	22.4	6.6	50.7
07	Jersey City	37.3	10.0	12.2	3.3	44.3
08	Newark	92.3	32.8	20.6	7.3	65.9
09	Buffalo	87.3	40.9	14.7	6.9	82.4
10	New York	940.2	433.6	11.9	5.5	87.1
11	Rochester	99.9	25.0	29.7	7.4	87.2
12	Syracuse	35.3	18.1	15.9	8.2	85.8
13	Philadelphia	328.6	125.8	15.7	6.0	88.8
14	Pittsburgh	81.4	63.2	11.7	9.0	68.6
15	Albany	10.5	10.6	7.8	7.9	64.6

Table 6-3. (cont.)

		Total		% of Population		Retailing City as % of SMSA
		Manufacturing	Retailing	Manufacturing	Retailing	
16	Providence	61.2	19.6	23.5	7.5	61.6
	Regional Mean	134.4	64.8	16.6	7.3	69.3
	Midwest					
17	Chicago	667.4	248.7	18.3	6.8	57.1
18	Fort Wayne	30.9	10.5	23.2	7.9	92.5
19	Indianapolis	79.8	30.8	18.7	7.2	94.8
20	Des Moines	14.1	14.4	8.1	8.3	95.0
21	Wichita	9.6	12.9	5.7	7.7	92.6
22	Detroit	338.4	114.0	17.8	6.0	83.0
23	Flint	53.8	10.6	33.7	6.6	84.1
24	Grand Rapids	44.2	14.1	25.1	8.0	82.7
25	Kansas City	46.7	46.2	10.1	10.0	93.9
26	St. Louis	172.9	63.0	19.5	7.1	83.1
27	Omaha	25.4	17.7	10.2	7.1	98.2
28	Akron	76.8	18.3	28.4	6.8	81.4
29	Cincinnati	97.5	38.6	19.2	7.6	85.1
30	Cleveland	223.6	68.8	24.1	7.4	83.5
31	Columbus, OH	41.4	28.9	11.2	7.8	93.0
32	Dayton	75.8	21.7	30.6	8.7	87.3
33	Toledo	59.5	22.3	19.5	7.3	90.7
34	Madison	9.2	7.6	9.7	8.0	76.7
35	Milwaukee	132.1	47.9	20.5	7.4	89.2
36	Gary	35.6	7.5	28.0	5.9	43.2
37	Minneapolis	61.9	46.5	11.6	8.7	93.6
38	St. Paul	40.6	25.3	13.1	8.1	97.4
	Regional Mean	106.2	41.7	18.5	7.6	86.7
	South					
39	Birmingham	26.5	22.2	8.1	6.8	81.7
40	Mobile	8.3	8.4	6.6	6.7	85.8
41	Jacksonville	12.2	15.0	5.9	7.3	91.7
42	Miami	7.1	22.4	3.0	9.5	66.6
43	Atlanta	36.2	35.3	10.8	10.5	86.6
44	Columbus, GA	15.1	4.7	24.6	7.7	96.8
45	Louisville	55.6	24.4	14.6	6.4	92.4
46	Baton Rouge	4.5	7.8	4.6	7.9	91.2
47	New Orleans	35.3	34.1	6.4	6.2	92.9
48	Shreveport	4.5	8.7	3.5	6.8	92.9
49	Jackson	4.8	6.6	5.1	7.0	91.5
50	Charlotte	13.5	10.5	10.3	8.0	95.3
51	Oklahoma City	8.6	17.4	3.6	7.2	92.0

126 Economic Growth and Decline

Table 6-3. (cont.)

		Total		% of Population		Retailing City as % of SMSA
		Manufacturing	Retailing	Manufacturing	Retailing	
52	Tulsa	7.9	13.4	4.2	7.1	92.7
53	Knoxville	19.3	11.4	15.0	8.9	92.8
54	Memphis	33.2	27.6	8.6	7.1	96.4
55	Nashville	21.7	14.2	12.2	8.0	86.1
56	Austin	2.2	8.5	1.7	6.7	97.2
57	Corpus Christi	2.8	7.1	3.0	7.6	88.8
58	Dallas	34.2	37.0	8.2	8.8	90.3
59	El Paso	5.0	9.1	4.0	7.3	91.1
60	Fort Worth	30.5	22.1	11.2	8.1	94.0
61	Houston	40.6	39.8	7.1	7.0	87.5
62	San Antonio	14.4	23.9	3.6	6.0	96.6
63	Richmond	28.1	21.0	12.0	9.0	97.5
64	Tampa	14.4	10.0	11.8	8.2	81.1
65	St. Petersburg	1.2	7.2	1.4	8.4	77.0
66	Norfolk	10.3	14.6	4.9	6.9	NA
	Regional Mean	17.7	17.3	7.5	7.6	89.9
	West					
67	Phoenix	3.0	10.6	2.8	9.9	70.7
68	Tucson	1.0	5.8	2.2	12.8	81.3
69	Fresno	3.3	8.9	3.6	9.6	72.4
70	Sacramento	5.7	12.1	4.2	8.8	86.0
71	San Diego	18.6	18.8	6.3	6.4	76.7
72	San Jose	8.7	7.5	9.4	8.1	55.9
73	Denver	30.9	30.7	7.7	7.6	91.9
74	Honolulu	NA	13.7	NC	5.9	NA
75	Albuquerque	1.5	6.3	1.9	8.0	95.1
76	Portland	33.8	30.4	9.0	8.1	94.3
77	Salt Lake City	7.9	14.2	4.4	7.8	87.3
78	Spokane	6.5	10.5	4.2	6.7	92.9
79	Tacoma	13.0	8.6	9.1	6.0	82.0
80	Los Angeles	161.2	131.7	8.8	7.2	56.6
81	Long Beach	8.1	15.3	3.4	6.4	6.6
82	San Francisco	61.6	55.8	7.8	7.1	58.8
83	Oakland	32.0	28.5	8.2	7.3	86.2
84	Seattle	50.2	34.1	10.8	7.3	86.6
	Regional Mean	26.2	24.6	6.1	7.9	75.4
	National Mean	65.4	34.3	11.9	7.6	82.0

relative to the same population standardized measure in the outside city areas.

This concentration of paid retailing employment in the cities was surprising, at least to this observer. It was presumed that the city was par excellence the manufacturing hub. Thus, it was true that the cities had considerably more employment in manufacturing than their proportion of the population would indicate. However, their relative concentration was at 13.12 per 100 persons as compared to 8.62 outside of their area, or about 152 percent greater manufacturing employment.

The increase in retailing employment far exceeded the observed increases in population, especially in the East and Midwest. Thus, a 7.2 percent increase in population in the East was associated with a 33 percent increase in retailing employment, with similar patterns in the case of the other regions. The vast increase occurred mainly after the War had ended. It was fueled by the sudden increase in populations, central nature of the city, particularly the central business districts and the trolley car.

Once again it was noted in the aforementioned study by McKenzie (13) that the process of suburbanization—i.e., nucleation— had begun in the earlier period, and that the changes after 1948 were to respond to the basic underlying forces as well as to the very high post-war concentration of retailing employment in the central city areas.

A distinction between the different classes of manufacturing workers apparently emerged prior to World War II and was carried through to at least the 1947 census of manufacturing, but it emphasized salaried officers and employees as opposed to wage earners. One whole class of manufacturing employees was excluded from the total. For the measurement of change between 1939 and 1947 this was not too critical, but for the measurement of change, using 1947 as a base year, this means underestimating the "true" level of employment of that year compared to later years. Excluded during this period were Central Administrative Office and Auxiliary Employment, and apparently some other non-production workers. This can be seen by comparing the years for which we have the Census of Manufacturing and the Bureau of Labor Statistics (BLS) data sets (Table 6-5).

The exclusion and then the inclusion of Central Administrative Office and Auxiliary Employment, as well as several other changes that occurred between 1947 and 1954, had deleterious consequences on some of the analyses that were based on the earlier year. For this analysis, it is recognized that 1947 represents an *underestimate* of

128 Economic Growth and Decline

the actual amount of manufacturing employment for that year. This means, if anything, that the rate of decline was greater than observed and the rates of increase were lower.

Part of this is shown in Table 6-4, which shows production workers as a fraction of total workers for 1947. These are distinctly higher than the situation in 1972 (Table 6-7). The decline is due to an actual decline in the proportionate share of production workers due to upgrading and the changing nature of manufacturing. This explains part of the anomalous results of John Kain, who wished to explain the "pervasive" decline in manufacturing between 1947 and 1954, and who had less than 50 percent of the cases he analyzed conform to the expected pattern. The decline in retailing employment was far more pervasive.

The relationship between the amount of manufacturing employment and the amount of retailing employment is of considerable interest. All cities had considerable retailing employment, while cities in 1947 varied greatly in the extent of manufacturing employment. The summary statistics are that in 1947 cities had 28.7 percent of the U.S. population, 38.0 percent of manufacturing employment, and 42.5 percent of all paid employees in retailing.

Thus, with a decline in the cities' proportion of population to 22.4 percent of the total in 1973, it would have been expected that other things being the same, the cities' proportion of total activity would

Table 6-4. Manufacturing Employment, 1947 (Thousands)

		Total	Production	Non-Production	Production %
	East				
01	Bridgeport	55.0	44.4	10.6	80.7%
02	Hartford	34.5	29.5	5.0	85.5
03	Washington	17.8	10.0	7.8	56.2
04	Baltimore	120.9	97.7	23.2	80.8
05	Boston	101.7	79.5	22.2	78.2
06	Worcester	46.8	37.8	9.0	80.8
07	Jersey City	37.3	29.7	7.6	79.6
08	Newark	92.3	73.6	18.7	79.7
09	Buffalo	87.3	71.7	15.6	82.1
10	New York	940.2	741.2	199.0	78.8
11	Rochester	99.9	76.3	23.6	76.4
12	Syracuse	35.3	28.3	7.0	80.2
13	Philadelphia	328.6	268.4	60.2	81.7
14	Pittsburgh	81.4	65.3	16.1	80.2

Table 6-4. (cont.)

		Total	Production	Non-Production	Production %
15	Albany	10.5	5.1	5.4	48.6
16	Providence	61.2	52.2	9.0	85.3
	Regional Mean	134.4	106.9	27.5	77.2
	Midwest				
17	Chicago	667.4	532.1	135.3	79.7
18	Fort Wayne	30.9	24.0	6.9	77.7
19	Indianapolis	79.8	63.1	16.7	79.1
20	Des Moines	14.1	10.4	3.7	73.8
21	Wichita	9.6	7.5	2.1	78.1
22	Detroit	338.4	281.5	56.9	83.2
23	Flint	53.8	46.6	7.2	86.6
24	Grand Rapids	44.2	37.6	6.6	85.1
25	Kansas City	46.7	35.9	10.8	76.9
26	St. Louis	172.9	141.2	31.7	81.7
27	Omaha	25.4	19.9	5.5	78.3
28	Akron	76.8	61.4	15.4	79.9
29	Cincinnati	97.5	77.4	20.1	79.4
30	Cleveland	223.6	181.7	41.9	81.3
31	Columbus, OH	41.4	32.0	9.4	77.3
32	Dayton	75.8	62.2	13.6	82.1
33	Toledo	59.5	49.0	10.5	82.4
34	Madison	9.2	7.0	2.2	76.1
35	Milwaukee	132.1	108.4	23.7	82.1
36	Gary	35.6	30.6	5.0	86.0
37	Minneapolis	61.9	48.0	13.9	77.5
38	St. Paul	40.6	32.0	8.6	78.8
	Regional Mean	106.2	85.8	20.3	80.1
	South				
39	Birmingham	26.5	21.7	4.8	81.9
40	Mobile	8.3	6.9	1.4	83.1
41	Jacksonville	12.2	10.5	1.7	86.1
42	Miami	7.1	5.2	1.9	73.2
43	Atlanta	36.2	29.4	6.8	81.2
44	Columbus, GA	15.1	13.0	2.1	86.1
45	Louisville	55.6	46.0	9.6	82.7
46	Baton Rouge	4.5	3.4	1.1	75.6
47	New Orleans	35.3	29.1	6.2	82.4
48	Shreveport	4.5	3.3	1.2	73.3
49	Jackson	4.8	3.8	1.0	79.2
50	Charlotte	13.5	11.3	2.2	83.7

Table 6-4. (cont.)

		Total	Production	Non-Production	Production %
51	Oklahoma City	8.6	6.2	2.4	72.1
52	Tulsa	7.9	5.8	2.1	73.4
53	Knoxville	19.3	16.8	2.5	87.0
54	Memphis	33.2	26.9	6.3	81.0
55	Nashville	21.7	17.4	4.3	80.2
56	Austin	2.2	1.5	0.7	68.2
57	Corpus Christi	2.8	2.2	0.6	78.6
58	Dallas	34.2	27.0	7.2	78.9
59	El Paso	5.0	4.1	0.9	82.0
60	Fort Worth	30.5	25.1	5.4	82.3
61	Houston	40.6	31.2	9.4	76.8
62	San Antonio	14.4	11.7	2.7	81.3
63	Richmond	28.1	24.1	4.0	85.8
64	Tampa	14.4	12.5	1.9	86.8
65	St. Petersburg	1.2	0.7	0.5	58.3
66	Norfolk	10.3	8.4	1.9	81.6
	Regional Mean	17.7	14.4	3.3	79.4
	West				
67	Phoenix	3.0	2.0	1.0	66.7
68	Tucson	1.0	0.8	0.2	80.0
69	Fresno	3.3	2.6	0.7	78.8
70	Sacramento	5.7	4.0	1.7	70.2
71	San Diego	18.6	13.0	5.6	69.9
72	San Jose	8.7	7.3	1.4	83.9
73	Denver	30.9	24.2	6.7	78.3
74	Honolulu	NA	NA	NA	NC
75	Albuquerque	1.5	1.2	0.3	80.0
76	Portland	33.8	27.1	6.7	80.2
77	Salt Lake City	7.9	6.0	1.9	75.9
78	Spokane	6.5	4.9	1.6	75.4
79	Tacoma	13.0	11.1	1.9	85.4
80	Los Angeles	161.2	132.5	28.7	82.2
81	Long Beach	8.1	6.3	1.8	77.8
82	San Francisco	61.6	45.8	15.8	74.4
83	Oakland	32.0	25.0	7.0	78.1
84	Seattle	50.2	41.0	9.2	81.7
	Regional Mean	26.2	21.0	5.2	77.8
	National Mean	65.4	52.5	12.8	78.9

Table 6-5. Manufacturing Employment Growth Rates (in Thousands)

	Census of Manufacturing	BLS*	Growth Rates C of M	Growth Rates BLS	C of M/BLS
1939	9,527	10,278			92.6%
1947	14,294	15,545	51.2%	50.0%	92.0
1954	16,014	16,314	12.6	4.9	98.7
1958	16,025	15,945	0.5	−2.3	100.5
1963	16,959	16,995	5.2	6.6	99.8
1967	19,323	19,497	13.9	14.7	99.1
1972	19,029	19,090	−1.5	−2.1	99.7
1974	19,884	20,040	4.5	5.0	99.2

*Bureau of Labor Statistics—Establishment Basis.

have declined. But the change was far more dramatic. As shown in Table 6-6, there were major changes in the spatial distribution of manufacturing.

These national patterns are of interest because they are at variance with some of the long term findings of this study. The changes were far more uniform in the case of retailing and more offsetting than has been presumed in the case of manufacturing. Table 6-8 summarizes the regional patterns of employment for the years 1947 and 1972 in the same format as the earlier analysis of the year 1947. The city patterns of change as shown in Table 6-8 are at variance with the national patterns of change of the same period. Between 1947 and 1972 manufacturing employment as a percent of population fell from a national average of 10.78 percent to 9.07 percent. At the same time, retailing employment rose from 4.71 percent in 1948 to 5.72 percent in 1972. While the national change in manufacturing is less than expected, the increase in retailing is more than expected. The unweighted city averages, on the other hand, indicate a much more substantial and uniform decline in retailing as compared to manufacturing during the period 1947 to 1972. The city decline in manufacturing followed the national decline in manufacturing, whereas the city decline in retailing took place while there was national growth in retailing relative to population.

THE REGIONAL PATTERN

The patterns that emerged showed a growing uniformity among regions, at least in the case of manufacturing. The regions which had

132 Economic Growth and Decline

Table 6-6. Employment Characteristics, 1972 (Thousands)

		Total		% of Population		Retailing City as % of SMSA
		Manufacturing	Retailing	Manufacturing	Retailing	
	East					
01	Bridgeport	29.6	7.9	20.4%	5.4%	17.1%
02	Hartford	13.0	11.3	8.8	7.6	20.9
03	Washington	19.0	53.6	2.6	7.3	42.4
04	Baltimore	91.0	52.9	10.4	6.0	57.0
05	Boston	59.0	53.2	9.5	8.6	26.3
06	Worcester	29.0	13.4	17.1	7.9	35.0
07	Jersey City	23.0	8.9	9.0	3.5	39.8
08	Newark	47.0	18.5	12.8	5.0	37.0
09	Buffalo	53.0	26.9	12.5	6.3	40.2
10	New York	757.0	385.9	9.9	5.0	64.4
11	Rochester	93.0	19.8	33.7	7.2	47.1
12	Syracuse	26.0	15.2	14.1	8.3	55.0
13	Philadelphia	203.0	95.6	10.4	4.9	68.0
14	Pittsburgh	63.0	34.8	12.1	6.7	39.5
15	Albany	6.7	7.5	6.0	6.8	36.6
16	Providence	34.8	12.4	20.5	7.3	33.4
	Regional Mean	96.6	51.1	13.1	6.5	41.2
	Midwest					
17	Chicago	430.0	203.0	13.6	6.4	58.0
18	Fort Wayne	36.0	17.5	19.5	9.5	85.0
19	Indianapolis	93.0	49.9	12.8	6.9	93.9
20	Des Moines	18.0	19.6	9.0	9.8	81.1
21	Wichita	23.0	19.6	8.8	7.5	92.0
22	Detroit	180.0	62.8	13.0	4.5	48.2
23	Flint	NA	13.1	NC	7.2	53.6
24	Grand Rapids	31.0	13.7	16.3	7.2	50.1
25	Kansas City	57.0	37.7	11.7	7.7	77.4
26	St. Louis	98.0	36.6	17.6	6.6	37.2
27	Omaha	32.0	27.4	8.6	7.4	96.4
28	Akron	51.0	16.7	19.5	6.4	55.0
29	Cincinnati	65.0	30.6	15.3	7.2	51.3
30	Cleveland	131.0	41.4	19.3	6.1	41.8
31	Columbus, OH	62.0	52.5	11.5	9.7	57.2
32	Dayton	72.0	17.0	33.6	7.9	44.1
33	Toledo	56.0	26.4	14.9	7.0	81.0
34	Madison	12.0	15.5	7.1	9.2	70.0
35	Milwaukee	106.0	42.6	15.4	6.2	63.3

Changes in Manufacturing/Retailing Employment in Medium-Size Cities 133

Table 6-6. (cont.)

		Total		% of Population		Retailing City as % of SMSA
		Manufacturing	Retailing	Manufacturing	Retailing	
36	Gary	30.4	9.1	17.2	5.1	30.6
37	Minneapolis	57.9	35.7	15.2	9.3	48.4
38	St. Paul	50.6	22.2	17.6	7.7	66.6
	Regional Mean	80.5	36.8	15.1	7.4	62.8
	South					
39	Birmingham	35.0	22.9	11.9	7.8	54.7
40	Mobile	14.0	15.1	7.6	8.2	52.1
41	Jacksonville	24.0	34.7	4.4	6.3	100.0
42	Miami	26.0	28.6	7.2	7.9	30.2
43	Atlanta	48.0	51.6	10.6	11.4	60.8
44	Columbus, GA	18.0	10.5	11.2	6.6	100.0
45	Louisville	60.0	24.5	17.9	7.3	58.2
46	Baton Rouge	13.0	15.1	4.5	5.2	89.5
47	New Orleans	29.0	34.5	5.1	6.0	62.7
48	Shreveport	15.0	12.1	8.2	6.6	93.0
49	Jackson	12.0	12.1	7.4	7.4	91.6
50	Charlotte	26.0	21.7	9.2	7.6	87.1
51	Oklahoma City	34.0	32.6	9.1	8.7	80.2
52	Tulsa	35.0	27.5	10.4	8.2	91.2
53	Knoxville	24.0	15.9	13.2	8.7	96.4
54	Memphis	54.0	42.3	8.2	6.4	92.4
55	Nashville	46.0	32.2	10.8	7.5	100.0
56	Austin	8.0	21.4	2.8	7.4	96.4
57	Corpus Christi	7.0	14.6	3.3	6.9	93.0
58	Dallas	107.0	66.4	13.1	8.1	71.6
59	El Paso	25.0	19.5	7.1	5.5	96.7
60	Fort Worth	47.0	27.2	13.1	7.6	60.1
61	Houston	105.0	90.3	8.1	7.0	79.0
62	San Antonio	28.0	42.8	3.7	5.7	87.5
63	Richmond	29.0	22.1	12.2	9.3	69.1
64	Tampa	25.0	24.9	9.1	9.0	77.4
65	St. Petersburg	11.0	17.2	4.7	7.4	43.7
66	Norfolk	11.9	19.8	4.2	7.0	NA
	Regional Mean	32.7	28.6	8.5	7.5	79.4
	West					
67	Phoenix	52.0	40.4	8.2	6.4	60.2
68	Tucson	8.0	26.5	2.6	8.8	89.7

Table 6-6. (cont.)

		Total		% of Population		Retailing City as % of SMSA
		Manufacturing	Retailing	Manufacturing	Retailing	
69	Fresno	7.0	16.1	4.0	9.3	67.2
70	Sacramento	12.0	17.3	4.5	6.5	46.5
71	San Diego	45.0	41.1	7.8	7.1	53.0
72	San Jose	39.0	24.8	7.5	4.7	40.1
73	Denver	42.0	38.8	8.2	7.5	54.6
74	Honolulu	17.0	39.0	5.1	11.7	79.4
75	Albuquerque	10.0	20.4	3.7	7.5	92.8
76	Portland	40.0	32.7	10.7	8.7	78.3
77	Salt Lake City	22.0	18.1	13.0	10.7	56.9
78	Spokane	6.0	12.8	3.5	7.4	75.1
79	Tacoma	16.0	11.1	10.7	7.4	56.9
80	Los Angeles	280.1	172.9	10.2	6.3	41.9
81	Long Beach	38.7	21.6	11.6	6.5	5.2
82	San Francisco	44.3	52.4	6.4	7.6	48.1
83	Oakland	25.9	32.2	7.5	9.3	56.9
84	Seattle	54.9	37.4	10.9	7.4	40.4
	Regional Mean	42.2	36.4	7.4	7.7	58.0
	National Mean	59.2	36.7	10.8	7.3	63.0

Table 6-7. Manufacturing Employment, 1972 (Thousands)

		Total	Production	Non-Production	Production %
	East				
01	Bridgeport	29.6	21.0	8.6	70.9%
02	Hartford	13.0	8.0	5.0	61.5
03	Washington	19.0	9.0	10.0	47.4
04	Baltimore	91.0	65.0	26.0	71.4
05	Boston	59.0	35.0	24.0	59.3
06	Worcester	29.0	20.0	9.0	69.0
07	Jersey City	23.0	17.0	6.0	73.9
08	Newark	47.0	34.0	13.0	72.3
09	Buffalo	53.0	38.0	15.0	71.7
10	New York	757.0	480.0	277.0	63.4
11	Rochester	93.0	52.0	41.0	55.9
12	Syracuse	26.0	14.0	12.0	53.8
13	Philadelphia	203.0	143.0	60.0	70.4
14	Pittsburgh	63.0	25.0	38.0	39.7

Table 6-7. (cont.)

		Total	Production	Non. Production	Production %
15	Albany	6.7	4.3	2.4	64.2
16	Providence	34.8	26.7	8.1	76.7
	Regional Mean	96.7	62.1	34.5	64.3
	Midwest				
17	Chicago	430.0	293.0	137.0	68.1
18	Fort Wayne	36.0	24.0	12.0	66.7
19	Indianapolis	93.0	63.0	30.0	67.7
20	Des Moines	18.0	11.0	7.0	61.1
21	Wichita	23.0	16.0	7.0	69.6
22	Detroit	180.0	126.0	54.0	70.0
23	Flint	NA	NA	NA	NC
24	Grand Rapids	31.0	23.0	8.0	74.2
25	Kansas City	57.0	33.0	24.0	57.9
26	St. Louis	98.0	63.0	35.0	64.3
27	Omaha	32.0	23.0	9.0	71.9
28	Akron	51.0	28.0	23.0	54.9
29	Cincinnati	65.0	38.0	27.0	58.5
30	Cleveland	131.0	85.0	46.0	64.9
31	Columbus, OH	62.0	39.0	23.0	62.9
32	Dayton	72.0	51.0	21.0	70.8
33	Toledo	56.0	36.0	20.0	64.3
34	Madison	12.0	8.0	4.0	66.7
35	Milwaukee	106.0	71.0	35.0	67.0
36	Gary	30.4	25.0	5.4	82.2
37	Minneapolis	57.9	33.6	24.3	58.0
38	St. Paul	50.6	27.7	22.9	54.7
	Regional Mean	80.6	53.2	27.4	65.5
	South				
39	Birmingham	35.0	26.0	9.0	74.3
40	Mobile	14.0	11.0	3.0	78.6
41	Jacksonville	24.0	18.0	6.0	75.0
42	Miami	26.0	19.0	7.0	73.1
43	Atlanta	48.0	32.0	16.0	66.7
44	Columbus, GA	18.0	14.0	4.0	77.8
45	Louisville	60.0	41.0	19.0	68.3
46	Baton Rouge	13.0	9.0	4.0	69.2
47	New Orleans	29.0	19.0	10.0	65.5
48	Shreveport	15.0	1.0	14.0	6.7
49	Jackson	12.0	9.0	3.0	75.0
50	Charlotte	26.0	17.0	9.0	65.4

Table 6-7. (cont.)

		Total	Production	Non-Production	Production %
51	Oklahoma City	34.0	22.0	12.0	64.7
52	Tulsa	35.0	22.0	13.0	62.9
53	Knoxville	24.0	19.0	5.0	79.2
54	Memphis	54.0	39.0	15.0	72.2
55	Nashville	46.0	31.0	15.0	67.4
56	Austin	8.0	5.0	3.0	62.5
57	Corpus Christi	7.0	4.0	3.0	57.1
58	Dallas	107.0	68.0	39.0	63.6
59	El Paso	25.0	20.0	5.0	80.0
60	Fort Worth	47.0	30.0	17.0	63.8
61	Houston	105.0	67.0	38.0	63.8
62	San Antonio	28.0	23.0	5.0	82.1
63	Richmond	29.0	18.0	11.0	62.1
64	Tampa	25.0	18.1	6.9	72.4
65	St. Petersburg	11.0	6.0	5.0	54.5
66	Norfolk	11.9	8.1	3.8	68.1
	Regional Mean	32.7	22.4	10.4	69.2
	West				
67	Phoenix	52.0	34.0	18.0	65.4
68	Tucson	8.0	4.0	4.0	50.0
69	Fresno	7.0	5.0	2.0	71.4
70	Sacramento	12.0	8.0	4.0	66.7
71	San Diego	45.0	28.0	17.0	62.2
72	San Jose	39.0	17.0	22.0	43.6
73	Denver	42.0	29.0	13.0	69.0
74	Honolulu	17.0	12.0	5.0	70.6
75	Albuquerque	10.0	7.0	3.0	70.0
76	Portland	40.0	28.0	12.0	70.0
77	Salt Lake City	22.0	19.0	3.0	86.4
78	Spokane	6.0	4.0	2.0	66.7
79	Tacoma	16.0	12.0	4.0	75.0
80	Los Angeles	280.1	185.7	94.4	66.3
81	Long Beach	38.7	22.8	15.9	58.9
82	San Francisco	44.3	25.5	18.8	57.6
83	Oakland	25.9	16.2	9.7	62.5
84	Seattle	54.9	31.1	23.8	56.6
	Regional Mean	42.2	27.1	15.1	64.9
	National Mean	57.3	37.2	20.1	66.4

above average levels of concentrations declined and those with below average levels increased. The increases were in addition to those associated with the increases in population, and the decreases were over and above those which would have been expected as a result of declines in population. In fact, the analysis shows the continued existence of two classes of American cities unrelated to size and far more related to region.

There are exceptions in many regions, but even these exceptions are mainly associated with the phenomenon of annexation. Thus, the population of cities increased between 1947 and 1972 by some 12.1 percent, while the unweighted average increased some 54.4 percent, indicating that it was the smaller cities, which on the average, increased more.* The small base, however, would operate in the case of manufacturing and retailing employment as well as in the case of population itself. This is brought out by the fact of the increases and

Table 6-8. Manufacturing and Retailing Employment as a Percent of Population, 1947 and 1972

(unweighted averages)

	Manufacturing					
	1947			1972		
	Mean	SD	Coefficient of Variation	Mean	SD	Coefficient of Variation
East	16.66%	8.11%	48.6%	13.06%	7.17%	54.9%
Midwest	18.46	7.82	42.4	15.11	5.64	37.3
South	7.50	4.43	59.1	8.51	3.69	43.4
West	6.10	2.91	47.7	7.44	3.16	42.4
U.S.	11.88	8.08	68.0	10.82	5.81	53.6
Entire U.S. (weighted)	10.78			9.07		
	Retailing					
East	7.32	1.57	21.4	6.50	1.41	21.6
Midwest	7.59	0.92	12.1	7.41	1.43	19.2
South	7.57	1.10	14.5	7.48	1.30	17.4
West	7.87	1.71	21.7	7.74	1.77	22.9
U.S.	7.59	1.39	17.1	7.33	1.58	20.5
Entire U.S. (weighted)	4.71			5.72		

*Derived from Tables 6-1 and 6-9.

decreases. The national increase in population was associated with a weighted 9.7 percent decline in the East, a 6.3 percent decline in the Midwest and increases of 68.5 and 53.0 percent in the South and West respectively. These general patterns hold in the case of manufacturing and retailing employment, but with notable differences.

The regional character of the manufacturing city is clear both in its cross-sectional and time series nature. The Northeast and Midwest still have higher proportions of their population engaged in manufacturing compared to the South and the West. The retailing city shows very little difference across regions and across time, but the absence of change, in a context of change, is what is important.

The patterns of long term change are shown in Tables 6-9 and 6-10. The first shows the absolute amounts of change for each of the critical variables, manufacturing, production workers and nonproduction workers. Also shown are the changes in retailing employment, population, and area.

The differential regional patterns indicate that the East and Midwest, with some exceptions, had their highest levels in 1947 while the South and the West had their highest levels in 1972. In the case of manufacturing there is probably an understatement of the decline, but it is more clearly seen in the case of production workers than in the case of total manufacturing employment. What is of great interest are the few cities which had reductions in the number of nonproduction workers over the long period. This occurs in spite of the fact that all the definitional biases and substantive changes were in favor of their increase.

The results are at variance with some of the analyses of Ganz and O'Brien, which indicated that at the end of the 1960s the cities had entered into a period of major recovery (14). That there was a recovery associated with the Vietnam buildup is now clear, but it was succeeded by major declines in the Midwest and East and continued increases in the South and West.

The large number of cities which showed declines in retailing employment, in part reflect three different forces, the overconcentration in 1947, the decline in population in many cities, and finally, the increased movement to suburban retailing activity. The third factor represents a return to the pattern of change reported by McKenzie (15). But again, the changes fall into two groups: in the East and Midwest declines; and in the South and West increases. In fact, what is of interest is that *only* San Francisco showed a decline in retailing employment outside of the East and Midwest.

The relative magnitudes of change are shown in Table 6-10. Here, an outlier has a distorting effect on the overall totals. Thus, an

Changes in Manufacturing/Retailing Employment in Medium-Size Cities   139

Table 6-9. Changes in City Employment, Population and Area, 1947-1972 (Thousands)

		Manufacturing					
		Total	Production	Non-Production	Retailing	Population	1972 Area Index
	East						
01	Bridgeport	−25.4	−23.4	−2.0	−3.1	−14.2	100.0
02	Hartford	−21.5	−21.5	0.0	−6.2	−33.8	100.0
03	Washington	1.2	−1.0	2.2	−18.9	−80.8	100.0
04	Baltimore	−29.9	−32.7	2.8	−14.8	−75.9	100.0
05	Boston	−42.7	−44.5	1.8	−21.1	−214.7	100.0
06	Worcester	−17.8	−17.8	0.0	−0.3	−38.5	100.0
07	Jersey City	−14.3	−12.7	−1.6	−1.1	−50.8	100.0
08	Newark	−45.3	−39.6	−5.7	−14.3	−81.8	100.0
09	Buffalo	−34.3	−33.7	−0.6	−14.0	−169.3	100.0
10	New York	−183.2	−261.2	78.0	−47.7	−278.9	100.0
11	Rochester	−6.9	−24.3	17.4	−5.2	−60.6	100.0
12	Syracuse	−9.3	−14.3	5.0	−2.9	−38.0	100.0
13	Philadelphia	−125.6	−125.4	−0.2	−30.2	−144.3	100.0
14	Pittsburgh	−18.4	−40.3	21.9	−28.4	−178.5	100.0
15	Albany	−3.8	−0.8	−3.0	−3.1	−23.5	109.8
16	Providence	−26.4	−25.5	−0.9	−7.2	−90.9	100.0
	Regional Mean	−37.7	−44.7	6.9	−13.6	−98.2	100.6
	Midwest						
17	Chicago	−237.4	−239.1	1.7	−45.7	−472.2	107.4
18	Fort Wayne	5.1	0.0	5.1	7.0	51.8	296.7
19	Indianapolis	13.2	−0.1	13.3	19.1	301.4	687.8
20	Des Moines	3.9	0.6	3.3	5.2	24.7	117.1
21	Wichita	13.4	8.5	4.9	6.7	93.6	365.2
22	Detroit	−158.4	−155.5	−2.9	−51.2	−517.3	100.0
23	Flint	NA	NA	NA	2.5	21.4	116.7
24	Grand Rapids	−13.2	−14.6	1.4	−0.4	13.6	191.3
25	Kansas City	10.3	−2.9	13.2	−8.5	23.5	392.2
26	St. Louis	−74.9	−78.2	3.3	−26.4	−330.6	100.0
27	Omaha	6.6	3.1	3.5	9.7	124.0	198.5
28	Akron	−25.8	−33.4	7.6	−1.6	−9.0	100.8
29	Cincinnati	−32.5	−39.4	6.9	−8.0	−80.6	104.0
30	Cleveland	−92.6	−96.7	4.1	−27.4	−248.4	100.0
31	Columbus, OH	20.6	7.0	13.6	23.6	170.1	399.6
32	Dayton	−3.8	−11.2	7.4	−4.7	−34.1	153.8
33	Toledo	−3.5	−13.0	9.5	4.1	72.0	212.2
34	Madison	2.8	1.0	1.8	7.9	73.8	335.4

Table 6-9. (cont.)

| | | | Manufacturing | | | | 1972 |
		Total	Production	Non-Production	Retailing	Population	Area Index
35	Milwaukee	−26.1	−37.4	11.3	−5.3	46.7	190.0
36	Gary	−5.2	−5.6	0.4	1.6	49.8	101.1
37	Minneapolis	−4.0	−14.4	10.4	−10.8	−151.3	100.0
38	St. Paul	10.0	−4.3	14.3	−3.1	−23.8	100.0
	Regional Mean	−28.1	−34.5	6.4	−4.8	−36.4	207.7
	South						
39	Birmingham	8.5	4.3	4.2	0.7	−30.3	125.4
40	Mobile	5.7	4.1	1.6	6.7	59.5	457.6
41	Jacksonville	11.8	7.5	4.3	19.7	341.5	2539.5
42	Miami	18.9	13.8	5.1	6.2	126.5	100.0
43	Atlanta	11.8	2.6	9.2	16.3	115.1	356.7
44	Columbus, GA	2.9	1.0	1.9	5.8	98.6	1828.7
45	Louisville	4.4	−5.0	9.4	0.1	−46.3	150.5
46	Baton Rouge	8.5	5.6	2.9	7.3	190.7	156.0
47	New Orleans	−6.3	−10.1	3.8	0.4	19.7	100.0
48	Shreveport	10.5	−2.3	12.8	3.4	56.8	277.9
49	Jackson	7.2	5.2	2.0	5.5	68.5	237.5
50	Charlotte	12.5	5.7	6.8	11.2	153.3	253.6
51	Oklahoma City	25.4	15.8	9.6	15.2	132.7	1252.0
52	Tulsa	27.1	16.2	10.9	14.1	145.6	657.3
53	Knoxville	4.7	2.2	2.5	4.5	53.4	303.1
54	Memphis	20.8	12.1	8.7	14.7	271.8	250.0
55	Nashville	24.3	13.6	10.7	18.0	249.5	2321.4
56	Austin	5.8	3.5	2.3	12.9	161.6	283.9
57	Corpus Christi	4.2	1.8	2.4	7.5	118.9	799.3
58	Dallas	72.8	41.0	31.8	29.4	396.1	242.0
59	El Paso	20.0	15.9	4.1	10.4	229.1	612.8
60	Fort Worth	16.5	4.9	11.6	5.1	86.5	245.2
61	Houston	64.4	35.8	28.6	50.5	727.1	311.5
62	San Antonio	13.6	11.3	2.3	18.9	359.5	364.9
63	Richmond	0.9	−6.1	7.0	1.1	4.7	162.9
64	Tampa	10.6	5.6	5.0	14.9	154.4	294.3
65	St. Petersburg	9.8	5.3	4.5	10.0	148.1	162.1
66	Norfolk	1.6	−0.3	1.9	5.2	70.8	157.2
	Regional Mean	14.9	7.8	7.1	11.2	158.3	536.9
	West						
67	Phoenix	49.0	32.0	17.0	29.8	524.2	1476.1
68	Tucson	7.0	3.2	3.8	20.7	256.7	945.1
69	Fresno	3.7	2.4	1.3	7.2	80.7	309.4

Table 6-9. (cont.)

		Manufacturing		Retailing	Population	1972 Area Index
	Total	Production	Non-Production			
70 Sacramento	6.3	4.0	2.3	5.2	129.9	555.5
71 San Diego	26.4	15.0	11.4	22.3	280.0	325.0
72 San Jose	30.3	9.7	20.6	17.3	430.6	858.7
73 Denver	11.1	4.8	6.3	8.1	111.2	168.7
74 Honolulu	NA	NA	NA	25.3	99.9	100.0
75 Albuquerque	8.5	5.8	2.7	14.1	194.6	182.8
76 Portland	6.2	0.9	5.3	2.3	−2.2	143.7
77 Salt Lake City	14.1	13.0	1.1	3.9	−11.9	110.1
78 Spokane	−0.5	−0.9	0.4	2.3	16.6	122.2
79 Tacoma	3.0	0.9	2.1	2.5	6.7	100.0
80 Los Angeles	118.9	53.2	65.7	41.2	916.5	102.9
81 Long Beach	30.6	16.5	14.1	6.3	93.6	144.6
82 San Francisco	−17.3	−20.3	3.0	−3.4	−98.8	100.0
83 Oakland	−6.1	−8.8	2.7	3.7	−43.6	100.0
84 Seattle	4.7	−9.9	14.6	3.3	36.5	119.2
Regional Mean	18.4	7.6	10.7	11.7	178.4	331.3
National Mean	−5.7	−19.0	7.6	2.4	61.3	323.5

Table 6-10. Percent Change in City Employment, Population and Area, 1947-1972

	Manufacturing			Retailing	Population	1972 Area Index
	Total	Production	Non-Production			
East						
01 Bridgeport	−46.2%	−52.7%	−18.9%	−28.2%	−8.9%	100.0
02 Hartford	−62.3	−72.9	0.0	−35.4	−18.6	100.0
03 Washington	6.7	−10.0	28.2	−26.1	−9.9	100.0
04 Baltimore	−24.7	−33.5	12.1	−21.9	−8.0	100.0
05 Boston	−42.0	−56.0	8.1	−28.4	−25.8	100.0
06 Worcester	−38.0	−47.1	0.0	−2.2	−18.5	100.0
07 Jersey City	−38.3	−42.8	−21.1	−11.0	−16.6	100.0
08 Newark	−49.1	−53.8	−30.5	−43.6	−18.2	100.0
09 Buffalo	−39.3	−47.0	−3.8	−34.2	−28.5	100.0
10 New York	−19.5	−35.2	39.2	−11.0	−3.5	100.0
11 Rochester	−6.9	−31.8	73.7	−20.8	−18.0	100.0
12 Syracuse	−26.3	−50.5	71.4	−16.0	−17.1	100.0

142 Economic Growth and Decline

Table 6-10. (cont.)

	Manufacturing			Retailing	Population	1972 Area Index
	Total	Production	Non-Production			
13 Philadelphia	−38.2	−46.7	−0.3	−24.0	−6.9	100.0
14 Pittsburgh	−22.6	−61.7	136.0	−44.9	−25.6	100.0
15 Albany	−36.2	−15.7	−55.6	−29.2	−17.5	109.8
16 Providence	−43.1	−48.9	−10.0	−36.7	−34.8	100.0
Regional Mean	−32.9	−43.9	13.1	−25.8	−17.2	100.6
Midwest						
17 Chicago	−35.6	−44.9	1.3	−18.4	−13.0	107.4
18 Fort Wayne	16.5	0.0	73.9	66.7	38.9	296.7
19 Indianapolis	16.5	−0.2	79.6	62.0	70.7	687.8
20 Des Moines	27.7	5.8	89.2	36.1	14.2	117.1
21 Wichita	139.6	113.3	233.3	51.9	55.9	365.2
22 Detroit	−46.8	−55.2	−5.1	−44.9	−27.2	100.0
23 Flint	NA	NA	NA	23.6	13.4	116.7
24 Grand Rapids	−29.9	−38.8	21.2	−2.8	7.7	191.3
25 Kansas City	22.1	−8.1	122.2	−18.4	5.1	392.2
26 St. Louis	−43.3	−55.4	10.4	−41.9	−37.2	100.0
27 Omaha	26.0	15.6	63.6	54.8	50.0	198.5
28 Akron	−33.6	−54.4	49.4	−8.7	−3.3	100.8
29 Cincinnati	−33.3	−50.9	34.3	−20.7	−15.9	104.0
30 Cleveland	−41.4	−53.2	9.8	−39.8	−26.8	100.0
31 Columbus, OH	49.8	21.9	144.7	81.7	46.0	399.6
32 Dayton	−5.0	−18.0	54.4	−21.7	−13.7	153.8
33 Toledo	−5.9	−26.5	90.5	18.4	23.6	212.2
34 Madison	30.4	14.3	81.8	103.9	77.5	335.4
35 Milwaukee	−19.8	−34.5	47.7	−11.1	7.3	190.0
36 Gary	−14.6	−18.3	8.0	21.3	39.2	101.1
37 Minneapolis	−6.5	−30.0	74.8	−23.2	−28.4	100.0
38 St. Paul	24.6	−13.4	166.3	−12.3	−7.7	100.0
Regional Mean	1.8	−15.8	69.3	11.5	12.5	207.7
South						
39 Birmingham	32.1	19.8	87.5	3.2	−9.3	125.4
40 Mobile	68.7	59.4	114.3	79.8	47.4	457.6
41 Jacksonville	96.7	71.4	252.9	131.3	166.2	2539.5
42 Miami	266.2	265.4	268.4	27.7	53.5	100.0
43 Atlanta	32.6	8.8	135.3	46.2	34.3	356.7
44 Columbus, GA	19.2	7.7	90.5	123.4	160.6	1828.7
45 Louisville	7.9	−10.9	97.9	0.4	−12.1	150.5
46 Baton Rouge	188.9	164.7	263.6	93.6	194.0	156.0
47 New Orleans	−17.8	−34.7	61.3	1.2	3.6	100.0
48 Shreveport	233.3	−69.7	1066.7	39.1	44.7	277.9

Changes in Manufacturing/Retailing Employment in Medium-Size Cities 143

Table 6-10. (cont.)

	Manufacturing			Retailing	Population	1972 Area Index
	Total	Production	Non-Production			
49 Jackson	150.0	136.8	200.0	83.3	72.5	237.5
50 Charlotte	92.6	50.4	309.1	106.7	117.3	253.6
51 Oklahoma City	295.3	254.8	400.0	87.4	55.2	1252.0
52 Tulsa	343.0	279.3	519.0	105.2	76.9	657.3
53 Knoxville	24.4	13.1	100.0	39.5	41.5	303.1
54 Memphis	62.7	45.0	138.1	53.3	70.4	250.0
55 Nashville	112.0	78.2	248.8	126.8	140.6	2321.4
56 Austin	263.6	233.3	328.6	151.8	126.8	283.9
57 Corpus Christi	150.0	81.8	400.0	105.6	127.7	799.3
58 Dallas	212.9	151.9	441.7	79.5	94.6	242.0
59 El Paso	400.0	387.8	455.6	114.3	184.9	612.8
60 Fort Worth	54.1	19.5	214.8	23.1	31.7	245.2
61 Houston	158.6	114.7	304.3	126.9	127.8	311.5
62 San Antonio	94.4	96.6	85.2	79.1	90.7	364.9
63 Richmond	3.2	−25.3	175.0	5.2	2.0	162.9
64 Tampa	73.6	44.8	263.2	149.0	127.0	294.3
65 St. Petersburg	816.7	757.1	900.0	138.9	172.4	162.1
66 Norfolk	15.5	−3.6	100.0	35.6	33.4	157.2
Regional Mean	151.8	125.1	256.7	76.6	82.4	536.9
West						
67 Phoenix	1633.3	1600.0	1700.0	281.1	490.8	1476.1
68 Tucson	700.0	400.0	1900.0	356.9	566.7	945.1
69 Fresno	112.1	92.3	185.7	80.9	87.4	309.4
70 Sacramento	110.5	100.0	135.3	43.0	94.7	555.5
71 San Diego	141.9	115.4	203.6	118.6	94.9	325.0
72 San Jose	348.3	132.9	1471.4	230.7	466.0	858.7
73 Denver	35.9	19.8	94.0	26.4	27.5	168.7
74 Honolulu	NA	NA	NA	184.7	42.7	100.0
75 Albuquerque	566.7	483.3	900.0	223.8	248.2	182.8
76 Portland	18.3	3.3	79.1	7.6	−0.6	143.7
77 Salt Lake City	178.5	216.7	57.9	27.5	−6.6	110.1
78 Spokane	−7.7	−18.4	25.0	21.9	10.6	122.2
79 Tacoma	23.1	8.1	110.5	29.1	4.7	100.0
80 Los Angeles	73.8	40.2	228.9	31.3	50.1	102.9
81 Long Beach	377.8	261.9	783.3	41.2	38.9	144.6
82 San Francisco	−28.1	−44.3	19.0	−6.1	−12.6	100.0
83 Oakland	−19.1	−35.2	38.6	13.0	−11.2	100.0
84 Seattle	9.4	−24.1	158.7	9.7	7.8	119.2
Regional Mean	251.5	197.0	477.6	95.2	125.8	331.3
National Mean	98.0	70.9	206.9	44.0	54.4	323.5

increase where there is a low initial level of manufacturing employment is converted into a massive relative change. This is due to the index number phenomenon. (The unweighted averages are shown purely for illustrative purposes.) However, if the data are converted into employment as a percent of population, the results are far more meaningful and show some distinct departures from the expected behavior.

The national patterns of change can be viewed in terms of the changes in population, adjusted or corrected for changes in population. Thus, in this period, the nation's population increased by 44.0 percent and, at the same time, there was 33.1 percent increase in manufacturing employment based on the underestimated level of 1947. The BLS figure for the same time period indicates an increase of only 22.8 percent. At the same time, retailing employment increased by 62.1 percent.

Measured in terms of employment as a percent of population, this resulted in a decline of manufacturing from 9.92 per 100 in 1947 to 9.14 in 1972. The BLS figure shows a much more substantial decline, from 10.78 in 1947 to 9.17 in 1972. At the same time, retailing increased from 4.71 in 1947 to 5.39 in 1972. These national trends are of interest because they were *not* predictive as to what was going to happen in the large cities.

MANUFACTURING AND RETAILING

The situation in the case of manufacturing stands in contrast with the changes in retailing. In the case of manufacturing there was an absolute decline in total city employment relative to population between 1947 and 1972 of 9.5 percent. This was the result of substantial declines in the East and the Midwest and substantial increases in the South and the West. As a proportion of the population, the declines in the East and the Midwest were lower and a good part of the increase in the South and the West was associated with the changes in population. These figures were shown in Table 6-9 and indicate the greatest losses in manufacturing relative to population occurred in the Midwest, where there was a 22.7 percent decline, and the greatest relative increase was only 11.1 percent in the West.

The reasons for the changes in manufacturing employment have been alluded to, but rarely have they been systematically analyzed. Thus, in many cities of the East there has not only been a decline in the city employment, but in the entire metropolitan area as well. It appears that where a city is doing badly, the metropolitan area is generally doing badly also, but not as badly as the central city. Further, the major increases in employment are associated (1) with a very small base in 1947 and (2) with the city encompassing more of the metropolitan area (i.e., annexation) or both (1) and (2). For the period under consideration, the employment and population data are dealt with in a consistent fashion.

The surprise finding, as already noted by this observer, concerns retailing. For while there were substantial changes in retailing, they were less than in the case of manufacturing. But most interesting, there were relative declines in the ratio of retailing employment to population at precisely the time that the national ratio was going up. In fact, in no region of the country did the ratio of retailing employment to population in the *cities* increase, even though there was 14.4 percent increase in the national relationship between retailing employment and population.

The result of all these forces was a reorientation of the cities relative to the areas which surround them. Prior to this period, specifically in 1947, the city was dominant and probably most dominant as a retailing center, since 28.7 percent of the population had 42.5 percent of retailing employment and 38.0 percent of manufacturing employment.

By 1973, the city proportion of the population had fallen to 22.4 percent of the national total. This explains the direction, but not the great magnitude of the decline. Manufacturing declined, but declined proportionately less than did retailing. The latter was due to the fact that there was a relative redistribution of manufacturing to the West and to the South. It was associated with an increase relative to the population. In the case of retailing, all areas lost relative to their populations.

The regional forces, however, clearly dominate the overall patterns. There were losses in the East and Midwest, except where there are offsetting annexations or special circumstances, and there were increases in the South and in the West. The issue in the latter regions was whether employment kept up with the growth of population. This was true of all population size groups. In the East and the Midwest the declines were more pervasive, although there were a few places which did not move along with the tide.

The pattern observed for the long period is also roughly the same as that observed for the shorter Census periods. Because of the importance of this in explaining the two classes of cities, a brief summary will be indicated at this point. Unlike prior analyses, the patterns will be shown on a regional basis. What is clear is that the secular patterns are not vitiated by the shorter term patterns. The

146 Economic Growth and Decline

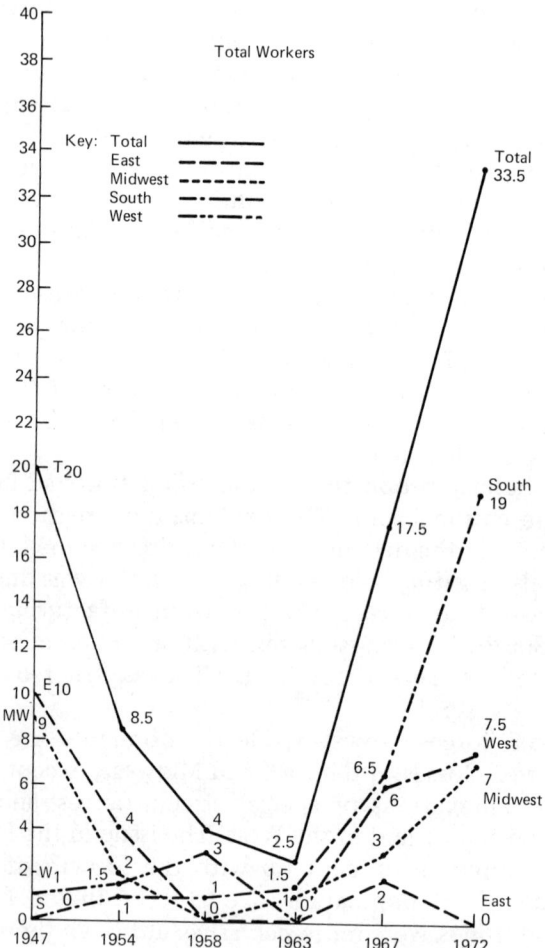

Source: Censuses of Manufacturing 1947 to 1972.

Figure 6-1. Year of Maximum Manufacturing Employment, for Total and Production Workers.

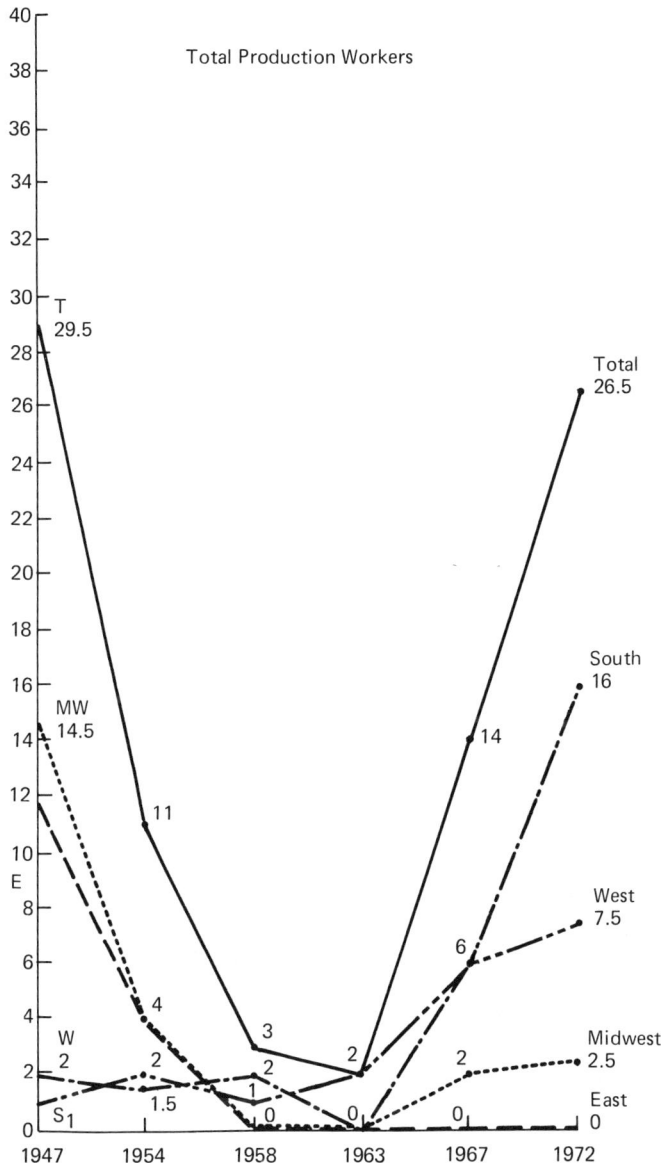

Figure 6-1. (cont.)

148 Economic Growth and Decline

situation in the case of the western and midwestern cities is not only true for the period, but has been roughly true for the subperiods as well. Similarly, the patterns for the South and the West are consistent with the longer term patterns.

The diagrams derived from all Censuses of Retailing and Manufacturing from 1947 to 1972 (Figures 6-1, 6-2, 6-3) help explain some of the anomalous results of Kain, and then of Harrison and others which took one part of the longer period and generalized the patterns of change from their most recent observations.

Before analyzing the separate periods, it should be noted that

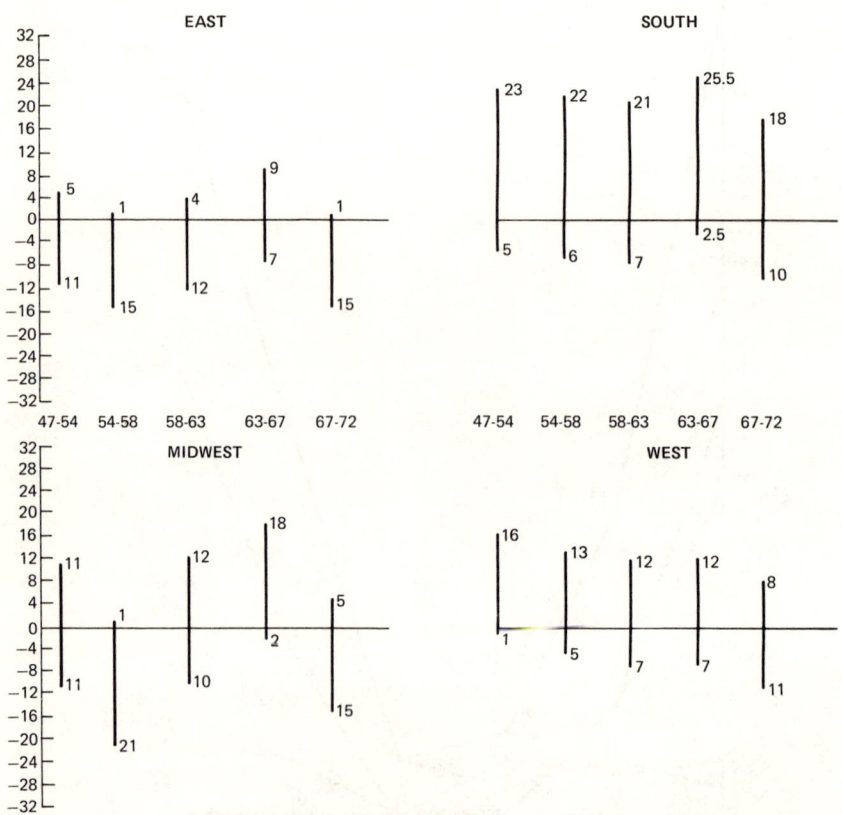

Source: Censuses of Manufacturing 1947 to 1972.

Figure 6-2. Manufacturing Employment by City: Changes in Employment Successive Censuses.

Changes in Manufacturing/Retailing Employment in Medium-Size Cities 149

from 1947 to 1954 the definitions of employment in manufacturing, added employment in Central Administrative Offices and Auxiliary Services and slightly redefined the number of production workers. The result was increased growth or reduced decline in the level of manufacturing employment concentrated in that one period of change. This is shown in Figure 6-2. Even with these biases it is clear that the East and Midwest behaved quite differently from the South and West.

The pattern also shows the differential effects of the Vietnam period, the only period in which there was a major increase in total

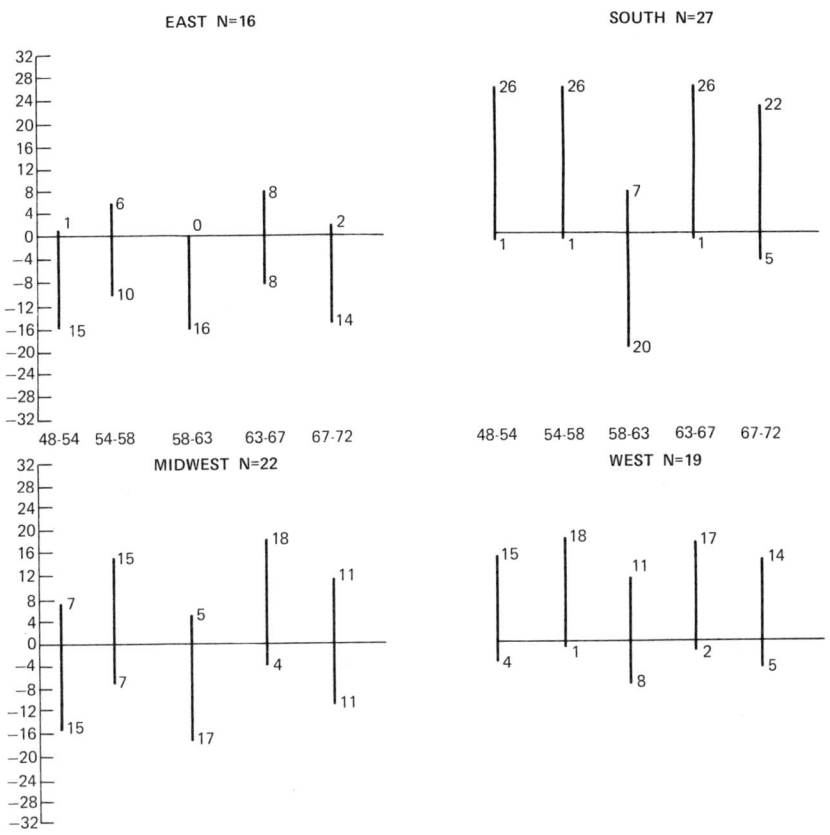

Source: Censuses of Retailing 1948 to 1972.
Figure 6-3. Retailing Employment by City: Changes in Employment Successive Censuses.

manufacturing employment. Thus, between 1958 and 1963 and again between 1963 and 1967, there were increases in manufacturing employment in some Eastern and many Midwestern cities, but those were shortlived as is indicated by the declines that occurred after 1967. At the same time, there were increases in the South throughout the entire period and growth, although of a slightly lesser intensity, in the West.

What is of importance is that by 1972, the overall level of manufacturing employment increased slightly, and in 1973 and 1974 it fell below the levels of 1972. The patterns indicate the movement of manufacturing activity from one region of the country to another, in the context of little or no change, except for that associated with the Vietnam era.

The pattern of change in the case of retailing shows the effects of regional change and cyclical behavior more clearly than do the manufacturing figures. Thus, the recession of 1958-63 appears rather pervasive nationally, but it was more severe in the East. The pattern also reveals that although the nation experienced prosperity between 1963 and 1968, about one-half the cities of the East did not participate in the growth. The differential effects of changing economic circumstances are apparent in every period. But what is quickly apparent are the positive indicators in the South and West, the negative indicators in the East, and the ambiguous picture in the Midwest.

All these patterns indicate that the improvements observed in the period 1958 to 1963, and then from 1963 to 1967, were not carried over to the next Census period as was the prognosis of many of the observers already cited. That this was true for manufacturing is clearly the case, but if one accounts for the general increase in retailing employment, as well as the increase in population, the favorable pattern of central cities in the South and West is also modified and appears to be more consistent with the other areas.

CONCLUSIONS

There are two regional patterns in the United States, which have been modified to a minor extent by special circumstances, but no exclusively medium-sized city patterns. In the first set, where there was an immense concentration of activity, especially associated with World War II, the cities entered into a period of decline. In many of these cases the decline was sufficiently great to be pervasive on a metropolitan basis. But this repeats some earlier changes. On the other hand, the increases in manufacturing and retailing in the South and in the West, even where they were concentrated in the cities, did not mean that the suburbs were left out. Indeed, except for the two unlikely cases—that the city became the central county or that annexation moved out to the sagebrush—the growth in city employment was exceeded in relative and, in most cases, absolute terms, by the suburban areas. In terms of employment, this meant that the dynamic was still there for the residents of the central city areas of the South and West. The result has been two worlds of cities primarily regional in nature. The first shows a long term decline from the concentrations of employment at the end of World War II and is associated with the decentralization of employment implicit in the high density city. The second world of cities, with low densities and with opportunities engendered by World War II and supplemented by annexation, showed enormous growth reaching peaks at the end of the period.

Part Four

Economic Characteristics of Small Cities

 *Chapter Seven*

The Relevance of City Size

David Puryear

DIVERSIFICATION AND URBAN SIZE

There is a substantial literature concerned with the relationship between urban size and the mix of urban activities. This literature suggests that small cities tend to be less diverse in the range of economic activities they perform and this tends to slow the pace of their economic growth. Many firms require a wide range of business services which are more likely to be available in larger cities and this influences their location decisions.

This aspect of city size implies that the planning and development efforts of small and medium-size cities should focus on development efforts in two areas. First, they should attempt to attract as wide a range of business service activities as possible to maximize their desirability as a business location. Second, they should attempt to attract industries with a relatively narrow range of business service needs. This two-pronged focus is more likely to generate economic growth than a broad, unfocused development effort.

Much of the literature in this topic grew out of the original contribution of Clark in 1945 (1). This classic paper noted the link between the size of a city and the type of activity occurring there. He observed that cities were centers for service production rather than manufacturing, that a city of 10,000 to 250,000 is required to

---

This material is based upon research supported by the National Science Foundation under Grant No. ERS74-21286 to the Joint Center for Political Studies-Howard University. Any opinions, findings, and conclusions expressed in this publication are those of the author(s) and do not necessarily reflect the views of the National Science Foundation.

provide an adequate range of commercial services, that a smaller city was sufficient for other services, that manufacturing is concentrated in older cities, and that a city of 200,000 to 500,000 is necessary for full development of manufacturing activity.

Several other authors published corroborating data in the decade following the appearance of Clark's paper, including Lillibridge (2), Schettler (3), and Schnore and Varley (4). These authors explored the question of city size and city function from essentially the same perspective as Clark; they all sought to identify an optimal city size in terms of the trade-off between the functions performed and the level of congestion and other disamenities associated with large city size.

In 1958, Berry and Garrison (5) looked at the relationship between size and function in a very different context. The principal intellectual debt was to Christaller and Lösch rather than to Clark. These authors investigated city functions for the purpose of developing an urban hierarchy. As in Clark's work, they found that larger places carried on a greater variety of activities, but this variety helped to locate the proper niche for the city in the system of cities. The work of Berry and Garrison in Snohomish County, Washington, was replicated by Stafford (6) for 31 towns in southern Illinois with results similar to the earlier study. This classification work was extended and applied to the national economy by Duncan et al. (7). More recently this work of Duncan and his co-authors was updated by Bean et al. (8).

Another strand of the literature on urban size and the mix of urban activities focuses on the greater diversity or its converse, specialization. The question of functional specialization or industrial diversification has been approached in two ways in the literature. In developing measures of diversification, a number of authors, including Bahl, Firestine, and Phares (9); Clemente and Sturgis (10); Crowley (11); Paraskevopoulos (12); Taylor (13); Thompson (14); and Ullman and Dacey (15), have noted that the cyclical economic stability of an economy is positively associated with the diversification of its industrial activities.

A second group, including Chinitz and Vernon (16); Duncan et al. (17); Hoover (18); Mills (19); and Puryear (20), has focused on specialization rather than diversification. These authors emphasize the comparative advantage which gives rise to urban areas and fosters specialization among them. Despite these differences in approach, the measures developed by these two groups of authors are quite similar and can generally be interpreted as opposite sides of the same coin. In other words, greater diversification implies less specialization and vice versa.

Both Mills and Puryear, the only studies to address the question of changes in specialization over time, find a decline in specialization among SMSAs. There are a number of possible explanations for this trend. Perhaps the most basic economic change that has contributed to the general decline in specialization is the massive shift of employment into the service industries.

Service producing industries accounted for about 40 percent of total employment in 1929. By 1967 their share of total employment had risen to 55 percent. This affects specialization for several reasons. Many services involve personal contact and are difficult to transport over long distances, so local production is more efficient economically. As services account for an increasing share of economic activity, employment growth shifts from national production centers toward local areas.

Services generally have fewer economies of scale in production, so there is less incentive for their production to be geographically concentrated. This too contributes to the decline in specialization as services become more important in the national economy. Finally, services are less closely tied to natural resource deposits than most other kinds of economic activity. Thus, they are free to locate close to their markets and their geographic distribution will reflect the distribution of the population more closely than most other activities.

Another important factor in the regional decentralization of economic activity may be the rise in the use of motor freight relative to railroads and water transport. Trucking has lowered costs for short hauls relative to longer ones and this has a decentralizing effect. Other things equal, average transportation distance increases with the volume of output in one location as close-by markets become saturated, and thus trucking lowers the average cost curve for relatively small volumes of output. This may lower the minimum cost volume of output and stimulate decentralization, but such an effect depends on the relationship between scale economies and transport costs for each commodity individually.

Industries that minimize costs by locating near their markets rather than near their sources of supply are said to be market oriented. Increases in market orientation lead to decentralization in industries whose markets are more widely dispersed than their sources of supply. Such industries make up a substantial fraction of economic activity. Factors that increase market orientation and thus tend to lead to decentralization include the growth of international trade in raw materials; the increasing share of secondary and tertiary goods in national product; the increasing number of steps in processing final goods; increasing labor mobility; and the decline of energy, transportation, and communication costs.

Finally, population growth itself may explain part of the decline since several of these studies show a negative relationship between specialization and population size—that is, greater diversity in larger urban areas (see Clemente and Sturgis (21), Crowley (22), and Paraskevopoulos (23)). This is a slightly different phenomenon from the size function relationships studied by Clark and his successors and by Berry and Garrison and their followers. Berry and Garrison were concerned with the presence or absence of activities in small centers, and Clark focused on the variety of services available in cities, while the specialization and diversification studies deal with the mix of activities in large urban areas (where all the activities are present, but in varying proportions). However, all three approaches are complementary and all three agree that the process of growth changes the nature of an urban area's specialization and, hence, changes its functional role in the economy.

The decline in specialization indicated by the results of Mills and Puryear is an aspect of urban growth and change that has important implications for future urban development. For example, future growth in urban areas is less likely to be the result of comparative advantage in a few specific industries. Urban areas with advantages which are attractive to a number of industries are more likely to experience rapid growth. A better understanding of the role of specialization in urban development is an essential part of any policy designed to influence the pattern of future urban growth in the United States.

EFFICIENCY AND URBAN SIZE

The views of Sundquist (24) are representative of many urban critics who feel that large urban areas have become too large to be economically or socially justified. Others, such as Mera (25), disagree. Mera argues, for example, that the rate of return on investments is at least as high in large urban areas as in small or medium-size areas. If it were not, investors would refuse to invest in large urban areas. In Mera's opinion, this productivity aspect of urban size is much more important than cost differences in urban areas of different sizes.

A policy to redistribute population from large urban areas to smaller ones must therefore be justified on the grounds of interregional or urban-rural equity and not on efficiency grounds. This fundamental disagreement has far-reaching significance for small and medium-size cities and for the most effective ways to plan for or stimulate their future growth. If big cities are too big to be sustained, then smaller places must plan for larger local growth than if big cities are likely to continue to grow and expand.

This section deals with the evidence on productivity and cost in relation to urban size. Since the overall efficiency of an urban area is the result of both productivity and cost considerations, it is necessary to examine both these questions before passing judgment on the relative efficiency of urban areas of different sizes. The issue of productivity and urban size is discussed first and then we turn to questions of the impact of urban size on the cost of both public and private activity in urban areas.

Benefits of Urban Size

There are two major types of benefits associated with urban size: greater productivity, and greater variety or diversification of economic activity. The question of diversification has already been discussed and the productivity question is at the heart of the issue of urban size, so this section will concentrate on productivity and urban size.

The literature on urban productivity is rather sparse, considering the attention that has been focused on the problems and prospects of urban areas in recent years. The best study of this issue, one that directly measures productivity, is by Sveikauskas (26). He uses a production function approach and estimates that a doubling of urban size results in an increase in the productivity of labor of roughly 6 percent. This relationship holds for all urban sizes including the very largest areas. There is no other reasonable explanation for this finding than that larger urban areas are simply more productive and by a substantial margin. According to this relationship, labor productivity in Chicago is nearly 25 percent greater than labor productivity in Tulsa, Oklahoma.

This analysis of productivity differentials requires careful evaluation, however, since it uses current money income or earnings as its measures of productivity. Personal satisfaction and preferences for a smaller urban environment may more than offset the measured differentials so that higher incomes and wages in larger urban areas represent a form of compensation for the less desirable nonpecuniary aspects of big-city life. This argument is examined by Hoch (27), along with a wealth of carefully documented evidence that larger urban areas pay higher wages. These higher wages can only be justified by greater productivity in larger urban areas. Any other situation would quickly lead to a very different pattern of population and employment distribution among urban areas.

Hoch's argument is worth a close look. He argues that different geographic locations have different levels of productivity deriving from a wide range of possible advantages including ports, rivers, mines, skilled labor, and available capital. Locations with high productivity attract concentrations of capital and labor and become urban areas. The higher the initial productivity of a location, the more capital and labor it can accommodate before its marginal product falls to the equilibrium level. Thus, large urban areas are large because they are highly productive.

Since workers are paid the value of their marginal product in a competitive labor market, this explanation of city size differentials would imply a constant wage rate regardless of urban size. But then Hoch adds another dimension of reality. Urban areas are places of congestion and pollution and other such disamenities roughly in proportion to their size. So Hoch contends that the significantly higher real wages in larger urban areas are a form of compensation for the greater number of disamenities associated with living and working there. Firms could not afford to locate in large urban areas and pay these higher wages unless the productivity of workers in larger urban areas justified such wages. Since the urban size-wages differential has persisted over many years, and firms have continued to locate in large urban areas, we can only conclude that productivity in larger urban areas is higher than in smaller places.

A similar chain of reasoning is advanced by Tolley (28) to explain differences in urban size and wage rates. Tolley adds the additional point that although the elimination of the inefficient externalities associated with congestion and pollution would impose additional pecuniary costs on urban residents, it would not necessarily result in a shrinkage of large urban areas. In fact, to the extent that workers found the greater traffic efficiency and cleaner environment worth more than their cost, the urban area might very well grow as a result of these policies.

Another argument for the higher productivity of large urban areas is found in the work of Lichtenberg (29). One alleged advantage of large urban areas is their greater variety of specialized business services. The availability of these services is an important economy for small new businesses trying to establish themselves. These new businesses are too small to employ their own attorneys, accountants, printers, machine shops, etc., on a full time basis. Therefore they cluster in large urban areas where these services and others even more specialized are readily available. This line of reasoning leads us to expect to find these firms, known as incubator industries, in relatively large proportions in the New York metropolitan area. Indeed, that is exactly what Lichtenberg found. New York had a larger than average share of small, single plant, labor intensive manufacturing firms.

Thus there is a very persuasive case that large cities have grown for good reasons and in fact represent a very real gain to society because of their high productivity. This point is not really disputed in the literature, although it is occasionally ignored (30). The real issue is not whether there are sound reasons for large urban areas to be large, but whether, because of the diseconomies of scale and externalities associated with urban size, large urban areas are too large. This question requires us to look at the relationship between urban size and the costs of economic activity.

THE COSTS OF URBAN SIZE

There are three aspects of urban size and its costs that we will discuss here. First, the impact of urban size on the cost of living will be examined. Then we will look at the question of economies of scale in urban public services and their implications for the optimal size of urban areas. Finally, we will discuss the issue of externalities and urban size.

Cost of Living

The available evidence suggests that the cost of living is higher in larger urban areas but not by nearly as large a margin as money wages. Thus larger urban areas offer higher real wages as well as higher money wages. Independent analyses by Alonso and Fajans (31), Hoch (32), and Tolley (33) reach this same conclusion. Land is more productive in larger urban areas and its higher price raises the cost of housing for both owners and renters. It also raises the cost of business establishments which pass on part of the higher costs to consumers as higher prices. Thus, there is nothing surprising in the higher cost of living in larger urban areas. The important point is that it is small in comparison to money wage differentials.

Economies of Scale in Public Services

There are two approaches to the question of scale economies in urban public services. One part of the literature focuses on expenditures per capita in urban jurisdictions of different sizes. The other approach is to estimate scale economies of specific urban public sector activities, usually with production function analysis. Both approaches focus on jurisdictions rather than entire urban areas because of the way in which public services are financed and produced in the U.S. This does not help us to compare benefits and costs, but it is the way the system works so we must see if the costs of public services vary significantly with jurisdiction size and then concern ourselves with the metropolitanwide implications if necessary.

Alonso (34) finds no significant relationship between expenditures per capita and city size. Bradford, Malt, and Oates (35) find that larger cities spend more per capita. Gabler (36) also finds that large cities spend more per capita. In a later article, Gabler (37) revises his conclusions on the basis of a larger sample of local jurisdictions. His more recent results indicate lower expenditures per capita as population rises up to 250,000 and rising expenditures per capita beyond that size. In evaluating Gabler's results, it should be noted that the statistical significance of his conclusions was very weak and that interstate and interregional variations in the pattern of expenditures per capita are relatively large.

Shapiro (38) also finds higher expenditures per capita for very small jurisdictions and very large jurisdictions, but Shapiro explicitly notes that no conclusion about the existence or extent of scale economies in the urban public sector is possible without examination of the actual level of output. This point applies to all of the articles which examine expenditures per capita. It may be the case that large urban governments provide a higher level of services so that their higher expenditures per capita reflect higher consumption of public goods and services rather than diseconomies of scale.

None of these authors (Alonso (39); Bradford, Malt, and Oates (40); Gabler (41); and Shapiro (42)) attempts to measure the level of services provided by larger governments, so their results tell us only that expenditures rise with size beyond some point and this may or may not indicate higher costs per unit of public service provided. If we knew that residents of large cities had the same preferences for the level of public sector activity as residents of smaller cities, higher expenditures would indicate the existence of diseconomies of two possible sorts.

Large cities might create extra costs so that larger expenditures were required to achieve the same standard of services as in smaller places, even though the actual production function of those services exhibited constant or slightly increasing returns to scale. The second possibility, of course, is that there are diseconomies of scale in these activities, at least beyond some threshold size.

If residents of large cities have a greater preference for public services than smaller city residents, then the higher expenditures in larger cities would appear to reflect those preferences, although we still do not know anything about actual economies of scale and we cannot know about them until we begin to try to measure the service or output levels of the public sector.

To complicate things still further, the higher expenditures per capita in large cities may reflect an entirely different kind of diseconomy altogether. It may be that larger cities have stronger public employee unions, which bargain effectively for higher wages than small city public employees receive. Thus, differences in expenditures per capita may reflect differences in factor costs rather than in the ratio of inputs to outputs.

Hirsch (43) discusses the manifold problems associated with trying to measure public output so that we can examine the issue of scale economies in the public sector. Since most public expenditures are for services rather than goods, and since virtually all public expenditures are provided without the benefit of market transactions, it is much more difficult to evaluate their quantity and quality than it is private sector goods and services which are evaluated by market prices.

Fire services are not sold to residents, they are provided as part of the public service package received by all residents without direct charge. Residents, of course, do pay for these services in the form of taxes, but there is no direct link between the level of taxes and the receipt of services and no option to forego fire services and save on taxes. In the national income accounts, government services are valued at cost, although this treatment does not really satisfy anyone.

In the past, the output of local public services was also measured by the level of expenditures on goods and services, but in recent years more sophisticated approaches have been developed and expenditures are no longer considered a satisfactory measure of output in the public sector. At the very least some disaggregation of expenditures into input price and input quantity components is expected. And many studies have used full-fledged production functions with a variety of service level measures as proxies for output.

Hirsch (44), Riew (45), and Walzer (46) all find some evidence of scale economies in public service production, but not enough to justify major changes in government structure to increase efficiency. Tiebout (47) argues that changes in government structure are justifiable on grounds of service quality rather than on the basis of scale economies. Duncan (48) surveys the "optimum" scale of providing a variety of public services and concludes that the "optimum" city size depends on the mix of goods provided since different goods have different levels of scale economies.

This evidence on expenditures per capita and economies of scale is consistent with the point made by Mera (49) that productivity differentials are more important than differences on the cost side. It suggests that small places may experience inefficiencies stemming from their size, but that larger places face a mixed situation with no very strong case for or against large cities on the basis of public service productivity. This is an area in which useful research could be done since there are so many unknowns, especially in terms of the relationship between jurisdiction costs and urban area costs, which will be discussed further.

Externalities and Urban Size

We turn now to the issue of externalities and urban size. A number of authors have noted that the existence of externalities leads to inefficient locational choices and may lead to urban areas that are too big (see Borukhov (50), Hoch (51), Mills (52), Neutze (53), and Tolley (54)). This argument is based on the deviation between social and private costs in the presence of external economies or diseconomies.

Industries that pollute urban areas have traditionally ignored the impact of their pollution on the general public. They were able to do so because the air and water they polluted were essentially free goods. They were not marketed and industries paid no price for using them as sewers. Industries based their location decisions on private productivity and ignored the social costs of pollution, so they located where the private return was highest, regardless of the social benefit or cost.

Thus, these externalities led to urban areas that were too big, given the level of pollution that exists in the absence of public controls. However, Hoch, Mills, and Tolley all note that proper pricing mechanisms which result in cleaner air and water in urban areas may well lead to larger urban areas than we have now as the reduction in disamenities makes large areas more desirable as economic and residential locations.

The most costly externality in urban areas, according to Mills (55), is not pollution but congestion. This problem results from the same economic situation as the pollution problem. In this case, roads and highways are free goods once they are built (obviously, toll roads are exceptions). Drivers do not consider the extra cost imposed on other road users when they enter a congested or crowded highway; they only consider their private cost. However, congestion slows down all traffic and each new entrant to a congested highway causes a slight additional slowing of traffic. Thus, private and social cost diverge and too many people use the highway. When location decisions are based on the private costs of congestion, too many activities will locate in large urban areas. Again, a rational road pricing mechanism which reduced congestion might increase the new equilibrium size of the urban area rather than decrease it.

The best study of the extra costs imposed on society by location in a large urban area instead of a small one is the analysis of Sydney, Australia, done by Neutze (56). Neutze measures the savings in congestion costs, including time costs, of shifting workers from Sydney (population 2,183,000 in 1961) to Wollongong (population 132,000 in 1961). His estimates indicate a savings equivalent to $300 (in 1964 dollars) per year for each worker shifted. Neutze is careful to point out that this amount assumes no loss of worker productivity, an unlikely circumstance in view of the work of Sveikauskas (57) and others.

Another important source of urban externalities in the past was interspersal of industrial and residential locations. For several decades, however, land use zoning has been used to deal with this externality. Babcock (58) examines the case for externalities zoning and discusses the practical application of this tool. A second type of zoning against externalities is fiscal zoning. This technique is used to exclude from consumption of local public goods those who cannot or would not under existing taxation systems pay their share of the costs of those public goods. Since most local revenues are derived from the property tax, fiscal zoning generally is a de facto mechanism to insure that local residents own enough housing to pay their share of property taxes. The usual approach is minimum lot size zoning for single family residences.

Fiscal zoning is much more controversial than traditional externalities zoning. It is closely related to the general question of efficiency in the provision of local public goods. The current paradigm in this area is the model of Tiebout (59), which provides a market analog for the provision of public goods. People select the level and mix of public goods they desire by "voting with their feet": they move to a local jurisdiction which provides just the combination of public goods they prefer. Exclusionary zoning is not necessary in Tiebout's model because residents pay their full share of the cost of the public goods they consume. In practice, reliance on local property taxes provides an incentive for zoning for homogeneous neighborhoods to share the local tax burden evenly.

One recent test of this practical implication of Tiebout's theory is Hamilton, Mills, and Puryear (60). This study presents evidence that local areas do indeed seem to behave in accordance with the Tiebout model. The larger the local share of school taxes (the smaller the state and federal aid share), the more homogeneous areas were in terms of incomes and house values.

Another perspective on the question of interjurisdictional spillovers of public goods is the work of Neenan (61). Neenan presents data which indicate that the suburbs of Detroit are exploiting the central city because they do not pay an amount equivalent to their full benefit from consuming various central city services. Auld and Cook (62) and Ramsey (63) take issue with this conclusion and point out that the Detroit suburbs pay very nearly the full costs of their consumption of public services, provided by the city of Detroit and it is not reasonable to expect them to pay the full value of their benefits. They also note that Neenan's results are very sensitive to the assumptions employed in the analysis and should be interpreted with extreme caution.

AN OPEN QUESTION STILL

It is clear that the question of the efficiency of urban size is still an open one. Some authors emphasize the benefits of higher productivity while others emphasize the diseconomies of size. On the whole, the productivity side seems to be more persuasive because there do not appear to be any market distortions of sufficient magnitude to radically affect the private location decisions which are ultimately responsible for urban growth.

In addition, the diseconomies, generally cited as evidence that urban areas are too big, are not tied to urban size with direct causal links. Urban externalities are better dealt with directly, on their own merits or demerits, than indirectly by shrinking the size of urban areas and hoping pollution and congestion will disappear.

Thus, small and medium-size cities appear to be less productive than larger cities, although the evidence is by no means conclusive. However, even if they are less productive in monetary terms, smaller urban areas may provide equivalent or greater satisfaction in nonmonetary rewards.

This suggests that planning for the growth and development of small and medium-size cities should place special emphasis on minimizing the undesirable consequences of larger urban size, even if this slows the growth of the area somewhat.

Chapter Eight

Fiscal Problems of Smaller Growing and Declining Cities

Thomas Muller

A considerable literature developed in the 1960s and early 1970s dealing almost exclusively with growth and its control. But the mid 1970s witnessed a decline in economic activity, with severe repercussions on the local and state public sectors, where employment had increased dramatically since the 1930s. As a consequence, the fiscal woes of large American cities replaced previous concerns over growth. This concern, however, was focused primarily on large declining cities such as New York and Detroit, with relatively little attention given to smaller urban areas. Although many of our larger cities are undergoing a decline, another group of mostly smaller cities, located primarily in the South and West, continue to grow.

This chapter examines two groups of central cities—those 50,000 to 200,000, and those 200,000 to 500,000 in population size. Cities below 50,000 are not considered "central cities," and larger cities have been the subject of previous analysis (1). The cities analyzed here contain about 42 million persons, or 20 percent of the total U.S. population in 1975. Actually, there are more people living in cities of this size than there are living in larger cities. The discussion will focus on three topics: fiscal characteristics of growing and declining cities, causes of growth and decline, and the response of cities to either growth pressure or declines in economic activity.

GENERAL CHARACTERISTICS OF GROWING AND DECLINING CITIES

A key characteristic of growing and declining cities is location. Most growing cities regardless of size are located in the South and West.

168 Economic Characteristics of Small Cities

Among the few exceptions are smaller cities, such as Nashua, New Hampshire, growing because of spillovers from Massachusetts which, together with New York, has the dubious distinction of leading other states in tax burden. New Hampshire, without an income tax, can therefore attract both commuters and business firms.

While declining cities, as seen in Table 8-1, are concentrated in the Northeast and in the mid-Western states, a number of older Southern cities have some of the most rapid declines. These include Savannah, Georgia; Charleston, South Carolina; and Birmingham, Alabama (cities which lost over 10 percent of their population between 1970 and 1973). In recent years, larger cities, such as Atlanta and Fort Worth, joined the list of cities with substantial population losses. As shown in Chapter Two, the South contains some of the fastest growing and declining small cities within the size-class 25,000 to 50,000.

Size is also a determinant of growth. Very few large cities are growing. The exceptions are those with massive annexation. On the other hand, the majority of cities with 10,000 to 50,000 residents continue to expand. Between 1970 and 1973, only ten of 28 cities with half a million or more residents had population growth, while

Table 8-1. Growing and Declining Cities, by Size and Region, 1970-73.

	50 to 200[a] thousand		200 to 500 thousand		500 thousand[b] and over		Total (Average)	
	Growing	Declining	Growing	Declining	Growing	Declining	Growing	Declining
Region:								
Northeast	1	10	1	5	0	4	2	19
North Central	4	7	0	8	1	8	5	13
South	8	1	6	7	5	2	19	10
West	17	1	7	2	4	3	28	6
U.S. Total	30	19	14	22	10	17	54	58
Income Per Capita (1972)	$3925	$3650	$3858	$3670	$4011	$3760	$3923	$3690
Density (persons per square mile) (1973)	3071	7533	2893	6136	4050[c]	11,760	3197	8219

Source:, Bureau of the Census, *Population Estimates and Projections*, Series P-25.
[a]Sample.
[b]Excludes New York City.
[c]Excludes areas added by city/county mergers.

only six had net in-migration. Among cities with 200,000 to 500,000 residents, 30 percent experienced growth, with the percentage rising to about 60 percent for cities with 50,000 to 200,000 residents.

Although most southern states have incomes below the national average, income in the majority of smaller growing cities in this region exceeds the level in declining northern jurisdictions. Since the cost of living is substantially lower in the South, differentials in real income between the regions are substantial (2). Few of the most rapidly growing cities are manufacturing centers. Most are concentrated in a relatively few southern and western states, particularly Florida, Arizona, and California. The common denominator associated with growing cities is annexation.

Many declining cities are older cities in the proximity of a major urban center. This would include such cities as Newark and Yonkers, which are near New York City, Camden near Philadelphia, Oakland near San Francisco, and East St. Louis, Illinois near St. Louis. These cities were historically in the shadow of their neighboring metropolis, and their housing stock consists primarily of moderately priced units.

A second category of declining cities consists of those with a strong manufacturing base which forms their own urban core. This includes such cities as Dayton, Ohio; Birmingham, Alabama; and Gary, Indiana. The third group has a diversified economic base but are nevertheless experiencing substantial out-migration. This group includes such large cities as Louisville, Minneapolis, St. Paul, and Atlanta, as well as a score of smaller cities.

FISCAL CHARACTERISTICS OF GROWING AND DECLINING CITIES

Size is important in distinguishing fiscal characteristics of cities. Therefore, the two groups of cities being discussed in this paper differ fiscally. Outlays for selected services, as shown in Table 8-2, vary considerably by city size, from $307 per capita in the largest cities to $111 in cities with fewer than 50,000 residents. These differences are primarily attributable to three factors: 95 percent more employees per capita to provide roughly the same type of services, 40 percent higher wages, four times higher debt (and interest payments on this debt), and more generous employee benefits. For example, the number of police varies from 22 per 10,000 residents in cities with 50 thousand to 200 thousand residents, to 41 per 10,000 in cities with a population of 1 million or more. Hence, size is important in distinguishing between characteristics of cities which have a fiscal effect. (Table 8-1 groups all cities

Table 8-2. Service Outlays, Municipal Wages, Employment, and Income as a Function of City Size.

	500,000 or more	200,000 to 500,000	50,000 to 200,000	Under 50,000	Ratio of Columns 1/3	Ratio of Columns 1/4
Number of jurisdictions (1973)	26	37	324	18,130	—	—
1973 population (In Millions)	31.2	12.2	29.3	63.0	—	—
Outlays per capita—selected services[a]	$307	$205	$165	$111	1.86	2.77
Total debt per capita[a]	$910	$601	$358	$279	2.54	3.26
Full faith and credit debt[a]	$492	$287	$198	$115	2.48	4.28
Interest payments per capita[a]	$37	$21	$12	$8	3.08	4.62
Municipal employees per 10,000 residents—selected services[b]	142	127	102	74	1.39	1.92
Police personnel per 10,000[b] residents	39	28	22	20	1.70	1.95
Monthly wages—all municipal employees[b]	$1159	$961	$961	$830	1.21	1.40
Monthly wages—selected services[b]	$1147	$981	$987	$815	1.16	1.41
Monthly wages—teachers[b]	$1438	$1233	$1120	$992	1.30	1.45
Annual payroll per capita—selected services[b]	$195	$149	$121	$72	1.61	2.70
Per capita income—1972	$3936	$3781	$3818	N/A	1.03	N/A

[a]Data for fiscal 1975 selected services are municipal functions other than education, welfare, hospital, housing, and utilities.
[b]Data for October, 1975.

Sources: Bureau of the Census, *City Government Finances, in 1974-1975*, October, 1976;
Bureau of the Census, *City Employment in 1975*;
Bureau of the Census, *Population Projections and Estimates*, Series P-25 and P-26, 1975.

with similar populations without distinguishing between those jurisdictions growing and those declining.)

To determine the fiscal and other characteristics of growing and declining cities with 50,000 to 200,000 residents, data from 30 cities with the most rapid growth in recent years (average net in-migration in excess of 15 percent of base population between 1970 and 1973), and 19 cities with the most rapid population decline (average out-migration of 10 percent between 1970 and 1973) were examined. (See Tables 8-4 and 8-5 below for list of jurisdictions.) The average population of the 49 cities in the sample was about 100,000. Thus, the 49 cities include about five million residents, or more than one-sixth of the population in this jurisdiction category. Other cities of this size had neither rapid growth nor decline in the three year interval.

As shown in Table 8-3 (column 1), per capita income in the growing cities was about 8 percent above the average of those losing population. Perhaps more important, the rate of increase in income among growing cities was more rapid than found in cities losing population, indicating a widening income gap attributable primarily

Table 8-3. Characteristics of Selected Cities.

	Population 50,000 to 200,000		Population 200,000 to 500,000	
	Growing	Declining	Growing	Declining
Number of cities	30	19	14	22
Basic employment per 10,000 residents[a]	73	91	82	101
Monthly wages–municipal workers (non-teachers)	$953	$904	$950	$1016
Monthly salaries–teachers[b]	–	$1172	$1111	$1268
Annual payroll per capita–selected services	$84	$94	$94	$119
Population outlays–basic services, fiscal 1975	$137	$203	$161	$235
Per capita income–1972	$3925	$3650	$3858	$3670
Change in per capita income–1969-1972	22%	19%	23%	19%
Average population–1973 (in thousands)	99	105	330	322
Population growth–1970-1973	17.7%	–7.3%	9.5%	–6.0%
Average area in square miles–1970	32	14	115	46
Long term debt full faith and credit (per capita)	$91	$228	$252	$309

[a]Basic employment includes police and fire protection, sewerage, sanitation, parks, financial administration, and general control. Employment and wage data for October 1975.
[b]Teacher salaries are based on cities which provide education services directly.
Sources: U.S. Bureau of the Census, *City Government Finances in 1974-1975*, October 1976;
U.S. Bureau of the Census, *City Employment in 1975*, July 1976.

Table 8-4. Growing and Declining Cities with 50,000 to 200,000 Population.

Growing		Declining
Montgomery, Alabama	Hialeah, Florida	Compton, California
Little Rock, Arkansas	Tallahassee, Florida	Hartford, Connecticut
Mesa, Arizona	Boise City, Idaho	Bridgeport, Connecticut
Tempe, Arizona	Sterling Heights, Michigan	East St. Louis, Illinois
Scottsdale, Arizona	Taylor, Michigan	Gary, Indiana
Anaheim, California	St. Joseph, Mississippi	Terre Haute, Indiana
El Cajon, California	Billings, Montana	Savannah, Georgia
Fremont, California	Lincoln, Nebraska	Brookline, Massachusetts
Huntington Beach, California	Las Vegas, Nevada	Somerville, Massachusetts
Modesto, California	Nashua, New Hampshire	Flint, Michigan
Santa Rosa, California	Eugene, Oregon	Kalamazoo, Michigan
Aurora, Colorado	Salem, Oregon	Syracuse, New York
Boulder, Colorado	Brownsville, Texas	Utica, New York
Colorado Springs, Colorado	Garland, Texas	Birmingham, New York
Clearwater, Florida	Laredo, Texas	Euclid, Ohio
		Youngstown, Ohio
		Harrisburg, Pennsylvania
		Chester, Pennsylvania
		Providence, Rhode Island

to out-migration. But the most significant difference between the two city categories was density: the declining cities had, in 1970, an average density of 7,553 compared to 3,071 in growing jurisdictions. This density ratio (shown in Table 8-1) also holds for larger growing and declining cities.

DENSITY AND COSTS

As noted previously, cities with rapidly declining populations have one common characteristic—high density. This in turn is associated with higher rents and older housing stock, higher cost of providing a unit of service, and greater per capita demand for many municipal services. This relationship is not new. The economics literature for several decades has shown the positive correlation between density and high public service costs, holding such variables as per capita income constant (3). However, recent work suggests that the contribution of density in explaining cost differentials may have increased (4).

Table 8-5. Growing and Declining Cities with 200,000 to 500,000 Population, 1970.

Growing[a] 1970-1973	Declining 1970-1973
Albuquerque	Atlanta*
Austin	Fort Worth*
Baton Rouge	Long Beach*
Charlotte	Norfolk*
Corpus Christie	Portland*
Oklahoma City	Richmond*
El Paso	Tampa*
Miami	Toledo*
Nashville	Wichita*
Omaha	Yonkers*
Sacramento	Akron
San Jose	Birmingham
Tucson	Dayton
Tulsa	Des Moines
	Louisville
	Jersey City
	Minneapolis
	Newark
	Oakland
	Rochester
	St. Paul
	Syracuse

[a]Including growth by annexation.
*Growing 1960-1970, Declining 1970-1973.

After population size and personal income are controlled for, density is shown to be a major explanatory variable accounting for differences in outlays among urban areas grouped by size. Cities with densities between 1,500 to 2,000 residents per mile have the lowest service costs, if service level differences are taken into account. Beyond a population density of 5,000 or so, a substantial increase in per capita outlays for common services can be observed.

Among cities with 200 to 500 thousand residents, three with highest densities, Jersey City—17,000, Newark—15,333, and Yonkers—10,888, all show out-migration. These cities have service outlays considerably above the area average. By contrast, Austin, San Jose, and Tucson, among the most rapidly growing jurisdictions in the nation, have densities well below 4,000. In the 50,000 to 200,000 population group, the five cities with highest density—Providence, Rhode Island; Chester, Pennsylvania; Bridgeport, Connecticut; Somerville, Massachusetts; and Harrisburg, Pennsylvania—had an average population decline of 8 percent between 1970 and 1973.

Cities which had the highest per capita outlays for services two and three decades ago continue to be highest today (5). But their ability to meet the rising cost of services from their own tax base has diminished due to out-migration of the more affluent households and loss of economic activity. Per capita income at the urban core is below the suburban level, offsetting the tax advantage of more commercial property.

In fact, the rapid growth of commercial activity at the urban periphery is reducing the economic viability of the Central Business District in many urban areas to a point where its future is uncertain (6). To meet the higher service costs in the face of a stable or declining revenue base, municipal taxes are increased. This, in turn, makes these areas less attractive as a relocation site for households or business firms.

Municipal Employees, Wages and Benefits

The group of fourteen growing cities between 200,000 and 500,000, as shown in column 1 of Table 8-3, required 82 persons per 10,000 residents in October 1975 to provide basic, or common, services. (These services are: police and fire protection, public education, sewerage, other sanitation, parks, financial administration, and general control.) These range from 47 in San Jose to 95 in Nashville. The twelve declining cities utilized 101 persons per 10,000 or 22 percent more than growing cities. Most personnel were on the municipal payroll in Newark, 113, and Louisville, 112, while the fewest were on the payroll in Des Moines, 63. A key service which explains part of the difference is police and fire protection. Newark had 77 persons per 10,000 on payroll; San Jose only 28.

Thus, three-quarters of the difference in personnel between these cities is explained by two services—police and fire protection. A similar relationship is found in other cities. Not only are there more personnel per capita in declining cities, but average monthly wages of personnel other than school teachers were $1,016 in 1975 compared to $950 in the growing group. Wages for teachers were also a few percent higher in declining cities. As a result of these differences, the payroll in declining cities, despite lower per capita income, is substantially higher.

In addition to somewhat higher salaries, benefit packages for employees in declining cities are usually more generous than found in growing jurisdictions, adding to the total personnel cost differential. Pension plan differences can be illustrated by several examples from the same state. Oakland contributed in fiscal 1975 $41 per capita to pension plans for its employees, while San Jose contributed only $11 per capita. Savannah, Georgia spent $12 per capita; Columbus, Georgia only half this amount. Minneapolis contributed $54 per capita, or 30 percent of its total payroll, St. Paul $17, or 11 percent of its payroll. Overall, however, the municipal contribution per capita is less in smaller cities, suggesting that employees in the very large cities are able to negotiate more favorable wages and benefits (7).

The 30 growing cities in this category, as shown in Table 8-3, employ 73 persons per 10,000 residents for common services, compared to 91 in the 19 declining cities, a difference of 29 percent. These values are almost the same as found among medium-size cities. Among cities requiring the most municipal employees, all in the declining category, are Hartford (137), Harrisburg (130), and Birmingham (113).

The average payroll (average annual wage × number of employees) for common services was $84 per capita in growing cities, $95 in declining cities. Declining cities have one relative advantage—their share of nonlocal revenues is several percentages above the level of growing cities (8). However, since declining cities have lower personal income and higher per capita outlays for services, this more than offsets higher state and federal contributions.

Debt and Interest Payments

Interest payments to repay debts are higher among declining cities in the 50 to 200 thousand population category. This is illustrated by differences in per capita debt—the average declining city had $228 compared to $91 in growing cities. Highest per capita debt during fiscal 1975 was found in Providence ($408), Hartford ($668), and Utica, New York ($403). Among growing cities, Las Vegas has the highest debt ($222) per capita, below the average of cities with declining population.

WHY DO SOME CITIES GROW, OTHERS DECLINE?

Conditions Leading to Growth

Population growth in medium sized cities can be the result of the following conditions.

Annexation of contiguous areas. Almost all population growth in recent years among cities with 100,000 or more residents is due to annexation rather than to natural increase, or net in-migration within its original boundaries.

Filling in of open areas (or redevelopment within existing municipal boundaries). Only a few examples of cities in this growth category exist. These examples are typically limited to areas with a particularly desirable environment, usually a seafront location, which attracts retired persons. These jurisdictions include Miami and St. Petersburg, Florida. In contrast to the recent pattern, a large share of urban growth during the 1920-1950 period was the result of the filling in of open space within fixed city boundaries.

Major new facility in a city (or more typically nearby), which attracts additional population within existing boundaries. This type of growth generator is typically found in smaller cities and rural areas. For example, the Cape Kennedy Space Center caused a major boom in nearby Melbourne, Florida, while Disneyworld encouraged growth in Orlando. At present, Kitsap County in Washington State is experiencing rapid growth attributable, in part, to the Trident submarine site under construction within county limits. Oil and coal extraction is causing the rise of numerous "boom towns" in rural areas of Alaska, Montana, and Wyoming. However, most communities undergoing rapid growth tend to be small, with almost all in the below 50,000 population category.

Causes Linked to Decline

The dominant cause of decline, defined as substantial net population out-migration over a decade or more, is related to aging of the housing stock and commercial-industrial facilities. There is a strong correlation between density and housing stock age, since high density usually means that a substantial share of housing is of pre-1950 vintage. Although more difficult to measure, some industrial plants, commercial facilities, and part of the public infrastructure is likely to be obsolete in cities where older housing is dominant.

Given these physical conditions, the choice has been to redevelop already urbanized areas or to build on the urban periphery. Increases in real income during the 1950s and 1960s, as well as life style changes, have led to an increased demand for larger, low density housing outside the boundaries of the urban core. Concurrently, technological changes, in the form of more sophisticated communication equipment, more efficient production methods, and improved transportation, have reduced the benefits of agglomeration that result from close physical proximity between producers, suppliers, workers, and consumers that in turn led to dense urban cores.

Transportation technology, in the form of subways, maintained the high density of Manhattan, New York, in the early parts of this century, and produced commuting patterns which would not be feasible in the absence of fixed rails tunneled beneath the city.

Within a few decades, the population movement from the urban core accelerated, made possible by technological improvements which created a comprehensive road network and mass availability of private vehicles. The early introduction of mass transit in New York and some other cities resulted in residential and commercial locational patterns which had no comparative advantage as the population and business firms decentralized to suburban locations. Thus, early introduction of mass transit may have worsened the fiscal problems facing high density cities today.

The sequence of events leading to decline appears independent of changes in regional economic activity. Two inner suburbs of Washington, D.C., Alexandria and Arlington, as well as the city of Richmond are experiencing substantial decline while other parts of their metropolitan areas and state continue to grow. Atlanta lost 9 percent of its population during a three year period, Savannah 11 percent, one of the most rapid rates of decline in the nation, although Georgia continues to attract in-migrants. Two smaller cities of Lancaster and Reading, in growing areas of Pennsylvania, and Scranton, in a declining area, share one common characteristic—population loss. Thus, location in a growing region has no impact on the decline of the urban core. There is, in fact, a very strong positive relationship between total SMSA population growth and the rate of growth outside the central city (9).

One contributing factor to the rate of decline appears to be the expansion of interstate or other limited access highways, such as beltways. One finds a positive relationship between the rate of suburban growth population and these roadways, after controlling for total regional in-migration.

A decline in population does not always result in an immediate reduction in business activity. However, a continuous decline leads to lower retail sales and loss of private sector jobs. If the rate of decline is low, there may be few abandoned housing units. However, rapid population loss, as in Newark or Camden, New Jersey, is accompanied by rising vacancy and abandonment rates.

Decline can also be accelerated by other conditions. There is a continuing debate on the association between school busing and loss of white families. Data from Richmond and Prince Georges County, Maryland, however, strongly implies a linkage between the two events. Thus, although a decline in nonminority students has been shown to take place independent of this issue, the rate may be accelerated in the absence of regional desegregation plans.

COPING WITH GROWTH AND DECLINE

Annexation Issues

Annexation, as shown earlier, is the major factor causing population growth. While there are a few exceptions, notably Miami and St. Petersburg, typically cities grow by annexing low density areas on the urban periphery. For example, Macon, Georgia, increased its area from 14 to 49 square miles in the 1960s, Columbus, Georgia from 25 to 70 square miles. In western states, Colorado Springs annexed areas three times its 1960 size. Among North Central cities, Fort Wayne, Indiana grew from 35 to 52 square miles, Cedar Rapids from 30 to 51 square miles. In all these instances, substantial loss of population would have taken place in the absence of annexation. While annexation is the only means by which a city, particularly an older one, can increase its population and open space, this process can create several economic and noneconomic problems.

Among the economic problems is the need for "up front" capital to provide the necessary infrastructure such as roads, utilities and other facilities. Typically, areas annexed have a less developed infrastructure than the core city, and there is a need to upgrade these facilities to the level of the core. For example, the City of Richmond had to increase its long-term debt substantially to provide facilities such as roads and sewer lines required as part of the annexation order (10). In Texas, a group of citizens can petition to "de-annex" from a city if adequate facilities are not provided.

Thus, cities are under substantial pressure to link their infrastructure with the annexed area. While this usually means that per capita debt service will rise substantially, revenues from the annexed area will presumably be sufficient to offset the cost of capital facilities over their useful life. Newly incorporated residents are also typically dissatisfied by the annexation process, since effective property tax rates are, without exception, higher in the core city. Thus, residents find that they pay higher taxes. While services received may improve, these benefits are typically discounted, as they were not asked for.

A second issue arising from annexation is education. Frequently, newly annexed areas are racially segregated, and the inclusion of schools into a multiracial school district leaves some residents dissatisfied. Whether or not this merger happens depends on state education laws. In some states, such as Virginia, an incorporated city or county boundary serves as the school district. Thus the annexed area automatically becomes part of the city's school district. In Texas, and most other states, school districts are independent of local government. Therefore, annexed area residents can maintain their children in their former school districts, leading to racially (and economically) segregated schools within municipal boundaries.

A political problem is triggered by dissatisfaction among some urban core minorities based on the premise that their vote and potential political influence is being diluted as a result of annexing predominantly white areas. The effect of annexation on minority voting power creates an interesting legal, political and economic dilemma. Indeed, this issue has been the focal point of legal challenges which twice reached the U.S. Supreme Court (11).

The basis for the challenge to annexation has been that either its intent or result has led to a dilution of the black vote in cities where this group was close to achieving a voting majority. An examination of 24 rapidly growing cities and 19 cities with substantial declines in the 50,000 to 500,000 population category shows that cities in the declining group, none with substantial annexation, had a 45 percent increase in the percentage of blacks between 1960 and 1970. By contrast, those growing by annexation had no change in racial composition. This implies that incorporating predominantly white households into these jurisdictions offset the outmigration of white households from the urban core. Thus the effect of annexations regardless of motive for these actions was to maintain the racial balance (12).

Annexation is not the only factor accounting for changes in the composition of population, but it nevertheless remains an important element. Although the Supreme Court has found that racial balance is not a compelling argument to prevent annexation, the issue of trading off a potential change in political power with a change in economic viability remains (13).

A social issue related to annexation is that persons being annexed believe the process may accelerate growth, which will result in changing prevailing lifestyles. Areas considered pastoral by residents become congested, and the sense of privacy can be lost. Annexation, by developing the infrastructure and changing land use regulations, frequently tends to accelerate development. This process, while benefiting some members of the community—particularly those owning land or involved in the development process financially—adds to the concerns of those residing on the urban periphery because it alters the semirural environment. Typically, the newest arrivals to the area are most vociferous in opposing additional growth.

Fiscal Response to Growth

In-migrants typically have higher personal income, and thus pay more taxes per capita than the existing population. These households also tend to be young, more likely to have school age children, and demand more services than older community residents. Thus, one finds both revenues and expenditures rising in growing jurisdictions. One difficulty facing growing communities, as noted previously, is the need for additional capital investment. Several approaches are used to cope with the demand for more facilities and operating funds when rapid growth takes place within existing boundaries.

Shifting Costs to Developer and Consumer. Costs are shifted by a more frequent use of fees, land dedication requirements and other means which require that the developer provide the land and build part or all of the infrastructure, including water and sewer lines, streets, and in some instances, fire stations (14). The shift from present residents to those purchasing the property increases the cost of new housing. Since the value of the existing housing stock tends to reflect the cost of new units, this benefits present residents who own their homes.

Constraining Development. Artificial constraints on new construction, using various land use controls and other mechanisms, limits the quantity and increases the cost of new construction. Zoning and other restrictions tend to drive up the price of land and housing, with the same impact on community residents as noted in the previous paragraph.

Seeking Assistance from Higher Level of Government. Two recent bills provide for assistance to communities affected by rapid growth attributable to promoting "the national interest." The first entitles assistance to an area where a large military facility is under construction if an adverse fiscal impact can be demonstrated (15). The second, under amendments to the Coastal Zone Management Act, provides up to $1.2 billion in loans and grants to communities which can demonstrate an adverse fiscal and environmental impact as a result of offshore energy development (16). Pressure from growing communities resulted in a state takeover of school construction in the state of Maryland several years ago. Federal revenue sharing and other legislation provide federal assistance based either in part or fully on population. Thus, holding income and tax burden constant, the level of federal assistance expands with population.

Changing Existing Tax Structure. Growing communities frequently diversify their tax base from one almost totally dependent on the assessed value of property to one that adds other revenue sources such as sales and business tax to decrease the reliance on the property tax. An additional effect of this diversification is to shift some of the tax to nonresidents such as shoppers and commuters. The level of flexibility local governments have to restructure their tax base varies from state to state.

Fiscal Response to Decline

Cities in the 200 to 500 thousand population category which had substantial population decline in recent years continued to increase the number of municipal employees between 1970 and 1975. The only exception to this pattern was Rochester, New York, which had an absolute decline in the number of personnel between 1970 and 1975. The number of employees in several declining cities, however, fell between 1975 and 1976, reflecting the fiscal crisis.

Wage increases were more moderate between 1973 and 1975 than in earlier periods, indicating a response to budget constraints resulting from the downward movement of the economy (17). In addition, many cities stabilized the number of municipal employees. Local revenue declined, in absolute terms, between fiscal 1973 and 1975 in some cities. Thus, taxes collected by Newark declined from $120 million to $115 million, in Jersey City from $74 million to $69 million, and in Syracuse from $33 million to $28 million (18). These reductions were attributable almost exclusively to lower property tax receipts.

While these reductions were offset by more state and federal dollars, if inflation is taken into account, these cities had actually less to spend in 1975 than in the prior two years. One means utilized to overcome the fund shortage was short term borrowing. Newark increased its short term debt by $2 million, Jersey City by $15 million to $43 million in fiscal 1975, and Syracuse by $10 million to $78 million. The record is held by Hartford, which borrowed on a short term basis an additional $30 million, part of which repaid long term notes. The need for borrowing in Hartford is attributed to payroll expanding by $8 million during a one-year period while revenue from its own sources declined.

These examples illustrate fiscal conditions during 1975 in the more severely depressed cities—municipal payrolls continuing to increase while revenues from own sources were reduced or stable. The resulting deficit was offset, at least temporarily, by more federal and state funds, with the balance of the gap eliminated by short term borrowing. However, not all cities with declining population had similar conditions. Rochester increased its property tax collection by over 15 percent, and its overall debt increased by only 1 percent between 1974 and 1975.

It is evident from these data that the immediate response of declining cities, borrowing and asking for more outside assistance, is only a stop-gap measure. In the absence of holding the line on municipal payrolls, their credit, failing direct state or federal intervention, will be exhausted during the next economic decline. An alternative, more fiscally sound, but difficult to implement approach, is to improve the fiscal structure of these cities by inducing business and middle income households to remain and expand, increasing the tax base.

Inducements to Business

Smaller cities faced with a decline in population and commercial activity have attempted several approaches to reverse the flow to outer areas. The most common approach is to conclude that the urban core lacks major attractions to bring families and business firms back. Thus, the construction of sports arenas, convention centers and similar public facilities. This is usually combined with the construction of public parking garages to facilitate more cars.

A second approach is to revitalize the urban core by restoring some of its buildings to their pre-twentieth century appearance, or by converting older structures, such as warehouses, into the type of residential units found attractive by families willing to move back to the urban core. Savannah, Georgia, and Charleston, South Carolina, are among cities finding this an attractive approach. The construction of subsidized residential units aimed at more affluent households was attempted in Newark, New Jersey and several other cities.

The results appear mixed. While Savannah appears to show signs of success, Newark's attempts failed, because other amenities were not provided. Tax abatement is a frequently used mechanism to encourage new development in older cities. Since property tax rates in central cities are in almost all instances higher than in adjacent suburbs, lowering or eliminating taxes for a given time period, it is thought, will encourage central city development which otherwise would not take place.

While numerous cities with declining population have attempted this fiscal device to entice commercial development, only limited success is evident. Several factors reduce the effectiveness of this approach. Granting tax abatement erodes the tax base further; in some instances, development would have taken place even in the absence of this inducement. If the business climate is poor, tax abatement is an insufficient incentive to capital investment. Tax increment financing is a device gaining favor in many communities, including Minneapolis. In this city, older buildings are purchased, razed and land cleared, with the operation financed by bonds which are anticipated to be repaid from property taxes accruing from privately constructed commercial development on sites cleared.

Tax increment financing has two basic weaknesses: anticipated development may not take place, which means that the city would have to repay its debt without offsetting revenue. If development indeed takes place, it does not add to the tax rolls. In fact, to the extent that retail stores or office space shifts its location from older structures within the city, there are no long term gains and possible revenue losses.

An alternative, high risk approach is to provide low interest loans backed by the local government or a special authority to business firms willing to expand their inner city facilities. Chester, Pennsylvania, one of the more depressed cities, is planning to construct and rebuild, with its own capital, retail facilities in its CBD, and lease these facilities to private business.

A fundamental weakness with most approaches to offset decline is that they focus only on retaining business firms, particularly commercial facilities in the inner city. However, these facilities to be economically viable, require a population base nearby. More important in the long run is the ability to retain middle income families, white and black, in the urban core. The level of retail activity and use of services is linked directly to disposable personal income. In most instances it is unrealistic to expect the CBD to be able to compete with new shopping centers on the urban periphery for suburban consumers. Therefore, it has to depend on its own population base. If this base continues to erode, loans and tax abatement will have little effect.

For example, Lancaster, Pennsylvania several years ago induced a large and reputable department store to locate in a redeveloped area of its business center. Although the building was new, incorporating the latest technological and marketing know-how, the department store closed its doors within two years, unable to compete with a newly opened regional shopping center located about eight miles from the city center. Similar examples of failure attributable to unrealistic expectations can be found in all regions of the nation.

To retain middle income households requires, at a minimum, that public schools provide a reasonable education and that crime be perceived to be minimal near residential and shopping areas. In both cases, it is perception, rather than reality, that matters. Chester will not be able to lease its space unless consumers feel comfortable to walk its streets in the evenings. Parents will not remain in Newark, Camden, or other older cities unless their children feel safe and comfortable in central city schools. While these are basic requirements, it is extremely difficult to improve these services, since they require dealing with the roots of the problem—particularly poverty, discrimination, and unemployment. Because urban renewal and tax abatement do not deal with these underlying issues, they are unlikely to meet their objective.

A totally different strategy is to accept the premise that some decline will take place due to market conditions and other factors which are beyond the control of a city. Since these conditions more than offset policies the city may adopt, providing inducements to business paid by local taxpayers is unlikely to be cost effective, as it will benefit the few at the expense of the many. The approach, then, is to provide an environment likely to keep much of what is already there, and reduce municipal outlays to a point where tax increases which can trigger further movement are unnecessary.

Such a strategy is somewhat risky, since inevitably some services will need to be cut back. If social services are retrenched, the poor will bear the burden; if services utilized by business or the more affluent are reduced, they may relocate elsewhere, reducing even further the ability of government to provide services. Municipal workers are typically unwilling to renegotiate these contracts. Nevertheless, this appears to be a more reasonable approach for many communities than borrowing more to improve the infrastructure with little likelihood of success.

This is not to argue that decline is inevitable in every older city, or that measures to improve facilities should not be undertaken. It does suggest, however, that the bricks and mortar approach, without taking into account serious social issues, may not accomplish much.

Unfortunately, it is easier to cope with growth, when demand exceeds supply, than decline. Therefore, the challenge we face is to develop strategies, particularly at the state and federal level, which will limit the adverse effects of decline without restricting the freedom to move.

FINDINGS

Several interesting findings emerge from the preceding analysis.

1. The fiscal situation in smaller cities with declining population is typically not as severe as in the very large declining cities, because per capita outlays for services, as a result of somewhat lower municipal wages and fewer public employees, are lower while personal income is stable within a wide range of city size.

2. From a fiscal perspective, there are no significant differences

between cities within the range of 100,000 to 500,000 residents. Below this population level, the fiscal posture tends to improve.

3. Smaller aging cities within the SMSAs of a large declining central city, such as Newark, Camden, and East St. Louis, have a particularly serious problem. These cities have a limited commercial base, and their population tends to be homogeneous—and poor. In the absence of large scale outside assistance, these cities cannot cope with decline.

4. As was found to be the case with the largest cities, practically all smaller cities gaining population and showing above average income gains have annexed adjoining areas, while declining cities have fixed boundaries.

5. As a result of annexation and regional location, growing cities have densities two or three times lower than those with rapidly declining population. Resulting differences in housing patterns and distribution of economic activity tend to result in a more stable fiscal situation than in cities with fixed boundaries.

6. With relatively few exceptions, whether a city is growing or not depends on its regional location. However, a considerable number of larger, older southern and western cities have levels of out-migration comparable to their northern counterparts. Thus, while location affects the probability of growth, age remains a more dominant factor.

7. Most approaches to cope with decline appear to have met only limited success. While growth controls have an uneven record, it is more realistic to expect a city, with its own resources, to minimize the adverse effects of rapid growth than to anticipate that a declining city will be able to cope with adverse economic consequences of decline.

8. The fiscal ability of local government to generate the necessary capital to encourage private employment or improve social conditions is limited. Therefore, if a national policy to stabilize the decline of older cities is formulated, substantial federal and state assistance will be necessary.

Part Five

Federal Impact on Cities

Chapter Nine

Cities: Their Increasing Dependence on State and Federal Aid

John Shannon and John Ross

One of the few facts that may be stated with certainty about our system of intergovernmental aid is that such aid is growing at a phenomenal rate. Both large and small cities are becoming increasingly dependent on financial aid from states and from the federal government.

From 1962 to 1975 federal aid to state and local governments increased by 494.9 percent, from about $7.9 billion to about $47 billion per year. It grew at an average annual rate of 14.6 percent per year. Over the same period, aid to local jurisdictions increased by 434.5 percent, from about $11.6 billion to about $62.0 billion, for an average annual rate of growth of 13.8 percent per year. Finally, aid to municipalities increased from $2.5 billion in 1962 to $19.6 billion in 1975. It increased by 684.0 percent, growing at an average annual rate of 17.1 percent per year.

Masked by this phenomenal growth in intergovernmental aid, a quiet revolution has occurred in municipal finance. Cities both large and small have joined the ranks of the financially dependent. Measuring dependency as the ratio of outside aid to own source revenues, cities as a class in 1962 were the least dependent unit of state-local general purpose government. By 1975, however, they were more than twice as dependent as the states on outside monies, had easily surpassed the dependency of townships, and were rapidly approaching the dependency of counties.

The authors wish to express their appreciation for substantial assistance to Gordon Folkman and Richard Reeder of the ACIR staff. The opinions expressed in the paper are those of the authors and do not necessarily reflect the views of the Advisory Commission on Intergovernmental Relations.

In the aggregate, over the thirteen-year period, their growth in dependency was more than three times as fast as counties. If the present rates of growth continue, cities in the not-too-distant future will achieve the dubious honor of being the unit of general purpose government with least direct control over its revenue sources.

A second unheralded aspect of this revolution is the fact that much of this increase in municipal dependency on outside monies is the result of increases in direct federal aid to cities. Over the past thirteen years such dependency has grown more than twice as fast as municipal dependency on state aid. When classed by population size, some large cities now receive more money in direct federal aid per dollar of own source revenue than does the average state. These increases in outside aid have already made the concept of the financially independent city a thing of the past and, if present trends continued, will make the city a financial arm of the federal rather than state governments.

While the blessings of increased aid to municipalities have been exalted by all those concerned with urban problems, the implications of increased dependency on outside monies—particularly the increased dependency on federal dollars—has received much less attention. The problems potentially associated with loss of municipal financial control, difficulties in reducing expenditures during times of recession, and more generally the effects of increased categorical aid have not been widely debated.

The purpose of this chapter is to examine the increase in municipal dependency and to discuss the implications of these changes for our system of fiscal federalism. The chapter is divided into two distinct parts. The first part simply describes the changes that have occurred over the last thirteen years, while the second part raises some of the issues and discusses some of the alternative directions available to solve the municipal financial dilemma.

MUNICIPAL DEPENDENCY AND ITS GROWTH WITHIN THE STATE-LOCAL FISCAL SYSTEM

In order to understand the magnitude and implications of increased municipal dependency, the position of cities within the intergovernmental fiscal system should first be examined.

Table 9-1 shows per capita expenditures, per capita aid, and the ratio of aid to own source revenue (dependency rates) for the states, all local units, and general purpose units of local governments. As would be expected, on a per capita basis cities outspent all other local government units and received more in aid than any other

Table 9-1. Per Capita Expenditures, Per Capita Aid, and Dependency by Jurisdictional Type; 1962, 1975, and Growth 1962-75

	Per Capita Expenditure* 1962	Per Capita Expenditure* 1975	Average Annual Rate of Growth in Per Capita Expenditure	Per Capita Aid 1962	Per Capita Aid 1975	Average Annual Rate of Growth in Per Capita Aid	Aid ÷ Own Source Revenues 1962	Aid ÷ Own Source Revenues 1975	Average Annual Rate of Growth of Dependence
State	$113.60	$424.75	10.6%	$41.70	$186.29	12.1%	31.6%	39.1%	1.6%
All Local	222.10	704.30	9.2	64.90	304.90	12.6	43.6	73.4	4.1
By Type of Government									
County	51.10	171.99	9.8	20.70	82.12	11.1	62.9	81.4	2.0
Municipality	113.56	358.65	9.2	22.66	144.76	15.3	25.8	65.1	7.3
Municipality aid less State education and welfare aid	—	—	—	—	—	—	15.3	44.8	8.5
Township	39.80	107.00	7.9	9.20	35.90	11.0	29.0	42.0	2.8

*Population figures are for 1960 and 1970.

Source: ACIR staff computations based on data from U.S. Department of Commerce, Bureau of the Census, *Census of Governments*, Vol. IV, 1962 and U.S. Department of Commerce, Bureau of the Census, *Governmental Finances in 1974-75*, various tables.

general purpose unit of local government in 1975. They were second to counties (and at that only slightly) in growth of per capita spending from 1962 to 1975, and first in growth of per capita aid, averaging an annual rate of growth of more than 15 percent per year.

Columns 7, 8, and 9 of Table 9-1 show the dependency rates of the various units of state-local general purpose government. Cities were the least dependent form of local government in 1962, receiving only about $0.26 in outside monies for every $1.00 of own source revenue. In the aggregate they were even less dependent than the states. By 1975 cities were receiving $0.65 for every $1.00 of own source revenue. Their dependency on outside aid increased at an average annual rate of 7.3 percent per year—well above the rate of increase of counties, townships, or the states. They now surpass the states in terms of dependency on outside aid.

If state educational and welfare aid to cities is excluded, the dependency rate drops to only 44.8 percent in 1975, but the growth rate for the thirteen-year period increased to 8.5 percent per year. Thus the rapid growth in dependency cannot be attributed primarily to increases in outside help in these two functional areas.

Table 9-2 breaks down the dependency rates by state aid and direct federal aid for general purpose units of local government.[a] In 1962 cities received only about $0.20 for every dollar of own source revenue in state aid as compared to counties, which were receiving more than $0.59, and townships, which were receiving $0.26. In 1975, cities were receiving about $0.43 for every dollar of own source revenue.

Municipalities grew in dependency on state aid at an average annual rate of 6.4 percent per year. At the same time their dependency on direct federal aid increased from about $0.05 in 1962 to $0.19 in 1975 for every dollar of own source revenue. Dependency on direct federal monies increased at an average annual rate of 10.4 percent per year.

Four general observations may be drawn from these two tables. First, municipal dependency on outside monies has more than doubled since 1962. Second, municipal dependency is growing at a faster rate than the dependency of the states, counties, or townships. Third, while the cities in the aggregate are more heavily dependent on state aid than on federal aid, their dependency on federal aid is growing almost twice as fast as their dependency on state aid.

---

[a]In this discussion "state" aid includes federal aid which is passed through the state to local governments. The reason for calculating dependency in this way is that except for years in which the census of government is taken it is impossible to separate direct state aid from federal pass-through money.

Table 9-2. General Purpose Local Government Dependency on State and Federal Aid—1962, 1975, and Growth 1962-1975

	State Aid ÷ Own Source Revenue 1962	State Aid ÷ Own Source Revenue 1975	Growth in State Aid ÷ Own Source Revenue 1962-1975	Federal Aid ÷ Own Source Revenue 1962	Federal Aid ÷ Own Source Revenue 1975	Growth in Federal Aid ÷ Own Source Revenue 1962-1975
All local governments	40.7%	60.5%	3.1%	2.9%	12.9%	12.1%
Counties	59.2	65.2	.7	1.1	13.1	21.8
Municipalities	20.5	43.2	6.4	5.3	19.3	10.4
Townships	26.6	30.6	1.1	1.03	9.1	18.2

Source: ACIR staff computations based on data from U.S. Department of Commerce, Bureau of the Census, *Census of Governments*, Vol. IV, 1962 and U.S. Department of Commerce, Bureau of the Census, *Governmental Finances in 1974-75*, various tables.

Finally, counties have experienced a very rapid increase in direct federal aid dependency but very little increase in state aid support.

MUNICIPAL DEPENDENCY AND ITS GROWTH BY CITY SIZE CLASS

As indicated by Table 9-3, per capita expenditures, per capita aid, and dependency rates vary appreciably among municipalities when grouped by population size. Cities of over one million not only had the greatest per capita expenditures and aid in 1975, but also showed the highest rates of growth in both categories from 1962 to 1975.

Columns 7, 8, and 9 of Table 9-3 show municipal dependency in 1962 and 1975 as well as the growth in dependency from 1962 to 1975. In 1975, cities of over one million received more than $0.90 in aid for every $1.00 of own source revenue. From 1962 to 1975 they grew in dependency at an average annual rate of about 9.25 percent per year. As indicated by the data, the rapid increase in dependency has also been experienced by small and medium-size cities.

Breaking down municipal dependency into its state and federal components, as is done in Table 9-4, provides an indication of where the growth in dependency has occurred. In 1975, all city size classes, including smaller cities, were more dependent on state aid than on federal aid. However, for all city size classes the growth in federal dependency has been much more rapid than the growth in state dependency. For example, for cities over one million, the ratio of municipal dependency on federal aid to municipal dependency on state aid was about 11 percent in 1962. By 1975 that ratio had increased to 19 percent.

The dependence of large cities on federal assistance has been much maligned in recent years. An objective picture, however, would show that this dependency is not an exclusive sin of large cities. While they might get more dollars, the growth in dependency rates is almost as large among small cities. As a matter of fact, the growth of dependency between 1962-1975 of federal aid to small cities of nearly 12 percent was almost as large as among cities over one million and more than all other city size classes. (For a graphic comparison, see Figure 9-1.) Furthermore, small cities generally have a larger percentage of their revenues coming from the federal government ($0.16 to $0.25 of each dollar of own source revenue).

Much of this increase in dependency on federal aid is a result of general revenue sharing. As shown in Table 9-5, for all municipalities GRS dollars accounted for about 38 percent of federal aid to cities in

Table 9-3. Per Capita Expenditure, Per Capita Aid, and Dependency, by City Population Size Class—1962, 1975, and Growth, 1962-75

City Size	Per Capita Expenditures 1962	Per Capita Expenditures 1975	Annual Average Rate of Growth in Per Capita Expenditures 1962-75	Per Capita Aid 1962	Per Capita Aid 1975	Annual Average Rate of Growth in Per Capita Aid 1962-75	Aid ÷ Own Source Revenue 1962	Aid ÷ Own Source Revenue 1975	Annual Average Rate of Growth in Dependency 1962-75	Number of Cities 1962	Number of Cities 1975
All municipalities	$113.56	$358.65	9.20%	$22.66	$144.76	15.27%	25.85%	65.1%	7.32%	—	—
1,000,000+	219.11	844.44	10.89	49.50	437.83	18.22	28.50	90.50	9.25	5	6
500,000-999,999	166.49	531.95	9.30	39.53	216.68	13.94	32.23	71.50	6.25	17	20
300,000-499,999	124.06	413.96	9.65	25.11	156.07	15.07	27.08	60.76	6.37	21	20
200,000-299,999	126.87	395.31	9.05	22.59	153.57	15.83	23.53	64.22	6.35	19	17
100,000-199,999	122.73	340.66	8.13	23.24	118.60	13.35	24.43	54.56	7.98	68	95
50,000-99,999	111.25	295.62	7.75	19.11	90.76	12.68	22.21	46.55	5.80	180	229
Less than 50,000	63.16	193.55	8.98	10.44	62.84	14.75	21.23	47.07	6.24	17,690	18,130

Source: ACIR Staff computations based on data from U.S. Department of Commerce, Bureau of the Census, *Compendium of City Government Finances in 1962* and U.S. Department of Commerce, Bureau of the Census, *Compendium of City Government Finances in 1975*, various tables.

Table 9-4. Municipal Dependency on State and Federal Aid 1962, 1975, and Growth 1962-75 by City Size Class

City Size	State Aid ÷ Own Source Revenue 1962	State Aid ÷ Own Source Revenue 1975	Annual Average Rate of Growth in Dependency on State Aid 1962-75	Federal Aid ÷ Own Source Revenue 1962	Federal Aid ÷ Own Source Revenue 1975	Annual Average Rate of Growth in Dependency on Federal Aid 1962-75
All municipalities	20.5%	43.2%	5.9%	5.3%	19.4%	10.4%
1,000,000+	25.6	74.9	8.5	2.9	14.5	13.2
500,000-999,999	22.3	34.7	3.4	9.9	33.3	9.6
300,000-499,999	16.8	31.7	5.0	10.3	25.2	7.1
200,000-299,999	16.4	34.1	5.8	7.1	25.5	9.7
100,000-199,999	17.9	31.5	4.4	6.6	19.7	8.7
50,000-99,999	18.1	27.7	3.3	4.1	17.2	11.6
Less than 50,000	17.3	27.8	3.7	3.9	16.4	11.7

Source: ACIR staff computations based on data from U.S. Department of Commerce, Bureau of the Census, *Compendium of City Government Finances in 1962* and U.S. Department of Commerce, Bureau of the Census, *Compendium of City Government Finances in 1975*, various tables.

1975, and ranged from 53 percent for municipalities of less than 50,000 people to about 21 percent of all federal aid for those cities between 500,000 and 999,999.

If CETA funds and Community Development Block Grants are also included, almost half the total direct federal aid to cities is accounted for. Table 9-5 also shows that GRS is much more important in relative terms to small cities. GRS amounts to approximately 8 to 9 percent of the revenues generated by these cities from their own source, compared to 5.5 percent for cities over one million or more.

MUNICIPAL DEPENDENCY AND ITS GROWTH AMONG THE VARIOUS STATES

Recognizing that municipalities in the various states have different functional responsibilities, it is still useful to examine the variation in

Cities: Their Increasing Dependence on State & Federal Aid 197

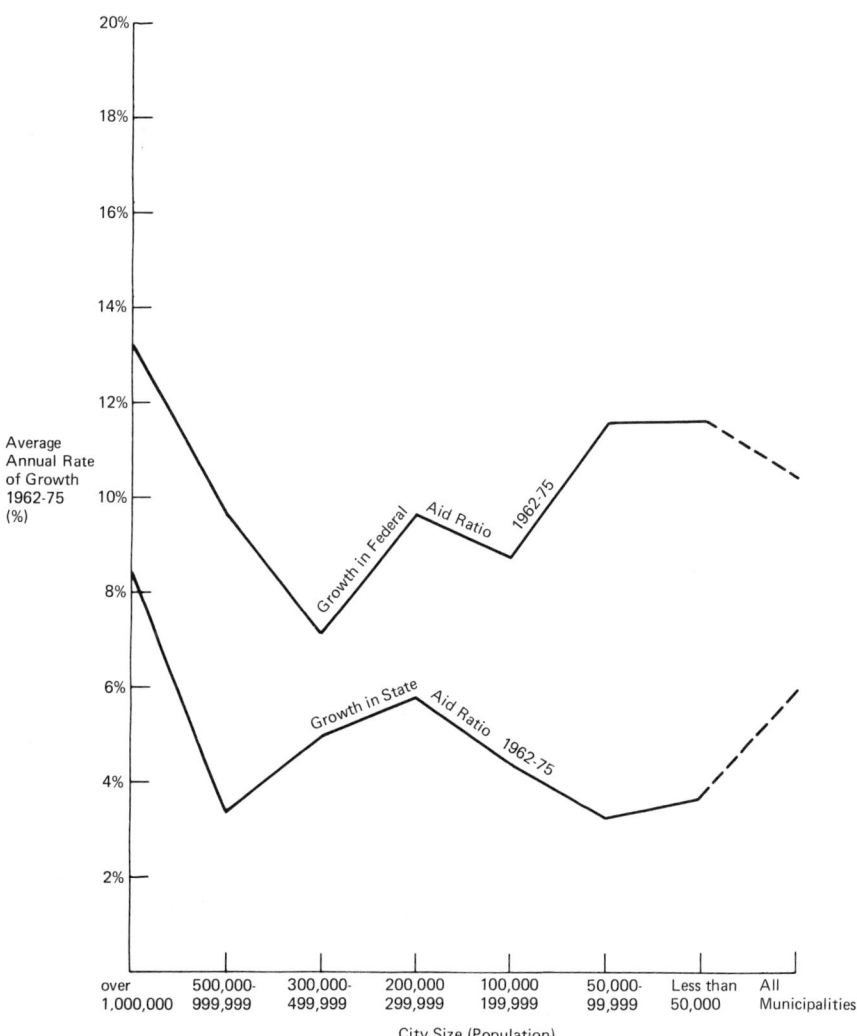

Source: ACIR staff computations.
Figure 9-1. Growth in Dependency by City Size Class, 1962-1975.

Table 9-5. Municipal Dependency, by Size Class, on General Revenue Sharing, 1975

City Size	GRS ÷ Total Aid 1975	GRS ÷ Federal Aid 1975	GRS ÷ Own Source Revenue 1975
All municipalities	11.2%	37.8%	7.3%
1,000,000+	6.0	37.6	5.5
500,000-999,999	9.9	21.6	7.0
300,000-499,999	12.7	30.6	7.7
200,000-299,999	12.9	32.5	8.3
100,000-199,999	14.5	40.4	7.9
50,000-99,999	16.2	43.9	7.5
Less than 50,000	18.7	53.9	8.8

Source: ACIR staff compilation from data in U.S. Department of Commerce, Bureau of the Census, *Compendium of City Government Finances in 1975*, various tables.

municipal dependency rates across states. Table 9-6 shows the municipal dependency rates by state for 1975 for state and federal aid, state aid, and federal aid, while Table 9-7 shows the growth in municipal dependency for these categories.

As would be expected, the variation is large. Municipal dependency on state and federal aid in 1975 ranged from 22.3 percent in Texas to 156.2 percent in Maryland, while the range in growth rates was from —4.6 percent per year in Arkansas to 33.4 percent per year in Florida. In 18 states, municipalities now receive more direct aid from the federal government than they do from their states. Also, as would be expected, the variation in state aid to municipalities is greater than the variation in federal aid to municipalities across the states.

The most interesting aspect of these tables is the relationship of dependency on state aid to the dependency on federal aid, both in 1975, and in growth from 1962 to 1975. If federal aid and state aid to municipalities are complementary, one would expect a strong positive correlation; if they are substitutes, one would expect a strong negative correlation.

Table 9-8 shows the correlation matrix between levels of depen-

Table 9-6. Municipal Dependency on State and Federal Aid, by State, 1975

State	State and Federal Aid ÷ Own Source Revenues			State Aid ÷ Own Source Revenues			Federal Aid ÷ Own Source Revenues		
	Dependency	Rank	Index	Dependency	Rank	Index	Dependency	Rank	Index
Alabama**	26.3%	50	53	6.9%	47	26	19.3%	36	81
Alaska	59.7	15	121	47.1	9	179	12.6	48	51
Arizona	68.2	11	138	40.1	11	152	28.1	16	119
Arkansas	57.5	17	116	28.9	23	110	28.6	13	121
California	39.8	37	80	26.8	25	102	13.0	46	55
Colorado**	36.4	41	74	17.1	36	65	19.4	34	82
Connecticut	48.0	29	97	33.8	18	129	14.2	45	60
Delaware	68.7	10	139	37.2	14	141	31.5	9	133
Dist. of Col.	89.7	6	181	—	—	—	89.7	1	378
Florida	40.1	36	81	24.4	28	93	15.6	40	66
Georgia**	32.4	46	65	8.7	44	33	23.7*	26	100*
Hawaii**	33.5	45	68	7.5	45	29	26.0	21	110
Idaho	59.9	14	121	25.1	27	95	34.9	7	147
Illinois	37.2	40	75	18.9	35	72	18.3	38	77
Indiana	67.9	12	137	41.0	10	156	26.8	20	113
Iowa	58.9	16	119	30.3	21	115	28.6	13	121
Kansas**	35.3	42	71	14.3	40	54	21.0	27	89
Kentucky**	34.3	44	69	5.0	48	19	29.3	12	124
Louisiana*	49.0	22	99	19.4	34	74	29.6	11	125
Maine	44.9	33	91	29.5	22	112	15.5	42	65
Maryland	156.2	1	316	127.5	1	485	28.7	13	121
Massachusetts	47.5	31	96	34.5	16	131	12.9	47	54
Michigan	50.9	22	103	27.0	24	103	23.9	25	101

Table 9-6. Municipal Dependency on State and Federal Aid, by State, 1975 (cont.)

State	State and Federal Aid ÷ Own Source Revenues			State Aid ÷ Own Source Revenues			Federal Aid ÷ Own Source Revenues		
	Dependency	Rank	Index	Dependency	Rank	Index	Dependency	Rank	Index
Minnesota	50.8	23	103	35.6	15	135	15.2	43	64
Mississippi	88.6	7	179	52.4	7	199	36.2	6	153
Missouri**	29.2	48	59	9.7	43	37	19.5	34	82
Montana**	42.2	34	85	14.8	39	56	27.5	17	116
Nebraska	46.3	32	94	26.3*	26	100*	20.1	32	85
Nevada	53.8	19	109	32.8	19	125	21.0	27	89
New Hampshire**	50.8	23	103	23.4	30	89	27.3	18	115
New Jersey	47.9	30	97	39.7	12	151	8.2	51	35
New Mexico	150.7	2	304	91.1	3	346	59.5	2	251
New York	105.5	4	213	93.3	2	355	12.1	49	51
North Carolina**	64.9	13	131	30.9	20	117	34.0	8	143
North Dakota	39.6	38	80	24.1	29	92	15.6	40	66
Ohio	41.3	35	83	20.6	32	78	20.7	31	87
Oklahoma**	37.7	39	76	10.4	41	40	27.3	18	115
Oregon**	50.0	25	101	19.6	33	75	30.4	10	128
Pennsylvania	48.1	28	97	22.7	31	86	25.4	23	107
Rhode Island	53.2	21	107	38.1	13	145	15.1	44	64
South Carolina**	54.1	18	109	17.1	36	65	37.0	5	156
South Dakota**	53.5	20	108	10.1	42	38	43.4	3	183
Tennessee	71.7	9	145	50.6	8	192	21.1	27	89
Texas**	22.3	51	45	2.2	49	8	20.1	32	85
Utah**	34.7	43	70	15.6	38	59	19.0	37	80

Cities: Their Increasing Dependence on State & Federal Aid 201

Table 9-6. Municipal Dependency on State and Federal Aid, by State, 1975 (cont.)

Vermont**	31.2	47	63	7.0	46	27	24.1	24	102
Virginia	78.1	8	158	57.1	6	217	21.0	27	89
Washington	49.5*	26	100*	33.1	17	126	16.3	39	69
West Virginia	27.7	49	56	2.2	49	8	25.5	22	108
Wisconsin	90.2	5	182	78.8	4	300	11.4	50	48
Wyoming	106.2	3	215	68.1	5	259	38.1	4	161

*Median State.
**Municipalities receive more aid from the Federal Government than they do from their State governments.

Source: ACIR staff compilations based on data from U.S. Department of Commerce, Bureau of the Census, *Census of Governments*, Vol. IV, 1962 and U.S. Department of Commerce, Bureau of the Census, *Governmental Finances in 1974-75*, various tables.

Table 9-7. Growth in Municipal Dependency on State and Federal Aid, by State, 1962-1975

State	State and Federal Aid ÷ Own Source Revenues			State Aid ÷ Own Source Revenues			Federal Aid ÷ Own Source Revenues		
	Dependency	Rank	Index	Dependency	Rank	Index	Dependency	Rank	Index
Alabama	10.7%	20	115	2.8%	31	70	18.5%	23	108
Alaska	9.3*	26	100*	8.2	16	205	15.1	37	88
Arizona	5.4	40	58	2.0	35	50	17.2*	26	100*
Arkansas	-4.6	51	49	-0.5	44	-13	28.6	7	166
California	6.7	32	72	4.4	25	110	15.8	34	172
Colorado	-0.1	49	-1	-4.8	48	-120	11.9	45	69
Connecticut	6.2	35	67	6.1	21	153	6.5	50	38
Delaware	2.7	46	29	-2.0	46	-50	40.2	1	234
Dist. of Col.	7.3	29	78	—	—	—	7.3	48	42
Florida	33.4	1	359	31.4	1	785	37.6	3	219
Georgia	18.7	4	201	12.7	10	318	22.8	14	133
Hawaii	-1.6	50	-17	-9.3	50	-233	4.6	51	27
Idaho	12.4	15	133	7.0	19	175	21.7	16	126
Illinois	5.9	37	63	1.7	36	43	16.6	29	97
Indiana	9.3	25	100	6.7	20	168	16.2	31	94
Iowa	6.5	33	70	2.5	33	63	16.5	30	96
Kansas	6.5	35	70	1.4	38	35	14.7	40	85
Kentucky	10.0	22	108	11.8	11	295	9.7	47	56
Louisiana	7.2	30	77	0.4	39	10	27.3	10	159
Maine	10.8	18	116	8.3	15	208	20.0	20	116
Maryland	6.2	34	148	5.5	23	138	10.2	46	59
Massachusetts	2.0	48	22	-0.2	43	-5	20.4	18	119
Michigan	3.9	44	42	0.0	41	0	15.0	39	87

Table 9-7. Growth in Municipal Dependency on State and Federal Aid, by State, 1962-1975 (cont.)

State									
Minnesota	11.2	17	120	8.6	13	215	28.2	8	164
Mississippi	18.2	5	196	16.3	4	408	22.0	15	128
Missouri	15.3	9	165	7.8	17	390	26.9	12	156
Montana	14.2	13	153	14.4	6	205	14.1	41	82
Nebraska	14.8	10	159	13.0	9	325	17.7	25	103
Nevada	18.0	6	194	20.6	3	515	15.1	37	88
New Hampshire	15.4	8	166	13.7	7	343	17.2	26	100
New Jersey	14.6	11	157	13.3	8	332	28.2	8	164
New Mexico	23.5	2	253	21.7	2	395	27.1	11	158
New York	10.0	22	108	9.4	12	235	16.9	28	92
North Carolina	10.1	21	109	5.9	22	148	18.1	24	105
North Dakota	14.3	12	154	16.1	5	403	12.2	44	71
Ohio	3.7	45	40	−0.1	42	−3	12.3	43	72
Oklahoma	5.6	38	60	−1.8	45	−45	13.2	42	77
Oregon	8.7	27	94	2.6	32	65	19.6	21	114
Pennsylvania	10.8	18	116	7.5	18	188	15.8	34	92
Rhode Island	5.6	38	60	3.7	28	93	15.3	36	89
South Carolina	13.8	14	148	4.9	24	123	32.2	5	187
South Dakota	16.7	7	180	3.6	29	90	35.9	4	209
Tennessee	2.4	47	26	0.1	40	3	16.1	32	94
Texas	9.8	24	105	−6.1	49	−153	20.9	17	122
Utah	7.9	28	85	3.4	30	85	16.0	33	93
Vermont	7.2	30	77	−2.9	47	−73	20.2	19	117
Virginia	4.7	43	51	4.0*	26	100*	6.8	49	40
Washington	5.0	42	54	2.4	34	60	18.6	22	108

Table 9-7. Growth in Municipal Dependency on State and Federal Aid, by State, 1962-1975 (cont.)

State	State and Federal Aid ÷ Own Source Revenues			State Aid ÷ Own Source Revenues			Federal Aid ÷ Own Source Revenue		
	Dependency	Rank	Index	Dependency	Rank	Index	Dependency	Rank	Index
West Virginia	19.9	3	214	1.7	36	43	29.7	6	173
Wisconsin	5.1	41	55	4.1	27	103	24.7	13	144
Wyoming	12.1	16	130	8.5	14	213	37.9	2	220

*Median State

Source: ACIR staff compilations.

Table 9-8. The Correlation of Municipal Dependency on State Aid with Municipal Dependency on Federal Aid

	\multicolumn{6}{c}{Correlation Matrix I (Levels 1962 and 1975)}					
	1.	2.	3.	4.	5.	6.
1.	1.00	.65	−.06	−.14	.30	.17
2.		1	−.18	−.06	.05	.42
3.			1.00	.62	.94	.47
4.				1.00	.54	.88
5.					1.00	.51
6.						1.00

	Correlation Matrix II Average Annual Growth Rates 1962-1975		
	7.	8.	9.
7.	1.00	.23	.48
8.		1.00	.84
9.			1.00

Definitions
1. Federal Aid ÷ Own Source Revenue – 1962
2. Federal Aid ÷ Own Source Revenue – 1975
3. State Aid ÷ Own Source Revenue – 1962
4. State Aid ÷ Own Source revenue – 1975
5. Total Aid ÷ Own Source Revenue – 1962
6. Total Aid ÷ Own Source Revenue – 1975
7. Growth in Dependency on Federal Aid – 1962-75
8. Growth in Dependency on State Aid – 1962-75
9. Growth in Dependency on Total Aid – 1962-75

Source: ACIR staff compilations.

dency in 1962 and 1975 and the correlation matrix for growth in municipal dependency over the thirteen-year period. What it shows is that there is basically no statistical relation between municipal dependency on state aid in 1962 and federal aid in 1962; no statistical relationship between municipal dependency on state aid in 1975 and dependency on federal aid in 1975; and little statistical relationship between the growth in municipal dependency on state aid and the growth in municipal dependency on federal aid from 1962 to 1975 across the states. Although unexpected, such a result may be explained by contending that these two types of aid have very different purposes and, therefore, respond to very different factors.

Given a lack of a statistical relationship between municipal dependency on state and federal aid across states, one may well question whether or not the federal aid is going to these cities most in need of outside funds. Richard P. Nathan and Charles Adams recently developed an index of central city hardship (1). If federal aid is going to those central cities most in need of such assistance, one would expect a high positive correlation between the Nathan-Adams index and municipal dependency on federal aid.

Table 9-9 shows the municipal hardship index, dependency on federal aid, and dependency on General Revenue Sharing by city for 1975, while Table 9-10 shows the simple correlation between these factors. Interestingly there is almost no statistical correlation between these factors. While the evidence presented in Tables 9-8 and 9-10 does not prove that federal aid is incorrectly targeted, it does at least lead one to question the ability of the federal government to provide funds to those cities most in need of aid.

POLICY IMPLICATIONS

The above discussion leaves no doubt that all municipalities—even small cities—are becoming increasingly dependent on outside funds to finance locally provided services. In addition, the federal government is becoming more important as a direct provider of that aid. These two rather straightforward findings have a number of implications with very serious policy ramifications.

First, the increase in dependency particularly when that increase is a result of increasing categorical aid causes a progressive reduction in municipal control over both revenue and expenditures.

Second, the increased dependency on direct federal aid increases uncertainty over funding and makes municipalities increasingly vulnerable to appropriation, regulation, and administrative decisions made in Washington and over which these municipalities have little control.

The growing dependency of municipalities on outside aid can be traced in no small measure to the inadequacy of the property tax. Heavy reliance on the property tax creates real problems, because most of the growth in the property tax base comes in the form of unrealized capital gains that bear no necessary relationship either to taxpayer cash flows or to the expenditure requirements of municipalities in a balkanized metropolitan area.

Both a "regionalization" role and a stronger state fiscal role have been suggested at various times as one way of reducing municipal

Table 9-9. Municipal Hardship Index, Dependency on Federal Aid, and Dependency on General Revenue Sharing, 1975

	Hardship Index	Federal	GRS
Newark	85.5	12.30	7.51
St. Louis	75.5	17.42	8.30
New Orleans	72.6	33.89	13.51
Gary	70.0	80.43	16.57
Miami	62.5	12.66	12.66
Birmingham	61.8	25.99	10.98
Youngstown	60.3	31.06	11.91
Baltimore	60.0	30.66	7.57
Cleveland	59.6	32.27	7.89
Detroit	58.6	42.07	10.90
Buffalo	57.2	26.18	6.19
Jersey City	56.6	14.48	6.55
Hartford	56.2	14.33	4.88
Louisville	55.9	38.86	11.23
Cincinnati	53.5	26.02	4.20
Providence	52.7	13.76	9.01
Springfield, Mass.	52.0	36.50	6.76
Tampa	50.9	38.34	10.91
Sacramento	50.4	16.88	6.13
Grand Rapids	50.3	55.75	12.38
Atlanta	50.1	27.09	5.10
Philadelphia	50.0	21.58	8.56
Chicago	49.3	22.39	9.46
Pittsburgh	47.1	32.54	18.31
Dayton	46.9	51.57	9.24
Rochester	46.3	8.41	3.93
Richmond	46.2	22.49	5.06
Boston	45.8	16.24	5.16
New York	45.3	10.11	4.28
Akron	43.4	23.27	7.36
Norfolk	43.4	29.92	7.87
Ft. Worth	42.8	15.83	8.14
Milwaukee	42.2	27.29	12.10
San Jose	41.9	13.74	5.54
Toledo	41.4	29.33	7.88
Syracuse	40.8	43.50	6.62
Indianapolis	40.3	26.70	8.54
Phoenix	40.1	34.91	9.24
Kansas City, Mo.	38.9	25.23	8.02
Houston	38.2	17.33	6.82
Los Angeles	37.9	16.40	5.25

Table 9-9. (cont.)

	Hardship Index*	Federal	GRS
Portland	37.7	36.49	12.59
Salt Lake City	57.6	13.34	13.34
Oklahoma City	35.5	28.37	9.66
Omaha	35.3	28.12	8.41
Columbus, Ohio	34.9	20.13	7.60
San Diego	33.2	24.07	5.97
Dallas	32.6	13.04	7.24
Denver	30.0	23.21	6.15
Allentown	29.1	18.09	13.90
Minneapolis	28.9	18.37	5.96
San Francisco	28.8	15.90	4.33
Seattle	28.5	21.26	8.17
Greensboro, N.C.	28.2	23.29	11.25
Ft. Lauderdale	24.0	5.88	4.01

*Nathan and Adams, p. 55.
Source: ACIR staff compilations from data in U.S. Department of Commerce, Bureau of the Census, *Compendium of City Government Finances in 1975*, various tables.

fiscal tensions. However, regionalization has proceeded at a slow pace over the past decade and most states have also moved very slowly in assuming the necessary responsibility. Indeed, some states, such as New York and Massachusetts, are themselves hard pressed.

Federal general revenue sharing was to provide the unrestricted revenue source needed by the local governments. There are, however, two basic problems with the assumption that GRS will restore most cities to fiscal well-being. First, GRS aid is only moderately equalizing because it is governed by an "iron rule"—everybody must get some of the action. And second, Congress has not been willing to increase the funding for this program so as to keep pace with economic growth and inflation. Chapter Twelve of this book offers some suggestions for improving the block allocation formula.

Thus the only hope for increased federal aid for cities appears to be in the form of categorical funds. But as Wes Uhlman, the mayor of Seattle, recently stated, "I don't believe we can really solve city problems by pumping more and more federal dollars into fragmented programs that patch surface symptoms instead of getting to the causes" (2).

A NEW APPROACH IS NECESSARY

Based on these considerations, it is time for a new approach for strenthening the fiscal position of municipalities. The most obvious

Table 9-10. Municipal Hardship and Municipal Dependency on Federal Aid, 1975

	Correlation Matrix		
	1.	2.	3.
1.	1.00	.28	.24
2.		1.00	.56
3.			1.00

Definitions
1. Nathan-Adams Hardship Index.
2. Municipal Dependency on Federal Aid, 1975.
3. Municipal Dependence on GRS, 1975.

Source: ACIR staff compilations.

candidate is federal direct assumption of welfare and medicaid programs.

Such an idea is not new and one of the major arguments against it has been the immediate strain on federal resources—an immediate takeover of all welfare and medicaid would impose an additional $20 billion cost on the federal government. However, the federal government could begin by assuming a part of the state-local welfare burden. It could hold all other categorical grants at their 1975 levels and use the average percent increase to finance the progressive takeover of health and welfare costs.

In order to target the fiscal relief most effectively, the federal government could extend aid first to those states with the heaviest welfare-medicaid burdens. (See Table 9-11.) Such a federal takeover plan should have a quid pro quo—that each state share a substantial part of its "freed-up" funds with cities and counties on a "no strings" equalizing basis.

It must be noted that the states that are carrying the heaviest welfare burdens in relation to their income are for the most part the very same states with the most acute urban fiscal problems: Massachusetts, Michigan, California, New York, Pennsylvania, Wisconsin, Ohio, and Illinois.

The federal takeover of welfare plans would appear to strengthen our system of fiscal federalism in three important ways:

1. It would provide for a more equitable financing of welfare and medicaid costs.
2. It would strengthen municipal finance by encouraging each state to share part of its revenues with its localities on an unconditional, equalizing basis.

Table 9-11. Public Welfare Circuit-Breaker Plan (Amount of Federal Reimbursement to States for Excess Public Welfare Payments, 1975)

States with Welfare Burden Above Median	Welfare Burden Exp. From Own Funds as % of State P.I. (FY)	($ in millions) S & L Welfare Exp. From Own Funds	Excess Payments	
			100 Percent Reimbursement	50 Percent Reimbursement
District of Col.	2.66%	$141.3	$100.9	$50.4
Massachusetts	2.16	739.4	479.5	239.8
Michigan	1.61	884.3	467.0	233.5
California	1.59	2,122.1	1,110.2	555.1
Rhode Island	1.58	82.2	42.5	21.2
New York	1.53	1,762.4	889.4	444.7
Hawaii	1.41	75.5	34.7	17.4
Pennsylvania	1.34	903.7	389.7	194.8
Wisconsin	1.29	324.3	133.5	66.8
Minnesota	1.25	274.8	107.1	53.6
Vermont	1.19	26.8	9.7	4.8
New Hampshire	1.13	47.5	15.7	7.8
Maine	1.12	55.2	17.8	8.9
New Jersey	1.09	519.4	158.8	79.4
Illinois	1.08	783.6	230.3	115.2
Ohio	1.02	621.3	159.9	80.0
Oregon	1.02	129.5	33.1	16.6
Iowa	0.92	153.5	26.9	13.4
Kentucky	0.90	144.0	22.9	11.4
Delaware	0.90	33.9	5.3	2.6
Maryland	0.88	224.5	36.2	18.1
Connecticut	0.82	169.6	11.5	5.8
Washington	0.81	169.1	9.8	4.9
Alaska	0.77	22.0	0.2	0.1
Colorado	0.77	111.4	0.7	0.4
Total		10,521.3	4,493.3	2,246.7

Excess payments means public welfare expenditures above those of the median State (above 0.76 percent of State personal income).
Source: ACIR staff computations.

3. It would slow down if not halt the trend toward growing municipal dependency on federal aid in general and on increasing numbers of federal conditional aids in particular.

Such a change would move the system back toward classical "federalism" with its clear lines of fiscal and functional responsibilities. It would encourage the states to assume a more active role in dealing with the financial plight of the major cities. By centralizing the fiscal system in one area we can centralize it in another thereby making it stronger.

Since the presentation of this paper, we have noted even greater municipal dependency on direct federal aid—rising to approximately 24% of own source general revenue for fiscal year 1976. With the addition of the counter-cyclical stimulation package we estimate municipal dependency will arise to about 30% for all cities and over 50% for many of our large central cities by fiscal 1978.

Chapter Ten

The Urban Impact of Federal Policies: Their Direct and Indirect Effects on the Local Public Sector

Stephen M. Barro

FEDERAL URBAN POLICY—AN OVERVIEW

One of the more promising recent developments in the urban field is the recognition that federal urban policy must be broadly defined. The federal influence on cities involves more than a handful of explicit urban programs—more even than the whole array of federal programs that channel funds to urban jurisdictions and their citizens.

Experts now recognize the "implicit" or "hidden" urban policy of the federal government (1). These terms encompass not only expenditure programs, but a spectrum of federal actions ranging from tax policy, to macroeconomic policy, to regulation of business, to enforcement of the civil rights laws. All these have been recognized as factors that affect the well-being of urban centers and their residents and that should be taken into account in formulating a comprehensive national urban policy. These policies in part explain the current transition of small cities as well as large ones.

But this broadened view of federal urban policy has not yet been assimilated into the policy making, policy analysis, or policy proposing processes.

For the most part, the list of action proposals still emphasizes the most direct and explicit forms of urban aid. An automatic response to fiscal problems of the cities is to ask for more federal grants to

---

This article summarizes portions of a Rand Corporation study of urban impacts of federal policies being conducted under a grant from The Charles F. Kettering Foundation.

local governments. Federal policies that operate less directly, less immediately, or less visibly have gotten much less attention.

A matter of particular concern is that the locational incentives created by federal policies have not been stressed by those seeking federal intervention on behalf of the cities. On this subject, the disjunction between diagnosis of the problem and prescription of solutions is clear-cut. The standard explanation of the economic difficulties of central cities and of the urban Northeast as a whole, is that a constellation of federal policies—highway programs, housing subsidies, the welfare system—created incentives for businesses and middle class households to move to the suburbs (smaller cities) or to the "sunbelt" and for the poor to concentrate in the central cities.

This diagnosis rests on the power of the locational incentives created by federal programs. Yet, few recent policy proposals have reflected the concept that locational incentives continue to operate and that it may be possible to alter them to work for rather than against the cities.

The consequences of neglecting locational incentives and other indirect effects of federal actions can be serious. One is that viable alternatives may be foregone. Another, perhaps more important, is that policies may be adopted without regard to their long term consequences. There are many instances of urban programs that had long run effects different from, or counter to, what was intended. They include highway programs that generated unanticipated patterns of development, welfare programs that increased poverty concentrations in the cities, and housing programs that facilitated and encouraged middle class flight. In all these cases, indirect effects on locational choices ultimately overshadowed the direct effects of the programs.

Policy makers have good, practical reasons for emphasizing programs that work directly and that aid people and businesses already in the cities. Some of the reasons are political: The direct programs seem to be quicker acting. They are more visible to the electorate. They usually place funds in the hands of local public officials, who can use the money to ease their fiscal and staffing problems and who stand to reap political benefits from fund disbursement.

But there are also cognitive reasons. It is much easier to understand and design direct aid policies and to analyze their short term effects than it is to work out locational incentive schemes and trace the long term consequences of more subtle modes of intervention. The difference is between, on the one hand, asking "who gets how much" from an aid program and, on the other hand, seeking to determine how the aid recipient's behavior will change over time because of his altered circumstances.

At this time, an analytical framework does not exist within which the full range of federal urban policies—including the indirect policies—can be formulated or evaluated. The problem is not so much that empirical information is unavailable on the effects of specific interventions (although such information is lacking, more often than not), but that a general conception has not been developed of the relationships between various kinds of federal policies and the urban outcomes that they are intended to affect. Without such a general framework, it is virtually impossible to do the kind of strategic analysis that is needed if a coherent, comprehensive urban policy is ever to emerge.

This chapter summarizes the approach to this analytical problem that has been developed in an ongoing Rand study of the urban impacts of federal policy. My purposes here are to outline our conceptual approach, to demonstrate how we have worked within the general conceptual framework to examine the effects of federal policies on specific urban outcomes, and to sketch some potential applications of the approach to the development of federal urban policy.

I believe that this type of analysis, when further refined, can contribute to the formulation of a richer array of policy alternatives than currently exists. It also may provide a framework within which policy analyses can be conducted of the indirect and long term urban repercussions of federal programs.

EXAMINING THE EFFECTS OF FEDERAL ACTION

The problem in developing a conceptual scheme of the relationships between federal policies and urban conditions is that there are a great many outcomes of interest, a large number of federal policies to consider, and a complex network of relationships between the policies and the outcomes. Some of the more important effects of federal actions on the cities are indirect. Typically, there are multiple channels of federal influence on particular urban outcomes and multiple links in the causal chains between policies and effects.

For instance, a federal pollution control program may raise the costs of doing business in a city, thereby discouraging investment, reducing employment, and lowering the local business tax base; meanwhile, the same policy may make the area more attractive to residents, increase the demand for housing, and raise the residential tax base. Even when the level of abstraction is kept relatively high, so that the detailed provisions and parameters of policies and the fine structure of outcomes do not enter into the analysis, the complexity of the system makes it unfeasible to examine the full range of urban outcomes or the full range of federal policies simultaneously.

It is necessary to break down the problem into manageable components. However, this must be done in such a way that an integrated view of the system will not be lost. Following is a general outline of one approach to dealing with the conceptual problem.

THE URBAN ECONOMY AS A THREE-SECTOR SYSTEM

First, we conceive of the urban economy as consisting of three distinct but interacting sectors: (1) the private business sector; (2) the residential, or household, sector; and (3) the urban public sector. Each sector is inhabited by a different type of operating or decision making unit.

In the business sector, the basic unit is the individual firm; in the residential sector it is the individual household; and in the urban public sector it is the local government (the term "local government" includes not only municipalities but such other jurisdictions as counties and school districts as well). Conceived of in this way, the problem of analyzing federal policy impacts on cities becomes the problem of analyzing federal impacts on the behaviors of business firms, households, and local governments in urban areas.

One purpose of the three-sector breakdown is to permit us to consider only a subset of urban conditions, or urban policy outcomes, at any one time. When we examine the effects of federal policies on the business sector, for example, the main outcomes of interest are levels of economic activity, income, employment, wages, and investment in urban areas. In the residential sector the principal outcome variables are the size, composition, and spatial distribution of the population, the makeup of the housing stock, and the match among people, housing units, and geographical areas. In the urban public sector, the major outcomes are the level and mix of public services and the magnitude and composition of the tax burdens imposed upon residents of urban areas.

Of course, one can argue endlessly about which are the "ultimate" outcomes of policy and which are only intermediate or intervening variables—e.g., is the quality of public services important "in itself" or only insofar as it affects the willingness of people and businesses to locate in the cities? Fortunately, it is not necessary to resolve such controversies to proceed with the analysis of federal impacts on the cities. Once relationships among the key variables within each sector are understood, it is not difficult to focus attention on whichever variable is salient in the context of a particular policy debate.

For many analytic purposes, it is less important to know how federal actions affect absolute levels of outcome variables than how they affect relative conditions in different places. What counts in assessing federal impacts on demographic patterns, for example, is the relative concentration of different population subgroups (classified by income, race, family structure, etc.) in urban and suburban areas, in cities of different sizes and types, and in different regions of the country. These variations are central to the discussion that follows.

The three-sector conceptual model also makes it possible for us to deal with one subset of federal policies at a time. This is not to say that there is one group of federal policies that affects only residential outcomes, a second group that affects economic activity, and a third that affects local public services and taxes. On the contrary, the point of this approach is to allow for the possibility that federal actions that appear to be aimed at one sector or to have their initial impacts in one sector may have indirect effects of comparable importance in other sectors.

For instance, the rate at which business activity has shifted from central cities to suburbs has been influenced *directly* by federal highway construction programs and federal support for development of suburban water and sewer systems. It has probably been influenced even more strongly—but *indirectly*—by such federal policies as tax benefits and subsidies for home ownership, which have encouraged shifts of population (consumers and workers) to the suburbs. Under our conceptual scheme, we would treat these federal interventions in housing as policies that have initial impacts in the residential sector, but that subsequently affect business location patterns via indirect, intersectoral linkages.

Adherence to the distinction between the direct and indirect federal policies can yield significant analytical economies. One can concentrate on the subset of federal policies that have initial effects in, say, the residential sector, recognizing that it will also be necessary to take account of the effects on residential location patterns of federally induced changes in the business and local public sectors. The key point is to separate the effects of federal policies that impinge directly upon a sector from the effects of policies that have their initial effects elsewhere.

The three-sector approach is illustrated schematically in Figure 10-1. Outcomes in the three sectors are shown as affecting one another. Different clusters of federal policies are shown as having direct impacts on each sector. For instance, the effect of a federal action that influences housing choices directly, such as a housing

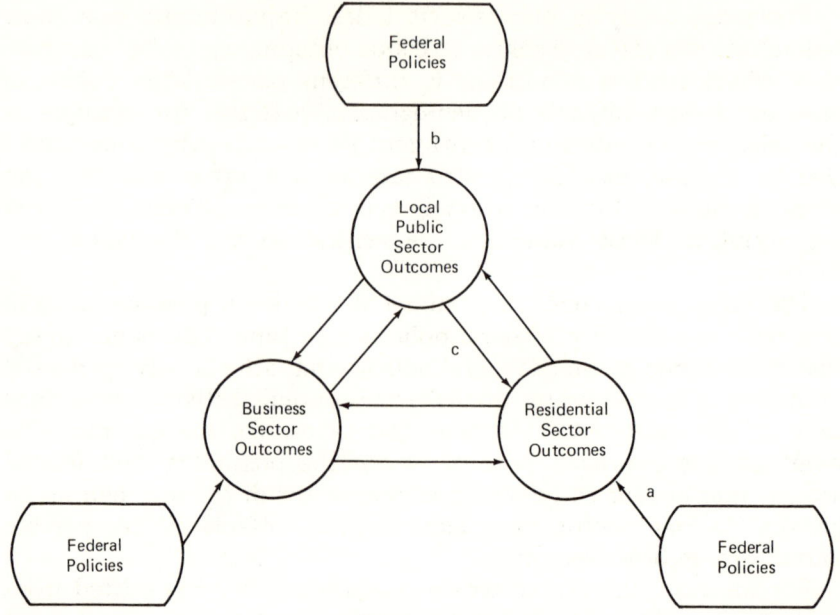

Figure 10-1. Schematic Diagram of the Three-Sector Approach to Urban Impact Analysis.

subsidy program, would be represented by the arrow labeled "a" in the diagram.

The effect of a federal policy that exerts an influence on housing choices by altering conditions in the public sector (e.g., a program of aid to education that improves urban schools, thereby making urban locations more attractive to families with children) would be represented by the pair of linkages labeled "b" and "c." The task of analyzing impacts of federal policy on the urban system can be subdivided into investigations of the three sets of direct impacts, such as "a" or "b," and the various intersectoral linkages, such as "c."

Determinants of Outcomes in Each Sector

Even with the system subdivided three ways, it is not feasible to proceed directly to the analysis of effects of specific federal policies on sectoral outcomes, for there are still too many policies to consider simultaneously within each of the sectors. Additional structuring of the problem is required. The approach we have taken is to divide into two steps the task of relating the policies to the outcomes within each sector.

The first step is to identify the major determinants of key urban outcomes. The second step is to analyze the federal policies that affect each major determinant. In this way, the problem of relating policies to consequences can be disassembled into several dozen manageable pieces. For instance, the determinants of the level of private economic activity in a given area include such things as the local labor supply and the availability and cost of freight transportation. Of the many federal policies that affect business location decisions, it is possible to identify some that operate specifically on the labor supply (e.g., federal manpower and training programs and enforcement of the wage and hour and occupational safety laws), and some that affect the characteristics of local transportation systems (e.g., highway construction grants, subsidies for railroads and airports, and regulation of freight rates and services). It is at this level that questions of cause and effect attain enough specificity to be researchable. Once the main determinants of outcomes have been identified and specific policies have been connected with specific determinants, it becomes reasonable to search the research literature for findings about the direction and magnitude of the policy impacts.

Different portions of the research literature pertain to each of the three sectors. In the case of the local public sector, the most relevant literature is the large body of work on determinants of state expenditure and tax choices. In the case of the business sector, it is the voluminous literature on industrial location. In the case of the residential sector, a number of fields are relevant, including studies of the housing market, of residential choice, and of interregional and intrametropolitan migration. Although the task varied in complexity among the sectors (it was easiest for the local public sector and most difficult for the residential sector), we were able to assemble lists for all three sectors of the main factors that have been touched on by researchers.

The table on the following page (Table 10-1) lists the major determinants of outcomes in the business, residential, and local public sectors. There are ten to twenty items on each list. Some of the variables listed are obviously influenced very strongly by federal policy. Examples of these are the amount of outside aid to local governments (in the public sector column), housing subsidies and tax benefits (in the residential column), and transfer payments to individuals (in both the business sector and residential columns). Other variables are influenced to a lesser degree by federal actions, but in every case there is at least some federal involvement.

There are a few instances in which a great many federal policies come to bear on a single variable. An example is the "amenities"

Table 10-1. Major Determinants of Outcomes in the Three Sectors of the Urban Economy

Sector	Decision-Making Units	Major Outcomes	Main Determinants of Outcomes
Private Business Sector	Firms	Output Investment Employment Wages: 　Magnitude 　Composition 　Spatial Distribution	Demand for output 　Consumer demand 　Population characteristics 　Income from economic activity 　Transfer payments 　Personal taxes 　Business demand (for intermediate goods) 　Public demand 　Federal purchases 　State/local purchases Factor supply 　Supply of labor 　Access 　Transportation of goods 　Transportation of persons 　Supply of raw materials 　Supply of energy 　Supply of land 　Supply of capital funds 　Public services and taxes 　Amenities 　Subsidies and restrictions 　Technology
Residential Sector	Households	Population and housing stock: 　Magnitude 　Composition 　Spatial distribution	Demand for housing 　Income (including transfer payments) 　Socioeconomic characteristics 　Neighborhood characteristics 　Access/transportation 　Amenities: Physical and social 　Public services and taxes 　Housing subsidies and tax benefits 　Availability and cost of mortgage credit Supply of housing 　Factor supply 　Housing construction 　Housing operation 　Public infrastructures 　Supplier subsidies and tax benefits 　Availability and cost of credit 　Production and marketing restrictions

Local Public Sector	Local Governments	Public Services:	Revenue sources
		Level	Local revenue base
		Mix	Residential/personal
		Distribution	Business
		Taxes:	Tax spillovers
		Level	Outside aid
		Composition	Federal and state grants
			Revenue subsidies (tax expenditures)
			Expenditure demands
			"Need" factors (population characteristics)
			Service costs
			Service spillovers
			Scope of local service responsibility
			Mandated expenditures

item in the residential column of the table. Many kinds of neighborhood amenities affect the demand for housing in different parts of urban areas. The federal policies that affect levels of amenities include such diverse things as antipollution programs, grants for law enforcement activities, and enforcement of open-housing laws.

A considerably more detailed substructure than can be shown in the table is needed to deal with that cluster of federal policies. Also, a single federal policy may have multiple effects. An example is the system of federal grants for income maintenance programs, which simultaneously affects the budgetary positions of local governments, the demographic makeup and demand for housing of the urban population, and the supply of low skill labor to the private sector. To determine how federal income maintenance policy affects the cities, it would be necessary to take into account all three channels of influence.

Note that a distinction is made in all three parts of the table between supply side and demand side influences on the behavior of a sector. This is of considerable analytical importance in appraising the effects of federal policies and the interactions among them. In some instances, the same federal policy will affect both the demand and supply sides of a market. One example is the dual effect of federal monetary and credit policy on the availability of construction credit to housing suppliers and the availability of mortgage credit to housing consumers. Another is the effect on both the demand for urban public services and the size of the per capita local tax base of federal policies that encourage the poor to migrate to cities. Recognition of the potentially offsetting or reinforcing multiple impacts of such policies is essential to an analysis of their overall effects.

What is accomplished by the taxonomic scheme summarized in Table 10-1? It contributes in two ways to the development of a comprehensive view of federal urban policy. First, it breaks down a grossly overbroad question—how do federal policies affect cities?—into several dozen questions that are potentially answerable by research such as:

- How do federal policies affect the magnitude of the residential component of the urban tax base?
- How do they affect the local labor supply in different types of cities, or in different regions of the country?
- How do they affect the relative costs of freight transportation in central cities and suburbs?

Although the ultimate analytical objective is to develop quantitative answers to these questions, it is useful at the outset to identify the points at which federal policies affect the urban system, to define the key intervening variables, and to trace the channels by which certain outcomes are obtained. Second, the conceptual scheme outlined here provides a framework within which information on the effects of individual federal policies on particular outcomes or intervening variables can be assembled and aggregated.

The next step in the analysis is to examine the linkages between specific federal policies or policy proposals and the variables represented in Table 10-1. Not surprisingly, little of the relevant information appears in the literature in forms that are directly usable. Most studies of business and residential location, for example, are motivated by concerns other than the influence of federal policy on locational choices. Therefore, we have had to rely a great deal on indirect inference and extrapolation of findings to be able to say anything about many of the linkages that our conceptual model tells us are relevant.

To convey the flavor of our analysis, I have selected one of the three sectors, the local public sector, for more detailed discussion. The reasons for this choice are (1) the relative simplicity of the network of federal policy effects pertaining to that sector, and (2) the predominance of public sector concerns in much of the recent public discussion of urban problems. The illustration serves to demonstrate the importance of intersectoral relationships in the urban economy and the central role of locational incentives in the arsenal of federal urban policies.

THE FEDERAL GOVERNMENT AND THE LOCAL PUBLIC SECTOR

The list of outcome determinants in the "public sector" column of Table 10-1 indicates that there are basically two ways that the federal government can influence the services and taxes of local governments in urban areas. One is by changing the financial resources available to the local governments (or the terms under which they are available); the other is by modifying the pattern of demands for local government outlays.

Local revenue sources consist of the various tax bases from which jurisdictions derive "revenue from own sources" and grant revenue from the federal government and the states. The demand for local government outlays may be decomposed into three factors: (1) "need-related" characteristics of the local population and area (defined further below), (2) costs of public services, and (3) the range of services for which local governments are responsible.

The overall fiscal condition of a locality can be summarized by comparing its revenue resource with the service demands placed upon it. This concept of fiscal condition, or fiscal well-being, of a locality can be defined in a precise, quantitative manner.[a] For the present purpose, however, all that is necessary is to recognize that federal policies aid local governments financially insofar as they tend to raise the local tax base and/or the amount of available outside aid, and to hurt them financially insofar as they tend to make the urban population more demanding of services, to raise service costs, or to expand the scope of local responsibility.

The question is which federal policies exert these kinds of leverage and to what degree. In this section, we provide a factor-by-factor summary of the types of federal policies that influence each major determinant of urban fiscal outcomes.

The Local Revenue Base

The revenue base of a local jurisdiction consists mainly of the assessed value of residences and businesses within its boundaries, but also of other taxable economic magnitudes, such as income, payrolls, and retail sales. The per capita revenue base is the most important single measure of a locality's access to revenue for financing public services. Although a large amount of state and federal revenue flows to the local public sector, revenue from own sources still accounts for approximately 62 percent of all general revenue of local governments in metropolitan areas (2).

The federal government can affect the urban tax base by adopting policies that increase the per capita value of the housing stock, that stimulate business activity and capital formation in urban areas, or that augment per capita incomes in urban areas by other means. From the point of view of local officials, nearly all such federal policies are indirect—that is, they do not involve transactions between federal and local governments. The main exceptions are federal transfer payment programs administered by local authorities and federally supported public employment programs, both of which combine grants to localities with stimulation of taxable economic activity. Most of the other policies that affect the per capita local

---

[a]In our study, we argue that the fiscal conditions of different cities, or of the same city at different times, should be quantified by comparing what we call their "fiscal opportunity schedules." These are mathematical expressions relating the levels of services that cities can provide (taking into account service costs and the nature of the population to be served) to levels of local fiscal effort. Using this method, it is possible to measure the fiscal well-being of each city relative to that of other cities and to measure the rate at which each city's condition is improving or deteriorating. The details are given in S.M. Barro, *The Urban Impact of Federal Policies:* Vol. 3, *Urban Fiscal Conditions*, The Rand Corporation, R-2114-KR/RC (forthcoming).

revenue base have their initial effects in the private residential and business sectors of the urban economy.

Among the federal policies that affect the residential or personal components of the tax base—i.e., the amount of taxable residential property in a jurisdiction and the levels of taxable income and retail sales—a logical distinction can be made between those that affect the economic circumstances of a given urban population and those that affect the makeup of the urban population itself. The policies in the former group include overt housing subsidies; less explicit housing subsidies, such as those provided by federal tax deductions for local property taxes and mortgage interest; and income maintenance programs, which augment the power of low income people to purchase housing as well as other goods. All these are policies that have their initial impacts in the household sector.

In addition, the taxpaying ability of a given population can be increased by policies that have their initial impacts in the private business sector and that stimulate employment and earnings. Federal policies in all the above categories have generally been adopted for the express purpose of raising the economic well-being of people. While that is not equivalent to a goal of raising local fiscal capacity, it is a closely related objective.

In contrast, the federal policies that have helped to induce major changes in urban populations during the last few decades were generally adopted for entirely different purposes and without anticipation of their demographic consequences. While attempting to accomplish a variety of social goals, ranging from improving transportation to redistributing income to the poor, the government created incentive systems that affected the attractiveness of cities relative to suburbs, small cities relative to large ones, and regions relative to one another. Moreover, the locational incentives have been different for members of different socioeconomic groups.

The most frequently cited examples of policies with strong locational effects include the federal highway programs, which have encouraged suburbanization and movement away from the urban Northeast; the provisions of federal housing programs that tend to favor one type of locality over another—e.g., tax and subsidy programs that favor owner-occupied housing and new construction and that are therefore skewed towards suburbs and growth regions; the provisions of the welfare laws that have resulted in much higher benefit levels in the urban Northeast than in other parts of the country, and thereby encouraged the concentration of the poor; and even enforcement of antidiscrimination laws in public schooling and housing, where such enforcement has taken forms that stimulate white and middle class flight from the cities.

The effects of these policies on local tax bases seem almost incidental compared to their overall economic and social consequences. Nevertheless, these and other federal actions that aided postwar suburbanization and the more recent sunbelt migration must be counted among the major sources of the current fiscal problems of the cities.

The research literature bearing on federal impacts on the urban population and its economic well-being cannot be reviewed or even summarized here. However, two major findings are relevant.

First, although it is possible to distinguish, in principle, between policies that affect the economic situation of the existing urban population and those that affect the urban population mix, it is apparent that some federal actions have both effects. Significantly, the two effects may operate in opposite directions.

For example, it might seem that the various indirect subsidy programs for housing could only exert a positive effect on the urban tax base. However, that neglects the locational incentive effect. As the indirect subsidy programs are now designed, they tend to favor types of housing that are more commonly found in suburbs than in cities—i.e., owner-occupied homes and newly constructed dwelling units. Therefore, although the subsidies benefit some city residents, they also provide inducements to other residents, especially in the middle and upper income groups, to move to the suburbs. It is not evident whether the net impact on the per capita residential tax base in the cities is positive or negative.

Similarly, the effect of federal income maintenance programs on the per capita income of city residents, and thus on the per capita urban tax base, might seem to be unambiguously positive; but this is true only if the population of transfer payment recipients remains constant. If (as many contend) the present welfare system has induced poor people to concentrate in the central cities, and if the influx of the poor has contributed to middle class flight, then the net impact of the welfare system on per capita income and property value in central cities could well be negative. These are only two examples of programs whose longer run locational effects may run counter to the initial effects of financial aid.

Second, although federal policies can increase local fiscal capacity either by aiding existing residents or by encouraging demographic changes that are fiscally favorable, the potential of the first approach is limited compared to that of the second. The revenue loss sustained by a city when a middle class household is replaced by a poor one can be only fractionally offset by income maintenance payments and housing subsidies.

This would still be true even if considerably more generous transfer payment programs than now exist were enacted into law. Moreover, the discussion thus far pertains only to the effects of demographic change on the revenue side of city budgets. For reasons explained below, the same population shifts that tend to reduce the per capita residential property tax base are also likely to increase per capita service demands, thereby compounding the fiscal problem.

The foregoing points underscore the importance of locational incentives as determinants of urban economic conditions. The key principle is that the residential tax base is economically, if not physically, portable. Other things being equal, residential property values reflect housing consumption expenditures, which reflect residents' incomes. A federal policy that tends to reduce the per capita income in cities relative to other places, either by inducing people with above-average incomes to move out or people with below-average incomes to move in, will almost inevitably result in a relative decrease in urban fiscal capacity.

The following qualifications should be noted.

1. Housing expenditures reflect family size and composition as well as income. The phenomena of middle class or white flight and in-migration of the poor and minorities entail simultaneous changes in the income and nonincome variables.

2. The response of the tax base to changes in the socioeconomic makeup of the population (and especially the *rate* of response) depends on the conditions of housing supply in each area. The same rate of relative decline should not be expected in areas that are experiencing absolute growth and those that are experiencing decline in the demand for housing units.

3. The emphasis on *relative* fiscal capacity is important. The downward influence on housing values in particular cities attributable to demographic change is likely to be much weaker, except in the most severely affected cities, than the upward influences that have caused housing prices to rise all over the country. Therefore, the demographic effect is likely to be evidenced only by differences in the rate of housing price increases in different areas.

Very similar remarks can be made about the federal impact on the business component of the urban tax base. The federal government has affected, and continues to affect, business property values and payrolls in urban areas through policies that alter the relative attractiveness to private firms of urban, suburban, and nonmetropolitan locations and of different regions of the country.

The central empirical issue is how federal policies affect the relative economic growth rates of the different areas. Although conclusive proof is difficult to assemble, there is evidence that the federal role in such areas as highway and rail transportation, provision of local public infrastructure, regulation of the labor market, and tax treatment of investments has contributed both to centrifugal tendencies within metropolitan areas and to the shift of economic activity to the Sunbelt (3). Here too, policies that were established with no intent to affect the public sector have significantly undercut the ability of central cities and older urban regions to sustain themselves.

A factor that makes it difficult to analyze the impacts of particular federal policies on the urban tax base is that changes in residential location and business location patterns are closely linked. Demographic changes imply changes in labor supply and consumer demand, both of which are important determinants of business location decisions. Shifts in the geographical pattern of business activity imply changes in the location of employment opportunities, which is a major determinant of the locational choices of households.

There are two consequences of these interactions: First, the underlying cause and effect relationships are obscure—does industry follow people or do people follow industry? Researchers have not yet succeeded in disentangling these complex, dynamic relationships (4). Hence, the available estimates of the magnitudes of policy impacts are suspect. Second, there is no clear-cut distinction between federal policies that affect the business component of the local revenue base and those that affect the residential component. It is usually clear in which sector the initial impact occurs, but the linkages between the two sets of outcomes are so strong that anything that affects urban demography is likely to affect urban business activity, and vice versa.

The Availability of Outside Aid

Federal decisions about the form, distribution, and funding level of grants to state and local governments have a relatively direct effect on the revenue available to urban local governments. The term "relatively direct" is used advisedly. Although it may seem that there is an unbroken connection between a federal decision to increase grant expenditures and an increment in funds available to the local public sector, that is not necessarily so.

What is too often omitted from discussions of federal grants is the role of the states. At present, only a minor fraction of all federal aid—on the order of 20 percent—flows directly from Washington to local jurisdictions. The most prominent direct aid programs are General Revenue Sharing and Community Development Block Grants. The bulk of federal intergovernmental aid flows initially to state governments and the bulk of the intergovernmental revenue of the local sector takes the form of state subventions.

Although some of the so-called state aid to localities is really passed-through federal aid, the relationship among the three levels of government is not as simple as the pass-through notion suggests. In such important program areas as welfare, education, and highways, what flows to the local level is commingled federal and state money. The significance of the states' involvement is that the local fiscal impact of a change in federal grant programs may depend, in part, on how state governments respond. State budgetary decisions may either offset or augment the impacts of federal aid on local budgets. Also, where states have some discretion over the distribution of federal aid funds, the fraction that goes to cities, as opposed to suburbs and rural areas, may depend on state preferences and state behavior.

The fiscal effects of intergovernmental aid on local jurisdictions depend on three sets of characteristics of the federal grant programs.

The Form of Aid. Major aspects of the form of grants are (a) whether they are categorical or block grants, (b) whether they are project or formula grants, and (c) whether they are lump-sum or matching grants.

The Distribution of Aid. In the case of formula grants, the key issue is the nature of the distribution formula: What measures of local "needs" for assistance does it contain? What allowances does it make for interjurisdictional variations in revenue-raising ability, fiscal effort, and service costs? In the case of project grants, the central issues are the procedures and criteria used in choosing among grant applicants.

The "Strings" Attached to Aid. The important characteristics of the constraints, or "strings" attached to grants are (a) how narrowly the use of aid funds is circumscribed, (b) the degree to which grantees are actually required to use resources for projects or activities that they would not have chosen to support themselves, and (c) the degree to which grant requirements are enforced.

During the last few years, those characteristics of grants have changed in ways that have significantly affected the relative positions of urban areas. Other proposals for change, which could have impacts of similar magnitude, remain on the federal agenda. Under the headings of "revenue sharing," "block grants," and "grant consolidation," there have been major shifts from relatively narrow, targeted grants to more general-purpose grants, from project grants to formula grants, and from detailed and specific to broader criteria for distributing funds.

Major legislation has included General Revenue Sharing (GRS), Community Development Block Grants (CDBG), and the Comprehensive Employment and Training Act (CETA). Block grant legislation has also been proposed in the education, health, and housing fields.

The changes in federal aid programs have affected the central cities and the older urbanized regions in several ways. The trend toward formula grants has neutralized the advantage that large cities enjoyed in project grants competitions because of their greater access to technical expertise. The shift from specific to broad allocation criteria has tended to spread out grant funds, instead of concentrating them in the areas with the most severe problems.

Under the CDBG program, for example, suburban counties and smaller cities that did not qualify for categorical urban funds are entitled to block grants. The formulas contained in the GRS and block grant legislation have certain features that generally favor southern and small areas over the urban centers of the Northeast. Typically, such formulas provide extra funds to low income areas, but they do not adjust for the significant cost of living differentials that exist among regions and between urban and rural areas. Also, they do not contain factors that reflect the deteriorated physical conditions of many urban areas or the obsolescence of the private and public capital stock; nor are the overall fiscal burdens on the cities taken into account, even in formulas that contain indices of local revenue raising ability.

There are some offsetting points. Some grant programs, notably General Revenue Sharing, contain fiscal effort factors, which tend to help the more urbanized areas. Certain new grant programs may be especially helpful to cities, notably the antirecessionary countercyclical aid and public employment programs. Also, the loosening of categorical restrictions may have given cities greater leeway to use their intergovernmental revenue in ways that seem desirable from the local perspective. Still, the recent changes in the grant system have probably had negative effects on the cities' relative fiscal position, even where increases in federal funding have prevented absolute reductions in amounts of aid.

There is no lack of awareness at the local level that the federal grant system is a major element of the implicit federal urban policy. Despite what was said about the role of the states, the intergovernmental grant is still the most certain and direct instrument available to the federal government for affecting the fiscal position of the local public sector. It is presumably for this reason that most policy proposals from the mayors and other urban interest groups are requests for expanded funding of existing grants or for the creation of new forms of intergovernmental aid for cities. However, there seems to have been some imbalance in the attention that has been given to various aspects of grants.

Local public officials have focused mainly on grant programs that are explicitly aimed at cities, such as the antirecessionary programs mentioned above. In comparison, less attention has been devoted to the urban implications of the design characteristics of grants that support broad social programs. The funding levels of the general social programs are so much larger than those of explicit urban programs that relatively narrow changes in the former's eligibility criteria and distribution formulas may have as much impact on urban fiscal conditions as the enactment of whole new programs of explicit urban aid.

Of course, the urban impacts of intergovernmental grants extend beyond their immediate effects on local budgets. Grants play a dual role in the urban economy. From the perspective of the public sector, grants are a source of revenue and, in many cases, a source of expenditure obligations.[b] At the same time, from the perspective of the private business sector and the household sector, the grant-aided programs modify the economic environment in each urban area. By influencing local transportation systems, local public infrastructures, and levels of social services and income maintenance payments in each area, the grant programs create significant locational incentives for both businesses and households.

A matter of some concern, from the standpoint of urban policy making, is that the short run budgetary impacts and the longer run locational impacts of grant programs may work in opposite directions. Examples of such possibilities abound in the literature. Grant-financed transportation improvements may attract more traffic, making urban congestion worse. Increased support for income maintenance and social services may relieve the local fiscal situation in the short run, but may attract so many new applicants that greater burdens are created in the future.

---

[b]Grant programs can generate expenditure obligations (a) when there are matching requirements (assuming that the grantee would not otherwise have devoted equivalent funds to the aided program), (b) when there are binding constraints on the uses of grant funds (i.e., the grantee is forced to spend more for the aided program than it would have spent in the absence of earmarking provisions), and (c) when grant provisions force the localities to incur higher costs than they would have otherwise (e.g., when certain service standards have to be met as a condition of eligibility for aid).

The attractiveness of grants to hard pressed local officials is such that it is difficult to draw attention to perverse long run consequences, much less to forego programs that may, after all, not have the hypothesized unpleasant aftermaths. A major contribution to more comprehensive urban policy making at the federal level would be to give fuller consideration to the long run locational effects as well as the short run fiscal benefits of grant programs. As it is, there is a tendency in times of fiscal stress to emphasize the latter exclusively, with the result that unanticipated and unwanted locational effects can occur.

Revenue Subsidies

Until recently, very little attention was given to the implicit subsidy to the state-local sector provided by the federal income tax system. During the last few years, however, the concept of federal "tax expenditures" has been developed and brought to national prominence. Tax expenditures are special provisions of the internal revenue laws that reduce the tax liability—by means of deductions, credits, or exemptions—of specified groups of taxpayers or of individuals or firms engaged in specified types of activity. These provisions can have allocative and distributional effects that are equivalent to those of overt federal spending for the same purposes and beneficiaries.

About $16 billion of federal tax expenditures in fiscal year 1976 can be interpreted as expenditures on behalf of state and local governments (5). These consist of the federal revenue losses attributable to the deductability of state and local taxes from federally taxable income and the exemption from federal income taxation of municipal bond interest. Although these benefits are received initially by individual taxpayers, there is reason to believe that they work, at least in part, to augment state and local revenue from own sources.

The basic mechanism—and the reason for referring to the tax expenditures as "revenue subsidies"—is that the special provisions lower the effective "price" to local taxpayers of supporting state and local government. An individual who pays a dollar of local property tax may receive back 20 to 50 cents in the form of a federal income tax reduction, depending on his tax bracket. There are both theoretical and empirical grounds for believing that this makes it easier for local jurisdictions to impose taxes and that tax receipts are higher than they would be otherwise. This is not to say that local revenues are augmented by the full amount of the federal revenue losses. A partial effect is more likely. Nevertheless, there is a multibillion dollar federal subsidy to the local sector that is not reflected in conventional tabulations of intergovernmental aid.

The federal tax expenditures on behalf of state and local governments do not loom large relative to the $60 billion or so per year that the federal government distributes as grants-in-aid. However, a different comparison is instructive. The General Revenue Sharing program, enacted in 1972, was hailed as the first major federal commitment to general purpose support of the state-local sector. That program distributes approximately $7 billion per year. The federal tax expenditure totals more than twice as much—all of it for use with no "strings" by local taxing jurisdictions.

"Needs" for Public Services

Far more attention has been given to the federal government's role in augmenting the revenue of the local sector than to its influence on the level of demand for local expenditures. As explained above, that demand can be decomposed into three factors, one of which represents the "needs" of the local population for public services. The term "needs" requires explanation. As used here, it does not refer to any sort of absolute service requirement, but rather to the relative levels of demand for local public services by households with different characteristics.

For instance, a household with school-age children "needs" more services, other things being equal, than a household with no children because of the demand for local elementary and secondary education; a low income household has greater than average "needs" because it receives transfer payments and consumes social services that higher income households do not consume; an automobile owning household represents more service "needs" than an otherwise similar household with no car because the former household makes use of streets and roads. Other household characteristics that may be related to service demands include family structure, the ages of household members, and the form of housing tenure.

In addition, there are two sets of nondemographic variables that would have to be taken into account in a full discussion of service needs: One is the characteristics of local business and industry that affect per capita levels of public service consumption by the business sector, such as industrial demands for water and sewer services and police protection. The other is the physical characteristics that can cause service demands to vary among areas even in the absence of demographic or business structure variations, such as differences in climate and topography.

One can conceive of an index of relative per capita needs for services that reflects the proportions of high and low service consuming households or individuals in each locality. Such an index would be constructed by assigning appropriate weights to each relevant demographic characteristic. One method would be to base the weights on the average costs of local services consumed by each class of citizen.

For instance, if it costs $500 per capita, on average, to support all local services other than public schooling, and if schooling costs $1000 per pupil, then each public school pupil would receive three times the weight in the need index as each citizen not enrolled in school. Other things being equal, high values of the need index will be associated with large proportions of the population in school, large proportions of poor or welfare eligible households, large numbers of female-headed households, and so forth.

Any federal policy that induces changes in the population composition of central cities and suburbs, or of different regions of the country, is likely to affect the relative service need indexes of more and less urbanized areas. For the most part, the relevant federal policies are the same ones cited earlier as influencing the per capita residential tax base. However, the linkages between specific federal policies and levels of service demand are more complicated than the linkages between the same policies and the residential tax base.

The revenue base represented by a given household depends mostly on its income. The service demands of a household are also associated with income, but other factors such as the number of children are important. Therefore, when a middle class family with an income, say, 30 percent above the mean moves from the city to a suburb, the result is a reasonably unambiguous modest decline in the per capita residential tax base; but if the family has children in school, it is not clear whether per capita service demands rise or fall as a result of the move. The question is, does the family's consumption of public schooling outweigh its nonconsumption of public welfare and related social services? Because of the uncertainty, it is difficult to say precisely what federal stimulation of outmigration from the cities has done to the per capita demands for urban services.

This discussion pertains to the impact of population changes on the fiscal position of the whole local public sector, not only the municipal, or general purpose, category of local government. Typically, the costs of schooling would be borne by an independent local school district rather than the municipality. Welfare costs may be borne by county units rather than cities. Thus, it is possible for a given population change to represent a net gain for the municipality and a net loss for the whole local public sector, or vice versa.

The foregoing underscores the importance of considering the net fiscal consequences of multiple effects of federal policy. Virtually any federal action that induces a change in the makeup of an urban population will affect both the local revenue base and the level of public service needs. The two effects may be offsetting or mutually reinforcing. The departure of the middle class family with school children provides an example of offsetting effects. The inmigration of a welfare-eligible family provides a case of reinforcing effects—doubly so if that family also has children in school.

Unfortunately, we do not know enough about the relationships between public service demands and demographic variables to compute the net fiscal surplus or deficit associated with each combination of household characteristics. But we can infer that some population shifts associated with federal policies have had significant effects—often adverse ones—on urban budgets.

The question of the net fiscal impact of demographic change is related to several ongoing controversies about federal social policy. One is the debate about welfare reform. If it is true that interstate differentials in income maintenance and social service programs are a cause of the poverty concentrations in the urban northeast, and if those concentrations, in turn, place financial burdens on the cities, then the design of a reformed welfare system could have major fiscal implications for the local public sector. These implications have received relatively little attention in the discussions of alternative reform proposals.

An even more controversy-laden subject is federal policy concerning school desegregation. A debate has been going on over the contribution of such policies—especially busing programs—to white and middle class flight. The potentially significant fiscal effects of the departure of families with school children, on cities as well as suburbs, have received little consideration during these discussions. In both areas, federal actions have been taken, and more actions are likely to be taken in the future, in the absence of information on either their locational effects or the consequent fiscal effects. This should indicate a high priority for efforts to predict both types of effects and to examine carefully the locational incentives implicit in program designs.

Costs of Public Services

The macroeconomic and regulatory policies followed by the federal government affect levels of wages and prices throughout the economy, including the wages of public employees and the prices that local governments must pay for energy, construction, contract services, and other inputs. The macroeconomic policies include the full range of instruments—fiscal and monetary policy, automatic stabilizers, targeted job creation programs, and controls—that federal authorities use to influence rates of economic activity, employment, and inflation. Regulatory policies include enforcement of the federal laws governing wages and hours and the collective bargaining process and policies that affect prices and supply conditions in specific sectors, such as construction, transportation, and energy.

Although the public sector as a whole has undoubtedly faced difficult adjustment problems because of general price inflation, it is difficult to identify federal policies that have had direct effects on service cost *differentials* among cities, suburbs, and rural areas or among different regions. One input price that federal policy has affected directly is the price of energy, but energy accounts for a very small fraction of public sector spending. To detect the federal influence on the most important component of public sector costs, the wages of public employees, one must look to indirect federal impacts via the private sector.

Regional differentials in private wages are attributable in part to federal policies that have affected the course of economic development (e.g., the rate of industrialization) in each region. Wage variations are also attributable, to some unknown degree, to the provisions of labor law that permit regional variations in the legal status and, thus, the effectiveness of unions (e.g., the provision authorizing state right-to-work laws).

It is well established that pay scales in the public sector reflect private sector wages. Therefore, to the extent that federal policy has contributed to private wage differentials, it has also contributed to differential public sector costs. However, the overall trend during the post-war period has been toward reduced interregional differences in wages. The effect of this trend should be pro-urban, in the sense that the cost advantages of the less urbanized regions are gradually being eroded.

One form of proposed federal intervention that could have had a major effect on public sector costs seems to have been sidetracked. That is the proposal for development of a national framework for collective bargaining in the state-local sector. The efforts to enact such legislation were blocked, at least for the time being, by the Supreme Court's decision in *National League of Cities* v. *Usery*, which has been interpreted by some to preclude that form of federal involvement in the affairs of state and local jurisdictions.[c] This inter-

---

[c]In the *Usery* case (96 S. Ct. 2465, 1976), the Supreme Court ruled that the federal government could not set a minimum wage for state and local employees. State sovereignty was said to transcend the justification for federal involvement under the commerce clause. By extension, this can be taken to preclude other forms of federal involvement in relations between subfederal governments and their employees.

pretation is not universally shared, and further attempts and consequent court tests may be forthcoming. No matter what the outcome, the growth of public sector collective bargaining is likely to have a major impact on public service costs in the future. The question is how much will federal involvement contribute?

Scope of Service Responsibilities

One important determinant of the fiscal well-being of local governments is the range of services for which they are responsible. There are now wide variations, both within and among states, in the pattern of assignment of functional roles and fiscal responsibilities to different levels of government. Functions that are performed by local authorities in some states are performed directly by the state government in others—an important example being administration of welfare. Functions that are performed locally are financed to widely varying degrees out of state government revenue.

There are also different divisions of responsibility within the local sector. Public school systems are run directly by municipal governments in a few instances, by county authorities in some states, and by independent local school districts in most of the country. Welfare systems are typically run by county governments when they are not administered directly by states, but a few cities (notably New York) are responsible for their own welfare systems. Any federal action that altered these assignments could have significant financial implications, either for particular classes of governments or for the whole local sector.

There are three ways in which the federal government can act to alter local responsibilities for service delivery and financing. One is by assuming added responsibility itself. There is recent precedent for this in the federalization of certain welfare programs under the Supplemental Security Income Program (SSI). It has been proposed that the other major welfare programs—Aid for Families with Dependent Children, and Medicaid—be federalized as well. That would provide several billion dollars of fiscal relief to the state-local sector.

Although most of the benefit would accrue initially to the states, there would probably be a significant longer run "pass-through" benefit to the local sector. Establishment of a national health insurance program could also have a major fiscal impact by shifting to the federal government the state-local share of Medicaid costs and some other costs of public health services and hospitals.

The second potential role of the federal government would be to induce states to assume some of the financial burdens now borne at the local level. Specifically, it has been proposed that the federal government should offer financial incentives to states to take over most or all of the burden of financing public schools (possibly with the federal government assuming some fraction of the burden itself). Since elementary and secondary education consumes the largest share of local revenue, there is probably no single change in the intergovernmental system that could offer more local fiscal relief.

The third possibility is that federal incentives could be offered for changes in local government structure that would reduce metropolitan fragmentation and encourage tax base sharing. There has been limited federal support for the formation of metropolitan area authorities in the past. A number of federal grant programs could be used to provide the incentives for more substantial structural change in the future.

A major change in the scope of local service responsibilities will alter the locational incentives facing business firms and households. Both shifts of responsibilities to higher level governments and reduction of metropolitan fragmentation would tend to reduce the importance of interjurisdictional fiscal disparities as factors affecting locational decisions. In most instances the effect would be to reduce the advantages that suburbs now enjoy relative to central cities and rural areas. However, there are places where cities are financially better off than suburbs and where the effects would be in the opposite direction. Direct federal assumption of state or local responsibilities could also affect the relative attractiveness of different regions by reducing interarea differentials in service levels and tax rates. The general effect would probably be to favor the lower income regions of the country by reducing service and tax differentials that are attributable to differences in "ability to pay."

FEDERAL POLICY IMPACTS

The diagram on the following page (Figure 10-2) summarizes the discussion of federal policy impacts on the finances of the local public sector. It depicts the major determinants of the ability of local governments to satisfy the service demands of their residents and the broad categories of federal policy that affect each determinant. The diagram is drawn to distinguish between the determinants of local fiscal resources (the four rectangles along the right side of the figure) and the determinants of demands for local public expenditures (the four rectangles on the left).

A distinction is also made between federal policies that impinge directly upon the local public sector and those that operate indirectly via the household and private business sectors or via state government (the indirect policy channels are represented by dashed lines).

The Urban Impact of Federal Policies 239

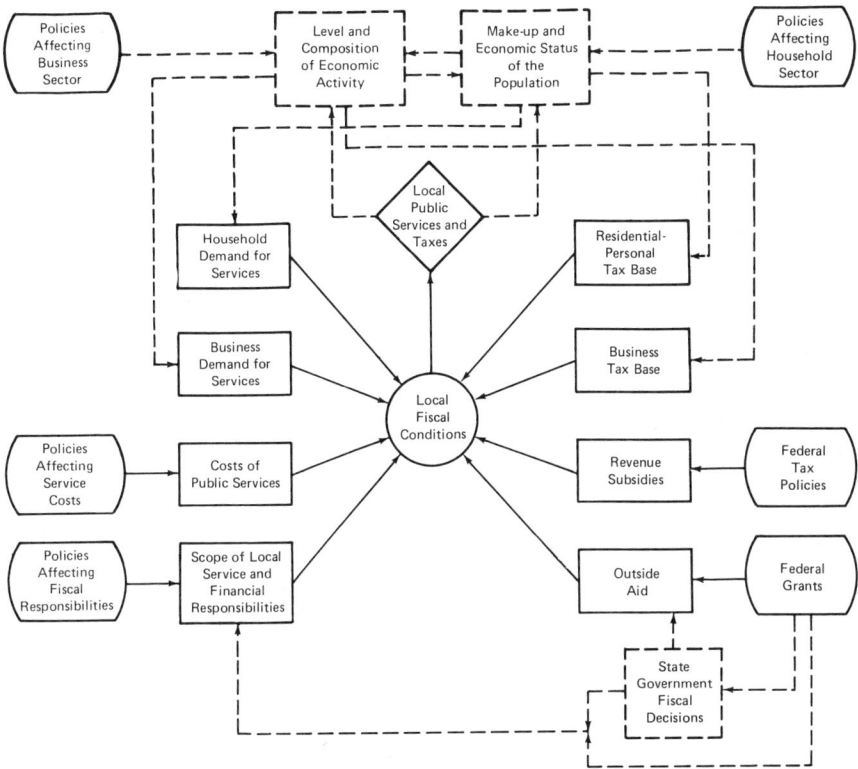

Figure 10-2. Federal Policy Impacts on the Local Public Sector.

The four major elements of local financial resources shown in the diagram are the residential/personal component of the local tax base, the business component of the tax base, grants-in-aid from federal and state sources, and federal revenue subsidies. It is shown that the federal government affects the first two by means of policies that alter the makeup and economic circumstances of the urban population and the level of urban economic activity, respectively. Federal grant policy is shown as operating both directly and through state government to influence the amount of outside aid available to the local sector. Federal tax policy is shown as the source of revenue subsidies to local governments.

On the expenditure side, demands for public services from urban households and businesses are shown as being influenced by the same federal policies that affect the household and business components of the tax base. Direct federal influences on local service costs and the scope of local responsibility are indicated. Also, the joint effects of state policies and federal grant policies on the financial and service obligations of the local sector are suggested by the network of dashed lines at the lower part of the diagram.

The most important point brought out by the diagram is that some of the main determinants of local fiscal conditions—the business and residential components of the local tax base and the level of local "needs" for public services—can be affected primarily, or exclusively, by federal policies directed at the *private* sector. Both the residential/personal component of the tax base and the characteristics of the urban population that generate service demands depend mainly on the locational decisions of households. Both the business component of the tax base and business demands for public services and facilities depend mainly on the locational decisions of business firms.

Although it is difficult to quantify the relative importance of the various determinants of local fiscal conditions, it seems likely (although we cannot be certain) that the federal policies aimed at the private sector have had a greater impact on local public sector outcomes over the years than have federal policies that affect the local public sector directly.

The diagram also reflects some of the major interactions that exist among the sectors of the urban economy, apart from the effects of private sector developments on local fiscal conditions. The two arrows connecting the economic activity and population composition boxes at the top of the diagram signify that developments in the business and residential sectors influence one another. This means that federal policies directed at the household sector are likely to affect business location decisions, and vice versa. The implication is that there are virtually no "pure" federal policies capable of influencing only one part of the system without disturbing others.

The connections between local services and taxes (the diamond-shaped figure in the diagram) and the economic activity and population boxes represent important feedback relationships between the public and private sectors. On the one hand, private sector outcomes affect the resources available to the public sector and the demand for public services; on the other hand, the adequacy of public services and the magnitudes of tax burdens are determinants of both business and residential locational choices. Therefore, any federal policy that improves local fiscal conditions (e.g., an increase in grants) is likely to have secondary effects on the demand for housing and the level of business activity. This further underscores the interrelatedness of the three sectors of the urban system.

IMPLICATIONS FOR FEDERAL POLICY DEVELOPMENT

Two general points about federal policy formulation emerge from the foregoing discussion. They are: (1) the potential importance of indirect federal policies—those that operate via linkages among the different sectors within the urban system; and (2) the central role of policies that affect the locational decisions of businesses and households.

Indirect Urban Strategies

Too little attention has been given to federal policies that operate indirectly. The strategies of working to affect the local business and residential tax bases or the levels of local demands for services deserve consideration as alternatives to the direct strategies of increased federal financial aid and federal (or state) assumption of local responsibilities. The longer the time horizon, the more attractive the indirect policies seem relative to the direct ones.

In the very short run, there is little that can be done to improve the fiscal conditions of urban areas other than to provide direct financial aid. However, if the aid funds go to support current social services, that will do nothing to attract business or to alter the makeup of the urban population in a fiscally favorable direction. In the long run, a federal policy limited to direct aid is likely to be self-defeating. Such a policy cannot eliminate conditions of economic decline or stagnation, and it virtually guarantees that increased amounts of aid will be needed in the future to sustain the urban public sector.

This does not mean that there are proven indirect policies waiting to be implemented. We know too little about the determinants of private sector behavior to be able to predict the magnitudes of indirect federal policy impacts, or to be sure that it is possible to design policies of sufficient potency to offset the underlying economic causes of urban decline. Still, the indirect route seems the more hopeful in the long run. It is the only route that is likely to help urban governments without making them completely dependent on federal largess—a concern mentioned in Chapters Nine and Eleven of this book.

Because developments in the private business sector and the household sector are closely related, there is considerable scope for creativity in the design of federal urban aid strategies. A policy that succeeds in attracting or retaining business in urban areas is likely to have indirect, fiscally favorable effects on the urban population; a policy that makes urban areas more attractive to middle income households is likely to have an indirect, positive effect on business activity and investment. This means that policies aimed at improving local fiscal conditions by the indirect, private sector route may be aimed at targets of opportunity in either the business or residential portions of the private sector without regard to whether it is private economic activity or the composition of the local population that the government ultimately hopes to influence.

Locational Incentives

The most important conclusion of this study is that locational incentives ought to be central elements in the development of a more comprehensive federal urban policy. Even with regard to the public sector, where locational incentives can have only indirect effects, the movements of people and industry in response to federal policy are of critical importance. Where the goal of policy is to affect the private sector of the urban economy, locational effects are of the essence. The objectives of stemming employment losses in central cities and reversing middle class or white flight can only be accomplished by policies that enhance the relative attractiveness of the urban centers.

Of course, it is easier to advocate that locational incentives be emphasized than it is to design them. There are two major obstacles to determining the potential effects of alternative locational strategies. One is that so many factors have influenced the pattern of urban development in the last two decades that it is extremely difficult to untangle them and assess their individual importance. Thus, although it is widely agreed that postwar suburbanization was stimulated by a combination of rising incomes, highway construction, housing subsidies, and minority migration to cities, no one has been able to quantify the relative influence of each of these major factors. The second problem is the irreversibility of many locational changes. The suburbs are built and the interstate highway system is in place. Nobody proposes to tear them down for the benefit of cities, even though, in retrospect, we might wish that they had developed differently.

The northward migration of the southern, rural poor is complete—a product among other things, of irreversible changes in agricultural technology. Therefore, even if the historical data yielded all their secrets, it would not be possible to help cities by operating the historical incentives in reverse. Although some may be reversible, for the most part, new locational incentives will have to be designed or discovered.

Recognition of the importance of locational incentives should lead to greater variety in the policy proposals put forth by spokesmen for the cities. Examples of policy alternatives that emphasize incentive effects rather than direct financial aid include the following.

1. Equalization of the tax treatment of housing expenditures by owner-occupants and tenants.
2. Extension of credit for housing rehabilitation and upgrading on terms comparable to credit for home purchases.
3. Revision of federal regulatory policies in the transportation field to eliminate anti-urban biases in services and rates.
4. Elimination of the bias in favor of new development that is inherent in federal water and sewer and other infrastructure grant programs by treating operation and maintenance of existing facilities on the same basis as construction of new ones.
5. Equalization of welfare benefits and social services among geographical areas.

In addition to options such as the above, all of which represent modifications of ongoing programs, it is possible to contemplate more thoroughgoing locational policies involving overt subsidies or tax benefits for "pro-urban" locational choices. These are in line with the concept of a comprehensive urban settlements policy, which some would make a central theme in the federal government's future role.

Chapter Eleven

Federal Aid for Cities: A Multiple Strategy

Richard P. Nathan and **Paul R. Dommel**

FRAMEWORK FOR ANALYSIS

In their pathbreaking Oakland study, Levy, Meltsner, and Wildavsky use three concepts of equity which provide a good starting point for this analysis. One is market equity, meaning that "an agency should give a citizen benefits in proportion to the taxes he pays" (1). A second is equal opportunity, giving each citizen the same dollar amount of services. Third is the equal results standard, "that an agency should allocate its resources so that all people are in an equal condition after the money is spent" (2). The third concept is, of course, the most liberal idea of equity in the way we customarily think of liberal and conservative.

These three equity concepts are shown in diagrammatic form in Figure 11-1, using somewhat different terms. We use the term "distributive" equity to refer to equal shares, and "opportunity" equity to refer to allocations according to poverty or income needs on the premise of bringing all recipients up to some equal opportunity starting point.

Several studies are brought together in this chapter on how the federal government can identify and deal with the needs of cities. Two ongoing monitoring projects examine the effects of the general revenue sharing and the community development block grant (CDBG) programs. Also underway is work to define urban "hardship" and possible alternative strategies for "welfare reform." These various projects have especially close interconnections for purposes of considering urban policy issues. The material presented here is the responsibility of the authors. Part of this chapter is based on work performed under a contract with the U.S. Department of Housing and Urban Development to monitor the Community Development Block Grant Program.

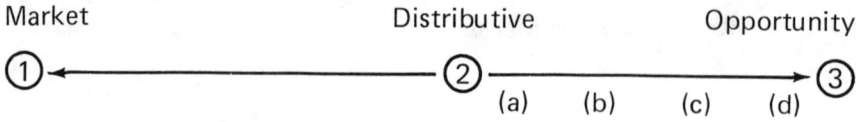

Figure 11-1. The Three Equity Concepts.

Beginning with market equity, many people said in 1969 when general revenue sharing was introduced by the Nixon administration that essentially it should pay money back according to the federal taxes paid by the residents of qualifying governments, the notion being that we should have one federal grant program that recognizes the proposition, "Him that gives, gets." Many citizens believe that they pay too much under government programs and do not receive a just amount of compensation for their tax payments. Here is one program, so the theory goes, that should work for the taxpayer.

To expand this analysis, we have marked four positions on the equity continuum. General revenue sharing, in the terms discussed above, would be at about position (a). The CDBG program as currently structured would be at about (b). The alternative approach to allocating CDBG funds presented in this paper would move it to (c). A transfer program like Food Stamps would be at about point (d), or perhaps all the way to the number 3 polar position. To this system, we would add two additional concepts as directional signals—spreading and targeting. Spreading moves from right to left on the diagram; targeting on the other hand refers to efforts to concentrate funds on "need," moving, therefore, from left to right.

Listed below are three general points applying to federal policy using this framework.

1. Transfer payments to families and individuals are better instruments than grants-in-aid for targeting, that is, moving towards the equity of opportunity position on the diagram above.
2. At the national level, we observe strong tendencies towards spreading under grants-in-aid to jurisdictions (state and local governments) in the distribution of grant funds.
3. Similarly, at the local level in the use of federal grant funds, our research on the CDBG program suggests that spreading often occurs in the use of federal grants-in-aid even on the part of communities with a significant low income population.

With these ideas and illustrations in place, we turn now to a discussion of federal aid policies for urban areas. We define "aid" as broadly encompassing both grants-in-aid to jurisdictions and transfer payments to individuals.

URBAN AID AND POLITICAL IMPERATIVES

The postwar period saw a great rise in the amounts of federal aid to state and local governments, increasing from about $2 billion in 1948 to $60 billion in 1976. Accompanying this increase in dollar amounts was the growth in the number of programs created to meet physical and human resource needs. For the most part, urban grant-in-aid programs were in the form of project grants, designed to provide funds for a specific project such as an urban renewal project or water and sewer development. Project grants permit considerable latitude of decisionmaking at the federal level in determining who will get such funding.

Besides making project grants, the federal government also makes formula grants, which provide funds to states and in some cases to local governments on the basis of certain measurable criteria, such as population and per capita income. Under most formula grants a fixed amount of money is available annually for a specific jurisdiction, subject to certain eligibility requirements. Allocating by formula gives less discretion to decisionmakers in the federal bureaucracy than does allocation on a project basis.

As the number of grants grew, so did dissatisfaction with the aid system. With growth came major problems of coordination, increased controls, and a greater degree of overlapping among programs. Several complaints were directed particularly at project grants. Among major objections were red tape and the attendant delays from application through final audit. Another frequent complaint was that the money was allocated on a basis favoring communities with the in-house expertise to develop project ideas quickly and make the necessary applications skillfully.

To a large extent because of the complaints, proposals for revenue sharing and block grants began to emerge. Revenue sharing was urged by some proponents in the mid 1960s as a means of providing funds to fiscally hard pressed state and local governments. To others it was perceived as a mechanism to substitute "no strings" money for some of the project and formula grants. Decentralization and equalization purposes were also stressed.

The idea of a block grant in this context was seen as a complementary allocation mechanism to revenue sharing as a means of reducing federal grant controls. Block grants were viewed as a means of consolidating a number of related, narrower purpose grants into a single block. Importantly, they were also perceived by some proponents as a distributive mechanism for converting "nothing for some" project grants into "something for everyone" formula grants. These new approaches brought national policy makers much more actively into the business of developing allocation systems. Allocation systems contain two distinct elements: (1) eligibility—stipulating who may participate in the program; (2) distribution—determining the amount of funds eligible units will receive.

We noted above that the redirection of aid policy from project to formula grants opened the way toward a "something for everyone" approach. This is nowhere more apparent than in the eligibility standard of general revenue sharing which provides entitlement grants to some 39,000 state and local government recipients. For all practical purposes, this decision was made in mid 1969 when the state and local coalition was being built to push for revenue sharing. This was more than three years before the legislation was passed; the decision in this case was never seriously challenged.

The second allocation decision, resource distribution, was not resolved until the House-Senate conference in 1972. Having adopted a broad entitlement standard, the issue then became how to provide for allocations based on objective measures that reasonably take complex and diverse organizational and fiscal arrangements into account among states and within states. Five factors were used—population, relative income, general tax effort, income tax collections, and urban population.

The effort to fix allocations was further complicated by the decision to include ceiling and floor provisions that have the effect of limiting the amount of funds some of the largest and neediest cities can receive and at the same time substantially increasing the amount of money received by many smaller communities and especially midwestern townships, which would have received a significantly lower allocation under a straight application of the formula. The net result is that central cities and rural poverty areas tend to do better than suburban areas—but not much better.

A second illustration, stressed in this chapter, is the Community Development Block Grant (CDBG) program, the biggest and, in our opinion, the most important of the block grants. As contrasted to the typical view of revenue sharing, block grants are not "new" money; they consolidate narrow purpose grants in a broad functional area and tend to involve relatively small amounts of additional funding. The CDBG program takes seven programs administered by HUD—particularly urban renewal and model cities—and puts them together in a single block, which goes to cities and some counties but not to states. The program has been in effect for more than two years. The Brookings Institution is currently engaged in a monitoring study of the program in 62 cities and counties, parallel to the Institution's monitoring study of the general revenue sharing program.

Under CDBG, all central cities, suburban cities with populations of 50,000 or more, and urban counties are so-called "entitlement" jurisdictions, involving in all nearly 600 recipient units. It should be no surprise that urban county governments and suburban communities generally are emerging as "winners in Washington." The demography of the United States indicates that suburbs are increasingly becoming the population centers of the nation, having a larger share of the nation's population than either central cities or rural areas. This is reflected (some would say overreflected) in the CDBG allocation system.

In addition to the entitlement areas, there are also discretionary funds for small metropolitan communities which, if the present formula is retained and fully implemented in fiscal 1980, will mean that in fiscal 1980 over half of the money would be going to these communities. In sum, the CDBG program as initially established represents a significant reallocation of urban funds away from central cities, who were the chief beneficiaries of the folded-in project grants as shown in the second and fourth columns of Table 11-1.[a] Referring to the introductory section of this paper, the combination of formula entitlements and discretionary funding of the CDBG program has a substantial spreading effect; funds are distributed to a much larger number of recipients than was the case for the folded-in project grants.

Next we look at the formula itself. In addition to the reallocations resulting from the eligibility decisions, a similar effect is seen as a result of the actual formula criteria. Allocations to the entitlement governments are based on population, overcrowded housing, and poverty weighted twice. These criteria result in a major bias toward southern cities because of the higher incidence of the poverty and

---

[a]In 1977 Congress adopted a dual formula system, an approach originally proposed in the Brookings Institution CDBG monitoring study which redirects a larger portion of funds back to older central cities. This change in the allocation system was incorporated into legislation extending the program through fiscal year 1981. Under the dual formula approach, a second formula weighted toward age of housing is added to the original poverty-based formula. An entitlement jurisdiction receives the higher amount computed under the two formulas.

Table 11-1. Folded-in Grant Distributions Compared with Projected 1980 Allocation of CDBG Funds Within Metropolitan Areas (1980 Projections Based on a Funding Assumption of $2.95 Billion)

Recipient Metropolitan area, by type	Folded-in (millions of dollars)	Percent of total	CDBG formula (millions of dollars)	Percent of total
Metropolitan areas				
Central cities	1,499	71.8	1,182	42.2
Suburban cities	94	4.5	140	5.0
Urban counties	67	3.2	290	10.3
Rest of SMSA	166	7.9	628	22.5
Total to metropolitan recipients	1,825	87.4	2,240	80
Total to non-metropolitan recipients	263	12.6	550	20

Source: The folded-in grant allocations were calculated from data supplied by the Department of Housing and Urban Development. The fiscal 1980 allocations were computed by applying the first-year data on objective needs to a projected fiscal 1980 appropriation.

overcrowded housing in that region as shown in Table 11-2 (columns 6 and 7). Suburban cities and urban counties in the western states also benefit significantly, but their principal benefits come as a consequence of the eligibility decisions. Many of these jurisdictions, particularly suburban communities, had not participated, or participated at a low level, in the folded-in project grants, but under the CDBG program they become "entitled" to an allocation. Taking both the eligibility and formula allocation decisions, the result is a significant reallocation of funds from the central cities of the Northeast Quadrant (the northeastern and midwestern states), as shown in Table 11-2 (column 5).

This brings us to one of the central issues of this chapter and our current CDBG research. How can we measure urban "need"? How can we target aid funds to such cities? Our research suggests that measurements of need are possible and that these objective measures can be translated into public policy. We emphasize that the approaches we consider are by no means the only approach. They are illustrative, however, of the kinds of steps that could be taken, depending on one's particular value preferences.

Federal Aid for Cities: A Multiple Strategy 251

Table 11-2. Folded-in Grant Distributions Compared with Projected 1980 Allocation of CDBG Funds Among Central Cities, by Region (Levels of Overcrowded Housing and Poverty)

Region	Number	Folded-in (millions of dollars) (1)	Percent of total (2)	Formula (millions of dollars) (3)	Percent of total (4)	Change in share (percent) (5)	OVH index (6)	Poverty index (7)
U.S. total	362	1,499	100.0	1,182	100.0	—	100	100
New England	34	159	10.6	53	4.5	−6.1	83	82
Middle Atlantic	43	332	22.1	259	21.9	−.2	107	101
East North Central	64	262	17.5	220	18.6	+1.1	92	89
West North Central	24	106	7.1	64	5.4	−1.7	85	84
South Atlantic	61	227	15.2	160	13.5	−1.7	105	120
East South Central	23	62	4.2	67	5.7	+1.5	106	131
West South Central	53	132	8.8	165	14.0	+5.2	121	124
Mountain	16	47	3.1	43	3.6	+.5	88	86
Pacific	44	172	11.4	151	12.8	+1.4	93	83

Sources: The folded-in grant allocations and the indices were calculated directly from hold-harmless determinations and data elements used by the Department of Housing and Urban Development in making first-year CDBG allocations. The fiscal 1980 allocations were computed by applying the first-year data on objective needs to a projected fiscal 1980 appropriation.

DEFINING URBAN NEED

How valid are the present CDBG formula criteria as measures of community development need? We discuss below each of the present formula criteria.

First is the population criterion. It can reasonably be argued that a population factor is an essential element in an urban focus. On the other hand, population contributes materially to the spreading effect of the CDBG program. Even if a suburban city with a population of 50,000 had no overcrowded housing and no poverty (and for some suburban cities this is nearly the case), that city still receives an entitlement based on population.

The second formula element, poverty, is more complicated. The CDBG program was not advertised by its proponents primarily as a means to eliminate poverty. The program is, however, aimed at alleviating the conditions of physical blight that accompany poverty. Viewed from the local level, poverty impacted communities tend to spend a higher proportion of their budgets on services for the poor, while deriving relatively fewer tax dollars from this group. In sum, the poverty factor can be said to serve as a proxy for both physical and fiscal need.

The overcrowded housing criterion is the most questionable of the three formula factors. Poverty and overcrowded housing are closely associated (a correlation coefficient of .6411). Given this association between overcrowded housing and poverty, the housing factor has the effect of further weighting the poverty criterion. The net result of this criterion is to further weight the formula toward the South.

What is missing from the formula is a measure of the condition of a community's physical plant—streets, sewers, public buildings, and other facilities, as well as actual dwellings. For this aspect of community development need, one statistical indicator that can be used is the amount of housing stock built before 1939. Not all housing built before 1939 is deteriorated or deteriorating, but the age of housing is quite clearly linked to the rehabilitation needs of urban communities and to the physical development purposes of the CDBG program.

The age-of-housing factor is particularly relevant to the needs of central cities, especially the cities of the Northeast Quadrant. Table 11-3 shows, using index numbers, the incidence of overcrowded housing, poverty, and pre-1939 housing in the various regions; it is shown that the cities in the Northeast and midwestern states would clearly benefit from the age-of-housing criterion. Similarly, the table shows that central cities as a whole would be benefited by this

Table 11-3. Indices of Overcrowded Housing, Poverty, and Extent of Pre-1939 Housing, by Region and Community Type

Region	OVH index	Poverty index	Pre-1939 housing index
New England	109	89	158
Middle Atlantic	96	96	143
East North Central	92	85	120
West North Central	92	88	107
South Atlantic	103	122	65
East South Central	112	147	74
West South Central	128	137	56
Mountain	95	96	55
Pacific	96	86	68
Community Type			
U.S.	100	100	100
Central cities	114	108	122
Suburban cities	84	53	70
Urban counties[a]	80	51	55

Source: Indices calculated from data used by the U.S. Department of Housing and Urban Development in making first-year allocations. Pre-1939 indices based on data from *1970 Census of Housing, Detailed Housing Characteristics*, Series HC(1)B, Table 35.

[a]The pre-1939 housing index for urban counties is based on an imputed number derived by assigning to urban counties by region, the same percentage of pre-1939 housing units outside of central and satellite cities as the urban county percentage of SMSA population outside of central and satellite cities.

criterion. Our research suggests that the CDBG allocation system needs to accommodate two different types of urban development need—needs that reflect physical condition and those that are more poverty related.

At this point, some readers may conclude that an accommodation should be arrived at by equally weighting these three criteria as measures of diverse needs—population, poverty, and age-of-housing. Table 11-4, comparing projected total allocations to metropolitan areas under the existing formula and such an alternative formula, shows the effects of this alternative approach.

Regionally, the Northeast Quadrant is benefited while the southern and western regions lose. Table 11-4 also shows the central cities deriving benefits from the alternative approach. At this point, however, the seemingly "logical" answers may conflict with the politics of CDBG. Adoption of this alternative would mean that existing CDBG entitlements would be lowered for some recipients;

other jurisdictions would receive bonuses in the form of reallocated funds. The history of general revenue sharing does not offer much encouragement about the prospects for such changes.

Extensive research was carried out at various places, including Brookings, suggesting ways to redesign the revenue sharing formula to better align the allocations with various measures of need. The Ford administration opposed any formula changes (except one advanced halfheartedly); the state and urban lobbies generally opposed any formula alterations; and there was little effective pressure from other groups in Congress for significant formula change. As a consequence, the original formula was retained. The problem is a familiar one. Once a recipient has an entitlement, it becomes as fixed as the stars in the firmament; the downward adjustment of some entitlements and upward adjustment of others is, to say the least, very difficult to achieve.

Table 11-4. Comparison of Projected CDBG Grants to Metropolitan Areas for Fiscal 1980 with Allocations Under an Alternative Formula Equally Weighting Population, Poverty, and pre-1939 Housing (by Region and Community Type)

Region	CDBG (millions of dollars)	Percent of CDBG total	Alternative formula (millions of dollars)	Percent of CDBG total
New England	111	4.0	144	5.2
Middle Atlantic	452	16.2	550	19.8
East North Central	409	14.6	453	16.3
West North Central	120	4.3	127	4.6
South Atlantic	336	12.0	279	10.0
East South Central	133	4.7	106	3.8
West South Central	264	9.4	201	7.2
Mountain	74	2.6	16	.6
Pacific	341	12.2	311	11.2
Community type				
Central cities	1,182	42.2	1,242	44.6
Suburban cities	140	5.0	148	5.3
Urban counties	290	10.3	290[a]	10.4
SMSA discretionary	628	22.5	552	19.7

Source: Calculated from data used by the U.S. Department of Housing and Urban Development in making first-year CDBG allocations. Data on pre-1939 housing are from *1970 Census of Housing, Detailed Housing Characteristics*, Series HC(1)B, Tables 35, 43, and 62.

[a]The urban county allocations are based on imputed figures to show the relative shift in shares and do not represent actual projected amounts or percentages.

The legislative history of general revenue sharing suggests another important lesson. In the final version, the House and Senate conferees adopted a Solomon-like compromise. Unable to agree on a single formula that accommodated the fundamentally incompatible versions adopted by the House and Senate, the conferees allocated to each state the greater of the amounts provided under the two bills. The same approach is possible with the CDBG program.

It would be both desirable and feasible to have a dual formula system for the CDBG program. Retain the present formula weighted toward poverty needs and adopt a second formula weighted toward the problems of the older cities. Each formula entitlement area would receive CDBG funds according to whichever formula yields the largest amount in its particular case. To make the two formulas approximately equal in their impact, the new alternative formula which is added could double weight the age-of-housing factor. The housing-age formula would be composed of population, poverty and pre-1939 housing counted twice.

The net result of the dual formula system is shown in Table 11-5,

Table 11-5. Comparison of Formula Allocations to Metropolitan Areas Under the CDBG Formula and the Dual Formula Alternative (by Region and Community Type)

Region	CDBG formula (millions of dollars)	Percent of CDBG total	Dual formula (millions of dollars)	Percent of CDBG total
New England	67	2.4	100	3.6
Middle Atlantic	348	12.5	462	16.6
East North Central	295	10.6	367	13.1
West North Central	84	3.0	104	3.7
South Atlantic	221	7.9	227	8.1
East South Central	75	2.7	76	2.7
West South Central	183	6.6	183	6.6
Mountain	51	1.8	53	1.9
Pacific	288	10.3	309	11.1
Community type				
Central cities	1,182	42.2	1,394	50.0
Suburban cities	140	5.0	169	6.1
Urban counties	290	10.3	318	11.4
SMSA discretionary	628	22.5	359	12.9

Source: Calculated from data used by the U.S. Department of Housing and Urban Development in making first-year CDBG allocations. Data on pre-1939 housing are from *1970 Census of Housing, Detailed Housing Characteristics*, Series HC(1)B, Tables 35, 43, and 62.

comparing formula allocations under the existing and dual systems. The most significant gains are made by communities in the Northeast Quadrant and by central cities, but no entitlement recipient loses funds. The additional money is obtained from the metropolitan discretionary funds which go to small suburban communities. Since the discretionary funds do not operate on a system of formula entitlements, there are no specific communities that lose. If it is felt that the discretionary funds are too greatly reduced, they can be augmented by adding additional funds.

The dual formula approach (one among countless possible formula iterations of CDBG), moves on the continuum towards the number three opportunity position, targeting additional resources on what are defined for purposes of this analysis as urban needs. A judicious mix (at least we could call it that) of analytical and feasibility considerations has gone into the analysis of alternative ways of allocating CDBG funds. We would stress that this approach is not put forward as an ideal or optimal solution, merely as a better way of recognizing values highlighted in the debate about CDBG but seemingly downplayed in the original formula. There is, however, another and in many respects more important way to move on the continuum in the targeting direction under the CDBG program.

AID TO NEEDIEST CITIES

We spoke earlier of the distinction between "nothing for some" and "something for everyone" approaches to federal grant-in-aid policy. The present CDBG program was characterized as "something for everyone" akin to general revenue sharing. Having established such a policy under CDBG, it may now be politically possible to talk about supplementing the basic system with funding limited to the more distressed cities. An additional formula factor important to the measurement of urban distress is included in this context—the decline of population.

In its present form, the CDBG formula favors growing communities over declining communities. There is implicit reasoning that more people mean more problems and greater burdens for a community. In a variety of ways, such as the need for additional streets, sewerage, police and fire protection, and water facilities, this is true. But growing cities tend to gain population with a higher income and growth increases property values, two important elements of a community's resource base. Declining cities, on the other hand, tend to have higher concentrations of low income population and a shrinking resource base.[b]

---

[b]Recognition of the special problems of declining and slow growing cities was incorporated into the dual formula system of the 1977 extension legislation. The

Table 11-6 divides the CDBG entitlement cities into two groups, those gaining and those losing population. The 150 declining cities show higher percentages of minority populations, lower income, and lower housing values. Highly significant also are the rates of changes in the two resource base factors, income and housing values. Between 1960 and 1970 per capita income grew faster in the growing cities by nearly 5 percent while housing values increased at a rate nearly 6 percent faster.

George E. Peterson, in a study of city finances, has focused the fiscal problems of declining cities and the contrasting opportunities of growing cities (3).

> The simple economics of overhead spreading then dictates that as population falls, the per capita costs associated with city operations must weigh more heavily on the remaining taxpayers.
>
> No city can withstand population losses of more than 20 percent in the space of 13 years, as has happened in Buffalo, Cleveland, Pittsburgh, and St. Louis, without suffering a decline in demand for the city's standing stock of housing. This is reflected in lower housing prices. . . .
>
> Growing cities, on the other hand, have benefited greatly from having their revenues tied to the property tax base. Not only are additions constantly being made to the cities' capital stock, but in-migration generates a vigorous demand for existing housing which drives up market prices.

We have combined three factors of poverty, community age

Table 11-6. Growing and Declining Cities in the CDBG Program During the Period 1960-70, Showing Black Population, Per Capita Incomes and Median Housing Values and Rates of Change for Income and Housing Values

Population experience 1960-70	Number (1)	Percent population change (2)	Average percent black (3)	Per capita income 1970 (dollars) (4)	Rate of income change 1960-70 (percent) (5)	Median house value 1970 ($000) (6)	Rate of value change 1960-70 (percent) (7)
Population losses	150	−6.7	17.3	3,062	57.0	15.9	32.5
Population gains	356[a]	20.5[b]	10.2	3,354	61.7	18.8	38.2

Source: Population, income and housing value data from U.S. Bureau of the Census, *County and City Data Book*, 1962 and 1972, Table 6.

[a]Does not include urban counties plus eight CDBG entitlement cities that did not exist as incorporated units in 1960.

[b]This is the median value. The calculated mean is 38.0 but this is high because of some extremely high values among a few communities gaining population.

second formula incorporates three factors—age of housing (.5 weighting), poverty (.3), and growth lag (.2). Growth lag measures the extent to which a locality has fallen below the average population growth of all CDBG formula entitlement cities.

(measured by pre-1939 housing stock), and population growth or decline into a formula for indexing community hardship (Figure 11-2). On the basis of this indexing of community hardship, needier communities are selected for supplemental CDBG funding. This formula was applied to determine eligibility for supplemental funding. Approximately one-third (196) of all CDBG entitlement cities are eligible on this basis. (Chapter Twelve of the Brookings report, "Block Grants for Community Development," shows all of the eligible cities.)

The next step is to calculate actual allocations. We use a formula equally weighting population, poverty, and pre-1939 housing, thus giving no weight advantage to any region through the poverty or age criteria. The coefficient for each jurisdiction is set against a given total of $500 million in supplemental funds to determine individual recipient allocations.[c] We feel it is also important to introduce a rate of change concept into the allocations by dividing this end coefficient by population change prior to calculating the final allocation. Applying these decision rules, we found that the neediest eligible city, East St. Louis, would receive $42.88 per capita while the 199th city, Bethlehem, Pennsylvania, would receive $5.24 per capita.

TARGETING URBAN AID: TRANSFER PAYMENTS

A central idea of this paper is that grant programs and transfer programs have to be looked at together in considering the policy of the federal government in relation to urban finances. The three general points in the introductory section of the paper suggest that transfer payments are better suited to targeting as a policy objective—that is, dealing with poverty in urban areas.

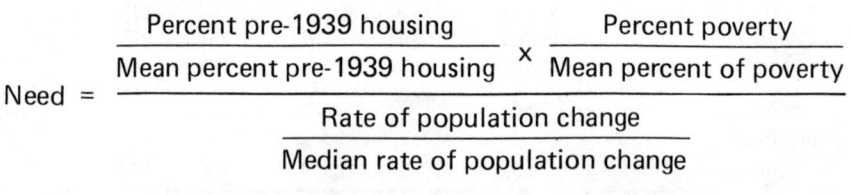

$$\text{Need} = \frac{\dfrac{\text{Percent pre-1939 housing}}{\text{Mean percent pre-1939 housing}} \times \dfrac{\text{Percent poverty}}{\text{Mean percent of poverty}}}{\dfrac{\text{Rate of population change}}{\text{Median rate of population change}}}$$

Figure 11-2. Formula for Indexing Community Hardship.

---

[c]The supplemental funding approach was incorporated into the 1977 extension legislation, adding $400 million to the basic block grant program. These additional funds for Urban Development Action Grants will be distributed on a discretionary basis by the Department of Housing and Urban Development to alleviate both physical and economic deterioration in severely distressed cities.

Underlying these ideas is an assumption that poverty is a special problem of the central city. The incidence of poverty was significantly higher outside of metropolitan areas—17.1 percent as compared to 13.4 percent in central cities in 1969. However, by 1974, the two areas were the same. The poverty rate of central cities is twice that of suburbs in 1974 as shown in Table 11-7.

The next question is, can we discern differences in the incidence among cities from the point of view of the burden of poverty on the public fisc. Here we are not looking so much at the poverty index as at the burden of the poor, recognizing that welfare benefits and eligibility levels are higher in cities generally and particularly in the older and declining cities of the Northeast Quadrant. Their higher benefit and eligibility levels, combined with their greater structural isolation, produce the conditions we would expect. Welfare incidence tends to be much higher in cities with higher hardship ratings (using the Brookings index) compared to cities with low hardship ratings. This is shown in Table 11-8.

This, of course, does not mean that the governments of central cities are burdened. Welfare is much more likely, even in these regions, to be a state or county responsibility. The city is more likely burdened both because of the diminished tax base and by virtue of the need to pay for what are often relatively expensive services for these groups.

John Shannon has presented a useful analysis of the welfare burden of the states, which shows as one would expect, that the states of the Northeast Quadrant (in large measure of their own doing) have the heaviest burdens. Boston is ranked first in Table 11-8 for its concentration of welfare cases. For Massachusetts as a whole, welfare expenditures as calculcated by the ACIR are 2.16 percent of state personal income—a ratio three times the national average,

Table 11-7. Percent of Persons in Poverty Status, 1974

	Percent
Central city	14.4
Negro	(29.6)
Suburban rings	7.1
Negro	(21.9)
Outside metropolitan areas	14.4
Negro	(42.0)

Source: U.S. Department of Commerce Document P-60, No. 102, *Current Population Reports—Consumer Income Characteristics of Population Below the Poverty Level: 1976*, pp. 38-40.

Table 11-8. Percent Central County Population Receiving Welfare Payments, Selected Cities and Central City Hardship Rankings

Top Six Welfare Percent	Welfare Percent	Hardship Rank
Boston	17.0	15
Baltimore	16.8	4
Philadelphia	16.5	14
St. Louis	15.8	6
Detroit	12.8	12
New York	12.6	11
Bottom Six		
Phoenix	3.1	49
Dallas	3.4	47
Houston	3.5	48
Seattle	4.3	53
Buffalo	4.7	17
Indianapolis	5.1	36

Source: Table 13, Chapter 2, "Finance," by George E. Peterson in *The Urban Predicament*, edited by William Gorham and Nathan Glazer. Hardship ranks, *Political Science Quarterly*, Spring 1976, DHEW Pub. No. (SRS) 76-03105, July 1975.

as shown in Table 11-9. He proposes a plan (a new Shannon plan) of fiscal relief under welfare according to the welfare burdens of the states (4).

In terms of benefit levels and coverage, welfare reforms that deal with current gaps and deficiencies in benefits under federally aided income maintenance programs would aid older and distressed central cities disproportionately because of (1) their relatively high proportions of recipients, as shown above, and (2) their generally higher benefits levels. In this setting, welfare reform is clearly part of the urban agenda; and yet "federalization" and other simplistic answers should not be. Federalization, which simply means Uncle Sam picks up the check, is really a nonpolicy.

No one seriously proposes that having the federal government pay as much as the states want to charge is a feasible policy. But more than this, even versions of federalization that involve a higher welfare matching ratio (e.g., the Abzug bill in the 94th Congress to raise the federal match to 75 percent) have glaring deficiencies. Such fiscal relief would focus on states, which in many cases are relatively well off, and county governments, with only a few cities (notably New York) benefiting at all. But even worse than that, such reforms are

Table 11-9. Welfare Burden, by State, NA = .76

States of Northeast Quadrant	Percent[a]
Massachusetts	2.66
Michigan	1.61
Rhode Island	1.58
New York	1.53
Pennsylvania	1.34
Wisconsin	1.29
Minnesota	1.25
Vermont	1.19
New Hampshire	1.13
Maine	1.12
New Jersey	1.09
Illinois	1.08
Ohio	1.02
Iowa	.92
Delaware	.90
Connecticut	.82
States Outside Northeast Quadrant	
California	1.59
Hawaii	1.41
Oregon	1.02
Kentucky	.90
Maryland	.88
Washington	.81
Alaska	.77
Colorado	.77

Source: Table C-1, "Measuring the Fiscal 'Blood Pressure' of the States," John Ross and John Shannon, October 15, 1976 (processed).

[a]Welfare burden is state-local spending from own funds for welfare as a percent of state personal income.

simply revenue sharing by another name and could end up not benefiting the poor in any way. Proper welfare reform, in the view of the authors, should include fiscal relief, but its primary focus should be welfare.

Welfare reform, as observed, contains both grant and transfer program features. Fiscal relief under welfare must be considered in a grant-in-aid framework; in this context there are considerable difficulties in targeting, moving towards the number three equity position, because states and counties are currently paying the bulk of the nonfederal share. However, on the benefits side, the targeting objective is much easier to achieve; in fact, we argue that transfer programs are on the whole a much better targeting device than grant-in-aid programs. We would further urge that whatever fiscal relief is part of a welfare reform plan, consideration be given to some version of the Shannon Plan, as referenced above, of relating fiscal relief in some way to above-average welfare burdens.

A MULTIPLE STRATEGY

In recent months, political leaders in the Northeast and Midwest have called national attention to the relative decline of the old industrial states compared to the Sunbelt. For a much longer time, urbanologists have been calling attention to the serious conditions of decay and hopelessness in the nation's older and infected core cities. These two themes come together for purposes of national policy. As we have discussed, the preponderance of infected core cities in the United States are in the Northeast Quadrant.

It should be stressed that in many healthy cities and suburban areas the nation's domestic problems are less serious and indeed are not perceived by residents in such critical and urgent terms. This is not to say that central cities outside the Northeast and suburban and rural areas don't have problems, only that their problems are not likely to be so compounded and acute as to warrant being described in crisis terms.

This chapter on federal aid policies affecting the cities deals with two main parts of what we suggest should be a multiple strategy: (1) revising current grant-in-aid distribution formulas to give greater attention to urban hardship conditions; and (2) parallel and incremental revisions of transfer programs, including both welfare policy changes and fiscal relief. One additional subject relating to federal aid should be added to this list. We increasingly see a role for some form of Urban Development Bank. Its function should be to assist investors in industrial and commercial development ventures for job creation in designated cities with hardship conditions.

Still another element of a multiple strategy is that the federal government could step in and deal on some basis with issues of state-local governmental structure. This subject, which has been examined in our research, requires further discussion. To a significant extent, the problems of urban distress involve boundaries. Old cities such as Cleveland, St. Louis, Baltimore, Detroit, Philadelphia, and Newark were established in the late nineteenth century. In St. Louis, for example, it was considered "liberal" to have the city include what was then a large territory. What happened is that these cities became surrounded by vast areas of closely settled incorporated territory.

When the automobile revolution occurred, it was difficult, if not impossible, to annex these adjacent areas because it would be necessary to add places that already existed as cities and did not choose to be annexed. Once the migration of poor and blacks from the South began to crest for the older cities, these boundary and political issues involved became rigidified. On the other hand, in the West and the South the city has tended to follow its tax base. Newer cities of the Sunbelt region are in many cases surrounded by unincorporated territory, which is easily annexed. Further state laws (e.g., Texas) often facilitate annexation.

This background is important, because a government that does not control functions and boundaries—the federal government in this case—is in a difficult position to deal equitably with political jurisdictions on problems of urban distress. The states as the arbiters of local governmental boundaries and functions have a central role to play in contemporary federalism. We see a need to consider federal policies to stimulate and support such efforts.[d]

---

[d]For further discussion of the Brookings CDBG monitoring study and urban policy research see: Brookings Institution, *Round Table Discussion on Urban Development Banking*, Washington, D.C., March 21, 1977; Richard P. Nathan, et al., *Block Grants for Community Development*, U.S. Department of Housing and Urban Development, February, 1977; Richard P. Nathan, et al., "Monitoring the Block Grant Program for Community Development," *Political Science Quarterly* (Summer 1977), pp. 219-44; and Richard P. Nathan and Paul R. Dommel, "The Cities," *Setting National Priorities, 1978*, edited by Joseph A. Pechman (Washington, D.C.: The Brookings Institution, 1977), pp. 283-316.

Part Six

The Metropolitan Setting and the Future of Small Cities

Chapter Twelve

The Coming Age of the Polynucleated Metropolis

Werner Z. Hirsch

Many scholars have convincingly argued that the forces which fostered the growth of the suburbs and led to the demise of the central city in the postwar period will continue to dominate the near future. However, little has been said about the probable spatial settlement pattern of tomorrow's suburbia. I agree with the prognosis of further suburbanization and see little hope for central cities to regain their earlier attractiveness and reverse the postwar migration trend. However, I would like to take the next step and point to a changing suburban settlement pattern that is emerging—the polynucleated metropolis. In such a development, medium-size cities will occupy a distinguished and major place.

THE SUBURBAN FRAMEWORK

What is the nature of the suburban configuration that is likely to emerge; why is it expected to develop and what implications is it likely to have? These issues are the subject of this chapter. To begin with, a framework will be presented within which the analysis will proceed.

The forces that affect spatial settlement patterns in America fall into several classes. Although there are strong interdependencies, it is

---

This paper, in part, originated from work in progress at the RAND Corporation, supported by the Energy Research and Development Administration.

useful to distinguish among these classes. Figure 12-1 provides a schematic view of the framework. The location of employment opportunities is affected by the demand for and supply of major resources, including energy, as well as by technological changes. Industrial location decisions affect employment opportunities and therefore have a bearing on trips-to-work, often considered to be the single most important urban transportation purpose.

Households in making their residential location decision tend to trade off housing and transportation costs. Usually, the further out the land is located in suburbia the lower its price; at the same time travel costs increase. Furthermore, a variety of demographic factors affect the demand for housing and transportation as well as the supply of urban labor. Important demographic factors include household size, age of head of household, number of school age children, number of gainfully employed in household, race, and so on. Finally, all these location decisions are made within a particular institutional environment. Among the important environmental factors are those that facilitate the movement into and within suburbia of various demographic groups: the tax system, zoning ordinances, and so forth.

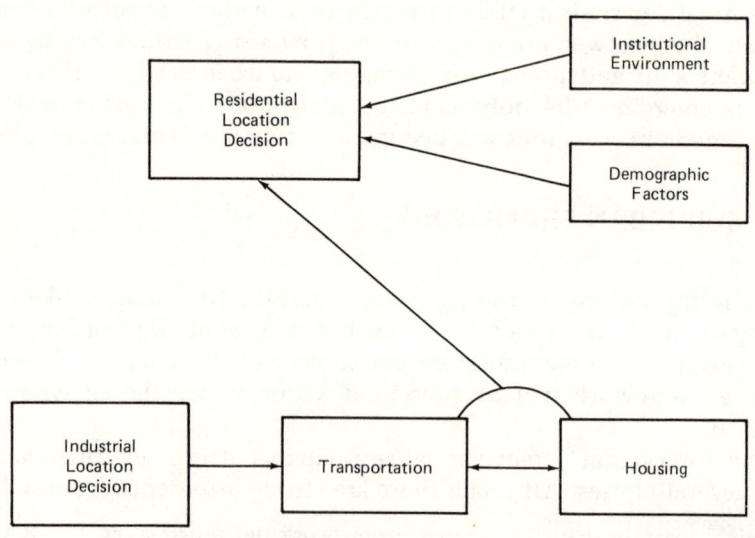

Figure 12-1. Factors Affecting Spatial Settlement Patterns.

INDUSTRIAL LOCATION PATTERNS

Interest in the spatial pattern of future employment opportunities stems from its relation to trip-to-work considerations by employees and their effects on residential location decisions.

The rapid growth of manufacturing enterprises has typified the U.S. in the first half of the twentieth century, accompanied by a decline in resource industries; this growth has been slowing down since the mid 1950s. Since then, manufacturing employment is no longer growing in relative terms. For example, the percentage of the labor force in manufacturing in 1970 was almost the same as in 1930. Manufacturing employment is expected to flatten out or decline in the near future, and service activities (which, no less than manufacturing, are subject to economies of agglomeration) will be the source of employment expansion in the future (1).

As to locating in the central city or suburb, the picture is quite clear. The share of employment located in central cities has been steadily declining. An examination of eight metropolitan areas indicates that the share of metropolitan manufacturing employment in central cities declined between 1900 and 1967 from 88.6 to 60.8 percent (2).

The suburb continues to be most attractive for commerce and industry because in many respects suburbs can furnish what was previously available only in the city—ease of communication, access to a large and diverse labor pool. Part of the reason relates to scale economies which appear to be more common in suburbia than in the core cities. For example, there are great cost advantages to using horizontal rather than vertical space for production and warehousing purposes. Moreover, land prices are lower in the suburbs. Manufacturing industries in the recent past have moved away from the city and even outside SMSAs because of automation, rapidly increasing costs of labor and improved techniques of quality control.

Another reason has been the increasing footlooseness of the manufacturing industry which, in part, is related to continued automation of production, the possibility of separating the different manufacturing processes, increasing miniaturization, and ease of transportation and communications through interstate highways and telecommunications advances. They, together with the high cost of land in the city, the difficulty of acquiring land for factory expansion, high taxes, the unpleasantness and personal insecurity of central city living, and costly congestion, all contribute to the increasing decentralization of manufacturing.

Not unlike manufacturing, office industries also have been moving out of the central city. Quante (3) studied headquarters relocations by analyzing the location listed by *Fortune* magazine of headquarters facilities of the largest 500 companies in the ten largest SMSAs in 1957 and 1971. The ten core cities lost 57 headquarters, or 19.5 percent of the total, while their suburbs gained 37. Of the ten SMSAs only Los Angeles had an increase in the number of headquarters in the central city (as well as in the suburbs).

RESIDENTIAL SETTLEMENT PATTERNS

The future residential settlement pattern of America will be heavily influenced by demographic changes now in the making, by housing and transportation cost trade-offs, and by certain government actions. The transportation costs directly relate to the industrial location patterns discussed above. The demographic variables that will be taken up next directly affect the demand for housing at specific locations (and to some extent the demand for transportation).

DEMOGRAPHIC CONSIDERATIONS

Population Growth and Family Size

The number of households in the United States is projected to increase somewhat more rapidly than population as family size diminishes and more people form separate households at various stages of life.[a] This differential will bring about a gradual decline in the average number of persons per household, or in other words, more dwelling units in the future than population growth alone would suggest. The outlook is for convergence on the two-child family as a national mode. Only a slight increase is projected in the number of married couples who will have no children.

Age Distribution of Household Heads

Based on fluctuations of the birth rate in recent decades, changes in the adult population's age composition over the next several decades can be expected. Specifically, we can expect a sharp reduction (and eventually cessation) of the currently high rates of increase in households with heads under 35 years, accelerating rates of increase of households headed by persons 35 to 44 years, and slow

---

[a]The discussion of anticipated demographic changes borrows heavily from work by Peter Morrison, for example, *Demographic Trends That Will Shape Future Housing Demand*, The Rand Corporation, P-5596, February 1976.

but steady increases in households with heads 65 years and older. (The 45-64 age group will not change to any notable degree.)

The large number of housing units that will be needed to accommodate the wave of households with special housing demands raises the question of whether many households may become committed to a specific pattern of spatial settlement—e.g., dispersed versus concentrated, urban versus suburban.

Household Composition and Its Effects on Living Arrangements

We can expect a decline in the average number of persons per household. The average size of households in 1976 was 2.89 persons, as compared to 3.14 in 1970 and 3.33 in 1960. The reasons for the shrinking household size are an increase in the number of primary individuals as a percent of all households, and the falling birth rate.

There is a growing tendency among young people to refrain from marriage. In the age group 20 to 24 years old, when most men and women had traditionally married, 60 percent of men and 40 percent of women remained unmarried in 1975, compared to 53 and 28 percent in 1960. Furthermore, there is a tendency to establish households in "nonfamily" living situations. Between 1970 and 1976, household heads who lived in their own homes entirely alone or with persons not related to them, i.e., primary individuals, increased by about 41 percent, from 11.95 to 16.81 million. This compares with a 9 percent increase for all other types of households, e.g., husband-wives, female-head of family, and so forth.

Primary-individual households are increasing most rapidly for the under-35 age group, which shot up between 1970 and 1976 by 136 percent, or from 1.95 to 4.60 million. This increase represents better than one-quarter of the total national increase in households of all ages and all types. Finally, we can continue to expect an increase in the percentage of elderly widows, and the duration of widowhood, since female life expectancy is increasingly exceeding that of males. In 1973 a 65-year-old white female could expect to outlive her male counterpart by 4.1 years, while in 1960 the expected difference was only 2.9 years.

Growth in Female Labor Force Participation

There has been a large increase in female labor force participation rates, together with many hints that these changes will be lasting ones—if anything, they will broaden. Thus for example, since the turn of the century, the percentage of "gainfully employed" wives increased from 5 to 10 in 1910, and to 22 in 1950 (4). A new series of labor force participation rates of wives shows a further increase from 23.8 percent in 1950 to 44.4 percent in 1975 (see Table 12-1).

Among major reasons for the increasing female labor force participation rate is women's increased orientation toward combining parenthood with away-from-home work. Research by Astin, based on interviews of women entering college, indicates an increasing broadly based intent to combine parenthood and work (5). The results of these national surveys indicate that while in 1967 about 44 percent of first-year college women endorsed the notion that women's roles be confined to home and family, only 18 percent did so in 1975. While in the 1950s labor force participation rates of wives were rising the fastest for women 45 years and older, after 1965 the sharpest increases have occurred among women under 35 (6).

In short, there is evidence that young wives in the 1960s began to view their careers as mothers and income earners in a different order. Perhaps the sharpest picture of this change and the most convincing one emerges from Figure 12-2, in which the labor force participation over a working life of cohorts of women born in selected intervals between 1886 and 1955 are compared. By far the sharpest rise in labor force participation at an early age is found among cohorts born after 1935. The likelihood is great, therefore, that a change in behavior has set in, and that more of today's young wives will be working in their older years than was true of their predecessors. Furthermore, labor force participation rates of married women with children have increased dramatically. For example, while in 1950 only 12 percent of married women with children under age six were in the labor force, the 1975 percentage was 37 (7).

Not only can we expect female labor force participation rates to continue rising, we also foresee continued increases in the number of women entering previously "male" occupations, particularly well paying ones. There have been notable increases in medicine and law; many more women will also assume managerial positions (8). Government enforcement of fair employment practice and affirmative action laws would make it highly probable that women workers will have access to a broader range of higher paying jobs in the future.

In addition to the sociological changes that accompany increasing female labor force participation rates, some major economic effects can be expected. Perhaps the single most important one will be increased family incomes. Median income of families with working wives has not only been substantially larger, but also has increased faster than that for families without working wives. For example, Table 12-1 indicates that between 1950 and 1974, real median

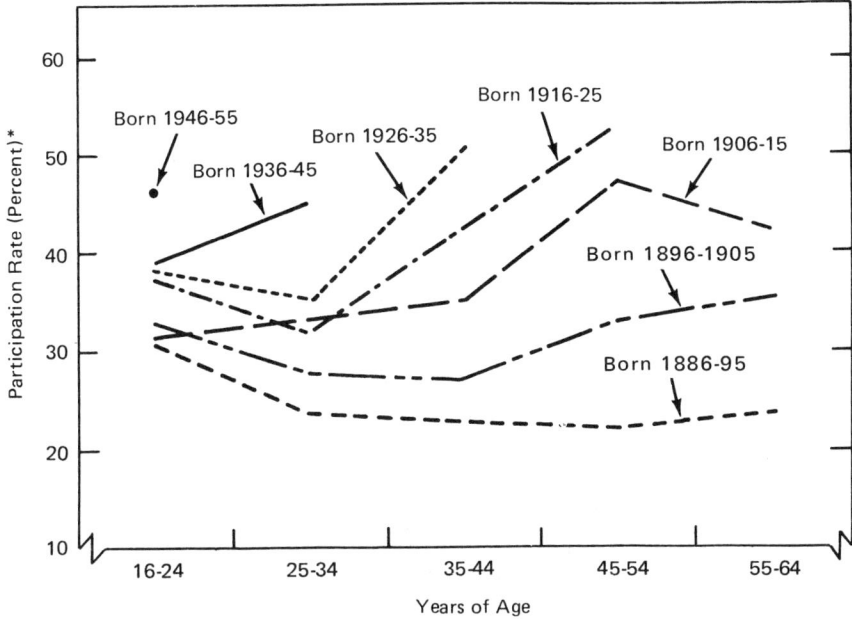

*Total labor force as percent of total noninstitutional population in group specified. Note: For women born between 1886 and 1915, the first age plotted is 14-24 years. Cohorts reach each age interval according to the midpoint of their birth years. Thus, the cohort born in 1886-95 reached ages 25-34 in 1920 and ages 55-64 in 1950. The cohort born 1916-25 reached ages 25-34 in 1950 and ages 45-54 in 1970.
Source: Department of Commerce
Source: *Economic Report to the President, January 1973*, p. 94.

Figure 12-2. Labor Force Participation Over a Working Life of Cohorts of Women Born in Selected Time Intervals, 1886-1955.

annual income of families of the former more than doubled, while that of the latter rose by only about four-fifths.

HOUSING AND TRANSPORTATION COSTS

William Alonso (9) and Richard Muth (10), among others, have developed residential location decision models that show how people trade off housing and transportation costs when incomes are constrained. These models consider not only money but time cost as well. They look at the process of location selection as a utility

Table 12-1. Median Family Income, with and Without Working Wives

	Median Family Income (in 1974 dollars)	
	Wife in Paid Labor Force	Wife Not in Paid Labor Force
1950	$ 8,200	$ 6,791
1960	11,490	9,192
1965	13,437	10,303
1970	15,759	11,816
1974	16,928	12,082

Source: Howard Hayghe, "Families and the Rise of Working Wives—An Overview," *Monthly Labor Review*, Vol. 99, No. 5, May 1976, p. 15.

maximization procedure constrained by the household's income. The Muth model combines land and structure size, as well as many other elements that affect the value of housing and treats them as housing services. The constrained maximum found in the model represents an equilibrium location from which no move in any direction can increase utility. The equilibrium location is determined by the land price and commuting cost function at the point where the marginal decrease in expenditures on housing is equal to the marginal increase in commuting costs for small changes in distance.

Households are induced to locate farther from the center because of the savings available from lower land cost; at the same time, they are induced to locate closer to the center because of the decrease in commuting costs available. (This and similar models assume a single nucleus metropolis.) During 1960-70 the housing cost-transportation cost trade-offs appeared to have favored the suburbs insofar as new dwellings are concerned. As can be seen from Table 12-2, in the Pittsburgh SMSA 85 percent of all new dwellings, for example, were built outside the central city.

The location of places of employment as well as the overall location pattern of industry is directly affected by all these forces that enter into the decision making process of industry (and commerce). In turn, because in urban areas work trips are the single most important commutation purpose, the location of employment opportunities enters significantly into the trade-off analysis of households as they consider housing and transportation costs. The supply and price of energy bears both on transportation costs, and heating and cooling costs of dwellings. Property taxes are also an element in housing costs; their location effect is discussed below.

Table 12-2. Proportion of New Dwelling Units Outside Six Central Cities, 1960-70

SMSA	Percent of New Dwelling Units Outside Central City Zones
Durham, N.C.	61
Austin, Texas	66
Portland, Oregon	81
Pittsburgh, Pa.	85
Washington, D.C.	82
Chicago, Illinois	74

Source: Frank de Leeuw and Raymond J. Struyk, *The Web of Urban Housing*, Washington, D.C., Urban Institute, 1975, p. 75.

In an age in which the previously core oriented metropolis is giving way to a dispersed, low density polynucleated pattern of settlement, energy saving public transportation becomes progressively less competitive with the private car. The exception is in cases where a number of densely populated nuclei emerge which can be connected by relatively densely populated transportation corridors. Likewise, higher heating and cooling costs will reinforce demographic trends favoring more compact dwellings, often parts of multiple dwelling units in one of the metropolis' major population centers.

GOVERNMENT ACTIVITIES

Residential settlement patterns, in addition to being affected by demographic forces and housing and transportation trade-offs, will also be affected by a number of government actions. Two are of particular interest—heavy reliance on local property taxes, and recent court decisions opening suburbia to minorities and low income groups.

Local Property Taxation and Fiscal Advantage

Residents can reap a fiscal advantage whenever their local government relies on a revenue source that is not a perfect benefit tax. This is particularly true if local government relies heavily on property taxation. Given the high per capita property values of many suburbs, public expenditures can be supported with a relatively low ad valorem tax rate. For example, a central city might have a property value per household of $40,000 and an actual property tax rate of 5 percent to raise $2,000 per household. A suburban jurisdiction might typically have a higher property value per household, e.g., $100,000 and so an actual tax rate of 3 percent would raise $3,000. A $40,000 structure located in such a suburb would generate only $1200 in tax revenues, while the occupant would receive the benefits of very high quality public services. Thus, there are strong incentives generated by the local property tax to locate low value structures outside the central city.

Thus, the owner of a structure with low value could pay very little in taxes while receiving the benefits of high quality services. The costs imposed on local government are probably of about the same magnitude as those generated by other members of the community. For education they are even higher.

Two empirical studies have shown that these fiscal advantages are substantial. Bradford and Kelejian have provided econometric evidence that fiscal advantages are significant in explaining interjurisdictional mobility (11). Likewise, Aronson and Schwartz have tested a model of fiscally induced movement. They found that 69 percent of migration in the fifties and 89 percent in the sixties resulted in fiscal advantages to movers (12). In summary, heavy reliance on the local property tax has resulted in situations in which governments with relatively high tax bases can offer either a lower ad valorem tax rate to provide a given level of public service, or better public services for a given tax rate, or some combination of the two. Since most jurisdictions with these characteristics are suburban communities, they have tended to attract urbanites.

Exclusionary Zoning and Court Actions

The preceding section has argued that heavy reliance on local property taxation furnishes strong inducements for out-migration from the core city into suburbia, including incentives for moves by low income groups. In order to "protect themselves" from such in-migrants, in the past middle and upper income suburbs have enacted exclusionary zoning ordinances. Such ordinances have been upheld by federal courts, mainly under the 1926 U.S. Supreme Court *Euclid* case (13). As recently as 1975, the Ninth Circuit Appeals Court overturned a lower federal court ruling against an exclusionary ordinance promulgated by the city of Petaluma (14).

Whereas the federal courts have consistently condoned exclusionary zoning ordinances, the highest courts in three states have recently taken opposite positions. The Pennsylvania Supreme Court (15), the New York Court of Appeals (16), and the New Jersey Supreme Court (17) all have ruled against exclusionary zoning ordinances in their states. The *Mt. Laurel* Court enunciated a "fair share housing obligation" to be met by all jurisdictions in the state.

Heavy reliance by local governments on property taxation has contributed much to migration out of core cities into suburbia, as was argued above. In the presence of exclusionary zoning ordinances sanctioned by the courts, most of this out-migration has been by the white middle and upper classes. These moves in turn have left central cities with increasingly large proportions of poor families, all too often members of minority groups. To the extent that the states of New Jersey, New York, and Pennsylvania will in the future invalidate exclusionary zoning laws, and other states follow suit, out-migration from core cities in the future will no longer be merely white and middle and upper class. Thus, even low income groups, including minorities, will increasingly seek to migrate to the suburbs.

THE EMERGING PATTERN: POLYNUCLEATED URBAN AREAS

By pulling together some of the strands developed in the preceding discussion, the tendency towards a polynucleated urban settlement pattern emerges. All indications are that employment opportunities will continue to move to the suburbs, mainly because industry and much of commerce favor suburban locations, and service industries follow residential locations.

Scale economies in the production and warehousing of goods on large lots permitting vertical operations will tend to favor employment centers in suburbia. In the face of such industry location tendencies, travel cost considerations, both in terms of money and time, will tend to continue to persuade people to reside in suburbs. But will the future residential pattern continue to be one of a sprawling suburbia? Most likely not, and for a number of reasons.

It is plausible to think that many of the forces that will shape the settlement pattern of suburbia in the future will tend to favor a polynucleated settlement pattern. First, the burgeoning number of households composed of unrelated members, of senior citizens (and particularly widows), and of two-worker families will foreshadow the day when many more households will be seeking the best that urban living can offer without its shortcomings. Specifically, these considerations in the foreseeable future can contribute to a greater demand for opportunities to live in relatively densely populated, self-contained urban or suburban centers, with close-in work, living, shopping, and recreational opportunities.

Many of these relatively small households are likely to choose to live in compact (often multiple) dwelling units with little if any private lawn and yard, the desire for which contributed in the fifties and sixties to urban sprawl. All these groups, the nonmarried, the divorced, the elderly and the two-worker families, it would seem, benefit relatively little from living far out in suburbia in unattached houses surrounded by lawns and yards (features most valued by families raising children). Moreover, they often have neither the time nor the skill to cope with plumbing, electrical, and gardening problems common to such living arrangements. While they are likely to have little desire to live in sprawling suburbia, neither do they appear to be attracted into core cities with all their social and economic ills. It is plausible to think that fears for their personal security among others will deter many of them from seeking homes inside core cities.

Such centers, with close-by shopping, employment and recreational facilities, appear to be emerging in many metropolitan areas. In most cases the central business district of the core city is just one of the numerous nuclei. The suburban centers spring up in response to the forces mentioned above, while the manifest initiative can be coming from a number of different sources. In some instances, the first step takes the form of a decision to build a large shopping center. In other instances, a large developer decides to create a new, almost self-contained community.

Examples are not merely Reston and Columbia, but also the decision of the Janss Corporation to develop Westwood Village adjacent to grounds donated earlier by the corporation to the University of California for a new campus—UCLA. Other examples are the development of Century City by the Century Fox Corporation and Alcoa into an office, service industry and residential center in West Los Angeles, and of Westlake Village in Northern Los Angeles County into a recreation oriented residential and service industry center.

A second consideration relates to the earlier discussed increase in the importance of households with two gainfully employed workers. It would be logical to expect such households to seek residential locations which will keep the work trip of each member to a minimum. Such an outcome is facilitated by the presence of a number of major residential-employment centers. Such centers are likely to resemble in their density patterns the metropolis of the 1920s and 1930s, though they will be much smaller. Specifically, the heart of a center is likely to be densely populated and have multi-dwelling units, and as one moves out from the center densities will substantially decline. Thus, there will be room for single dwelling units at the outskirts of each and every one of the nuclei.

Third, declining energy supply and rising energy prices in the future, it would appear, can tend to reinforce most of the tendencies which earlier pointed towards a polynucleated metropolis. For example, high energy costs will tend to persuade families to prefer apartment house living to single family dwelling living. Research by Hittman Associates Inc. indicates, for example, that the annual energy requirement for heating and cooling housing units in the Baltimore-Washington area are the highest per unit in single family, attached dwellings and lowest in high rise dwellings.[b] However, this is not necessarily the case on a per-occupant basis, where the smallest households tend to live in high rise dwellings. Thus, the Hittman Associates studies indicate that the annual energy requirements for heating and cooling of single family, detached dwellings is 1300-1400 therms a unit, that of townhouses 896, of low rise dwellings 575, and of high rise dwellings 493 (18).

Moreover, Dale Keyes reports on two studies that simulate the energy requirements under two different residential development patterns—all new residential development is in the form of (1) high rise buildings and (2) single-family detached units (19). Comparing the two alternatives, Hittman Associates estimate that a development of type (1) compared to type (2) would result in an energy saving of 20 to 30 percent for residential space heating and cooling. Arthur D. Little, making a similar comparison, estimates an even greater difference between the two development types: a 65 percent energy saving of type (1) over type (2).

We turn from cost comparisons of space heating and cooling of the different housing types to comparisons of gasoline requirements of different size families. Under present settlement and transportation arrangements, according to data collected by the U.S. Bureau of Labor Statistics, smaller families tend to require more gasoline per family member than do larger ones. Specifically, data collected between July 1973 and June 1974 indicate that average weekly per capita expenditures for gasoline, motor oil, coolant, etc., amounted to $3.40, $2.93, $2.54 and $1.99 for families of sizes of 2, 3, 4, and 5 respectively (20). Accordingly, unless their after-tax incomes are very high, small families will have a stronger incentive to reduce their gasoline bill than will large families.

There also exists some limited empirical evidence of energy consumption for commutation in urban areas with different settlement patterns. For example, Fels and Munson estimate that a fourfold difference in per capita energy consumed for transportation in Trenton is possible, in the extreme, by the year 1985 (21). This is

---

[b]High rise dwellings require disproportionately large amounts of energy in their public areas.

the difference between the "everybody wants a luxury car" option (where long and more frequent trips are taken by richer people living farther apart and driving less efficient autos) and the "energy consciousness" option (where fewer and shorter trips are taken by people living closer to each other and to work, and traveling by more efficient modes and more efficient autos). The first scenario approximates a sprawling suburbia, the second a polynucleated metropolis.

Clearly, studies that attempt to look many years into the future involve many uncertainties. But the general direction of the difference in energy consumption between the two settlement patterns appears to be valid. The result appears to be consistent with that of another recent study, of the Washington, D.C. SMSA by Roberts (22). It compares, among others, a "sprawl" settlement pattern with a "transit oriented" pattern in which all new housing and commercial employment is located along radial transit lines, primarily at new stations, and industrial employment is located peripherally. Roberts estimates transportation energy consumption to be about 1.7 times as large in the first than in the second pattern.

There is also evidence that a polynucleated metropolis is efficient. Before exploring the dimensions of the efficiency issue, I would like to point out that efficiency is not the main reason why I expect this settlement pattern to emerge as the pattern of the future. In addition to being efficient, polynucleated urban areas tend to be beneficial to various interest groups and therefore attractive to a number of important decisionmakers.

The efficiency of polynucleated settlement patterns can be deduced from work done by Irving Hoch. He regressed wage rates in individual occupations to city size, measured by the logarithm of SMSA population (23). In 24 out of 25 cases he found positive and statistically significant relationships. Wage rates, on average, increased by about 9 percent per order of magnitude of population. Thus, a place with one million people had a 9 percent higher wage rate than did a place of 100,000 for the same work. Half this increase is required to compensate for the cost of living increases. The other half is explained by such nonmarket costs as the value of time spent in the journey to work, the value of risks not covered by insurance, and the cost of air pollution.

If we were to compare metropolitan areas of different sizes with one another, we would have to consider not only the cost effects of size, but also the benefit effects. However, to the extent that a metropolitan area is composed of a number of smaller centers (for example, a metropolis with 3 million inhabitants may have ten centers, with about 300,000 people, on the average, in each), benefits usually associated with metropolitan life are not lost. Economies of scale are present and make possible the existence in the metropolis of specialized medical facilities, great cultural facilities—e.g., museums, symphony orchestra, ballet companies, as well as major league sports. It is not clear whether the emergence of a polynucleated metropolis will have an effect on taxes, environmental quality and crime.

SOME CONCLUDING THOUGHTS

If we look hard, we can detect some early signs of polynucleation of urban areas. While these signs are strongest in the western and southwestern parts of the United States, they can also be seen, at least to some extent, in the older parts of the country. Even though such a spatial arrangement is likely to be more efficient than the present one, it will leave core cities with enormous fiscal problems. Large scale federal participation may be required for their solution.

Polynucleation may not only be stimulated by urban transportation considerations, but in turn it may give impetus to some slow shift towards more public transportation. For example, not every working member of a household may be able to afford a private car, especially in the presence of very high gasoline prices. Moreover, emerging densities in the new popluation centers may give rise to relatively densely populated transportation corridors, which in turn could facilitate and justify public transportation.

The emergence of numerous population centers within metropolitan areas will be a challenge to local governments. Some of the centers will be coterminous with existing municipalities, while others will extend into two or more municipalities. In either case, municipalities will have to adjust themselves to the emergence of major population centers with high levels of economic activity demanding large amounts of public services, and yet at the same time offering a major tax base.

In conclusion, the medium-sized city, part of a polynucleated metropolis, promises to be the city of the future. It promises to be the linchpin in tomorrow's urban America, and public officials, no less than private industry, may want to start preparing for the newly emerging urban settlement pattern.

Chapter Thirteen

Transformation of the Nation's Urban System: Small City Growth as a Zero-Sum Game

Brian J.L. Berry

Opposing trends are conspiring to make small city growth a zero-sum game. The United States has moved from being merely a political entity comprising diverse regions held together by a common symbolism, to a true national society in which changes taking place in one section of the society have immediate effects in all others. Commensurate with this movement, the national system of cities has been transformed from being merely a set of regional hierarchies held together by heartland-hinterland relationships among its metropolitan centers, to a true national urban system in which specialized interdependence transcends the traditional constraints of size and region.

Yet the nation's economic and demographic growth is slackening. The eventual number of births expected per woman is barely at replacement levels for today's younger age cohorts, implying that we are approaching a zero-growth situation in which differential attractiveness to migrants is becoming ever more critical. For small cities and nonmetropolitan areas to grow, other places must decline, and what are declining are the big cities of the old manufacturing belt heartland which have lost their traditional position as centers of innovative leadership. In this chapter, I examine these trends, and explore some of the policy implications of the trade-offs now occurring between size and location in the nation's settlement system.

A NATIONAL SOCIETY

The emergence of a national society is due in large measure to the revolution in communication and transportation that has occurred in the past quarter-century: the rise of national network television, coast-to-coast telephone dialing, simultaneous publication of national news media, and jet transport. The result is that Americans share in common many daily experiences as a national community, with the same retail chains, the same network news programs, the same televised sports events, and the same type of large employers, either business or government.

This coalescence into a national society has profound political implications. It has led to efforts towards national rather than regional and local solutions to social problems, and, by definition, the expansion of central government into the field of social policy. Yet it has also produced a new localism. Increasing population mobility within a nationwide framework has fostered the growth of smaller scale communities, both within and outside each of the nation's urban regions, among which Americans now move without disturbing the rhythms of their daily lives.

There is a resulting tension between increasing scale and mobility in a truly national society on the one hand, and increasing insistence upon a mosaic of small and coherent communities on the other. As Scott Greer has so graphically pointed out, increasing societal scale means a widening of the radii of interdependence, so that whether men know it or not, they become mutual means to individual ends; the intensity of interdependence increases (1).

As a concomitant, increasing scale produces an increasing range and content of the communications flow. This results in a widening span of compliance and control within social organizations, the salience of large scale organizations, their nationwide span of control, and the similarity of their division of labor and rewards, tending to develop a stratification system cutting across widely varying geographical and cultural subregions of the country, and creating national citizens.

This nationwide quality varies for different social groups, however. The high mobiles are those with some college education, higher incomes, working for large corporate or government organizations, in the mid-twenty to mid-forty age span. The low mobiles are the blue collar employees and other working class people, whose lives are built around kinship and ethnic ties within local neighborhoods.

When the high mobiles move, according to Vance Packard, it involves shift from one region to another, but in moving they scarcely change their life style; there is a tendency to move between near identical social environments, and indeed, their assessment of the quality of life in a community centers on the characteristics of its social environment (2). This fact is important in understanding the recent emergence of small town growth.

Professional real estate consultants aid them in their search for communities that offer the same environment in terms of schools and neighbors, income levels, education, family background, and clubs. This attachment to a type of environment that sustains a particular life style is the key to the way in which contemporary Americans have adjusted the need to retain a locally based sense of security and stability of the emergence of a nationwide highly mobile society.

When the heterogeneity of American cities was caused primarily by the influx of successive immigrant waves, a policy of encouraging assimilation was taken for granted ideologically. Citizens might demonstrate a wide range of behaviors and preferences, but this variety was viewed as being both temporary and expendable. A white, middle class, "Americanized" standard could be imposed from the outside and justified in terms of the shared higher goal of assimilation. People behaved in the way they did only because they had not yet learned the "better way."

The segregated local community was regarded as a passing entity, which might be maintained only so long as temporary patterns of racial and socioeconomic segregation persisted, but ultimately the local community would decline as people found nonterritorial bases for association. Territorial groups were, it was felt, coercive in character and far less attractive than voluntary forms of association. The latter would shortly replace local community ties and these so-called interest communities would result in a more faithful response from government and big business. The local community would decline then as racial and socioeconomic segregation declined and interest communities replaced residential communities.

What is indicated today, however, is that a new type of heterogeneity exists and is intensifying. This heterogeneity results from internal differentiation and may be understood from the different position of cultural pluralism. In such a framework, the forms of community that emerge are in no way vestigial remnants of a more fragmented localized society, but rather new specialized components of a national society. Among these components are smaller towns in formerly declining regions.

A major advance in understanding these new forms of community has been made by sociologists such as Gerald Suttles, who argue that a useful point at which to begin is by retrieving the cognitive maps of childhood (3). For the child, awareness of the city radiates outward, with the density of information diminishing rapidly with the distance from home. The area of comfortable familiarity constitutes the experience of neighborhood. Yet cities do not consist of an infinitely large number of neighborhoods each centering on one of millions of inhabitants. Rather there is a small number of social labels applied to definable geographic areas. Because population characteristics of a city are continuously variable, with no clear demarcation between one side of the street and the other, society imposes categorical labels on specific areas. Neighborhoods are not simply found in nature, but are consensually imposed.

A neighborhood label, once affixed, has real consequences. For outsiders it reduces decision making to more manageable terms. Instead of dealing with the variegated reality of numerous city streets, the resident can form a set of attitudes about a limited number of social categories and act accordingly. For those who live within it, the neighborhood defines areas relatively free of intruders, identifies where potential friends are to be found or where they are to be cultivated, minimizes the prospects of status insult, and simplifies innumerable daily decisions dealing with spatial activities. Thus the mental map of neighborhoods is not superfluous cognitive baggage, but performs important psychological and social functions.

The neighborhoods in which Americans live vary: in their ethnic and socioeconomic composition, and in their available life styles; in their physical features, which can be used to create images and boundaries; and in their historic claims to a distinct reputation or identity. Members of a mobile society select among communities in terms of the neighborhood life styles they are perceived to offer. Most metropolitan regions offer them an entire shopping basket of alternatives, and rural areas yet others.

What, then, are some of the principal life style differences that are to be found within American society today? They appear to arise from two common developmental processes experienced by all Americans: (1) passage through stages of the life cycle, with especially sharp breaks associated with the transition from one state to another (as in leaving home, marriage, family expansion, entry into the labor force, retirement); and (2) occupational career trajectories that may necessitate, preclude, or otherwise pattern geographic mobility alongside social mobility.

These developmental processes are cross-but by several different value systems: (1) familism, in which a high value is placed upon family living and a corresponding devotion of time and resources to family life; (2) careerism, in which there is an orientation toward upward social mobility and a corresponding disposition to engage in career related activities, at least to a partial neglect of family ties;

(3) localism, a parochial orientation implying interests confined to a neighborhood and reference to groups whose scope is local; and (4) cosmopolitanism, an ecumenical orientation implying freedom from the binding ties to a locality and reference to groups whose scope is national rather than local, so that the cosmopolitan resides in a place but inhabits the nation.

What appears to have emerged in America as a result of these changes is a mosaic culture, a society with a number of parallel and distinctively different life styles repeated in each of the nation's regions. While one result is divisive tendencies for the society as a whole within the broader framework of interdependence, at another level, the mosaic of homogeneous communities maintains different life styles that are internally cohesive and exclusive, yet externally nonaggressive, unless threatened. Mobility within the mosaic leads to a high degree of expressed satisfaction by residents with their communities, and the option for those who are dissatisifed to move to an alternative that is more in keeping with their life style requirements.

THE NATION'S URBAN SYSTEM: CLASSICAL PATTERNS

These social trends have been supported by the growth of a post-industrial economy, which in turn has enabled a national urban system to emerge. The post-industrial economy can be outlined schematically along five dimensions, according to Daniel Bell: the creation of a service economy; the preeminence of the professional and technical class; the centrality of theoretical knowledge as the source of innovation and policy formulation in society; the possibility of self-sustaining technological growth and transformation; and the emergence of a new intellectual technology centering on information and information processing, leading to the growth of a quarternary sector in the economy (4).

Such ingredients of a post-industrial economy tend to be footloose rather than transport oriented, either to raw materials or markets; and they use high grade, highly skilled, high priced labor. Amenities for this labor—the preferred residential settings that support the desired life style—loom ever larger in their locational decisions. The employees form part of a national rather than any local labor market. And the nature of the talent used is such that it is the source of the new ideas that breed further growth. The result has been to break down the classical urban-regional patterns so ably documented by John Friedmann (5).

According to this traditional theory, it is the nation's metropolitan centers that stand at the center of each region and at the top of each regional hierarchy—centers of activity and of innovation, focal points of the transport and communications networks, locations of superior accessibility, at which firms can most easily reap economies of scale, and at which industrial complexes can obtain the economies of localization and urbanization, encouraging labor specialization, areal specialization in productive activities, and efficiency in the provision of services.

One consequence is agricultural enterprise that is more efficient in the vicinity of cities; another is that net economic welfare increases with city size due to externalities. Three major elements stand out in this classical city oriented organization of economic activities in space:

1. A heartland-hinterland arrangement of industrial and resource regions linked by intermetropolitan flows.
2. A system of cities within each region, arranged in a hierarchy according to the functions performed by each.
3. Corresponding areas of urban influence or urban fields surrounding each of the cities in the system.

In such a system, impulses of economic change are transmitted simultaneously along three planes:

1. Outward from heartland metropoles to those of the regional hinterlands on a national scale.
2. From each regional metropolis to centers of lower level in the hierarchy, in a pattern of "hierarchical diffusion" within each of the nation's major regions.
3. Outward from urban centers into their surrounding urban fields, in radiating "spread effects," at the scale of the local labor market.

Part of the diffusion mechanism has been shown to reside in the operation of urban labor markets. When growth is sustained over long periods in the heartland's urban industrial centers, regional income inequality should be reduced because any general expansion in a high income area will result in some industries being priced out of the high income labor market. There will be a shift of that industry to lower income regions, especially to smaller urban centers in more peripheral areas.

The significance of this filtering or "trickle-down" process lies not only in its direct but also in its indirect effects. If the boom originates in the high income region, the multiplier effects will be larger in the initiating region, although the relative rise in income may be greater in the underdeveloped region. But the induced effects on real income and employment may be considerably greater in the low income region if prices there are likely to rise less and/or if the increase in output per worker is greater.

Both are likely, because of decreasing cost due to external economies stemming from urbanization of the labor force. If the boom can be maintained, industries of higher labor productivity will shift units into lower income areas, and the low wage industries will be forced to move into even smaller towns and more isolated areas. The net result is that the following properties characterize such classical urban-regional hierarchical systems.

1. The size and functions of a central city, the size of its urban field, and the spatial extent of developmental "spread effects" radiating outwards from it are proportional.
2. Since impulses of economic change are transmitted in order from higher to lower centers in the urban hierarchy, continued innovation in large cities remains critical for extension of growth over the complete economic system.
3. The resulting spatial incidence of economic growth will be a function of distance from the central city. Troughs of economic backwardness will lie in the most inaccessible lower level centers in the hierarchy.
4. Further, the growth potential of any area situated along an axis between two cities is a function of the intensity of interaction between them, which in turn is a function of their relative location and the quality of transportation arteries connecting them.

In this scheme, the driving mechanism is the continuing viability of the major metropolis—which in Wilbur Thompson's view resides ultimately in its continuing capacity to innovate. As Thompson has said, (see his chapter in this book) the economic base of the larger metropolis is the creativity of its universities and research parks, the sophistication of its engineering firms and financial institutions, the persuasiveness of its public relations and advertising agencies, the flexibility of its transportation networks and utility systems, and all the dimensions of infrastructure that facilitate the quick and orderly transfer from old dying economic bases to new growing ones (6).

Larger urban regions combine a favorable industry mix for growth with a steadily declining share of the various growth industries. High wage rates of the innovating area, quite consonant with the high skills needed at the beginning of the learning process, become excessive when skill requirements decline, and the industry (or parts of it) filters down to the smaller, less industrially sophisticated regions where the cheaper labor can meet the declining skill demands of the filtering industry, thus creating the phenomenon of small towns with low wage, slow growth filtered down industry (at the time when the metropolis has moved on to new bases).

Thus, when metropolitan growth is sustained over long periods, it results in progressive integration of the space economy by outward flows of growth impulses through the urban hierarchy and inward migration of labor to cities. Troughs of economic backwardness at the intermetropolitan periphery should thereby be eroded, and each area should find itself within the spheres of influence of a variety of urban centers of a variety of sizes.

URBAN-REGIONAL GROWTH AND DECLINE: NEW DIRECTIONS

This traditional pattern of urban-regional organization is being transformed by contemporary demographic and economic changes (7). Dominating all demographic and settlement trends is the continuation of a long term decline in the rate of national population increase. The population of the United States continues to grow, but at a steadily decreasing rate that points towards zero population growth as an emerging reality.

During the 1950s the national population grew 19.0 percent, during the 1960s, 13.3 percent, and if current growth rates continue through the close of this decade, the national population will have increased by 8.4 percent during the 1970s.

The components of change are as follows: The annual death rate, after falling continuously throughout the twentieth century, appears to have stabilized at 8.9 to 9.0 deaths per thousand. Meanwhile, following the anomaly of the post-World War II baby boom, the birth rate has continued to fall. It was 19.4 per thousand in 1940, rose to 24.9 per thousand in 1955, but has declined continuously since, dropping to 14.7 per thousand by 1975, the lowest level in American history. When all women are taken into account, the eventual number of births expected per woman averages to 2.1 children for today's younger age cohorts, barely at the replacement level required for a stable population.

Superimposed upon this long term decline in population growth there are, of course, the continuing consequences of earlier fluctuations in birth rates. The population of individuals aged 18 to 24 and

25 to 34, age groups now occupied by members of the postwar baby boom, has grown 13 and 23 percent respectively since 1970. The aging of these large cohorts will continue to play a primary role in raising the average age of the nation's population and in changing housing needs and locational preferences. Major changes in the populations of other age groups during the first half of the 1970s include a decline in the number of youths and an ever increasing number of elderly.

The lower birth rates of the latter 1960s have produced a decline of 8 percent in the number of children aged 13 and under, while the declining mortality rate has served to increase the size of the 65 and over age group by 12 percent. Continued declines in the birth rate, coupled with the stable death rate, will produce a population that contains proportionately more elderly persons year by year. The median age of the population, which dropped from 30.2 years in 1950 to a low of 27.9 years in 1970 has already begun to rise and as of 1975, stood at 28.8 years.

Alongside these shifts in the demographic structure of the nation's population are changes in the overall structure of marital relations. As the large birth cohorts of the late 1940s and early 1950s move through young adult ages, marriage rates are declining, median age at first marriage is increasing, divorce rates are increasing (from 35 per 1,000 in 1960 to 47 per 1,000 in 1970), more young unmarried adults are maintaining their own homes, and more children are living at home with a single parent.

Since 1970, the largest increase among family groups has been in those headed by a woman who had no husband living with her; half of this increase was accounted for by women who were divorced. The combination of falling birth rates and changing household composition is reflected in the sharp decline in the average number of persons per household. Again, there are obvious housing and locational implications.

Accompanying these national shifts are changes at the regional and interregional level. Signs of a reversal of the long term pattern of metropolitan growth rates exceeding those of nonmetropolitan areas first appeared during the 1960s. During this time, several nonmetropolitan regions experienced a turnaround from population decline to modest increase and it appeared that at least in some of these areas, out-migration had peaked during the previous decade.

The metropolitan population growth of 22 million persons during the 1960s resulted in part (one-third) from growth through the addition of new land area, while the remaining two-thirds was derived from population increases within the 1960 boundaries. Of the growth within these earlier boundaries, three-quarters was due to natural increase, and of the remaining quarter, a larger proportion resulted from inmigrants from overseas than from the inmigration of former rural area residents. Thus, only a small proportion of the increase in America's metropolitan population during the 1960s was attributable to rural out-migration.

Nonetheless, while the nation's total population increased 13.3 percent during the 1960s, the number of individuals residing in metropolitan areas increased 16.6 percent, or 8.5 times the rate for nonmetropolitan areas. Since 1970, however, a reversal has occurred, resulting in the growth rates for nonmetropolitan areas exceeding those of metropolitan locations. Nationwide statistics for the first half of the 1970s indicate that population has increased 6.3 percent in nonmetropolitan areas and only 3.6 percent in metropolitan areas.

When the nation's metropolitan areas are divided between their central cities and surrounding suburbs, an even more dramatic pattern is evident. The lower metropolitan area population growth of the 1970s has resulted from a combination of the depopulation of the central cities and a slackening of the suburban boom. Since 1970, central cities have experienced an absolute population loss of nearly two million persons, or 3 percent of the total number of residents at the beginning of the decade. Net out-migration from the central cities to the suburbs and to nonmetropolitan areas during this same period exceeds seven million persons, for a central city population loss of 11.2 percent.

What is new, of course, is the current nationwide trend of absolute central city population decline: the proportion of metropolitan residents living in the central city rather than the suburbs reached a peak during the 1920s and has declined continually since. In 1920, central city dwellers accounted for 66 percent of America's metropolitan residents, with the remaining 34 percent being suburban residents. By 1960 metropolitan residents were about equally divided between central cities and suburbs, and by 1975 central city residents accounted for only 43 percent of the nation's metropolitan population.

Absolute losses of population in certain central cities did occur prior to 1970; however gains in the remaining central cities always more than offset these losses to create overall central city growth. The decade of the 1950s saw 56 central cities lose population while the national total of central city residents increased 11.6 percent. During the 1960s, while nationwide central city population increased 6.5 percent, the number of central cities which lost population increased to 95, or 39 percent of all central cities in the nation.

Altogether, the central cities of 47 of the nation's metropolitan areas lost population continuously throughout the twenty-year period from 1950 through 1970. With an aggregate central city population decline of 3.1 percent between 1970 and 1975, the number of central cities experiencing losses may be expected only to increase.

While central city population losses during the 1950s and 1960s occurred in a relatively large number of metropolitan areas, they were in large measure confined to the industrial heartland cities of the North Central and Northeast regions of the country. During the 1950s, 81 percent of the central cities that lost population were located in this northern region extending from the Midwest through New England.

In the 1970s, the greatest concentration of central cities losing residents again continues to lie within this northern region. In the South, the central city portions of metropolitan areas containing over one million total residents lost population, while the central cities of metropolitan areas of less than one million increased. In the West, the number of residents in metropolitan places of all sizes increased with the largest gains occurring in the central cities of areas with less than one million total residents.

The experience of nonmetropolitan America has been the opposite of the foregoing. From the 1940s through the 1950s, out-migration from the nation's rural areas continued apace. Certain rural areas reached a turning point where they were no longer losing residents during the 1960s, but it was not until the 1970s that nonmetropolitan areas as a whole shifted to the status not only of retaining residents, but also of gaining population through net inmigration from metropolitan areas.

The number of individuals residing in the nation's nonmetropolitan areas during the 1960s grew by 6.8 percent, a rate of increase that was only half the national average. During the first half of this decade, however, the nonmetropolitan population increase of 6.3 percent was above the national average of 4.4 percent and well above the increase of 3.6 percent for metropolitan areas.

More significant for nonmetropolitan areas than their current faster growth rate is the turnaround that has occurred in migration between the nonmetropolitan and metropolitan portions of the nation. During the 1950s, nonmetropolitan areas lost over five million persons. This high level of out-migration continued into the 1960s. But since 1970, nonmetropolitan areas have experienced a net in-migration of approximately two million persons, thus reversing the trend of population loss.

While not all nonmetropolitan areas are sharing equally in this new pattern of growth, it is true that net migration reversals have occurred in almost every nonmetropolitan subregion of the country. Actual population increases in the four major regions of the country vary from a low of 1.8 percent in the North Central region, to 5.1 and 5.4 percent respectively in the Northeast and South, to a high of 11.6 percent in the West. Intraregionally, overall population decline continues in those nonmetropolitan counties that contain the smallest settlements—those with less than 2,500 residents. This is especially true in the Northeast, where such areas lost 31.9 percent of their 1970 population between 1970 and 1975.

Sparsely settled areas in the South have grown by 11.6 percent in the South, however. Even though the West has experienced the highest overall nonmetropolitan growth, the South has been the region of the country with the most widespread nonmetropolitan gains, with population increases in counties with both smaller and larger sized urban centers.

Generally, those nonmetropolitan areas located immediately adjacent to metropolitan centers (accounting for 51.5 percent of all nonmetropolitan residents) have experienced the highest nonmetropolitan growth rates during the 1970s: a 4.7 percent increase through 1973 for adjacent counties compared with 3.7 percent for nonadjacent counties. Nonmetropolitan areas that have a high level of integration of their residents into metropolitan labor markets, in particular have experienced larger recent growth rates.

Through 1974, population has increased 9.1 percent in those nonmetropolitan areas where 20 percent or more of the residents commute to a metropolitan place for work, but only 4.8 percent in those areas where less than 3 percent of the residents commute to metropolitan places for employment. Even this relatively lower nonmetropolitan growth of 4.8 percent in the latter case is, however, higher than the average growth rate of metropolitan places during this same period.

The subregions of nonmetropolitan America that underwent turnarounds from population decline during the 1960s to growth during the 1970s are quite diverse. In the South, defined here as the region extending from the Ozarks through eastern Texas and containing a predominantly white population, underwent a shift during the 1960s from reliance upon agricultural employment to development of manufacturing, as well as benefitting from newly developed recreational areas.

The Upper Great Lakes area, bordering the southern coast of Lake Superior, is a second nonmetropolitan region that experienced growth throughout the 1960s and 1970s—again primarily as the result of manufacturing decentralization and the development of recreational facilities and retirement communities.

The nonmetropolitan areas of the Blue Ridge-Piedmont, Florida, the Southwest, and the northern Pacific Coast regions all experienced growth in both the 1960s and 1970s as the result of either decentralization of manufacturing, recreational-retirement developments, the opening up of new resources, or the expansion of improved transportation facilities (the interstate highway system) which enable persons to reside in rural areas yet participate in metropolitan labor markets.

During the 1970s, nonmetropolitan growth has spread to a greater number of the nation's rural subregions. For example, a new growth axis now cuts through central Maine along the route of the interstate highway. While only those six rural areas discussed in the previous paragraph experienced net in-migration during the 1960s, there is now only one rural subregion that continues to lose population through new out-migration: the old tobacco and cotton belt extending from the North Carolina Cape to the delta area of the Mississippi River. This subregion, which contains a large rural black population, has not benefitted significantly from the decentralization of manufacturing, and its residents continue to migrate to the cities of the North.

THEORIES OF THE GROWTH TRANSITION

The evidence is clear. An increasing number of United States central cities, and a widening ring of their older suburbs, must now learn to cope with population decline. Half-way through the decade, the central cities of U.S. metropolitan areas already have lost 3.1 percent of their 1970 residential population. During the same period, suburban areas have grown by 9.3 percent.

Suburban areas are now the home of 38.9 percent of the nation's population, as compared with 29.2 percent for central cities and 32.0 percent for nonmetropolitan areas, which are growing once again. As the nation's growth rate slackens these relative shares will shift as part of a zero-sum game—some regions will gain, but only because other regions lose. In short, a turning point has been reached in the American urban experience.

To those who wrote about nineteenth and early twentieth century industrial urbanization, the essence was size, density, and heterogeneity in an atmosphere of continuing growth. "Urbanization is a process of population concentration," wrote Hope Tisdale in 1942 (8). "It implies a movement from a state of less concentration to a state of more concentration." But since 1970 American metropolitan regions have grown less rapidly than the nation, and have actually lost population to nonmetropolitan territory. A new low-slung far-flung settlement pattern is emerging as we move from a state of more concentration to a state of less concentration—as a process of counterurbanization runs its course.

There are two important theoretical models that bear on this decline of the industrial metropolis in the northeastern industrial heartland and the growth of smaller places in the hinterlands, according to William Alonso and Harvey Garn in a paper prepared recently for HUD, the efficiency model and the disamenities model. These models both offer explanations for the existence and viability of large urban areas in terms of the positive correlation between wage differentials and city size that was discussed earlier. The explanations aim at answering the question of what traditionally has motivated the flow of labor and capital into large places, and why counterurbanization now is the dominant force shaping the nation's settlement patterns as labor and capital flow in the opposite direction. Let us repeat what Alonso and Garn have to say.

The Efficiency Model

The efficiency model argues that income differentials in cities of different sizes result from the greater efficiency of the larger places. There are two versions of this explanation.

According to the first, the larger city is efficient because of its ability to facilitate production due both to the availability of markets and efficient arrangements among needed inputs provided by concentration and centrality. Higher wages for comparably productive labor inputs result from the city's efficiency. These relatively higher wages then continue to attract productive labor and the city grows. That is, it becomes larger because it is efficient. Technological advantages and agglomeration economies associated with size produce a situation in which, if the city gets big enough, it will continue to grow due to induced migration.

The second version of the efficiency model is that the places with efficient labor will continue to attract capital. Wage rates are high because labor is efficient. Additional productive labor is attracted. Thus a city becomes large because its labor is efficient rather than because of efficiencies associated with size per se. Obviously, there is some validity to both versions. Most probably they work interdependently in a process of circular and cumulative causation.

What might stop growth, given this view of persistent wage differentials? In the first version, growth will stop if either of two things happen: (1) changes in the arrangement of production that result in smaller places or more dispersed spatial arrangements being able to achieve economies heretofore associated with larger and more dense agglomerations, or (2) changes in large cities that create technological disadvantages and diseconomies reducing the competitive edge of the large city.

In the second version, growth will stop if the quality of the labor force deteriorates, the city is therefore unable to attract capital and, in the second round, additional productive labor. This could be especially serious if the high wages associated with more productive labor persist—for example as a consequence of unionization—since the high costs would further reduce the incentive for additional capital to flow into the area. The relative absence of capital causes a second round, not of attraction of productive labor, but of an exodus of the most productive members of the current labor force.

Depending upon which version of the forces breaking the cycle of cumulative causation is adjudged to be more in accord with the facts, policy solutions for rectifying the situation will differ. In the first case, efforts would be devoted to improvements in technology, while in the second case, efforts would be devoted to improving the productivity of labor (e.g., through training and education) or attempting to reduce wages to be more in line with productivity. In both cases where the accepted explanation of wage differentials rests on efficiency, the emphasis would be on dealing with those things that fairly directly affect the cost of doing business or the probability of business profit.

The Disamenities Model

The disamenities model starts from the premise that, with fairly free mobility of labor and capital, there is no reason to suppose that wage rates for equally productive labor would be unequal across city sizes and regions. But differentials do persist. The explanation, according to this model, is that a premium must be paid to compensate labor for social costs that grow with increasing city size.

Wages and incomes consist in this view of two parts: a productivity payment, which tends to be equal across cities for equally productive labor; and a disamenity premium, which increases with city size. So long as this premium is not so large that it seriously threatens profits it will continue to be paid because of the productivity associated with an industry and employment mix that benefits most from external economies within larger cities, and, on the second round, additional labor will be attracted by the apparent promise of higher money income.

What stops growth in this view is that disamenities get so large and pervasive that the premium can no longer be paid. If this happens, capital is no longer attracted, making it more difficult to pay the premiums, or productive labor begins to feel that the disamenities are larger than the compensation provided by the premium and workers migrate to places where the disamenities are less.

Possible policy approaches in this case differ from those of the efficiency case. There are two general approaches. The first is to do nothing to stem the exodus. Since disamenities are a function of size, they would presumably be diminished by the exodus so that lower premiums would have to be paid. But then the other advantages of size and concentration would also be lost. The second approach is to attempt to reduce a portion of the disamenities which are causing people to leave, either by ameliorating the disamenities themselves or by instituting preventive measures. Housing programs, transportation improvements or expansions, provision of improved public services (such as education, health facilities and care, police, fire), generation of community pride and association, noise and pollution control, code enforcement—all possible approaches to resolving this problem.

SOLVENTS FOR METROPOLITAN GLUE

Size, concentration, and centrality are interdependent in the efficiency model, and they were certainly basic to traditional urban-regional growth. Yet the concentrated industrial metropolis only developed because proximity meant lower transportation and communication costs for those interdependent specialists who had to interact with each other frequently or intensively.

One of the most important forces contributing to the new urbanization is the erosion of centrality by time-space convergence. As Melvin Webber has emphasized, virtually all technological developments of industrial times have had the effect of reducing the constraints of geographic space (9). Developments in transportation and communications have made it possible for each generation to live farther from activity centers and for information users to rely upon information sources that are spatially distant. In other words, in line with the efficiency model, large dense urban concentrations are no longer necessary for external economies to be present.

Contemporary developments in communications are supplying better channels for transmitting information and improving the capacities of partners in social intercourse to transact their business at great distances. It was the demand for ease of communication that first brought men into cities. The time eliminating properties of long distance communication and the space spanning capacities of the new communication technologies are combining to concoct a solvent that has dissolved the core oriented city in both time and space, creating what some now refer to as an urban civilization without cities. Under such circumstances, it is little wonder that smaller cities and towns, as well as nonmetropolitan regions, are now sharing in the nation's growth.

But as growth slackens, the newly discovered advantages of these outlying areas are being counterposed against the older industrial metropolitan centers in a zero-sum game, and the disamenities model is also becoming more relevant. What is implied is what J.J. Servan-Schreiber has called the essence of "the American challenge," the compression of time and space and the acceleration of change, with intensification of human experience alongside lessening demands for face-to-face contact because of the centralized information sources and instantaneous communication (10).

The revolutionary aspect of the new electronic technologies is that they not only reduce the frictions in moving goods and people; they can move the experience instead to the body. The body can, therefore, be located where it finds the nonelectronic experiences most satisfying, and thus the second part of the change—increasing interdependence has as its complement the increasing localism noted in the first part of this discussion, in which the nature and quality of the local environment are of growing importance.

Already, as we have seen, population is tending accordingly. Settlement patterns are spreading broadly over the continental surface, localized at those places where the climate and landscape are most pleasant. Densities are settling down at the scale of the exurban fringes of the eastern metropolitan areas. The edges of many of the nation's urban systems have now pushed one hundred miles and more from the traditional city centers. More important, the core orientation implied in use of the term "central city" is fast on the wane.

Today's urban systems appear to be multinodal, multiconnected social systems, sharing in national growth and offering a variety of life styles in a variety of environments. What are being abandoned are those environments that were keys in the traditional metropolis driven growth process: the high density, congested, face-to-face center city settings, now perceived as being aging, polluted, and crime ridden, with declining services and employment bases, and escalating taxes.

It is no accident that the suburbanization of city dwellers and of center city jobs has increased, supported by rising real incomes and increased leisure time, as persons of greater wealth and leisure seek homes and work among the more remote environments of hills, water, and forest, while most aspire to such an ideal. It is no accident that smaller cities and towns, and nonmetropolitan areas are in consequence experiencing accelerating growth.

Chapter Fourteen

The Future of Suburban Cities and Their Black Populations

Phillip L. Clay

Conventional wisdom characterizies the mature metropolitan area as a dying core surrounded by a ring of new growth. This is inaccurate. There are significant age and cycle determined differences within the central cities and suburbs. Both areas contain aspects of the old and new, as well as transition zones. Both are experiencing selective population and economic gains and losses.

This chapter will focus on one component of the metropolis—the older suburban city. Comparisons may be drawn between the cycle of decline which devastated portions of the central city and the emerging demographic and economic trends associated with the suburban city. Unless urban policy recognizes the complexities of the metropolitan organism and begins to manage the trends related to the movement of blacks into small and medium sized suburban cities, we shall witness the creation of sectors in our metropolitan areas undergoing rapid decline and racial resegregation, producing a situation not unlike that in some central city neighborhoods.[a]

THE SHAPE OF THE METROPOLITAN AREA

Urban ecologists theorize that communities are conceived, born, mature, decline and may be restored, albeit sometimes in a different form. While there has been some debate about the precise character-

---
[a]Many of the same issues raised here in reference to blacks occur in suburban cities to which blacks have not moved. While the present analysis is for the purpose of planning to deal with racial change, the income issue is also pertinent.

istics of each stage, there is some consensus that community life cycles do exist. As the city and suburbs move through stages in the cycle at various rates, differentiation between the city and the suburbs is produced (1) (2) (3).

Visualize the metropolis as having: 1) a central city, 2) small and medium sized suburban cities, and 3) a suburban fringe—or exurbia— (including unincorporated areas as well as towns). Some suburban cities are nearly as old as their central city hub. On the other hand, suburban fringe communities vary considerably in age. In general, the rate of growth of suburban cities' populations peaked between 1950 and 1960, when the suburban fringe (drawing population from the central and suburban city) entered its "take-off" stage.

The Central City

Some urban planning experts suggest that the central city is dying (4). They cite the abandonment of housing, increased crime rates, loss of jobs and tax bases, welfare dependency, and reduced public services as evidence of the demise of the central city as a viable entity. The picture is not entirely accurate. The central city is not a single entity, but consists of several "cities." Within the political boundaries, real growth and improvement exists alongside of decay and neglect. The central city may be thought of as including "economic city," "high-rise city," and "poor city." Each has its own character, and each is at a different stage in the cycle of growth and decline. The entire central city is a constantly renewing entity: some functions disappear as others (with the aid of improved technology in such areas as transportation and communication) persevere. Urban renewal often serves as the vehicle of improvements. New investment and the residual value of prior investment in the central city make it inconceivable that the total demise predicted by the nay-sayers will ever occur. But what about its component "cities?"

"Economic City." This is the complex of office buildings, institutions, and service facilities (convention centers, exhibition halls, sports arenas) existing primarily in or near the central business district. It generates white collar and service jobs, produces information, and serves as a decision-making center.[b] Historically, central cities have performed key economic functions affecting manufacturing, administration, and business in general.

After World War II, much of "economic city's" industrial base, especially manufacturing, moved to the suburbs, relocating in indus-

---

[b]I am grateful to Prof. David Smith of the University of Massachusetts-Boston for first calling my attention to "economic city," especially as it exists in Boston.

trial parks. This led observers to suggest that many of the economic functions of the central city have been assumed by the suburbs and that the city will soon be a center only for government, culture, and business requiring face-to-face contact. This has not occurred.

Perhaps the best measure of the economic esteem in which the central city is held is the level of investment in office space. In the last dozen years, there has been a substantial increase in office space in the "economic city." The square footage of office space increased between 60 and 90 percent in New York, Atlanta, Boston, Cleveland, and Dallas. St. Louis, San Francisco, and Minneapolis-St. Paul added over 100 percent (5). Even Detroit has added several major central business district offices in its Renaissance Center and institutional complexes in its downtown medical area. And more development is on the drawing board.

The increase in office space parallels the growth of white collar, professional, and service jobs in the city. The growth experienced by "economic city" is a result of strong business and political leadership, public investment incentives, urban renewal, and the continuing attractiveness of a central location.

"High-rise city." Residential clusters represent the beginnings of new, "high-rise cities"—small islands of luxury in or near the "economic city." These towers are typically self-sufficient communities with shopping, parking, work, and recreation within easy access, if not actually in the same building. They have private security forces and community services. Residents do not interact with the surrounding urban neighbors (6).

"Poor City." This is the "city" which gets the most publicity and about which the more dire predictions are made. The predictions, partially valid and tragically self-fulfilling, are then applied to the entire central city. While the central city as a whole is experiencing an upswing in the number of well-to-do residents it still has large concentrations of the poor and near poor. "Poor City" also has large numbers of undermaintained or decayed residential stock, and the quality of its services is becoming less satisfactory as fiscal problems mount.

"Poor City" comprises segregated black and white working class families, each fighting for a piece of what is becoming a smaller pie of urban services. They benefit little from "economic city" or "high rise city." Needless to say, they cannot afford housing in redeveloped areas. Many householders, excluded by income or exclusionary zoning, remain in the central city because they have no choice.

It is largely in "poor city" that urban disinvestment occurs. Billions of dollars are invested in stabilizing or increasing "economic city" and "high rise city" facilities. But, building rehabilitation, and urban renewal programs have not succeeded in stabilizing the housing stock or improving conditions in "Poor City."

The Suburban City

Exodus from the central city to the suburban city is an old phenomenon. Suburban cities have existed in larger metropolitan areas for decades (7), serving primarily as residential "bedroom" communities, with some larger industrial satellites serving economic functions. The condition of the suburban city depends on its location, age, and economic or residential roles.

At the end of the 1960s, suburban cities adjacent to the central city received an influx of blacks, usually into a segregated area. Examples of such communities are Pasadena, Compton, and Pomona in Los Angeles; East Cleveland and Cleveland Heights in Cleveland; and Yonkers and New Rochelle in New York.

In recent years these suburban cities have been the major frontiers for black families. For whites, the frontier was the new suburban fringe with its new development of detached and multifamily housing, as well as the reclaimed parts of the central city.

The Suburban Fringe (Exurbia)

The suburban fringe is the largest area of recent growth and development. It absorbs population from the central city, suburban city, and other metropolitan areas. People moving to the suburban fringe are searching for more land, modern and spacious homes, greater amenity and public services. Though some move specifically in search of jobs in the new suburban fringe plants and offices, accessibility to jobs in the rest of the metropolis is maintained by transportation networks (8).

To service the population and industry, services and retail outlets have clustered on major transportation arteries in the outer ring. Vast shopping centers, industrial parks office complexes, sports arenas, and research and development firms have sprung up. These are the areas which represent sprawl. Fringe communities are booming, representing some of the fastest growing areas of the country.[c]

---

[c]There are more than 18,000 suburban places. This chapter deals with only a selected sample of older suburban cities to which blacks have migrated. The small suburban communities and the newer developing areas are referred to here as the "suburban fringe." More particularly, the argument made here is limited to urban areas in the Northeast, North Central, and West Coast, and not in the Sunbelt states. This chapter does not deal with the wealthy suburban cities (such as Newton, Massachusetts, or Dearborn Heights), but with the more modest suburbs for moderate income families.

THE SUBURBAN CRISIS

Concentration on downtown development was detrimental to "poor city." A similar concentration on development of the suburban fringe or exurbia has been to the disadvantage of the suburban city.

Suburban cities are faced with many of the same problems faced by older central cities: a stable or declining tax base while inflation and the demand for more and improved services are creating severe fiscal pressures. Many of these communities are unable to attract the better-off households and/or new or relocated businesses. Until the inception of revenue-sharing programs, they received relatively little federal assistance for social service programs. In suburban cities the demand for new housing, especially single detached units, has not grown as rapidly as in new fringe communities in the metropolitan area. Consequently, prices for existing housing in suburban cities have not risen as rapidly, and a great deal of housing, in various states of repair, has come within the price range of many low and moderate income families.

Suburban cities have begun to attract substantial numbers of blacks because of the availability of moderately priced housing and despite the problems outlined above.

DEMOGRAPHIC TRENDS

Table 14-1 lists the SMSAs accounting for most of the black migration during the decade of the sixties. Of the 800,000 blacks who moved to the suburbs, almost 600,000 moved to within the ten SMSAs listed in Table 14-1.

Among these ten SMSAs, New York, Los Angeles, and Washington, D.C. showed the greatest increase in the level of black suburbanization, although several other cities also had large increases. Another significant fact shown in Table 14-1 is the percentage of suburban blacks who are concentrated in the largest of the suburban cities within each of the ten SMSAs. With the exceptions of New York and Philadelphia, where there are more blacks scattered in much smaller communities and townships, all of the SMSAs show most blacks are located within just a few of the suburban cities.[d]

What changes in relative status among sectors of the metropolis might be reflected in this increase in the number of black suburban-

---

[d]In compiling Table 14-1, all suburban municipalities with black populations greater than 1 percent in 1970 were considered. The present list includes only those communities which meet this criteria and which were municipal (or other general purpose) government entities.

Table 14-1. 1960 and 1970 Black Suburban Population and Concentration of Blacks in Major Suburban Cities of Selected SMSAs

SMSA	1960 Black Suburban Population	1970 Black Suburban Population	Percent of Suburban Blacks in the Selected Suburban Cities	Percent of Total SMSA Census Tracts included in Selected Cities**
New York	139,694	216,656	38[a]	12
Los Angeles	117,099	240,247	68	12
Chicago	77,517	128,299	57	14
Philadelphia	142,064	190,509	38[b]	6
Washington, D.C.	83,746	166,033	65	36
Detroit	76,647	96,655	65	5
St. Louis	81,039	124,625	52	8
Cleveland	8,099	44,773	71	16
Newark	86,049	140,884	79	21
San Francisco	68,012	109,319	55[c]	13

Source: U.S. Bureau of Census, *Census of Population and Housing*, 1970, PH C(2)-1 and appropriate volumes.

a. Includes mainly the larger suburban cities in Westchester County below(*) and not the many smaller townships on Long Island.
b. Includes only larger cities (*) below, not small townships in the urbanized counties.
c. Does not include Oakland.

*The specific cities included in these calculations are: New York (Freeport, Hempstead, Mt. Vernon, New Rochelle, Port Chester, White Plains, and Yonkers); Los Angeles (Altadena, Carson, Compton, Florence–Graham, Inglewood, Willowbrook, Pomona, Pasadena); Chicago (Chicago Heights, Evanston, Harvey, Maywood, North Chicago, Waukegan, Joliet and Aurora); Philadelphia (Camden, Chester and Norristown); Detroit (Pontiac, Hamtramck, Highland Park and Inkster); St. Louis (Alton, East St. Louis, University City, and Webster Groves); Cleveland (East Cleveland, Cleveland Heights, Garfield Heights; and Shaker Heights); Newark (East Orange, Plainfield, Linden, Rahway, Irvington, Elizabeth, Montclair); and San Francisco (Alameda, Berkeley, Haywood, and Richmond). In the Washington, D.C. SMSA, Prince Georges County, Alexandria are included. included.
**Split and adjacent tracts as well as tracts inclusive in suburban ring.

ites and their concentration in only a few suburban cities? Where did these cities stand relative to the rest of the SMSA and to each other in 1960 as compared to 1970?

Table 14-2 presents data on the value of owner-occupied homes in 1960 and 1970. This measure was chosen because of all the single measures which are widely available, home values in various communities best reflect the variation in physical characteristics, estimates of fair market value, and attractiveness.

Table 14-2 shows that most of the suburban cities to which blacks moved were of relatively lower status (i.e., lower priced housing).

Table 14-2. Trends in Relative Value of Owner-Occupied Homes Among Selected Suburban Cities in Selected SMSAs, 1960 to 1970*

SMSA/Suburban City	1960 Value Ratio	1970 Value Ratio
New York SMSA		
Mt. Vernon	1.21	1.10
Freeport	.97	.89
New Rochelle	1.55	1.55
Yonkers	1.29	1.24
Los Angeles SMSA		
Carson	.81	1.06
Compton	.81	.74
Inglewood	1.18	1.57
Pasadena	1.10	1.08
Pomona	.80	.71
Chicago SMSA		
Harvey	.76	.72
Maywood	.88	.80
Joliet	.77	.95
Chicago Heights	.97	.86
Evanston	1.31	1.39
Philadelphia SMSA		
Camden	.60	.56
Chester	.82	.68
Norristown	.96	.87
Detroit SMSA		
Pontiac	.77	.79
Hamtramck	.65	.52
Highland Park	.80	.69
Inkster	.95	.90
Cleveland SMSA		
East Cleveland	.85	.72
Cleveland Heights	1.18	1.02
Shaker Heights	1.95	1.82
St. Louis SMSA		
East St. Louis	.57	.54
University City	1.43	1.14
Alton	.83	.77
Webster Groves	1.36	1.23
Newark SMSA		
E. Orange	.81	.69
Orange	.81	.70
Plainfield	.94	.80

Table 14-2. (cont.)

SMSA/Suburban City	1960 Value Ratio	1970 Value Ratio
Elizabeth	.81	.73
Montclair	1.22	1.13
San Francisco SMSA		
Alameda	.91	.97
Berkeley	1.02	.99
Hayward	.95	.84
Oakland	.87	.79
Richmond	.80	.74
Washington, D.C. SMSA		
Prince Georges County	.88	1.15
Alexandria	.96	.95

Source: U.S. Bureau of Census, *Census of Population and Housing: 1970,* PHC (2)-1 and appropriate volumes.

*This table gives a ratio of median value of owner-occupied housing in selected suburban cities to the SMSA median for 1960 and 1970. A value less than 1.00 indicates the housing is less valuable while greater than 1.00 means it is more valuable. Since the ratio refers to the whole SMSA, the ratio understates the relatively less value of housing in these selected communities to housing in suburban fringe communities. The inter-decade comparisons show the relative position of the given suburban city in 1960 compared to 1970.

This does not mean that there was a decline in housing values as blacks moved in. On the contrary, blacks, having lower incomes, might have been attracted to these less expensive communities. In addition, in 28 of the 40 suburban cities, the median value of housing was often much less than the SMSA median. Thus, the relative status held by these communities pre-existed black migration to them. No doubt slack demand for older housing and alternative opportunities for whites helped to open the doors to blacks in suburban cities.

Characteristics of people and households of black suburban populations are presented in Table 14-3. The average size and age of the black family in the suburbs showed little change between 1960 and 1970, while the average size of the central city black family increased and became younger.

Table 14-3. General Characteristics of Metropolitan Population by Race and Place, 1960/1970

Characteristics	Black		White	
	Central City	Suburban	Central City	Suburban
Median income of families (1969 dollars)	4840/6794	4383/6986	7881/9797	8486/11,155
Average family size	4.0/4.1	4.5/4.4	3.4/3.3	3.7/3.7
Percent adults (over 25 years) with high school education	43/63	38/55	62/74	67/81
Percent of all families below poverty line (1969 dollars)	40.8/24.7	50.9/23.2	13.8/10.2	10.4/5.4
Median age (both sexes)	25.5/22.5	23.1/23.6	32.9/32.7	28.6/27.3
Labor force participation rates				
(a) male	80.7/78.2	81.3/76.6	80.7/78.2	81.3/76.6
(b) female	46.8/51.9	46.0/54.2	39.8/44.1	34.3/41.9
Black median earnings as percent of white median earnings for employed males	63/75.3	50/64.9		

Source: U.S. Bureau of Census, *Current Population Reports*, P-23 # 37, 1971.

The decade began with a large proportion of poor among the suburban black population, but by the end of the decade, the pattern had reversed as more non-poor families moved in. Recent black suburban migrants were, as a group, of much higher income, smaller families, higher education, and more likely to be skilled workers (9). Some of the migrating black families were of higher income; but most families with incomes greater than $20,000 per year had two people working.

As a group, these blacks had resources with which to negotiate in the suburban housing markets, but few had the substantial wealth or savings necessary to buy the new or more expensive dwellings. Table 14-3 shows that in 1960 the difference between income of black suburbanites and central city blacks was $500 per year. By 1970, their positions were reversed and blacks in the suburbs earned slightly more.

Housing in Suburban Cities. A look at the housing situation suggests substantial differences exist between housing opportunities available to blacks in older suburban cities and whites in newer suburban or exurban areas (see Table 14-4).

The situation with respect to housing in some older suburban cities is much like that faced by inner city neighborhoods in the late 1950s and the early 1960s (10). As units come on the market, they

Table 14-4. Comparison of Selected Housing Variables, by Race, in Areas Outside the South, 1970

N = 717

Variable	Percent White	Percent Black
Unit has 6 rooms or more	51.0	36.0
Unit has complete plumbing facilities	98.6	97.3
Unit is owner-occupied	68.3	49.7
Unit is valued at $25,000 or more	35.9	20.1
Unit was built pre-1940	30.7	39.3
Unit was built since 1960	27.9	20.9
Unit is single family structure	77.0	71.8
Unit has no more than 1.01 persons per room	93.7	81.8
Household spends 25 percent or less for rent	67.3	57.4

Computed from Public Use Sample Tape of the 1970 U.S. Census.

go to blacks—the group for whom mobility is most limited and for whom resources are most scarce. Table 14-4 shows that the suburban units occupied by whites were larger, newer, and more valuable than those occupied by blacks. For some urban blacks suburbanization might be involuntary (i.e., no suitable housing is available in the central city because of demolition, condemnation, or rezoning regulations) or the result of "spillover" (where suburbanization is more technical and not just a choice of housing and community services). While many black suburbanites are no better off than blacks in the central city, they are, at least for the time being, more satisfied with their neighborhoods. There is an average to above-average level of political participation and civic leadership. In many neighborhoods there is even the skeleton of *gemeinschaft* (11).

The supply of suburban housing, while currently quite sound, poses some interesting questions, especially in view of racial transition and the evidence of a lag in property values relative to the larger metropolitan housing market. The major question is whether the present situation is the beginning of the process of disinvestment, like that which devastated central cities in the 60s, or a new, long term equilibrium of modestly priced homes.

East Orange, New Jersey is a good case in point. Blacks began to move into East Orange in substantial numbers early in the 1960s, and by 1970, the racial balance had shifted. A review of census data on rents, housing values, and change in value between 1960 and 1970 shows that despite the fact that housing values increased in the entire

Newark SMSA by 21 percent (in constant dollars) during the decade, and by substantially more in the suburban fringe areas, East Orange had only a 3 percent increase in its estimated housing values. Other small and medium-sized cities in the metropolitan area showed correspondingly small increases, i.e., Bloomfield (6.7%), Irvington (5.0%), Plainfield (2.7%) and Elizabeth (10.0%). Even the substantially middle-class community of Montclair showed an increase of only 14.7 percent.

While the shortage of housing and other problems in Newark will bolster the housing demand in these suburban communities, the relative position of the suburban city versus other suburban areas discourages private developers and investors. The failure of the tax base to increase substantially makes it unlikely that local public investment (assuming no massive state or federal aid) will be sufficient to fund the needed services and public capital improvements. Indeed, in East Orange, a decline in investment confidence has already begun, evidenced by a second wave of out-migration from the community. This time it is the middle class blacks who are moving out.

For many black families, as for other groups, suburban cities have served as "zones of emergence." See Table 14-5. These communities were originally settled by whites who wished to escape the central city and who had amassed enough money to buy a modest home. They wanted to raise their children in a community of similarly emerging migrants (12). As whites improved their financial situations, they left. It appears that blacks will do likewise. Recent

Table 14-5. Comparison of Housing Units Occupied by Blacks in the Central City vs. the Suburbs, Outside the South, 1970

$N = 703$

Variable	Percent Central City	Percent Suburban
Unit has 6 rooms or more	28.0	36.0
Unit has complete plumbing facilities	97.0	97.3
Unit is owner-occupied	30.0	49.7
Unit is valued at $25,000 or more	6.6	20.1
Unit was built pre-1940	51.9	39.3
Unit was built since 1960	11.8	20.9
Unit is single family structure	53.7	71.8
Unit has no more than 1.01 persons per room	83.3	81.8
Household spends 25 percent or less for rent	62.6	57.4

Computed from Public Use Sample Tape of the 1970 U.S. Census.

experience with "zones of transition" adjoining the central city should alert us to the significance of the following signs:

1. Suburban cities are showing rapid increase in some social problems long associated with the central city. These include increases in crime, traffic congestion, unemployment, welfare dependency, and lagging investment in housing maintenance which threatens the housing stock (13).

2. Suburban property taxes have increased significantly. A survey in suburban cities outside of New York shows that average property taxes on a modest home ($30,000) increased from less than $900 in 1960 to more than $2000 in 1975, in spite of cutbacks in public services.

3. Funds for federal and state programs to assist communities in meeting the needs of their poorer citizens and in supporting housing development are not being allocated at a satisfactory level. General Revenue Sharing and Community Development Block Grants remain as major sources of funds, and they are often used for "safe" public works projects and not human or social services.

The reading of this tells us clearly that these are signs of trouble, especially when combined with increasing black concentrations and a psychology of disinvestment in older suburbs. Public policy must respond to these problems to avoid a "suburban crisis."

 *Part Seven*

Conclusions: Planning for the Future

Chapter Fifteen

Planning the Needs of Small Cities

Herrington J. Bryce, Gloria J. Cousar, and Stephanie Fain

PLANNING BACKGROUND

Cities need to plan for growth and for decline so that change might be orderly and efficient; cities plan because of legal requirements by state, federal, and even local laws as stipulated in their charters. Clearly, there is a strong imperative for planning by cities of all sizes.

Planning in small cities is not new. Mel Scott, in his *American City Planning Since 1890*, documented that 75 of at least 100 plans produced between 1920 and 1926 had been prepared for cities under 100,000 in population (1). But planning in many of these cities had a sharp decline during the Depression. In California, for example, by 1932 more than half the planning commissions and staff in cities 25,000 to 100,000 in population had gone out of existence (2).

But planning has since been revived in many small cities, although the scope of the planning function is often not as wide as in many of the larger cities. It is generally recognized that the planning functions of small cities are not free of significant handicaps and difficulties that in so many cases make planning in the traditional sense a near impossible task for many small cities. Many lack adequate planning resources.

This material is based upon research supported by the National Science Foundation under Grant No. ERS74-21286 to the Joint Center for Political Studies-Howard University. Any opinions, findings, and conclusions expressed in this publication are those of the author(s) and do not necessarily reflect the views of the National Science Foundation. Prepared with the assistance of William McCoy and Clevie Gladney. Only the authors hold responsibility for the errors in this article.

This fact was recognized by the federal government when it established the 701 program as part of the Housing Act of 1954. The initial purpose of Section 701 of this Act was to facilitate planning for small communities (those under 25,000 in population). Since 1954, however, this assistance is made available to all sizes of government and quasi-government planning authorities.

A review of the literature reveals that there have only been limited attempts to systematically analyze the planning needs of small cities even though there are several floating hypotheses about the character of needs.

There have been few systematic efforts to ask local government officials to rank their priorities. One such effort was conducted in 1973 by the National League of Cities and the U.S. Conference of Mayors. The study, entitled "America's Mayors and Councilmen: Their Problems and Frustrations," is based on a survey of 4,000 locally elected public officials (Mayors and Council). Among other things, these officials were asked to indicate which of 28 specific functions of local government represented major problems for them. In the April, 1974 issue of *Nation's Cities*, results indicated that refuse/solid waste was mentioned most frequently as a serious problem. It was followed by law enforcement and streets and highways.

This same data, when regrouped into eight major functional categories, showed that community development problems were the most frequently mentioned concerns for cities of all sizes. However, by size, the expression of needs by functional responsibility varied considerably. Cities under 10,000 in population most frequently saw their community development problem as one related to parks and recreational facilities, cities 10,000 to 25,000, like cities 25,000 to 50,000 and cities 50,000 to 100,000, were most often concerned with downtown development.

In the National League of Cities Study, items receiving the highest numerical response were not necessarily the most important needs, although they were the most common (3). Furthermore, needs are likely to differ for a host of reasons other than size. These reasons include growth rates, age, region, income, and metropolitan status. Because of the limited systematic knowledge of the needs of small cities and because of the imperative of these cities to plan, the objective of the present study is to identify their planning needs and priorities.

The cities studied are 10,000 and 100,000 in population size (1970) and are incorporated areas. These cities are very different in numerous ways which are important to planning. They have different forms of government; some are free standing while others are suburban; some are rural rather than urban, some are metropolitan rather than nonmetropolitan. They are also different in terms of economic orientation and even in age. Consequently, by focusing on such a diverse group of cities, it is possible to address key questions such as the following: Do small cities have similar needs even though they are different in terms of certain important characteristics? What are the key characteristics which distinguish between the planning needs among small cities?

Specifically:

1. Do cities of different size have different needs? Cities will be broken down into three population size classes using 1970 data: 10,000-24,999; 25,000-49,999; and 50,000-100,000.
2. Do cities of different urban orientation have different needs? Cities will be classified according to whether they are part of a nonmetropolitan or a metropolitan area.
3. Do cities of different vintage have different needs? Do older cities have functional needs which are greater than and different from younger cities?
4. Do poorer cities have different planning needs from richer ones?
5. Do northern cities have different planning needs than southern or western cities?
6. Do planning needs differ among cities with different growth rates?

DEFINITION OF PLANNING AND PLANNING NEEDS

What is planning? Planning has been variously defined as a process of decision making, as a source of political power to bring about changes, as a technique of continuous adjustment to societal changes, as the organization of a clear statement of intent, and so on (4). More formally, planning has been defined by the Office of Management and Budget through Circular A-95 as including:

1. The preparation of a guide for governmental policies and action relating to the pattern and intensity of land use, the provision of public facilities and other government services, and the effective development and utilization of human and natural resources.
2. The preparation of long range physical and fiscal plans for such action.
3. The programming of capital improvements and other major expenditures, based on a determination of relative urgency, together with definitive financing plans for such expenditures in the earlier years of the program.

318 Conclusions: Planning for the Future

4. The coordination of all related plans and activities of the state and local governments and agencies concerned.
5. The preparation of regulatory and administrative measures in support of the foregoing.

In an insightful summary definition, Dorn C. McGrath, Jr., formerly president of the American Institute of Planners, writes that planning is the means by which a unit of government may fulfill its commitment to people by anticipating and preparing for future needs inherent in the process of urban growth and change (5).

For the purpose of this study, one aspect of planning needs is emphasized. The study will identify the functional or policy areas of need. According to local officials, in which function of city government (housing, transportation, economic development, water and sewer, etc.) occurs the greatest need for planning?

METHODOLOGY

A questionnaire was sent to 1,330 cities, and information from 522 cities has been received. All (687) incorporated cities between 25,000 and 100,000 in population in 1970 received questionnaires. One-half the cities 10,000 to 25,000 in population received questionnaires. The response rate was 46.6 percent for the first group, 31.2 percent for the second. Respondents who ranked priorities in the survey included elected officials and municipal administrators from 460 cities 10,000 to 100,000 in population. Nearly 63.5 percent of these participants represented cities located in standard metropolitan statistical areas, while 168 of the questionnaires were identified as nonmetropolitan in character.

By city size class, 174 of the responses to priority needs came from municipalities 10,000 to 25,000 in population; 182 were from cities 25,000 to 50,000 in population; and 104 were identified with cities 50,000 to 100,000 in population. A majority of the questionnaires were completed by planning directors; the survey was explicitly directed to persons with responsibility for administering planning activities.

The following question was asked:

In which of the following areas is planning most needed in your city?

Please indicate at least 3 in the order of their importance.

Land use/zoning	_____	Manpower programs	_____
Transportation	_____	Welfare	_____
Housing	_____	Day Care	_____

Planning the Needs of Small Cities 319

Economic development _____	Elderly services _____
Sewer/water services _____	Recreation/open space _____
Enrivonmental protection _____	Historic preservation _____
Health _____	Crime prevention/
Education _____	criminal justice _____
	Other _____

(specify)

FINDINGS

The findings are divided into two sections. The first shows the most common (modal) responses. The second shows the first priority (ranked) responses. In many cases, the most common planning concerns of cities are not the ones which are of the highest priority.

Table 15-1 shows the most common planning needs by city size. Land-use planning is the most common planning need among the smallest size cities, while housing is the most common need of the other cities. Interestingly enough, human resource planning is about equally common regardless of city size. But planning of recreational facilities is distinctly a more common need among the smaller cities.

Does the planning need of small cities vary by region? Economic development planning is the most common need in the Northeast—a fact undoubtedly related to the adverse economic conditions in that part of the country. Among cities located in the North Central states, land use/zoning is the most common need; but among cities in the South, housing and land use are equally important. In the West, housing is just slightly more common a planning need than land use.

Table 15-2 shows that planning for recreation is not a marked concern of small cities in any region, although substantial population growth throughout the South and in Northeast states like Vermont have been due to the attraction of recreational possibilities. Also, a much smaller percentage of Northeast and North Central cities responded to the need for environmental planning, as compared with southern, and especially western cities. For cities in the northern regions, higher priorities are assigned to economic development (as shown below in Table 15-7), even though many of these places are faced with serious environmental problems. Thus, given a trade-off between planning for environmental protection and economic development planning, the declining industrialized areas show a preference for the latter.

One clear difference emerges when cities are divided within regions between those which are metropolitan and those which are non-

Table 15-1. Distribution of Common Planning Needs in Small Cities, by Size

Major Planning Needs	City Size Classes						Total	
	I. 10,000-25,000		II. 25,000-50,000		III. 50,000-100,000			
	No.	(%)	No.	(%)	No.	(%)	No.	(%)
1. Land use	130	(18.7)	112	(16.0)	72	(17.9)	314	(17.5)
2. Transportation	79	(11.3)	89	(12.8)	45	(11.2)	213	(11.9)
3. Housing	103	(14.8)	122	(17.5)	80	(19.9)	305	(17.0)
4. Economic development	95	(13.6)	108	(15.5)	51	(12.7)	254	(14.1)
5. Water/sewer facilities	68	(9.8)	63	(9.0)	24	(6.0)	155	(8.6)
6. Environmental protection	31	(4.4)	39	(5.6)	25	(6.2)	95	(5.3)
7. Human resources[a]	70	(10.0)	69	(9.8)	44	(10.9)	183	(10.2)
8. Recreation	62	(8.9)	30	(4.3)	15	(4.0)	107	(6.0)
9. Crime	33	(4.7)	36	(5.1)	19	(5.0)	88	(5.0)
10. Other	26	(3.7)	30	(4.3)	27	(7.0)	83	(4.6)
Totals	697	(100.0)	698	(100.0)	402	(100.0)	1797	(100.0)

In this and other tables, percentages may not add to 100 percent because of rounding.

[a]Human resources includes the following functions or service areas of local government: manpower programming, welfare, day care, health, education, and elderly services.

metropolitan. That difference is within the South. The most common need among metropolitan cities is for land use planning; but among the nonmetro cities in this region, it is for housing. This undoubtedly reflects the growth of metro cities, compared to the high rates of substandard housing located in the nonmetro South.

To what extent do growth rates affect the planning needs of cities? The most common need of declining cities is in planning for better housing. Over 20 percent of the declining cities indicated this. Economic development and land use planning are second. For the moderately growing cities (those with a growth rate from 0 to 13.13 percent—the national average), housing is the most common need. But for the rapidly growing cities, the need is for more comprehensive planning as indicated by the frequency with which these cities emphasize land use planning. These findings hold even when metropolitan status is taken into account. In addition to these aspects,

Table 15-2. Distribution of Common Planning Needs in Small Cities, by Region and Metropolitan Status

	United States							
Major Planning Needs	Northeast		North Central		South		West	
	No.	(%)	No.	(%)	No.	(%)	No.	(%)
1. Land use	65	(16.7)	93	(19.2)	82	(17.4)	74	(17.1)
2. Transportation	42	(10.8)	56	(11.6)	51	(10.8)	54	(12.5)
3. Housing	60	(15.4)	81	(16.8)	83	(17.6)	81	(18.8)
4. Economic development	71	(18.2)	73	(15.1)	53	(11.3)	57	(13.2)
5. Water/sewer facilities	36	(9.2)	46	(9.5)	52	(11.0)	21	(4.3)
6. Environmental protection	13	(3.3)	18	(4.0)	30	(6.4)	34	(8.0)
7. Human resources	40	(10.2)	41	(8.5)	46	(9.8)	47	(11.0)
8. Recreation	25	(6.4)	29	(6.0)	32	(6.8)	21	(5.0)
9. Crime	17	(4.3)	25	(5.2)	24	(5.1)	22	(5.0)
10. Other	21	(5.3)	21	(4.3)	18	(3.8)	21	(5.0)
Totals	390	(100.0)	483	(100.0)	471	(100.0)	432	(100.0)

	Metropolitan							
Major Planning Needs	Northeast		North Central		South		West	
	No.	(%)	No.	(%)	No.	(%)	No.	(%)
1. Land use	50	(17.6)	55	(18.3)	47	(19.9)	50	(16.1)
2. Transportation	29	(10.2)	32	(10.7)	24	(10.1)	39	(12.5)
3. Housing	44	(15.5)	50	(16.6)	37	(15.6)	56	(18.0)
4. Economic development	49	(17.3)	45	(15.0)	23	(9.7)	40	(12.9)
5. Water/sewer facilities	24	(8.4)	30	(10.0)	26	(11.0)	14	(4.5)
6. Environmental protection	10	(3.5)	10	(3.3)	18	(7.6)	27	(8.7)
7. Human resources	30	(10.5)	27	(9.0)	25	(10.5)	36	(11.6)
8. Recreation	17	(6.0)	19	(6.3)	17	(7.2)	15	(4.8)
9. Crime	14	(5.0)	18	(6.0)	12	(5.1)	18	(5.8)
10. Other	17	(6.0)	14	(4.6)	7	(3.0)	16	(5.2)
Totals	284	(100.0)	300	(100.0)	236	(100.0)	311	(100.0)

Table 15-2. (cont.)

Major Planning Needs	Nonmetropolitan							
	Northeast		North Central		South		West	
	No.	(%)	No.	(%)	No.	(%)	No.	(%)
1. Land use	15	(13.9)	38	(20.5)	35	(14.3)	24	(19.8)
2. Transportation	13	(12.3)	24	(13.0)	37	(15.2)	15	(12.4)
3. Housing	16	(14.8)	31	(16.8)	46	(18.9)	25	(20.7)
4. Economic development	22	(20.4)	28	(15.1)	30	(12.3)	17	(14.0)
5. Water/sewer facilities	12	(11.1)	16	(8.6)	26	(10.6)	7	(5.7)
6. Environmental protection	12	(11.1)	14	(7.5)	20	(8.1)	11	(9.0)
7. Human resources	3	(2.7)	8	(4.3)	12	(5.0)	7	(5.7)
8. Recreation	8	(7.4)	10	(5.4)	15	(6.1)	6	(5.0)
9. Crime	3	(2.7)	7	(3.7)	12	(5.0)	4	(3.3)
10. Other	4	(3.7)	9	(4.8)	11	(4.5)	5	(4.1)
Totals	108	(100.0)	185	(100.0)	244	(100.0)	121	(100.0)

Table 15-3 shows that there is a higher level of concern for environmental planning among the faster growing cities.

Table 15-4 shows the relationship between planning needs and the age of housing which is used as a proxy for age of city. There seems to be one noticeable difference. The most frequently mentioned need among the youngest cities is for land use planning, particularly those in metropolitan areas. Youngest nonmetropolitan cities expressed a greater concern for housing. The youngest cities also expressed greater needs for environmental planning and noticeably less need for human resources planning. Among the oldest cities, the most common need for planning is for housing services, and there is no difference between metropolitan and nonmetropolitan cities in this respect.

In cities where the poverty rates are high, physical planning is a more common concern than social planning; the only exception to this finding occurred among the poorest metropolitan cities, for whom human resources planning was indicated as the most common need. It should also be noted that among those cities with high rates of poverty, the most frequently mentioned need is for planning housing services. This is especially true among nonmetropolitan cities (see Table 15-5).

Table 15-3. Distribution of Common Planning Needs in Small Cities, by Percentage 1960-70 Population Change and Metropolitan Status

Major Planning Needs	United States							
	Less than 0		0-13.3%		13.4%-49.9%		50% & above	
	No.	(%)	No.	(%)	No.	(%)	No.	(%)
1. Land use	53	(15.0)	73	(14.4)	109	(19.3)	74	(19.9)
2. Transportation	36	(10.2)	58	(11.5)	73	(12.9)	46	(12.4)
3. Housing	73	(20.6)	88	(17.4)	87	(15.4)	56	(15.1)
4. Economic development	56	(15.8)	79	(15.6)	68	(12.1)	51	(13.7)
5. Water/sewer facilities	37	(10.4)	43	(8.4)	48	(8.5)	27	(7.2)
6. Environmental protection	9	(2.5)	31	(6.1)	36	(6.4)	29	(7.8)
7. Human resources	39	(11.0)	60	(11.8)	51	(9.0)	26	(7.0)
8. Recreation	15	(4.2)	27	(5.3)	36	(6.4)	29	(7.8)
9. Crime	22	(6.2)	27	(5.3)	21	(3.7)	18	(4.8)
10. Other	14	(4.0)	19	(3.7)	35	(6.2)	15	(4.0)
Totals	354	(100.0)	505	(100.0)	564	(100.0)	371	(100.0)

Major Planning Needs	Metropolitan							
	Less than 0		0-13.3%		13.4%-49.9%		50% & above	
	No.	(%)	No.	(%)	No.	(%)	No.	(%)
1. Land use	31	(16.8)	45	(16.0)	53	(16.9)	63	(19.7)
2. Transportation	13	(7.0)	30	(10.7)	42	(13.4)	39	(12.2)
3. Housing	37	(20.0)	44	(15.7)	45	(14.4)	47	(14.7)
4. Economic development	28	(15.1)	45	(16.0)	41	(13.1)	43	(13.5)
5. Water/sewer facilities	18	(9.7)	23	(8.2)	32	(10.2)	21	(6.6)
6. Environmental protection	5	(2.7)	14	(5.0)	20	(6.4)	26	(8.2)
7. Human resources	20	(10.8)	39	(13.9)	23	(7.3)	27	(8.5)
8. Recreation	10	(5.4)	11	(3.9)	22	(7.0)	25	(7.8)
9. Crime	14	(7.6)	17	(6.0)	15	(4.8)	16	(5.0)
10. Other	9	(4.9)	13	(4.6)	20	(6.4)	12	(3.8)
Totals	185	(100.0)	281	(100.0)	313	(100.0)	319	(100.0)

Table 15-3. (cont.)

Major Planning Needs	Nonmetropolitan							
	Less than 0		0-13.3%		13.4%-49.9%		50% & above	
	No.	(%)	No.	(%)	No.	(%)	No.	(%)
1. Land use	22	(13.3)	38	(17.7)	41	(18.3)	11	(21.1)
2. Transportation	23	(13.9)	28	(13.0)	31	(13.8)	7	(13.5)
3. Housing	32	(19.4)	35	(16.3)	42	(18.8)	7	(13.5)
4. Economic development	28	(17.0)	34	(15.8)	27	(12.0)	8	(15.4)
5. Water/sewer facilities	19	(11.5)	20	(9.3)	16	(7.1)	6	(11.5)
6. Environmental protection	4	(2.4)	7	(3.3)	16	(7.1)	3	(5.8)
7. Human resources	19	(11.5)	21	(9.8)	16	(7.1)	1	(1.9)
8. Recreation	5	(3.0)	16	(7.4)	14	(6.5)	4	(7.7)
9. Crime	8	(4.9)	10	(4.7)	6	(2.8)	2	(3.8)
10. Other	5	(3.0)	6	(2.8)	15	(6.7)	3	(5.8)
Totals	165	(100.0)	215	(100.0)	224	(100.0)	52	(100.0)

PRIORITIES

The fact that a need is the most common might not necessarily indicate that it has the greatest priority. Among those cities which indicated a priority, nearly one-third indicate that their number one priority is land use planning. The high priority given to land use planning holds across city size. Thus, land use planning is not only the most common need, but it is the most important. This finding holds even when cities are divided by region, with one major exception: the nonmetropolitan city of the Northeast, where economic development rivals land use planning as the number one need (see Table 15-6).

In addition, differences in first priorities by region, although numerically small, are worth noting. While land use planning had an almost unchallengeable priority in other regions, it was slightly lower than the priority given to economic development in the Northeast. Thus, economic development was not only the most common need in that region; it also had the highest priority (see Table 15-7).

Priority is also related to rate of growth. Generally, cities which

Table 15-4. Distribution of Common Planning Needs in Small Cities, by Percentage Housing Built Prior to 1950 and Metropolitan Status

Major Planning Needs	United States							
	Under 30%		30-49.9%		50-69.9%		70% and above	
	No.	(%)	No.	(%)	No.	(%)	No.	(%)
1. Land use	64	(18.6)	66	(19.9)	69	(17.6)	115	(15.8)
2. Transportation	47	(13.7)	44	(13.3)	41	(10.5)	81	(11.2)
3. Housing	50	(14.5)	60	(18.1)	66	(16.8)	129	(17.8)
4. Economic development	49	(14.2)	36	(10.9)	54	(13.8)	115	(15.8)
5. Water/sewer facilities	27	(7.8)	27	(8.2)	33	(8.4)	68	(9.4)
6. Environmental protection	29	(8.4)	21	(6.3)	19	(4.8)	26	(3.6)
7. Human resources	23	(6.7)	29	(8.8)	49	(12.5)	78	(10.7)
8. Recreation	21	(6.1)	16	(4.8)	25	(6.4)	45	(6.2)
9. Crime	17	(4.9)	17	(5.1)	21	(5.4)	33	(4.5)
10. Other	17	(4.9)	15	(4.5)	15	(3.8)	36	(5.0)
Totals	344	(100.0)	331	(100.0)	392	(100.0)	726	(100.0)

Major Planning Needs	Metropolitan							
	Under 30%		30-49.9%		50-69.9%		70% and above	
	No.	(%)	No.	(%)	No.	(%)	No.	(%)
1. Land use	60	(19.0)	45	(19.1)	47	(18.8)	50	(15.6)
2. Transportation	43	(13.6)	30	(12.7)	23	(9.2)	28	(8.8)
3. Housing	44	(13.9)	41	(17.4)	44	(17.6)	58	(18.1)
4. Economic development	44	(13.9)	28	(11.9)	35	(14.0)	50	(15.6)
5. Water/sewer facilities	25	(8.0)	16	(6.8)	21	(8.4)	32	(10.0)
6. Environmental protection	27	(8.5)	16	(6.8)	8	(3.2)	14	(4.4)
7. Human resources	24	(7.5)	22	(9.3)	32	(12.8)	31	(9.7)
8. Recreation	18	(5.6)	13	(5.5)	18	(7.2)	19	(5.9)
9. Crime	15	(4.7)	11	(4.7)	14	(5.6)	22	(6.9)
10. Other	16	(5.0)	14	(5.9)	8	(3.2)	16	(5.0)
Totals	316	(100.0)	236	(100.0)	250	(100.0)	320	(100.0)

Table 15.4 (cont.)

Major Planning Needs	Nonmetropolitan							
	Under 30%		30-49.9%		50-69.9%		70% and above	
	No.	(%)	No.	(%)	No.	(%)	No.	(%)
1. Land use	4	(14.3)	21	(22.1)	22	(16.1)	65	(16.4)
2. Transportation	4	(14.3)	14	(14.7)	18	(13.1)	53	(13.4)
3. Housing	6	(21.4)	19	(20.0)	22	(16.1)	71	(17.9)
4. Economic development	5	(17.9)	8	(8.4)	19	(13.9)	65	(16.4)
5. Water/sewer facilities	2	(7.1)	11	(11.6)	12	(8.7)	36	(9.0)
6. Environmental protection	2	(7.1)	5	(5.3)	11	(8.0)	12	(3.0)
7. Human resources	1	(3.6)	7	(7.4)	12	(8.7)	37	(9.3)
8. Recreation	1	(3.6)	3	(3.2)	7	(5.1)	26	(6.6)
9. Crime	2	(7.1)	6	(6.3)	7	(5.1)	11	(2.8)
10. Other	.1	(3.6)	1	(1.0)	7	(5.1)	20	(5.0)
Totals	28	(100.0)	95	(100.0)	137	(100.0)	396	(100.0)

experienced a positive growth rate place land use planning on the top of the list. Declining cities in general see economic development as their number one need. This is particularly interesting, since the most common need among declining cities is housing. Thus, while we may conclude that planning for housing is the most common need among declining cities, it is clearly not their first priority. Economic development is. (See Table 15-8.)

There are several results that deserve discussion. First, the evidence indicates that declining cities see their number one priority as economic development planning which includes downtown development. This is not unexpected. On the other hand, their most common need is in the planning of better housing services. One reason for this result is that many small cities see their comparative advantage in being residential rather than industrial centers and hope to improve their tax base by attracting middle and upper level income individuals. Another reason is that many cities which have experienced decline have an old housing stock which either has to be upgraded or replaced. According to William Alonso (see Part I of this book), the major housing problem of stable and declining small cities is that of maintenance, as opposed to the problem of increasing housing supply which is the case for rapidly growing cities.

Table 15-5. Distribution of Common Planning Needs in Small Cities, by Percentage of Persons Below 1970 Poverty Income Level and Metropolitan Status

Major Planning Needs	United States					
	Under 5%		5-14.9%		15% and above	
	No.	(%)	No.	(%)	No.	(%)
1. Land use	93	(17.3)	189	(18.3)	31	(14.0)
2. Transportation	73	(13.6)	114	(11.1)	26	(11.7)
3. Housing	83	(15.9)	190	(18.5)	42	(18.9)
4. Economic development	64	(11.9)	162	(15.8)	28	(12.6)
5. Water/sewer facilities	48	(9.0)	86	(8.3)	21	(9.5)
6. Environmental protection	32	(6.0)	47	(4.5)	16	(7.2)
7. Human resources	56	(10.4)	99	(9.5)	21	(9.5)
8. Recreation	36	(6.7)	50	(4.8)	17	(7.7)
9. Crime	24	(4.4)	54	(5.2)	10	(4.5)
10. Other	28	(5.2)	47	(4.5)	10	(4.5)
Totals	537	(100.0)	1038	(100.0)	222	(100.0)

Major Planning Needs	Metropolitan					
	Under 5%		5-14.9%		15% and above	
	No.	(%)	No.	(%)	No.	(%)
1. Land use	83	(17.5)	110	(18.6)	9	(13.4)
2. Transportation	67	(14.1)	52	(8.8)	5	(7.5)
3. Housing	67	(14.1)	110	(18.6)	10	(14.9)
4. Economic development	55	(11.6)	94	(15.9)	8	(11.9)
5. Water/sewer facilities	42	(8.9)	48	(8.1)	4	(6.0)
6. Environmental protection	30	(6.3)	28	(4.7)	7	(10.4)
7. Human resources	51	(10.7)	56	(9.5)	12	(17.9)
8. Recreation	32	(6.7)	31	(5.2)	5	(7.5)
9. Crime	24	(5.0)	34	(5.7)	4	(6.0)
10. Other	23	(4.9)	28	(4.7)	3	(4.5)
Totals	474	(100.0)	591	(100.0)	67	(100.0)

Major Planning Needs	Nonmetropolitan					
	Under 5%		5-14.9%		15% and above	
	No.	(%)	No.	(%)	No.	(%)
1. Land use	10	(18.6)	79	(17.7)	22	(14.3)
2. Transportation	6	(10.9)	62	(13.9)	21	(13.6)
3. Housing	6	(10.9)	80	(17.9)	32	(20.8)

Table 15-5. (cont.)

Major Planning Needs	Nonmetropolitan					
	Under 5%		5-14.9%		15% and above	
	No.	(%)	No.	(%)	No.	(%)
4. Economic development	9	(16.4)	68	(15.2)	20	(13.7)
5. Water/sewer facilities	6	(10.9)	38	(8.5)	17	(11.0)
6. Environmental protection	2	(3.6)	19	(4.2)	9	(5.8)
7. Human resources	5	(9.0)	43	(9.6)	9	(5.8)
8. Recreation	6	(10.9)	21	(4.7)	12	(7.8)
9. Crime	0	(0.0)	20	(4.5)	5	(3.2)
10. Other	5	(9.0)	17	(3.8)	7	(4.5)
Totals	55	(100.0)	447	(100.0)	154	(100.0)

A third reason is that many declining cities do experience high vacancy rates and rates of abandonment. This is true of such cities as Compton, California and Highland Park, Michigan, both of which are in our sample. A fourth reason for the high mention given housing by cities which are declining is that many of them have a reasonably

Table 15-6. First Priority Planning Needs in Small Cities, by Size

Major Planning Needs	City Size Classes							
	I 10,000-25,000		II 25,000-50,000		III 50,000-100,000		Total	
	No.	(%)	No.	(%)	No.	(%)	No.	(%)
1. Land use	64	(36.8)	53	(29.1)	30	(28.8)	147	(32.0)
2. Transportation	15	(8.6)	14	(7.7)	11	(10.6)	40	(8.7)
3. Housing	29	(16.7)	31	(17.0)	18	(17.3)	78	(17.0)
4. Economic development	28	(16.1)	42	(23.1)	16	(15.4)	86	(18.7)
5. Water/sewer facilities	17	(9.8)	22	(12.0)	5	(4.8)	44	(9.6)
6. Environmental protection	6	(3.4)	6	(3.3)	5	(4.8)	17	(3.7)
7. Human resources	4	(2.3)	3	(1.6)	4	(3.8)	11	(2.4)
8. Recreation	6	(3.4)	3	(1.6)	0	(0.0)	9	(2.0)
9. Crime	1	(0.5)	5	(2.7)	3	(2.9)	9	(2.0)
10. Other	4	(2.3)	3	(1.6)	12	(11.5)	19	(4.1)
Totals	174	(100.0)	182	(100.0)	104	(100.0)	460	(100.0)

Table 15-7. First Priority Planning Needs in Small Cities, by Region

Major Planning Needs	Regions							
	Northeast		North Central		South		West	
	No.	(%)	No.	(%)	No.	(%)	No.	(%)
1. Land use	27	(28.1)	46	(34.8)	42	(33.1)	32	(30.5)
2. Transportation	9	(9.4)	6	(4.5)	12	(9.4)	13	(12.4)
3. Housing	11	(11.5)	22	(16.7)	22	(17.3)	23	(21.9)
4. Economic development	29	(30.2)	24	(18.2)	19	(15.0)	14	(13.3)
5. Water/sewer facilities	11	(11.5)	12	(9.0)	17	(13.4)	4	(3.8)
6. Environmental protection	1	(1.0)	1	(0.7)	5	(3.9)	10	(9.5)
7. Human resources	1	(1.0)	5	(3.8)	2	(1.6)	3	(2.8)
8. Recreation	1	(1.0)	4	(3.0)	3	(2.4)	1	(0.9)
9. Crime	1	(1.0)	3	(2.3)	2	(1.6)	3	(2.8)
10. Other	5	(5.2)	9	(6.8)	3	(2.4)	2	(1.9)
Totals	96	(100.0)	132	(100.0)	127	(100.0)	105	(100.0)

Table 15-8. First Priority Planning Needs in Small Cities, by Percentage 1960-70 Population Change

Major Planning Needs	Less than 0		0-13.3%		13.4-49.9%		50% and above	
	No.	(%)	No.	(%)	No.	(%)	No.	(%)
1. Land use	21	(23.3)	33	(26.0)	52	(36.4)	41	(41.8)
2. Transportation	5	(5.6)	8	(6.3)	18	(12.6)	9	(9.2)
3. Housing	19	(21.1)	28	(22.0)	19	(13.3)	12	(12.2)
4. Economic development	25	(27.8)	24	(18.9)	23	(16.1)	14	(14.3)
5. Water/sewer facilities	12	(13.3)	15	(11.8)	10	(7.0)	7	(7.1)
6. Environmental protection	2	(2.2)	2	(1.6)	8	(5.6)	5	(5.1)
7. Human resources	2	(2.2)	4	(3.1)	2	(1.4)	1	(1.0)
8. Recreation	0	(0.0)	3	(2.4)	3	(2.1)	3	(3.0)
9. Crime	3	(3.3)	4	(3.1)	2	(1.4)	0	(0.0)
10. Other	1	(1.1)	6	(4.7)	6	(4.2)	6	(6.1)
Totals	90	(100.0)	127	(100.0)	143	(100.0)	98	(100.0)

high rate of poverty and many are recipients of the Community Development Block Grant funds, which require a housing assistance plan.

Land use planning is the most common need among cities and ranks reasonably high even among cities which are declining. One reason for this is clearly due to the fact that land use planning and zoning is the most common tool available to small cities for charting their destinies, and it is probably the most common function among cities. A second reason is that many states do have stringent land use laws. In some cases land use planning is mandated by law, or by federal grant requirements. A third reason for the frequency of response for the need for land use planning is that even older cities which are fully developed find that one hope to reverse decline is to change the configuration of the city by zoning.

Among rapidly growing cities it is understandable that land use planning is a top priority. Many of these cities have been involved in annexation, and land use planning becomes the hope for rational integration of new land. Furthermore, land use planning and zoning is seen as the underlying approach to growth control. In addition, it underlies planning for better housing, economic development, environmental protection, recreation, historical preservation, and a host of other government planning functions.

Of particular interest is the difference between metro and nonmetro areas in the South. As we found earlier (in Chapter Two), the South is not homogeneous; unlike other regions, there is a distinct difference there between the planning needs of metropolitan and nonmetropolitan cities. The most common need in the former is the need for land use planning. This undoubtedly reflects growth. The latter see their needs mostly in terms of housing, which probably reflects the fact that the housing conditions in the nonmetropolitan south are among the worst in the country.

Chapter Sixteen

Summing Up: Adjustment to Growth and Decline, Population Size and Production Diversification

Herrington J. Bryce

Small cities are not homogeneous. Within any given population size there are those cities which are growing and those which are declining. Both growth and decline can be aided by sound planning and an orderly adjustment process. Why do declining cities find it so difficult to adjust to their decline? It is argued (with some truth) that decline can be a disguised blessing, for it offers an opportunity for lower densities and an improved ambience.

Cities find it hard to adjust to decline for several reasons. First, decline is associated with underutilization of existing capital, and abandonment. Abandonment leads to higher social costs such as fires, vandalism, and blight. Decline leads to an erosion of the property tax base. Decline also leads to the possible loss of intergovernmental transfers to the extent that those transfers are calibrated to a population size or population-sensitive indicator.

Frequently, the cutting of services is not readily attainable, (although cities do find ways to accomplish this) not only because of

---

This material is based upon research supported by the National Science Foundation under Grant No. ERS74-21286 to the Joint Center for Political Studies—Howard University. Any opinions, findings, and conclusions expressed in this publication are those of the author(s) and do not necessarily reflect the views of the National Science Foundation.

the expectations of citizens but because of contractual arrangements which cities have with personnel, civil service, unions or quasi-union bodies. Furthermore, many programs that could be eliminated often have only a small proportion of their costs coming out of the city budget and some become increasingly important in dealing with the problems attendant to decline.

Decline can also affect the ability of a city to sell its bonds and increases the average costs of services to the citizens who are left behind. Decline also has a negative image which often makes it difficult for a city to attract firms and households. Finally, while some cities have succeeded in managing and even in reversing decline, few elected officials want to be associated with the decline of their cities or have reason to be confident that once such a decline begins they will have within their power the tools to arrest it. Citizens often oppose changes in their communities, even though these might attract a younger population. These problems are not necessarily impossible to deal with, but they certainly make decline an uncomfortable experience.

LOCAL CONTROL

One problem is the limited control many cities have over their own destinies. It is one thing to plan, it is another to achieve. The ability of a locally appointed or elected official to implement a policy is circumscribed first by the federal government and the Constitution, and then by the state and city charters. It is further circumscribed by regional governments.

But perhaps one of the most profound limitations is the national economy. A survey of over 500 small cities, which asked the extent to which the recession-inflation of 1974-75 affected their cities, showed the results displayed in Table 16-1. Clearly, cities of all sizes were affected by the economic crisis. Regardless of size, nearly 60 percent of these cities reported the cancellation or postponement of planned projects. One-fourth of the smaller cities, a third of the middle-sized, and over 40 percent of the larger cities cut services.

In an economy where there is freedom of choice, a city might plan extensively for in-migration or the attraction of new firms; but may have very little success in either. Cities in the final analysis must compete both for people and firms. Furthermore, the location decisions of firms are often not made in local offices, where there might be a strong attachment to the individual city.

Table 16-1. The Impact of the Current Economic Crisis on Small and Medium Size Cities

Policy Undertaken	City Size 10,000-25,000	City Size 25,000-50,000	City Size 50,000-100,000	All Cities
Increased taxes	36.5	34.7	36.3	35.7
Reduction or cutback on city services	25.1	33.2	41.6	31.9
Reduction or cutback on city employment	33.5	46.0	46.9	41.3
Postponed or cancelled projects	60.1	61.4	62.8	61.2
Utilized CETA funds	72.9	77.7	77.0	75.7
Postponed wage increases	19.2	26.2	23.9	23.0
Others (including not affected)	3.0	3.0	0.9	2.5

Copyrighted Original Data: Herrington J. Bryce and The Joint Center for Political Studies.

GEOGRAPHIC REGION AND POLICY

The issue of the relevance of size appears in many papers in this book. As one can be critical of the issue of size, so can one be critical of the use of regions. Regions (in the traditional geographic sense) are not decision making bodies and have no political accountability. Furthermore, within regions there are significant variations; hence, regions may be weak targets for public policy. Some policies are better targeted to cities according to age, growth rates, and some other "behavioral" variables.

SIZE AND DIVERSIFICATION

Indeed, size is often less relevant than other variables such as the age of city, the regional location of the city, or its metropolitan status. But there are at least three instances in which size cannot be ignored. Size does appear to have some effect on the cost of providing services, upon efficiency, and upon diversification.

As indicated by Puryear in Chapter Seven, empirical studies have clearly shown a relationship between population size and diversification. This relationship suggests that as population gets larger, a local economy tends to become more diversified. But does diversification increase at a constant rate, a diminishing rate or at an increasing rate with respect to growth in population? This is, in a sense, the crux of what appears to be a difference between Thompson (Chapter Five) and Berry (Chapter Thirteen). Thompson clearly argues that as places become larger they have the capacity of becoming more diversified. Berry suggests that the inherent advantages to which Thompson refers are broken by the rise of efficient transportation and communication networks which reduce the advantages that size has. Both authors admit to the fact that diseconomies of size do exist and can affect the rate of growth (and I would presume diversification) in a city. But the larger the population size, the greater are likely to be some of the diseconomies as noted by Puryear. Furthermore, the integration of production activities can mask diversification as large production units integrate a number of production lines. A countervailing force, of course, is that as production becomes more routine (or physically independent) and requires less skill, it is possible to break off independent units and locate elsewhere.

In spite of these issues, some empirical work continues to fit models which suggest that diversification is a constant function of population size. If this were true, then the larger a city gets the more diversified it would be without limits. A 2 percent increase in population size, for example, would mean a 2 percent increase in diversification, and so on.

A more probable assumption is that because of diseconomies of size, the role of transport and communication systems in making firms footloose, and internal economies of production, diversification might increase as population size increases, but this increase occurs at a diminishing rate.

It is certainly possible that as places get larger and larger up to some size, diversification increases more rapidly than population; then as these factors come into play, the rate of increase in diversification diminishes as population grows. For these reasons, it is worthwhile to test the hypothesis that diversification is a diminishing function of population size. But is this true of the United States as a whole, the North, the South?

THE MODEL AND DATA

The Model which is fitted is:

$$\log D = a + b \log P \qquad (1)$$

where P is population size and a and b are constants and where D is an index of regional diversification. Specifically, D is defined as:

$$D = \frac{\sum_{k=1}^{40} \left| \frac{e_{kj}}{e_{tj}} - \frac{E_{ko}}{E_{to}} \right|}{2} = \frac{\sum_{k=1}^{40} |d|}{2} \qquad (2)$$

where:

e_{kj} is employment in the kth industry in the jth region.

e_{tj} is total employment in the jth region.

E_{ko} is employment in the kth industry in all regions.

E_{to} is total employment in the kth industry.

Its limits are 0—a proportional mix exactly equal to the nation, and 1—a complete centralization or specialization of employment in one industry.

The usual shortcomings of these indices which are standard in regional analysis are given in Isard (1). The index is computed on the basis of forty Census (roughly 2-digit S.I.C.) industrial classifications (2). The data used are drawn from *The United States Census of Population 1960, General Social and Economic Characteristics.*

THE RESULTS

Regressing P on D in a test of the hypothesis gave the following results first for the country as a whole and then for the metropolitan areas of the North and South taken separately:

United States (222 SMSAs):

$$D = 1.8359 - 0.1965 P^{**} \qquad (1)$$
$$(0.0148)$$

$R^2 = 0.669 \qquad Se = 0.0931 \qquad df = 220.$

**Significant at .01 level

North (134 SMSAs):

$$D = 1.8356 - 0.1966 P^{**} \qquad (2)$$
$$(0.0180)$$

$R^2 = 0.689 \qquad Se = 0.0936 \qquad df = 132$

**Significant at .01 level

South (88 SMSAs):

$$D = 1.8335 - 0.1950P^{**} \qquad (3)$$
$$(0.0274)$$

$$R^2 = 0.609 \qquad Se = 0.0932 \qquad df = 86$$
**Significant at .01 level

The results indicate that for the United States, as well as for the North and South taken separately, the elasticity of diversification is negative and less than unity ($b < 1$). It is roughly -0.20 in the regions, as well as in the country as a whole. It is apparent, then, that as population increases, diversification increases but less than proportionately. The elasticity coefficient is similar within and across regions.

This relationship between size and economic activity underlies much of what Sacks reported in this volume for individual cities. The link between individual cities and their larger area (i.e., metropolitan area) is commonly noted. This link also holds for growth. Thus, Sternlieb and Hughes report that growth rates of cities are closely linked to the growth rates of their metropolitan areas (3). The growth of many small cities is a function of their proximity to larger metropolitan areas (4).

Finally, while we have focused on the small city, we are reminded that cities are units within a larger system. Cities might adjust to decline by changing their relationship to that larger system. Thus, Danbury, Connecticut has been transformed from an agricultural center to a textile center and has now become a fairly diversified, thriving small city. For many cities, the successful adjustment to change might ultimately involve fundamental changes in their economic structure, say by changing either to a more diversified economy or by changing their competitive advantage in a single industry. Thus, Aspen, Colorado changed from a mining community to a recreational center.

For other cities, the change might be less drastic. Thus, Hoboken, New Jersey has managed to deal with its decline by an imaginative housing and community development policy. And Jamestown, New York was successful by using another strategy—coordinating the influence and concerns of labor, management, and city hall. The policy possibilities vary.

Epilogue

1: A Note on Variations in Leading Streams of Migration to the Washington, D.C. Metropolitan Area

Vera J. Banks

Beckman and Rose (Part II) are concerned with the movement of people among jurisdictions or regions. The dynamics and the character of movement in and out of a metropolitan region provide a rather interesting phenomenon of cross flows of people. A metropolitan area which declines does not necessarily have zero in-migration. The areas that surround a central city might grow as a consequence of net in-migration but they all might differ in the source of people. The decline of a central city and the rise of its suburbs does not necessarily mean that the growth of the suburban region was simply at the expense of the central city.

Let us look at the Washington, D.C. metropolitan area. The uniqueness of the geographic boundaries of the Washington Standard Metropolitan Statistical Area (SMSA) permits an analysis of migration streams to the central city of Washington and its Maryland and Virginia suburban rings separately. Each of these parts is identified by the census as a separate State economic area and we can examine the volume and sources of migration by race.[a]

The pattern of population changes between 1960 and 1970 in the Washington, D.C. SMSA was typical for a metro area of its size. During that decade the white population declined in the central city and grew in the Maryland and Virginia suburbs. The black population of the metro area increased both inside and outside the central city.

---

[a]The Maryland suburbs are identified as Md. SEA B and include Montgomery and Prince Georges counties; the Virginia suburbs are Virginia SEA B and include Arlington and Fairfax counties, and Alexandria, Fairfax, and Falls Church cities.

Although there was a net loss of whites from the central city, what was the source of population growth in the balance of the SMSA? Between 1965 and 1970, the Washington metro area as a whole attracted 568,000 migrants.

The leading white and black migration streams were determined for each of the three parts of the D.C. metro area.[b] Migration to the Washington, D.C. SMSA was mainly from other metropolitan areas in the same general region of the country. As expected, for the entire area the top two sending states were Maryland and Virginia, especially from areas adjacent to the Washington SMSA. Other leading states, Pennsylvania and New York, are in the vicinity of Washington, D.C. The fifth state was California—the only major source state not located on the east coast. If the remaining parts of Maryland and Virginia are excluded, North Carolina and South Carolina join the list of major exporters to the D.C. metro area.

Of the more than half-million migrants who moved to the D.C. SMSA between 1965 and 1970, only 14 percent moved to the central city. There were about 49,000 white migrants and 32,000 black migrants and for both races Maryland, Virginia and New York were among the top states of origin. The remaining major sending states were northern Pennsylvania and western California for whites, and North Carolina and South Carolina for blacks. However, whites were more likely to move to Washington from Maryland and New York, while blacks more often came from Virginia and North Carolina. The majority of the migrants to the central city came from metropolitan parts of other states. Metro migrants comprised 81 percent of all whites and 57 percent of all blacks who moved to D.C.

The Virginia suburbs of the D.C. metro area attracted 209,000 migrants between 1965 and 1970. About 19 out of every 20 of these migrants were white, and two out of three came from another metropolitan area. Virginia was the main contributor to the Virginia ring and the volume of white migration was about evenly divided among the remaining sending states of California, Maryland, Pennsylvania, and New York. This was the only racial-suburban group where the migration from the District to the suburbs was not one of the dominant streams. However, Washington, D.C. is still considered a prime source since it sent only 1,300 fewer migrants than fifth-ranking New York.

White migrants were a mixture of short and long distance movers, while the majority of the relatively few black migrants were from nearby. About one-third of the blacks who moved to the Virginia

---

[b]The term white refers to whites and minority races other than blacks. Published Census data does not permit the separation of other racial minorities.

ring of the D.C. SMSA came from the central city of Washington and a fifth were from parts of Virginia outside the SMSA. The larger Maryland suburbs of the Washington SMSA received about half the total migration to the area in the 1965-70 period. The central city was the major source of these migrants—particularly blacks. Over two-thirds of total black migration to the Maryland ring was from Washington.

Although there were differences in relative ranking, New York, Virginia and that part of Maryland outside the SMSA were also major source states regardless of race. The only difference by race in the leading migration stream to suburban Maryland was that Pennsylvania ranked among the top five for whites and North Carolina was in the black group. In general, white migration to the Washington SMSA was geographically more diverse than the black. Among whites the top five streams comprised a consistently lower proportion of all migrants. Blacks, on the other hand, had very dominant streams.

The major sources of migration accounted for more than 60 percent of all black migrants regardless of their destination. The data also suggest a strong geographic preference among migrants from the central city to the suburban rings. Between 1965 and 1970, more than 90 percent of the black movers from the District to the suburbs of the SMSA went to adjacent (Montgomery and Prince Georges) counties in Maryland.

The data do not permit an examination of the migration into these two counties separately for the 1965-70 period. However, county net migration estimates for the 1960-70 decade as a whole reveal Prince Georges County to be the dominant receiver. During this period there was a net in-movement of blacks and other minority races of 56,000 to Prince Georges County, compared to 13,000 to Montgomery County. Census income data show Prince Georges to be the less affluent county: in 1970 median family income was $17,000 and $12,000 in Montgomery and Prince Georges Counties, respectively. Blacks comprised 4 and 14 percent of the total population of these two counties respectively.

2: City Employment and Economic Development

Carolyn Shaw Bell

Seymour Sacks's examination of employment in medium-size cities since World War II can be taken as an exercise in the analysis of economic development. Arguing that the nature of the city is defined by manufacturing and retailing employment, Sacks examines "economic growth" and the "medium-size city" for the period since World War II, which, Sacks argues, concentrated population and employment so as to obscure the secular decline of cities.

The trouble is that his fascinating analysis, in detail, diverts attention from what else is going on. Specifically, we lack a complete model of development to explain the changes he finds so significant. For example, he examines retailing employment as a function of population and shows that very little change occurred between 1947 and 1973, except in those cities where the population grew because of annexation. As for manufacturing, he argues that the exodus of manufacturing workers from the city differs by region. What is needed is to put these two phenomena into a larger framework.

For the country as a whole, employment rose by about 75 percent during the period; depending on one's definition of the term, labor force growth may have been somewhat larger. Gross national product, income, and other measures of aggregate economic activity more or less tripled. Manufacturing employment declined as a percentage of the total from 35 to 26 percent, while retailing remained almost constant: 15 to 16 percent of total employment. Both retailing and manufacturing are private sector industries; during the period public sector employment increased so that the number of private workers, as a percent of total employment, declined by 8 percent.

In what sense was this "economic development"? For that matter, what does economic development mean to the post-World War American economy? Were the structural changes that took place during this period so sweeping as to nullify any useful deductions about economic development from examining employment? Can development conclusions be generalized from data on employment in selected cities, restricted to only one sector, and to two relatively small divisions of that sector?

Should we retain the notion of a "mature economy" as one heavily concentrated on the production of services. For if indeed this is what economic development brings, it should be argued that cities losing their manufacturing industries were developing more rapidly than the rest of the country. Manufacturing employment for the entire country declined by 26 percent. Sacks shows a decline of 33 percent for the East, and increases for the Midwest, South, and West, of 11, 150, and 70 percent respectively. Employment in the eastern cities consisted more and more of jobs in financial, transportation, and public utilities, as well as federal and in particular state and local government. These "service sector" employers showed a rising trend over the period involved.

If, on the other hand, one defines economic development in terms of higher per capita income or a growth in productivity, then what do employment data disclose, for the cities involved? How does a loss of manufacturing jobs, per se, become either cause or effect of lower incomes, relative to those areas that gained manufacturing jobs?

At the time of accelerating industrialization and the growth of cities, manufacturing employment certainly appeared to offer higher wages than the nonagricultural alternatives of mining, construction, trade, transport, and services. (In 1890, the Census year in which agricultural employment fell below half the total, domestic service workers were ten times as numerous as government employees or those engaged in financial, insurance, or real estate services.)

But the wage relationship has not been constant over time, or for particular types of manufacturing and of "other" employment. Presumably the enormous influx of workers into government, financial, transportation, and utility employment has reflected the inducement of higher wages. So examining employment in retailing and manufacturing does not seem to lead to any useful conclusion about relative incomes in cities.

If, to take another definition of economic development, rising productivity describes economic growth, then employment data become less and less useful to analyze an economy with a larger and larger output of services. Productivity measures relate outputs to inputs defined in terms of labor or capital—more frequently the former. In manufacturing and other types of industrial production, output can be measured in physical units and the input of labor in nonmonetary quantitative units like "person hours." Such a measure is impossible to compute for many services in which labor is a very large percentage of total input and also makes up a large fraction of output. (This of course excepts such "service industries" as transportation and public utilities whose output can also be measured in terms of physical units like passenger miles and kilowatt hours.) Any "productivity ratio" in the sense of input/output would necessarily be close to 1. It follows that as more and more employment is shifted to service industries, productivity inevitably declines because of the nature of the measure.

The importance of this argument should not be overlooked. It appears strikingly in the contrast of retailing with manufacturing. By measuring retailing output in terms of dollar sales (a common enough practice), productivity (sales per employee) seems to have grown very little from 1947 to 1976. But this measure clearly does not apply over time because of the technological change in retailing, including the extension of self-service, prepackaging, extended shopping hours, the development of shopping malls, discount houses, catalogue and mail order proliferation, and so on. What the employee is selling, in the way of personal service, is totally different in 1976 than it was in 1947.

It is likely that the amount of consumer satisfaction with the retailing system is much greater in 1976 than it was in 1947. It may also be that the consumer's efficiency in shopping has been greatly improved; to measure total productivity, this, too, should be taken into account. In manufacturing, however, where the physical units can be counted, technological change increases their number per employee and we note significant rises in productivity. As in retailing, we ignore the fact that what the worker is doing or making has become totally different. It can be argued that the increase in productivity does not represent an increase in consumer satisfaction because of the social costs of manufacturing. Productivity has been accompanied with an increase of pollutants, traffic congestion, industrial accidents, and the like.

My point is that the measures used to calculate productivity are not necessarily appropriate as an indication of economic growth. It follows that employment data cannot be reliable indicators of economic development when so much else about the structure of the economy is left unexamined.

Finally, the notion of economic development requires, of course, the identification of "an economy," that which develops. It is not yet clear what coherent or rational economic model can describe development for a unit like a city or region within a national economy. Over any time period, the economic change occurring in the United States will have an impact on all kinds of its subdivisions. They may be seen in economic terms, like the structure of the labor force or of industrial output or the types of household saving. But they may also show up as social subdivisions of the country like the structure of the family, the nature of "the community," racial attitudes, or the sense of social responsibility. And of course, they may also show up in political subdivisions of the country, which are more or less arbitrarily drawn. But to expect the process of "economic development" within a national economy to be somehow paralleled in small within a state or city has not, it seems to me, been justified.

Rising incomes, wider employment opportunities, higher productivity and output spell economic growth. But it is people, as workers and consumers, who benefit, and the individual human beings involved somehow get overlooked in models based on political subdivisions.

Why, therefore, do we use data on cities? Because they exist. Economic development will remain with us as a goal or at least a good thing for a long time. But this does not necessarily imply that economic development need be defined as a goal for every sector of the American economy, for every region, or for cities. Somehow, development economics needs to refocus on the citizen as the economic unit.

3: A Fourth Stage in Our National Development?

Ralph R. Widner

Have we entered a distinctly new phase in our national development? Some would argue that we are, indeed, into a fourth since the founding of the Republic. The first lasted up until shortly after the Civil War. The frontier stage in our development, the national objective during this period was to fill up the heartland of the country with as many settlers and entrepreneurs as possible. Our purpose was to get the continent's resources under development. We succeeded.

The second, or industrial stage, came into its own in the last quarter of the nineteenth and first two decades of the twentieth centuries. Burgeoning manufactures birthed a generation of factory towns and industrial cities especially in the Northeast and lower Great Lakes regions. And the mechanization of agriculture combined with the rapid expansion of manufactures catalyzed the rural-to-urban population exodus that began to empty out the agricultural heartland so recently populated.

With the coming of the commuter railroad and the automobile we thence moved into a third, or metropolitan, stage of national growth. The industrial city burst its bounds as urban residents exploited their newfound mobility and increasing affluence. We suburbanized. The older, core industrial cities spun out their old economic and social functions to the suburbs, while the influx of poor, rural migrants continued to move in to take advantage of the housing abandoned by the suburbanizing middle and upper income groups. The familiar problems of metropolitanization occupied our national agenda.

Then, some time in the latter half of the 1960s, we entered still another, perhaps post-industrial phase.

- The rural-to-urban population exodus dwindled toward an end.
- Manufacturing continued to decentralize to areas beyond the suburbs into interstitial nonmetropolitan counties.
- Retail and other services began following suit.
- The largest metropolitan areas stopped growing in population—and in many cases, in employment as well.
- Population losses from the old, industrial core cities, mostly in the Northeast and lower Great Lakes, accelerated as the combined result of declining birth and fertility rates, a cessation of in-migration, and increased out-migration.
- The South and West, after decades of lag behind the old economic core regions, began to catch up in terms of social and economic well-being, while signs of deterioration increased in the old industrial belt.
- The old relationships between metropolitan and nonmetropolitan economies became blurred as transportation and communications seemed to be leading toward a far more diffuse and decentralized pattern of settlement and economic activity. Statistics told us nonmetropolitan economies and population are growing more rapidly than metropolitan.

How do we read these signs? Are they statistical artifacts; or do they, in fact, argue for a new form of post-industrial human settlement? Is Irving Kristol right in asserting that we are moving toward an urban civilization without cities? Have modern transportation and communications enabled us to abandon the city as a locus for dense face-to-face interaction and are now moving us toward a decentralized, diffuse network of commuting fields with many centers rather than the old city center?

If that is true, should we not be looking for a new statistical definition of what is urban, what is metropolitan, what is rural? Would not we gain a more accurate picture of what is happening if we used Brian Berry's commuting fields or functional economic areas as the territorial base for our reporting systems? Or are we not seeing, as Wilbur Thompson argues, a transition in our urban systems that reflects a change in economic and employment base?

Old industrial metropolitan areas are shrinking back in size to meet the conditions of lower labor intensivity in manufacturing, while a new crop of service-based cities is growing in the "newer" sections of the country. And are we, as Thompson hypothesizes, seeing the costs of congestion in very large places overtaking their former locational benefits, so that metropolitan centers of one million to one and a half million seem to appeal as about the right size for metropolitan diversity and quality of life without high costs of congestion?

What is so interesting about these speculations is that the form now emerging was, just a decade ago, the state of aspiration of many advocates for a "national growth policy" and for a policy of population dispersal. Many economists argued that the aspiration was futile; that the forces moving toward concentration in large metropolitan areas were massive and irreversible. Yet a brief decade later we are in the midst of debate about not whether such a result can happen, but whether it is a problem rather than an aspiration realized.

4: The Urban Fiscal Dilemma

Ransford W. Palmer

The purpose of these comments is to focus on the problem of the declining city discussed by Thomas Muller in Chapter Eight. Two characteristics of the declining city that Muller discusses are important for understanding its predicament.

One is that while per capita income of growing cities was larger and grew at a greater rate than that of declining cities, declining cities had larger public payrolls and more generous benefit packages for their employees. The other is that these larger public expenditures exist side by side with declining economic opportunities in what may be described as stagnant economies (1).

Muller attributes the decline of cities principally to substantial out-migration over a decade or more. This in turn is due to the aging of the housing stock and commercial industrial facilities, which is a manifestation of declining economic opportunities. The substantial out-migration from declining cities does not mean a one-way flow of people; it represents an excess of out-migrants over in-migrants. The important question here is: Who are the out-migrants from—and the in-migrants to—the declining cities?

Some recent research on interstate and intermetropolitan migration suggests that the principal factor influencing the migration of blacks are high welfare payments in the destination city or state, while the principal factor influencing white migration are better economic opportunities (2). If this conclusion is correct, then the declining cities with their high welfare payments and high public payrolls would tend to attract the poor and unskilled, who are predominantly black. Thus, a historically high income city which is now declining could be viewed as exporting skilled workers with high incomes and importing unskilled workers with low incomes. The net effect of this is to further decrease per capita income or to restrain its growth.

If this process continues, then the question of the impact of the concentration of low income persons on the fiscal capacity of the declining city becomes important. It is generally argued that such a concentration will impose a fiscal burden on the city since increased expenditures for welfare and other public services cannot be met from a contracting taxable capacity.

Reischauer, on the other hand, argues that "the fiscal impact that concentrations of low income persons may have on a city depends very much on the way in which each state has chosen to divide provision of services and financing responsibilities between the state and local government and among the local governments." Furthermore, he points out that the impact of low income persons on a city's fiscal capacity is not clear-cut because "most large cities rely on revenue sources that are only indirectly related to the economic well-being of their residents," since the income tax accounts for a relatively small share of total tax receipts and a substantial share of the sales tax revenues collected comes from taxable sales to commuters and suburbanites (3).

The fact remains that whether we are talking about large, medium, or small cities, as the housing stock ages and more low income people occupy it, the property tax base does not grow fast enough and the additional revenues from increases in existing taxes and from alternative sources of revenue are usually inadequate. Many cities resort to borrowing, which results in the accumulation of debt, the interest on which imposes a further burden on the taxpayer.

Can additional federal funds save the city? If one accepts the theory that the rise or decline of the city is merely a passive index of the development of the region in which it is located, then additional federal funds ought to be directed to that region. On the other hand, if one views the city as an active ingredient of industrial development, then additional federal funds to the city may be just what is needed to revitalize its inner dynamism (4).

The answer appears to lie in a transfer of some of the fiscal responsibilities of the city to both the state and the federal government. This may not reverse the inexorable economic forces that alter the structure and location of industry over time, but it would reduce the burden these forces now impose on declining cities.

5: Urban Governments and Economic Policies

Selma J. Mushkin

Two questions are paramount in the current economic and fiscal scene.

1. What economic compensatory policies would help synchronize the fiscal decisions of the 80,000 local governments on the one hand and national economic policy on the other.

2. What policies would help encourage structural reform in local areas that could improve the prospects of long term economic growth and achievement of high employment.

Each of these questions has two different aspects. One aspect concerns the characteristic behavior of local governments and the states, and raises the issue of how to get the governments to harmonize their action with that of the nation. The other aspect concerns national policies on state-local aids. Are these aids causing economic problems or mitigating them?

Economists appear to find themselves in the position of a physician without the tools for either a genuine diagnosis or therapy, with the consequence of too much ignorance to warrant action. Whatever the cause of the lack of policy, it is plain that both the local governments and the states impact on the economy not only of the small areas within the jurisdictions of those governments but on the nation as well. State and local governments that had an appropriate national policy could play an important role in assuring full and productive employment by the way in which they orient public spending, fashion their tax systems, and perform their regulatory activities.

Making 80,000 Governments Work Toward Synchronizing Countercyclical Behavior

While there have been differences in findings about the cyclical impact of state and local government, few dispute that in past decades state and local governments have been a strong stabilizing factor in the economy. Their demand for goods and services moved up despite economic swings, providing a sort of built-in stabilizer against the downturns. Not so long ago, in late 1972 and 1973, state and local government finances served also as a damper on inflationary forces. The subsequent period witnessed a reversal of past performances. Indeed, state and local governments have tended by their fiscal practices to contribute to the recent recession rather than to cushion it. See Chapter Sixteen for some of the ways in which small cities reacted. Assuming that the national government was seeking to reduce unemployment and encourage an increase in demand at that time, the machinery of the state and local governments was going in the wrong direction.

What incentives can be designed by the national government to make operations of states and localities supportive of federal policies rather than counteractive to them? Perhaps it would be useful to think in terms of a set of collaborating institutions (despite the bureaucracies involved) to discuss the joint concerns of all governments about unemployment, industrial production and income flows. When the national economy is weak, the economies of most of the states and local governments—although not all—are weak too. The interaction has been described in this way: "When the national economy has a cold, some states and cities get pneumonia." State and local governments in their own self-interests are concerned about the state of the national economy.

Ways might be developed to achieve collaborative policies, building on the common interests and objectives of the different governments. If the economy has heated up, joint consideration might well be given to "staying" some state and local capital projects, not as a matter of federal budget recisions, but as a collaborative effort of governments. If it is depressed, then choices about methods of counteracting the decline, such as public works, public jobs, and so forth, could then be jointly considered.

Encouragements to this end might be: planning assistance for economic stabilization and growth purposes; informational exchanges on economic behavior (including sharing of projection resources and development of a state-by-state economic indicator series); and introduction of stabilization objectives in the regular grant programs.

Removing Structural Barriers to Economic Growth

Barriers to economic growth could be overcome or lessened by collaborative policies. One potential contribution to the national economy may be outlined in terms of the relationships between price changes and the percentage level of unemployment (or in terms of the Phillips curve). It is now widely assumed that policies can be designed to shift the position of the curve. Recent experience with quite high levels of unemployment associated with price rise suggests a tendency for the curve to shift to the right. Any policy that would counteract this tendency would result in less national unemployment or less upward pressures on price.

While the evidence is scant, there are some study findings that suggest that the change in the rate of inflation associated with a given change in unemployment tends to be greater in the regions with low unemployment than in those with high unemployment. By determining where to target measures to check unemployment, it becomes possible then to influence the national relation between unemployment and prices.

Operations in cities and states are replete with those structural or legal barriers that economists view as preventing the market from operating efficiently and that impede price stability or high employment. Public utility operations, employment exchanges, and labor protections are some examples. Despite the importance of the small area economies in economic stabilization, the past has been characterized by a tendency to disregard local and state governments in economic stabilization. Just a fragmentary list makes plain the activities of the states and local governments that have a bearing on structural economic stabilization.

- Developing labor market skills sufficient for the job market.
- Labor protections (at present labor statutes deter employment by raising costs of employment relative to capital costs).
- Housing codes and zoning laws (these often adversely affect the supply of housing in the cities).
- Sales taxation (sales taxes raise the prices of consumer goods and where there are differentials also influence consumption patterns).
- Property taxation (these taxes impede property repair and maintenance and have been a factor deterring investment and contributing to central city decay).

Because economic stabilization is viewed as a national affair, the national government has no policy about these state and local governmental structural barriers. Appropriate incentives do not exist for hard reviews in the local governments of activities that would help over the longer run to restore the economy of the smaller areas and the nation.

Introducing an Economic Stabilization Purpose in Federal Grants-in-Aid

Federal aid policies have perhaps aggravated the unevenness in geographic growth that makes for more serious barriers to economic progress and high employment in some parts of the country than in others, and unevenness in taxing burdens as a consequence of differential prices for goods and services, both private and public.

A few words on national responsibilities for this uneven economic growth as a backdrop for consideration of the introduction of economic stabilization purposes in grants: It was the federal aid programs that unintentionally encouraged the population movements from agricultural areas to urban centers. Federal aid for agricultural experimentation and extension brought about a dramatic productivity rise in farming. The number of farms and farmer workers declined sharply. And the number of city dwellers rose. It was the federal government's procurement (especially for the wars) that generated jobs away from the farming areas. People moved when economic opportunities closed on the farm and opened in the city.

There are other national programs that have been charged with responsibility for much of the incentive to population movement from center city to suburb, namely, the veterans' housing program, the highway construction program, the FHA mortgage insurance preferences for owner-occupied dwellings, and so forth. School desegregation and the lack of controls over the crime rates perhaps have been recent additions to the earlier incentives to move. As indicated, with few exceptions, the national government in its grants-in-aid has paid little attention to geographic variations in industrial and employment growth. One exception to the general "no policy" is the regional development program such as EDA and Appalachian Regional Commission, but these programs are essentially designed to bring backward places into the mainstream of economic life. The slow growth areas today are the have-beens of a former period.

Existing aid programs tend to aggravate employment and industrial growth differentials. The very concern with equalization has had this uneven impact. But even the equalization provisions are based on inadequate information that works to the detriment of the sections of the country that are already disadvantaged by their age, social policies, and perhaps outmoded technology. In grant provisions it is assumed that prices are uniform throughout the United States, both prices for public services and for private goods and services. Neither of these assumptions is accurate. Yet this uniformity—assumed by the federal government—has been costly for the high price states such as in New England.

Equalization as a grant purpose was first discussed when there were very wide differentials in income levels among the states in a 3.5 or 4 to 1 ratio. The spread was so wide that partial offset, constrained within much narrower limits, by aid grant formulas, posed no special problems. Recently per capita income variations are in the range of a ratio of less than 2 to 1. But this variation fails to tell the full story or tell it accurately. Corrected for price, differences in per capita income are now likely to be very small indeed. The highest income state is Alaska but it has a high price structure. Moreover, the lower income states are growth states and are relatively prosperous, with incomes moving up.

Regional price differences and regional growth rate differences do not tend to offset each other. On the contrary, they reinforce each other in redistributing federal tax funds collected in slow growth states, such as New York and Massachusetts, to the more rapidly growing states, including, for example, Texas.

Preliminary analysis shows that in the industrial states, the size of federal grants per capita varies directly with the state's growth rates; grants are higher per capita where state growth rates are higher.

It is possible to take corrective action: (1) to introduce price variations into grant formulas; (2) to introduce growth indexes that will capture the direction of economic change in grant formulas; (3) to introduce an incremental fiscal effort measure (perhaps with a trigger provision).

Summary

The need for a policy on geographic impact has not gone unnoticed. From time to time there have been some urgings that the national government anticipate the effect of its actions on different sections of the country and take preventive steps so that adjustments may be made to the changes in federal activities, without undue hardships, such as that involved in reduced military spending, the closing of a base, or the termination of a major contract for airplanes.

In studies of national policy impacts, not only direct effects but also the triggered repercussions on private investment and employment are often considered. Little has been achieved, however, over the decades toward the development of an overall policy.

358 Epilogue

Issues of uncompensated structural and cyclical impacts of the economy on local government describe but one facet of the problem. There is the other, the past failure of the national government to take full account of, or be responsive to, the role that could be played in correcting those imbalances by subnational governments.

6: Federal Programs to Assist the Cities

George E. Peterson

The papers in this book illustrate one of the principal paradoxes involved in designing federal programs to assist the cities. Municipal dependence upon external aid, as demonstrated by Ross and Shannon (Chapter Nine), has grown dramatically over the last decade. With this financial dependence has come a reduction in local budgetary discretion and increasing vulnerability to the economic conditions of higher levels of government, as well as to changes in their policy initiatives. Yet the remedy most commonly prescribed for this situation is *more* external assistance, whether in the form of revised allocation formulas (Nathan and Dommel, Chapter Eleven), federal assumption of state and local spending responsibilities (Ross and Shannon), or federal adjustment of basic market incentives (Barro, Chapter Ten).

At the heart of the dilemma of federal program design is the simple fact that the cities—especially the older and larger cities—have become high cost producers, both of private goods and of public services. It is largely for this reason that their tax obligations have become burdensome and their "hardship indices" so high. All the authors in this section implicitly accept the proposition that federal resources should be used to redress, or at least to mitigate, the competitive imbalance under which many cities labor. But there are other views as to what the federal role should be, and it may be helpful to consider the federal government's choices from a somewhat broader perspective.

Smoothing Market Adjustments

Private markets are generally well equipped to make their own adjustments to cost differentials. The migration of jobs and people away from most central cities—and away from the older and colder regions of the country—is a strong private market response to the cost differentials that have emerged.

Instead of trying to stem or reverse this flow, the federal government might try to smooth its operation. This would involve such programs as national job banks, which make it easier for citizens to locate job opportunities in other parts of the country; migration allowances, which subsidize the cost of moving to accept new job openings; and a continuation of present federal programs that subsidize new investment in plant and equipment, thus accelerating the process of national adjustment to changed market incentives. Policies of this description would attempt to work *with* the private market rather than against it. The national objective would be to make it easier for individual households and individual firms to respond to market signals.

Such programs, of course, need not displace federal efforts to cushion the adverse impact that market forces have on the cities. But they imply sharp limits to federal objectives. Rather than trying to "revitalize" the cities, such a policy would encourage the scaling down of most of the nation's older cities. Federal assistance to the cities (as opposed to assistance for the individuals emigrating from them) would be restricted to facilitating the transition to a smaller scale.

Restoring Market Neutrality

As Stephen Barro argues, federal policies in the past often have skewed the terms of market competition against the cities. A good case can be made that federal tax and expenditure policies have subsidized suburban development at the expense of the central city; have encouraged new capital formation at the expense of maintenance and repair of older capital; and have indirectly subsidized the development of newer regions of the country.

One who believes in the desirability of entrusting national development decisions to the marketplace might then argue that the first federal objective should be to restore neutrality to the development market by removing the locational bias inherent in present federal programs. A truly neutral federal posture is probably impossible to achieve. But establishing a goal of approximate neutrality would encourage federal authorities to overhaul present tax, aid, and economic development programs with an eye to reducing the federal impact on private markets.

There are actually two versions of the argument in favor of "market neutrality." One version concentrates on making today's federal programs approximately neutral in their impact. The other, stronger version argues that federal policies since World War II, ranging from FHA subsidies and highway programs to federal tax incentives, have systematically tended to weaken the competitive position of the cities.

Some of these programs are now less important than formerly— FHA mortgages, for example, currently finance but a small proportion of new homes, and federal support for highway construction has diminished in importance. The strong version of the argument for neutrality maintains that federal intervention should go beyond removing the remaining locational bias in present federal programs. It is proper now to tilt federal policy in favor of the cities (it is said) in recognition of the past incentives the government has provided to the cities' economic competitors. Over the long term, however, federal policy would still pursue the objective of approximate neutrality.

Compensating Cities for Their Cost Disadvantages

The final set of policy alternatives would acknowledge that cities are high cost producers of public and private services and would set about restoring their competitiveness through permanent federal subsidy. This position is most apparent in the debate over federal assistance programs. Recommendations that federal aid formulas allocate funds to government recipients in proportion to age of the capital stock, rate of population loss, cost of living levels, tax burdens, or hardship indices, all assume that it is proper for cities to be compensated for their high costs of service provision.

A similar debate is now being conducted in most European countries. West Germany, for example, adjusts the per capita revenue sharing contributions it makes to local governments by the size of jurisdiction, on the grounds that it is more expensive, per capita, for big cities to provide public services than for small cities. This policy has engendered a good deal of criticism from those who complain that it artificially sustains big cities when market forces should lead to their shrinkage.

As long as cities incur higher public sector costs because of the special populations they house, it is easier to defend compensatory federal aid than if the additional costs are the result of higher wages, higher benefit levels, or less efficient production. The case for uniform federal provision of health and welfare benefits, for example, is a persuasive one. The case for federal assumption of the financial burdens of health and welfare in those states with the heaviest Medicaid or welfare loads is necessarily more controversial, however, since it involves compensating states in part for costs that were voluntarily assumed and in part for their overall higher costs of service provision.

Direct compensation of cost differentials incurred in the provision of standard public services, such as police and fire protection, schooling, and sewer and water supply, generally is justified by either (or both) of two arguments. One argument emphasizes equity considerations and the limitations of private markets. Private market forces, such as job and population migration, cannot correct the full imbalance that now exists, at least in any socially acceptable period of time.

Since many households do not realistically have the option of moving to locales where jobs are available and public services cheaper to provide, equity might seem to require that the federal government step in and spread over the entire taxpaying public the extra costs that are currently confronted by city dwellers. Fair treatment of the urban poor, it is claimed, would provide them with greater fiscal relief, even at the cost of encouraging some continuation of high cost service conditions.

Alternatively, it has been asserted that the apparently higher costs of public sector operations in cities is merely an artifact of the accounting system. We are not in the habit of computing the full capital costs that would be required if the capital facilities now found in older cities were scrapped and replaced with new capital in the suburbs or in other parts of the country. Some economists and planners have argued that a full cost accounting would reveal it to be inefficient, even in narrow dollar and cents terms, to allow urban decentralization to continue unchecked.

Any national development policy will have to resolve the larger question of what the federal attitude toward urban decline should be, as well as the more specific question of how federal aid and incentive programs can best be restructured to achieve agreed-upon objectives. The choice of a national development policy is in large degree a value question.

There are, however, analytical issues that remain unclear and can shed some light on the question. How far do present federal policies deviate from market neutrality? How rapidly can private market forces be expected to equilibrate urban cost differentials, if allowed to operate unhindered? If a proper accounting were made of the national investment in present urban capital facilities, would it prove to be cheaper to encourage growth within current metropolitan areas than to permit continued decentralization? And, given any agreed-upon national policy toward cities, what is the most effective manner of redesigning federal programs to achieve this policy?

The papers in this book will help inform the national debate on these issues. They offer a good deal of specific analysis, and at the same time point to information gaps that should be filled and policy choices that need to be weighed.

7: The Borrowing Costs of Small City Borrowers

John E. Petersen

A possible constraint on small city growth and prosperity might be their higher cost of financial capital. A common view is that small communities (small governmental borrowers such as towns and cities) have only limited access to the credit markets and must rely on local sources of credit. This limitation has been responsible for the creation of a variety of federal and state programs through the years.

However, most of these have been directed toward assisting borrowing for certain purposes, such as local school building, wastewater treatment plants, or water and sewer projects. Outside of some well advertised, but limited, use of state bond banks, the small city, county, or special district has been left to fend for itself in the capital markets.

As we discuss below, there indeed are ways in which small borrowers are disadvantaged in the municipal bond market because of their size. Correspondingly, there are a variety of things that states in particular can do to help small cities to improve their acceptance in the credit market and to lower their cost of borrowing. However, it does not appear—except for the very smallest borrower—that the higher cost of borrowed capital is a very significant burden on small unit public finance. Once a borrower has obtained a size where it markets bond issues of about $5 million in size, it has reasonable access to the national markets and has probably overcome most systematic diseconomies associated with small size.

The higher costs of the very small borrower stem from several sources. (For purposes of this discussion, a small borrower can be viewed as one selling a bond issue of $1 million or less in size.)

Costs of Flotation

There are certain costs involved in preparing a bond issue for sale, including legal fees, printing expenses, publishing bond notices, and the like. These costs are largely fixed, and decline rapidly per dollar of borrowed funds as the issue size increases. A survey taken in the early 1970s found that for bond issues of less than $2 million in size, costs of flotation averaged about $9 per $1,000 borrowed (for general obligation bonds)—over ten times as much per dollar borrowed as for issues in excess of $20 million in size.

Net Interest Costs

The most important cost to be considered for the small issue is the money it must pay out in interest charges over the life of the bond issue. The net interest cost, which is a simple interest cost concept unique to the municipal bond market, actually reflects two elements of cost: (1) the underwriting cost or "spread" that represents the underwriter's charge for buying and reselling the issue to final investors, and (2) the interest yield required by the final investor for the loan of his money. In both cases the smaller issuer tends to pay more.

Looking at the net interest cost, studies indicate that small bond issues ($1 million), regardless of credit rating, tend to pay 15 to 25 basis points (one hundredths of a percentage point) more in interest cost than bond issuers of $20 million or more in size. If the credit ratings given by Moody's or Standard and Poor's are held constant, the interest cost difference is more on the order of 10 to 15 basis points. The present value of 10 basis points of additional interest is equal to about $10 per $1000 bond (6 percent coupon, 15-year maturity), to put it in terms equivalent to those costs of flotation discussed above.

Underwriting Costs

The higher net interest cost derives from several factors. First, underwriters tend to exact a higher unit charge for their services on small issues. Their costs are largely fixed in handling a bond issue, no matter what its size. Furthermore, there is considerable evidence that there is less competition among underwriters for small issues. This is seen in the fewer number of bids submitted for small issues. Generally, underwriters appear to charge about $2 to $3 more per $1000 on bond issues of less than $2 million than those of $20 million in size.

Final Investor Demand

The largest impact on cost per unit is found in the higher interest rates demanded by final investors. Small bond issues are less marketable and generally more cumbersome for investors. Record keeping is about the same whether the issue is large or small and smaller issues definitely present more of an information problem since their current reporting is typically deficient, if not nonexistent. No secondary market may exist for the bonds of a small, lesser known issuer. Thus, the investor who attempts to sell his bonds before maturity may have to take a considerable price reduction in order to find another borrower. For these reasons, the evidence is that final investors demand roughly 1 to 1 1/2 basis points in extra yield per million dollar decrease in the size of the bond issue. That is equal to about $1 in present value of added interest costs per $1000 of a 6 percent coupon bond.

Adding all these efforts up, it appears that small issues of $1 million or less can expect to pay approximately $20 to $35 more in borrowing costs per $1000 than bond issues of $20 million or more and of equivalent credit quality. This can mean an added $20,000 to $35,000 in overall costs (in present value terms) on a $1 million issue. Considering, however, that a 15-year, 6 percent issue would pay out $900,000 in interest over the life of the bonds, the amount of added cost is not of overpowering significance.

Other Factors

Of course, other factors in the loan that are hard to measure can be inhibiting to small issuers. For example, small issuers may not be able to borrow for as long a period as they would like. Moreover, as noted, smallness is highly correlated to lower credit ratings or to having none at all. Lower quality borrowers must pay more to borrow, and the added costs for lower bond ratings have increased substantially since 1975 and the great concern surrounding New York City. The costs are also regional in their composition, with borrowers in the Northeast and Middle Atlantic areas experiencing the largest increases. During the height of the New York City crises these regional cost differentials overpowered the other effects, and bonds sold by issuers in those regions were requiring 50 to 100 basis points more in yield than similar securities sold in other regions.

Conclusion

In conclusion, it is clear that economies are to be enjoyed by enlarging the market for smaller municipal bond issues. However, not too much emphasis should be given either to the constraints (additional costs) placed on communities because of small size or to the cost advantages that will occur from consolidations of borrowing or other forms of credit assistance. Outside of obvious credit problems having to do with the intrinsic riskiness of projects or borrowers, there do not appear to be major obstacles to small cities receiving an adequate share of capital at a reasonable cost.

8: The Metropolitan Future: Accidental or Designed?

James L. Sundquist

Professor Werner Hirsch's chapter is of interest for not just one but two vivid portraits that it draws. One, intentionally sketched, is of the future urban sprawl, to which he applies another name: the "polynucleated metropolis." The other, subliminal and unintended, is of impotent government in a laissez-faire society.

When he speaks of "forces" that will "dominate the near future," he does not list government among them, except for two kinds of governmental "actions." One is reliance on the property tax for financing local government—which is not really "action" at all, but inertia. The other is a series of three state court decisions overturning exclusionary suburban zoning laws, which he manages to project as a major influence despite the opposite trend of recent United States Supreme Court civil rights decisions.

But there is no suggestion anywhere that a factor in the future might be Congress, or state legislatures, or governors, or Presidents. No suggestion that the nature of the coming metropolitan configurations might be influenced by the concepts of planning bodies at any level. Indeed, it is a significant commentary on our society that the word "planning" does not once appear in a chapter outlining the factors influencing the shape of megalopolises of the future.

Not that government is left wholly without a role! In his final section, Professor Hirsch acknowledges a place for government. "Large scale federal participation" may be required, he tells us, to help solve the "enormous fiscal problems" of the core cities as they are deserted in the future not only by the rich but by the poor as well—the black as well as the white. While the mess is being made of the modern metropolis, the federal government is a spectator. But when the time comes to pay for that mess, it becomes a large scale participant.

This is not to suggest that Hirsch is wrong. Any projection of the forces that are actually at work now in our society would be less than honest if it gave government a much greater role, if it paid much heed to planning. Perhaps the word "planning" should at least appear in a chapter such as this one (once, say), in recognition of some intriguing experiments in state planning now getting underway, especially in New England, in the West, in Florida, and in Hawaii. Even so, one cannot truly speak of instances where the general pattern of metropolitan sprawl has yet been influenced profoundly by any kind of planning process. The ambitious federal innovations of the "Great Society" period and even earlier times to shape urban and metropolitan growth—urban renewal, and model cities, and planned new communities—have now been pronounced failures and been abandoned. City planners influence the form of urban sprawl in minor particulars but not in basic patterns. Those are indeed drawn by the economic and demographic factors that Hirsch skillfully enumerates.

But suppose one were to undertake to do more than simply project the present trends? Suppose one looks not just at economic and demographic factors but also at the world of politics. Has a pervasive dissatisfaction with existing growth patterns set in motion new *political* forces that may one day become powerful enough to deflect the Hirsch projections?

Nobody said it better than Richard Nixon in his first State of the Union Message, in 1970. He deplored "the vast areas of rural America emptying out of people and of promise." He went on to identify "the violent and decayed central cities of our great metropolitan complexes" as "the most conspicuous area of failure in American life today." And, finally, he proposed "that before these problems become insoluble, the nation develop a national growth policy.... If we seize our growth as a challenge, we can make the 1970s an historic period when by conscious choice we transformed our land into what we want it to become."

President Nixon did not seize his own challenge, of course. Nor did anybody else. Now the 1970s are drawing to a close. But that does not mean the chance is lost. Substitute "1980s" for "1970s," and the Nixon language still possesses its original vitality. The conscious choice can still be made.

If we are to speculate seriously about the nature of the "coming age," we cannot omit entirely the prospect that the choice will be made, that some degree of rational planning will be imposed upon the pattern that would otherwise be the blind creation of economic and demographic forces. There are many signs of such a prospect. Nixon backed off from his 1970 commitment to the goal of planning, but before he did so the Congress passed two laws calling for the establishment of the kind of national growth policy he then endorsed. The next biennial national growth report (as required by one of those laws, and due in February 1978) will be prepared under the direction not of Richard Nixon nor of Gerald Ford but of Jimmy Carter, whose record as governor of Georgia and as an official of one of the regional planning bodies of that state gives every evidence of a belief in planning.

A White House Conference on balanced national growth will be held early in 1978. The states are stirring, as mentioned earlier, and so are many suburban jurisdictions concerned about the consequences of unrestrained, too rapid growth. Even against Presidential opposition in the Republican years, Congress came close on two occasions to passing a bill that would have provided federal stimulus and aid for state planning.

But, above all, there is the impetus from those "violent and decayed central cities," newly dramatized by the fiscal collapse of the greatest central city of them all, New York. It is hard to believe that the cities' plight can fail to force the metropolitan areas, and the states, and the federal government (as the ultimate receiver in bankruptcy) to confront—and soon—a range of choices as to the form that metropolitan growth shall take.

At one extreme is the unplanned and undirected polynucleation (I still say "sprawl") that Professor Hirsch describes. At the other is a planned metropolis. I would not expect the choice to be for total control of the urban form through planning, on the British or Dutch or Swedish model—not right away, anyhow. But I would expect enough movement along the scale from the present laissez faire extreme to require a rewriting of the Hirsch scenario to provide a new and crucial role for government.

And what would be the nature of the metropolis of the coming age, given a new role for government as planner? Polynucleation, in all likelihood. That seems to be the lesson to be learned from the planners of London and Edinburgh, Paris and The Hague, all of whom are still trying to create the satellite "Garden Cities of Tomorrow" that Ebenezer Howard dreamed of close to a century ago. But quite a different kind of polynucleation from the one that Hirsch foresees.

A consciously-adopted metropolitan growth policy would not be insensate to the destruction of the central cities. It would not be blind to resource and energy costs. It would surely give a high priority to encouraging investment and hence employment in the central cities, where the people live, rather than at random on vacant tracts in the outer metropolitan fringes where employment depends upon vast and wasteful expenditure—both in dollar terms and in energy terms—for transportation, for infrastructure, for housing, and for all the supporting services required by residential and industrial development.

"Bring the work to the workers" is the slogan of the government planners whose ideas control the location of investment in Europe. Not a bad policy anywhere. In this country, as across the Atlantic, to bring the work to the workers concentrated in the central cities would be both more humane and more economical than to pursue either of the two available alternatives: forcing the workers to relocate, or building incredibly expensive new transportation systems. For those reasons, it would also be the course that would most nearly reflect the desires of a great many urban voters, who are bound to find political expression at some point.

And so, in sum, it is hard to believe with Professor Hirsch that rationality, backed up by political weight, will not one day be introduced as a factor influencing the shape of metropolitan America.

9: Local Economic Development Policy

Benjamin Chinitz

Professor Brian Berry (Chapter Thirteen) has given us a clear picture of recent trends in the geographic distribution of population in the United States by type of place: urban vs. rural, metropolitan vs. nonmetropolitan, central cities vs. suburbs. He observes—I believe correctly—a reversal in the long term trends for the first two categories and an acceleration of long term trends in the third.

Rural and nonmetropolitan areas are faring better in the 1970s than they had before, central cities worse. Between 1960 and 1970, 95 central cities experienced population declines, while the overall central city population increased 6.5 percent. Since 1970, the total U.S. central city population has declined by 3.1 percent.

Berry suggests "the number of central cities experiencing losses may be expected only to increase." He may be right, but it is also true that specific central cities have experienced much steeper declines than they had in the past. The acceleration of decline in specific cities has greater policy significance than the diffusion of decline among a larger number of central cities.

On an annual basis, the population of the following cities (whose 1950 populations exceeded 500,000) has declined more rapidly since 1970 than previously:

> Baltimore   Cincinnati
> Boston   Cleveland
> Buffalo   Detroit
> Chicago   Milwaukee

Minneapolis-St. Paul   Pittsburgh
New Orleans   St. Louis
New York   San Francisco-Oakland
Philadelphia   Seattle

Smaller cities have also experienced a more rapid rate of decline in the 1970s than in the 1960s. For both large and small cities the trend in the 1970s reflects not only the well heralded decline in the U.S. birth rate, but also an acceleration of suburbanization; that is, the share of the metropolitan population residing in central cities has declined at a more rapid rate in the 1970s than in the 1960s.

In this brief comment, I cannot deal with all the causes and consequences of the acceleration of central city decline. Clearly one cause is the decline of job opportunity in the central city, and one consequence is the weakening of the tax base of the central city. There seems to be no doubt that the demand for labor in the central city is decreasing at a fiscally alarming rate.

There may or may not be a national stake in either the economic or fiscal health of our central cities, but from the city's standpoint there is no question but that the preservation of the economic base is crucial to fiscal survival. What can a city do to stimulate the private sector within its borders? Should cities as an interest group lobby for urban economic development assistance from the federal government?

Conventional economic wisdom emphasizes the inevitability, due to market forces, of job losses in the central city and the futility of trying to combat these forces. While I do not discount market forces, I think it is appropriate to assign them a limited role in explaining the decline of the central city economy. By the same token, I do believe that there is a role for public policy in combating the downward slide.

The private decision to locate or to expand at a given location is undoubtedly, at times, significantly influenced by local public policy as it affects the cost of doing business at that location. Local tax rates, the scope and quality of local public services, and the quality of the local environment and "business climate" are bound to have some influence on private management choices with regard to location. The fact that econometric analysis may have failed to produce a significant partial coefficient on such variables is frustrating but not decisive.

The decline of economic activity in the central city is also viewed as detrimental to the welfare of central city residents, particularly minority ghetto populations. The logic of the argument and its policy implications would seem to be straightforward. The demand is shifting to the suburbs and the workers are stuck in the city; ergo, their economic opportunity is diminished. Demand must be stimulated in areas close by.

But research has shown that the logic is faulty. A recent monograph issued by the Institute for Research on Poverty at the University of Wisconsin concludes that racial discrimination in the labor market and deficiencies in human capital are far more important than housing segregation in explaining the low earnings of inner city minority populations (1). Such findings undermine the logic of job creation in ghetto areas as a remedy for high unemployment and low income in the central city.

It would be unwise, in any case, to view local economic development efforts as serving simultaneously the fiscal needs of the city and the job needs of city residents. Any private sector expansion occurring anywhere within the city's boundaries employing any kind of people, including suburbanites, will improve the city's fiscal situation, provided that the costs of stimulating that expansion and the public service needs of the facility do not exceed the additional revenues. To meet the job needs of inner city residents, however, the expansion must be fine tuned as to location within the city and the skill mix required.

Making the distinction between the fiscal needs of the local jurisdiction and the job needs of local unemployed residents should not, however, be interpreted as opting for a "place oriented" versus a "people oriented" strategy. In the final analysis, the fiscal viability of the local jurisdiction is crucial to the welfare of its residents.

Even if we are suspicious of macroeconomic policies which favor the encouragement of business investment over direct job creation, we should be sympathetic to filtering down strategies at the local level. The physical and human capital needs of disadvantaged city residents will be better served by a fiscally healthy city government.

Furthermore, there is no reason why the objective of expanding the revenue base must necessarily compete with the objective of employing inner city residents, as long as we do not seek to accomplish both objectives simultaneously in each case.

10: The Future of Small Communities

Ann C. Macaluso

Do small communities have a future in urbanizing America? It is tempting to romanticize the potential role of small, particularly rural, towns. America's conventional wisdom recalls the idyllic and bucolic vision of the nineteenth century, when neighbors cared for each other, the air was fresh, and the trilling of birds permeated peaceful countrysides.

But even small towns are today part of a national, urbanizing culture. Developing communications networks, including television, and improved transportation have changed the values and aspirations of all the nation. We are not faced, any longer, with an exodus of less skilled, less educated individuals from rural to urban areas, but rather, with a transformation toward urbanization of the whole society, including rural and urban, metro and nonmetro and the interdependencies among them.

Clearly, there is a need that small communities have for upgrading their planning, managerial and programming skills to provide more responsive services to an increasingly sophisticated constituency. One city manager in a town of 1,800 in Oklahoma recently said: "The people in my community expect to be able to go to a library, as much as the people in Oklahoma City." (Thanks to general revenue sharing, that small town *did* provide a library.)

Except for general revenue sharing, however, it is not clear that the federal government has recognized the role that small communities play in an urbanized nation. They still are excluded, by failing to meet program formula factors, from most grant-in-aid programs. Such exclusion means that small communities are forced to rely on their own revenue sources for paying salaries to managers and administrators.

Since local revenue sources are often inadequate to permit offering of competitive salaries for jurisdictional managers, small communities have a great need for the technical assistance and information that will improve their planning and management capability. In addition, small communities need increased expertise in applying for those few federal programs for which they are eligible and in responding to the regulatory demands and information requests levied upon them by the federal government.

Currently, many institutions either offer directly, or have the potential for offering, such information and assistance directly to small communities. They include state departments of community affairs; economic development districts; state, municipal, and county leagues; and some university extension programs. Many of these institutions are acutely aware of the problems faced by small communities in dealing with federal red tape and in obtaining planning information.

In hearings before the Subcommittee on Census and Population of the House Committee on Post Office and Civil Service in the spring of 1976, Pamela R. Grimm, research director of the East Tennessee Development District, made the following comments:

> Initially we did planning and very little else. While planning is still a major part of our program, we have become more and more involved in what we call technical assistance, which generally means helping our member governments with applications for federal or state funds, explaining new regulations and guidelines, and helping them through a maze of red tape.

Increasingly, similar technical assistance organizations complain about both the red tape requirements levied by the federal government and its failure to make available general purpose statistical information and data which can be used for small community planning. For example, the Census Bureau does not disaggregate its data to a small community level. It does furnish Census data for cities of 50,000 and above.

Since federal funding applications often require census data, small communities are placed at a distinct disadvantage in securing such funds. They are similarly disadvantaged in being able to obtain adequate census data for purposes of planning and managing their own jurisdictions, without turning to intermediaries to secure such data on their behalf.

Government officials in the major statistical agencies (including

The Future of Small Communities 379

Census and Bureau of Labor Statistics) acknowledge that their estimates for small communities, particularly in rural areas, are far less accurate than their estimates for large, urban centers.

Finally, then, small communities are penalized by the federal government in being required to respond to red tape, regulation and information requests for which they lack adequate data; and in not being able to obtain adequate data for their own planning and federal grant application purposes.

Notes

Notes

INTRODUCTION

1. For further discussion of Lee's views see Howard Lee, "Managing the Small City," in *Urban Governance and Minorities*, edited by Herrington J. Bryce (New York: Praeger Publishers, 1976), pp. 86-90.

CHAPTER ONE

1. Beale, Calvin L. (1975) "The Revival of Population Growth in Nonmetropolitan America." Washington, D.C.: Economic Development Division, Economic Research Service, U.S. Department of Agriculture, ERS-605.

2. Beale, Calvin L. and Glenn V. Fuguitt (1975), "The New Pattern of Nonmetropolitan Population Change." Madison, Wisc.: Center for Demography and Ecology, University of Wisconsin, CDE Working Paper 75-22.

3. Morrison, Peter A., with Judith P. Wheeler (1976), "Rural Renaissance in America?" *Population Bulletin* 31 (October):1-26.

CHAPTER TWO

1. Fuguitt, Glenn and Calvin Beale, "Population Change in Non-Metropolitan Cities and Towns," Agricultural Economics Report No. 323, Economic Research Service, U.S. Department of Agriculture, February 1976.

2. For another discussion of the growth and decline of small cities see Leonard F. Wheat, *Urban Growth in the Non-Metropolitan South* (Lexington, Mass.: Heath, Lexington Books, 1976).

3. Beale, Calvin L. "The Revival of Population Growth in Non-Metropolitan America," (ERS 605) Economic Research Service, U.S. Department of Agriculture, pp. 4 and 11.

4. *Ibid.*, pp. 4 and 11.

CHAPTER THREE

1. Sundquist, J.L. "Where Shall They Live?" *The Public Interest*, (Winter 1970): 91.

2. Kirp, D.L. " 'Growth Management' Zoning, Population Policy and the Courts." *Policy Analysis*, (Summer 1976):436-437.

3. U.S. Congress. House Committee on Public Works. Science Advisory Panel. *A National Public Works Investment Policy*. Task Force Report (Committee Print). Washington, D.C., 1974.

4. U.S. Department of Agriculture. *Rural Development Goals, Second Annual Report of the Secretary of Agriculture to the Congress*, Washington, D.C., 1975, p. 2.

5. Housing Assistance Council, Inc., *The Housing and Community Development Act of 1974: Implications for Rural America*, Washington, D.C., 1974, p. 27.

6. *President's 1974 Report on National Growth and Development*, Washington, D.C., pp. 46-47.

7. U.S. Department of Commerce. Economic Development Administration. *A Myth in the Making: The Southern Economic Challenge and the Northern Economic Decline*, Washington, D.C., 1976.

8. U.S. Department of Housing and Urban Development. *State Growth Management.* Washington, D.C., May 1976, pp. 51-53.

9. Whiting, Vaughn. "A Community Development Experiment in State Government," *Missouri Municipal Review*, vol. 39 (August 1974):18-21.

10. U.S. Advisory Commission on Intergovernmental Relations. *State Actions in 1976.* July, 1976. Washington, D.C., M-102, pp. 37-38.

11. *President's 1976 Report on National Growth and Development. The Changing Issues for National Growth*, Washington, D.C., February 1976, p. 122.

12. *Ibid.*, p. 121.

13. U.S. Department of Housing and Urban Development. *Urban Growth Management, Summary of Evaluation Research.* Washington, D.C., May 1976, pp. 4-5.

14. U.S. Congress. Joint Economic Committee, *Toward a National Growth Policy: Federal and State Development, 1975* (Committee Print), Washington, D.C. (forthcoming), Introduction.

15. U.S. Congress. House Committee on Public Works (1974). *A National Public Works Investment Policy*, Washington, D.C., p. 33.

16. *Ibid.*, pp. 9-10.

17. U.S. Department of Agriculture, Economic Research Service, Clark Edwards, *Strategies for Balanced Rural-Urban Growth*, Agriculture Info. Bulletin #392, p. 2.

18. *Ibid.*, p. 9.

19. Sundquist, James, cited in the *Congressional Record*, Senate, June 3, 1975.

20. Morrison, Peter A., *How Population Movements Shape National Growth*, The RAND Corporation, P-50007 (Multilith), May 1973, p. 19.

20A. Advisory Commission on Intergovernmental Relations, *Improving Urban America: A Challenge to Federalism*, M-107, September 1976, pp. 242-244.

20B. *Ibid.*

21. Library of Congress, Congressional Research Service, Schussheim, Morton J., *Rural Development Goals: Critique of the Second Annual Report of the Secretary of Agriculture to the Congress*, August 22, 1975.

22. Humphrey, Hubert H., National Policy Planning: Roosevelt to Nixon. Remarks in the Senate, *Congressional Record* (daily ed.), vol. 122, March 1, 1976, S 2538.

23. U.S. Congress, Joint Economic Committee, *Toward a National Growth Policy: Federal and State Developments in 1975* (Joint Committee Print, May 19, 1977) Conclusions, pp. 205-209. Washington, D.C., U.S. Govt. Printing Office.

24. Public Law 93-426, Section 720 i (2).

25. Rainey, Kenneth D., "Realism and Ruralism: The State Role in Non-Metropolitan Development," *State Government*, XLVII (Autumn 1974):199-203.

26. "The Second War Between the States," *Business Week*, May 17, 1976, pp. 112-113.

CHAPTER FOUR

1. Irene B. Taeuber, "Migration, Mobility, and the Assimilation of the Negro," *Population Bulletin*, November 1958, pp. 137-138.

2. Harold M. Rose, 'The All-Negro Town: Its Evolution and Function," *The Geographical Review*, July 1965, pp. 362-381.

3. Carter G. Woodson, *The Rural Negro*, Association of Negro Life and History, Washington, D.C., 1930, pp. 110-119.

4. Reynolds Farley, "The Changing Distribution of Negroes within Metropolitan Areas: The Emergence of Black Suburbs," *American Journal of Sociology*, January 1970, pp. 512-529.

5. Harold X. Connolly, "Black Movement into The Suburbs," *Urban Affairs Quarterly*, September 1973.

6. William W. Pendelton, "Blacks in Suburbs," *The Urbanization of the Suburbs*, edited by Louis H. Masotti and Jeffrey K. Hadden, Beverly Hills, Calif.: Sage Publications, 1973.

7. Leo F. Schnore, Carolyn D. André, and Harry Sharp, "Black Suburbanization, 1930-1970," *The Changing Face of The Suburbs*, ed., Barry Schwartz, The University of Chicago Press, Chicago, 1976, pp. 69-94.

8. Brian J.L. Berry and others, "Attitudes toward Integration: The Role of Status in Community Response to Social Change," *The Changing Face of The Suburbs*, ed. Barry Schwartz, The University of Chicago Press, Chicago, 1976, pp. 221-264.

9. Harold M. Rose, *Black Suburbanization: Access to Improved Quality of Life or Maintenance of the Status Quo?*, Cambridge, Mass.: Ballinger, 1976, p. 9.

10. Connolly, *op. cit.*

11. Francine F. Rabinovitz, *Minorities in Suburbs: The Los Angeles Experience*, Working Paper No. 31, Joint Center for Urban Studies, Cambridge, Massachusetts, 1975, p. 16.

12. Robert C. Weaver, "Housing and Associate Problems of Minorities," *Modernizing Urban Land Policy*, Marion Clawson, editor, Baltimore: The Johns Hopkins University Press, 1973, pp. 73-77.

13. Brian J.L. Berry, "Short Term Housing Cycles in a Dualistic Metropolis," *The Social Economy of Cities*, ed. Gary Gappert and Harold M. Rose, Beverly Hills, Calif.: Sage Publications, 1975, p. 170.

14. Reeve D. Vanneman and Thomas A. Pettigrew, "Race and Relative Deprivation in the Urban United States," *Race*, 13 (4) (1972), p. 478 (see Table 9).

15. Thomas F. Pettigrew, "Attitudes on Race and Housing: A Social Psychological View," *Segregation in Residential Areas*, National Academy of Sciences, Washington, D.C., 1973, p. 43.

16. St. Clair Drake and Horace R. Cayton, *Black Metropolis*, New York: Harcourt, Brace, 1945, pp. 495-525.

17. Jessie Bernard, *Marriage and the Family Among Negroes*, Englewood Cliffs, N.J.: Prentice-Hall, 1966, pp. 28-30.

18. Harold X. Connolly, "Black Movement into the Suburbs," *Urban Affairs Quarterly*, September 1973, p. 92.

19. Sarah M. Mazie and Steve Rawlings, "Public Attitude Towards Population Distribution Issues," *Population Distribution and Policy, Commission on Population Growth and the American Future*, Vol. 5, editor Sarah Mills Mazie, Washington, D.C.: U.S. Government Printing Office, 1973, p. 605.

CHAPTER FIVE

1. While the basic conceptual framework of this chapter was set in place in a work written over a decade ago (*A Preface to Urban Economics*, Baltimore: Johns Hopkins Press, 1965), important modifications and additions have been drawn from numerous subsequent writings, most notably: "Internal and External Factors in the Development of Urban Economies," in Harvey S. Perloff and Lowdon Wingo, Jr., *Issues in Urban Economics*, Baltimore: Johns Hopkins Press, 1968; "The Economic Base of Urban Problems," in Neil W. Chamberlain, *Contemporary Economic Issues*, Homewood, Ill.: Richard D. Irwin, 1969; "Problems that Sprout in the Shadow of No-Growth," *AIA Journal*, December, 1973; and unpublished material from a manuscript currently in preparation.

CHAPTER SIX

1. Roderick C. McKenzie, *The Metropolitan Community* (New York: McGraw-Hill Book Co., 1933), but also see the earlier work of Robert Murray Haig, "Towards an Understanding of the Metropolis," *Quarterly Journal of Economics* (May 1926), pp. 402-434 and Adna F. Weber, *The Growth of Cities in the Nineteenth Century* (New York: MacMillan Company, 1899).

2. Daniel B. Creamer has dealt with the problem of manufacturing employment both before World War II and after World War II. The earlier analysis appeared in his monograph *Is Industry Decentralizing?* (Philadelphia: University of Pennsylvania Press, 1935) and with Herman C. Brunck in Carter Goodrich, et al., *Migration and Economic Opportunity* (Philadelphia: University of Pennsylvania Press, 1935), pp. 314-392. In *Changing Location of Manufacturing Employment* (New York: National Industrial Conference Board, 1963). In his *Studies in Business Economics* #83 Creamer viewed the problem from a postwar perspective.

3. John F. Kain has written the most influential explicit statement of the

problem in an essay which has appeared in several variants as "The Distribution and Movement of Jobs and Industry." The most up-to-date version appears in John F. Kain (ed.), *Essays in Urban Spatial Structure* (Cambridge, Mass.: Ballinger Publishing Company, 1975), pp. 79-114.

4. *Urban Economic Development* (Washington, D.C.: The Urban Institute, 1974), pp. 3-59.

5. McKenzie, pp. 191-198.

6. "Industrial Location and Urban Redevelopment" in Coleman Woodbury, ed., *The Future of the Cities and Urban Redevelopment* (Chicago: University of Chicago Press, 1953), pp. 103-286.

7. Kain, pp. 79-86.

8. McKenzie, pp. 55-58.

9. McKenzie, pp. 250-266.

10. The growth was known but was obscured by a preoccupation with the distribution among types of localities. See Woodbury, pp. 251-269.

11. McKenzie, p. 113.

12. Kain, pp. 90-91.

13. McKenzie, pp. 173-190.

14. Alexander Ganz and Thomas O'Brien, "The City: Sandbox, Reservation or Dynamo?" *Public Policy* (Winter 1973); but see also other studies which generalized on the Vietnam experience including Bennett Harrison, *op. cit.*, pp. 14-20; and Benjamin Cohen, "Trends in Negro Employment within Large Metropolitan Areas," *Public Policy* (Fall 1974), pp. 614-615. The regional characteristics appear to have been ignored throughout.

15. McKenzie, pp. 56-88.

CHAPTER SEVEN

1. C. Clark, "The Economic Functions of a City in Relation to Its Size," *Econometrica* 13 (1945):97-113.

2. R.M. Lillibridge, "Urban Size: An Assessment," *Land Economics* 28 (1952):341-352.

3. Clarence Schettler, "Relations of City-Size to Economic Services," *American Sociological Review* 8 (1953):60-62.

4. Leo F. Schnore and D.W. Varley, "Some Concomitants of Metropolitan Size," *American Sociological Review* 20 (1955):408-414.

5. B. Berry and W. Garrison, "The Functional Bases of the Central Place Hierarchy," *Economic Geography* 34 (1958):145-154.

6. H.A. Stafford, Jr., "The Functional Bases of Small Towns," *Economic Geography* 39 (1963):165-175.

7. O. Duncan, W. Scott, S. Lieberson, B. Duncan, and H. Winsborough, *Metropolis and Region*, Baltimore: Johns Hopkins Press, 1960.

8. F.D. Bean, D.L. Poston, Jr., and H. Winsborough, "Size, Functional Specialization, and the Classification of Cities," *Social Science Quarterly* 53 (1972):20-32.

9. R.W. Bahl, R. Firestine, and D. Phares, "Industrial Diversity in Urban Areas: Alternative Measures and Intermetropolitan Comparisons," *Economic Geography* 47 (1971):414-425.

10. F. Clemente and R.B. Sturgis, "Population Size and Industrial Diversification," *Urban Studies* 8 (1971):65-68.

11. R.W. Crowley, "Reflections and Further Evidence on Population Size and Industrial Diversification," *Urban Studies* 10 (1973):91-94.

12. C. Paraskevopoulos, "Population Size and the Extent of Industrial Diversification: An Alternative View," *Urban Studies* 12 (1975):105-107.

13. J. Taylor, "A Note on the Definition of Industrial Diversification," *Journal of Economic Studies* (1967):105-113.

14. W. Thompson, *A Preface to Urban Economics*, Baltimore: Johns Hopkins Press, 1965.

15. E.L. Ullman and M.F. Dacey, "The Minimum Requirements Approach to the Urban Economic Base," *Papers of the Regional Science Association* 6 (1960):175-194.

16. B. Chinitz and R. Vernon, "Changing Forces in Industrial Location," *Harvard Business Review* 38 (1960):126-136.

17. Duncan, et al., *Metropolis*.

18. E. Hoover, *An Introduction to Regional Economics*, New York: A. Alfred Knopf, 1971.

19. E. Mills, *Studies in the Structure of the Urban Economy*, Baltimore: Johns Hopkins Press, 1972.

20. D. Puryear, "A Programming Model of Central Place Theory," *Journal of Regional Science* 15 (1975):307-316.

21. Clemente and Sturgis, "Population Size."

22. Crowley, "Reflections."

23. Paraskevopoulos, "Population Size."

24. J. Sundquist, "Where Shall They Live?" *Public Interest* 18 (1970): 88-100.

25. K. Mera, "On the Urban Agglomeration and Economic Efficiency," *Economic Development and Cultural Change* 21 (1972):309-324.

26. L. Sveikauskas, "The Productivity of Cities," *Quarterly Journal of Economics* 89 (1975):393-413.

27. I. Hoch, "Income and City Size," *Urban Studies* 9 (1972):299-328; and "Urban Scale and Environmental Quality," U.S., Commission on Population Growth and the American Future, *Population, Resources, and the Environment.* R. Ridker (ed.) Vol. III of Commission research reports, Washington, D.C.: Government Printing Office, 1972, pp. 231-286.

28. G. Tolley, "The Welfare Economics of City Bigness," *Journal of Urban Economics* 1 (1974):324-345.

29. R. Lichtenberg, *One-Tenth of a Nation*, Cambridge, Mass.: Harvard University Press, 1960.

30. Sundquist, "Where Shall They Live?"

31. W. Alonso and M. Fajans., *Cost of Living and Income by Urban Size.* Working Paper No. 128 (University of California, Berkeley: Center for Planning and Development, 1970).

32. Hoch, "Income" and "Urban Scale."

33. Tolley, "Welfare Economics."

34. W. Alonso, *The Economics of Urban Size.* Working Paper No. 138 (University of California, Berkeley: Center for Planning and Development, 1970).

35. D. Bradford, R. Malt, and W. Oates, "The Rising Cost of Local Public Services: Some Evidence and Reflections," *National Tax Journal* 22 (1969):185-202.

36. L.R. Gabler, "Economies and Diseconomies of Scale in Urban Public Sectors," *Land Economics* 45 (1969):425-434.

37. L.R. Gabler, "Population Size as a Determinant of City Expenditures and Employment: Some Further Evidence," *Land Economics* 47 (1971):130-138.

38. Harvey Shapiro, "Economies of Scale and Local Government Finance," *Land Economics* 39 (1963):175-186.

39. Alonso, *Economics.*

40. Bradford, "Rising Cost."

41. Gabler, "Economies and Diseconomies" and "Population Size."

42. Shapiro, "Economies of Scale."

43. W. Hirsch, "The Supply of Urban Public Services," in H. Perloff and L. Wings, *Issues in Urban Economics*, Baltimore: Johns Hopkins Press, 1968, pp. 81-140.

44. W. Hirsch, "Cost Functions of an Urban Government Service: Refuse Collection," *Review of Economics and Statistics* 47 (1965):87-92; and "Expenditure Implications of Metropolitan Growth and Consolidation," *Review of Economics and Statistics* 41 (1959):232-241.

45. J. Riew, "Economies of Scale in High School Operation," *Review of Economics and Statistics* 48 (1966):280-287.

46. N. Walzer, "Economies of Scale and Metropolitan Governments," *Review of Economics and Statistics* 54 (1972):431-438.

47. C. Tiebout, "Economies of Scale and Metropolitan Governments," *Review of Economics and Statistics* 42 (1960):442-444.

48. O.D. Duncan, "Optimum Size of Cities," in J. Spengler and O.D. Duncan (eds.), *Demographic Analysis: Selected Readings*, Glencoe, Ill.: The Free Press, 1956, pp. 632-645.

49. Mera, "Urban Agglomeration."

50. E. Borukhov, "Optimal Service Areas for Provision and Financing of Local Public Goods," *Public Finance* 27 (1972):267-281.

51. Hoch, "Income and City Size," and "Urban Scale."

52. E. Mills, "Economic Aspects of City Sizes," in U.S. Commission on Population Growth and the American Future, *Population Distribution and Policy*, S.M. Mazie (ed.), Vol. V of Commission research reports, Washington, D.C.: Government Printing Office, 1972, pp. 383-394; and "Welfare Aspects of National Policy Toward City Size," *Urban Studies* 9 (1972).

53. G.M. Neutze, *Economic Policy and the Size of Cities.* Clifton, N.J.: Augustus M. Kelley, 1965.

54. Tolley, "Welfare Economics."

55. E. Mills, "Economic Aspects of City Sizes"; and *Urban Economics*, Glenview, Ill.: Scott, Foresman, 1972.

56. Neutze, *Economic Policy.*

57. Sveikauskas, "Productivity."

58. R. Babcock, *The Zoning Game*, Madison: University of Wisconsin Press, 1969.

59. C. Tiebout, "A Pure Theory of Local Expenditures," *Journal of Political Economy* 64 (1956):416-424.

60. B. Hamilton, E. Mills, and D. Puryear, "The Tiebout Hypothesis and Residential Income Segregation," in E. Mills and W. Oates (eds.), *Fiscal Zoning and Land Use Controls*, Lexington, Mass.: D.C. Heath, 1975, pp. 101-118.

61. W. Neenan, "Suburban-Central City Exploitation Thesis: One City's Tale," *National Tax Journal* 23 (1970):117-139.

62. D. Auld and G. Cook, "Suburban-Central City Exploitation Thesis: A Comment," *National Tax Journal* 25 (1972):595-597.

63. D. Ramsey, "Suburban-Central City Exploitation Thesis: Comment," *National Tax Journal* 25 (1972):599-604.

CHAPTER EIGHT

1. See Thomas Muller, *Growing and Declining Urban Areas: A Fiscal Comparison*, The Urban Institute 1975 and George Peterson, *The Urban Predicament*, William Gorham and Nathan Glazer, eds. The Urban Institute, 1976.

2. Per capita money income during 1974 for smaller cities for which such data are available (adjusted for cost of living) was as follows: Austin, $5,176; Orlando, $5,268; Baton Rouge, $4,723; Dayton, $4,471; Hartford, $758; Newark, $3,087.

3. For example, Harvey E. Brazer, *City Expenditures in the United States*, National Bureau of Economic Research, New York, 1969; and Roy W. Bahl, *Metropolitan Population and Municipal Government Expenditures in Central Cities*, University of Kentucky Press, Lexington, 1969.

4. Thomas Muller and George Peterson, *Public Service Costs*, Draft, The Urban Institute, 1976.

5. New York, Boston, and San Francisco had the highest per capita outlays in the 1950s and the 1970s.

6. Changes in CBD activity are discussed in Thomas Muller, Kevin Neels, John Tilney and Grace Dawson, *The Economic Impact of I-295 on the Richmond Central Business District*, The Urban Institute, 1977.

7. For a discussion of population size and regional location effects on wages, see Thomas Muller *Intergovernmental and Intrametropolitan Cost Differentials*, The Urban Institute, forthcoming 1977.

8. This is attributable primarily to higher intergovernmental funding for social services and higher tax burden.

9. Muller et al., *The Economic Impact of I-295*.

10. Thomas Muller and Grace Dawson, *The Economic Effects of Annexation*, The Urban Institute, 1976.

11. *Holt v. Richmond* 406 U.S. 903 (1972), *City of Petersburg v. U.S., et al.*

12. Shifts in racial balance continued into the 1970s. Between 1970 and 1976 the white population in central cities nationally decreased by 3.7 million, black and other race populations increased by 1.5 million. Change continued to be most rapid in cities without annexation.

13. Interestingly, a Richmond special City Council election held in March 1977 after a six year delay awaiting the outcome of the court challenge to annexation by the city resulted in a Black majority, although this group has less than fifty percent of the voting age population. The shift in racial balance was made possible by a city agreement to change from at-large elections to a nine ward plan. This agreement is the reason cited by the U.S. Supreme Court (422 U.S. at 385 (1975)) for not finding the annexation a violation of the Voting Rights Act.

14. This is usually the case in suburbs of such growing states as California and Florida. For example, see Thomas Muller and Cathy Christensen, *State-Mandated Impact Evaluation: A Preliminary Assessment*, The Urban Institute, 1976.

15. Public Law 93-552 Section 608. This section is aimed at offsetting the fiscal impact of the Trident submarine program. As of July, 1977, Congress appropriated $27 million to offset fiscal deficits.

16. *Coastal Zone Environment Act* P.L. 94-370, 94th Congress 2nd Session.

17. Average wages of municipal and state employees in 1970 were six percent above the private sector. By 1975, they were only marginally higher.

18. For these and similar data, see Bureau of the Census, *City Government Finances in 1974-1975*, Washington, D.C., 1976.

CHAPTER NINE

1. Richard P. Nathan and Charles Adams, "Understanding Central City Hardship," *Political Science Quarterly*, Vol. 91 (1) (Spring 1976):47-62. In this article, relative need is defined by a number of factors including unemployment, persons less than 18 or over 65, education, income, housing, and poverty.

2. Wes Uhlman, "Beyond the City Limits," The *Washington Post*, Tuesday, December 14, 1976, p. A-19.

CHAPTER TEN

1. See, e.g., National League of Cities, "State of the Cities: 1975—A New Urban Crisis?" Washington, D.C., 1976.

2. U.S. Bureau of the Census, *1972 Census of Governments*, Vol. 5, *Local Government in Metropolitan Areas*, Washington, D.C., 1975, Table 9.

3. See Roger J. Vaughan, *The Urban Impacts of Federal Policies:* Vol. 2, *Economic Development*, The Rand Corporation, R-2028-KF, forthcoming.

4. The research issues are discussed in Vaughan, Section IV.

5. *Budget of the United States Government, Fiscal Year 1977*, Special Analysis F, "Tax Expenditures."

CHAPTER ELEVEN

1. Frank Levy, Arnold J. Meltsner, and Aaron Wildavsky, *Urban Outcomes: Streets, Schools, and Libraries*, University of California Press, 1974, p. 17. See also Chapter 4, pp. 240-245.

2. *Urban Outcomes*, p. 17.

3. George E. Peterson, "Finance," in *The Urban Predicament*, William Gorham and Nathan Glazer, (eds.), Washington, D.C.: The Urban Institute, 1976, pp. 46, 54-55.

4. "Measuring the Fiscal 'Blood Pressure' of the States," John Ross and John Shannon, October 15, 1976 (processed).

CHAPTER TWELVE

1. U.S. Bureau of the Census, *Statistical Abstract of the United States, 1975*, U.S. Government Printing Office, Washington, D.C., pp. 343-60.

2. Charlotte Fremon, *The Occupational Patterns in Urban Employment Change*, The Urban Institute Paper No. 7000, Washington, D.C., 1970.

3. Wolfgang Quante, "The Relocation of Corporate Headquarters from New York City," unpublished Ph.D. thesis, Columbia University, 1974.

4. Howard Hayghe, "Families and the Rise of Working Wives—An Overview," *Monthly Labor Review*, Vol. 99, No. 5, May 1976, p. 13.

5. Alexander W. Astin, *et al.*, *National Norms for Entering College Freshmen—Fall 1966*, *ACE Research Reports*, Vol. 2, No. 1, 1967; Robert J. Panos, *et al.*, *National Norms for Entering College Freshmen—Fall 1967*, Vol. 2, No. 7, 1967; Alexander W. Astin, *et al.*, *The American Freshman: National Norms for Fall 1975*, Laboratory for Research on Higher Education, Graduate School of Education, UCLA.

6. Howard Hayghe, *op. cit.*, p. 14.

7. U.S. Bureau of Census, *Current Population Reports*, P-23, No. 58, April 1976.

8. Stuart H. Garfinkle, "Occupations of Women and Black Workers, 1962-74," *Monthly Labor Review*, Vol. 98, No. 11, November 1975, Table 3.

9. William Alonso, *Location and Land Use: Toward a General Theory of Land Rent*, Cambridge, Mass., Harvard, 1964.

10. Richard Muth, *Cities and Housing*, Chicago, The University of Chicago Press, 1969.

11. David Bradford and Harry Kelejian, "An Economic Model of Flight to the Suburbs," *Journal of Political Economy*, Vol. 81 (March/April, 1973), p. 566.

12. J. Richard Aronson and Eli Schwartz, "Financing Public Goods and the Distribution of Population in a System of Local Government," *National Tax Journal*, Vol. 26, 1973, p. 137.

13. *Euclid v. Ambler Real Estate Co.*, 272 U.S. 395 (1926).

14. *Construction Industry Association of Sonoma County v. City of Petaluma*, 522 F.2b 897 (1975).

15. *National Land Investment Company v. Kohn* 419 Pa. 504, 532, 215A 2d 597, 612 (1965).

16. *Berenson v. Town of New Castle*, No. 430, December 2, 1975.

17. *Southern Burlington County NAACP v. Township of Mt. Laurel*, 67 NJ 151, 336A 2b713 (1975).

18. R.W. Anderson, *Residential Energy Consumption, Single Family Housing*, Hittman Associates, Inc., Columbia, Maryland, March 1975; and M. Tokman-

hekin and D.G. Harvey, *Residential Energy Consumption, Multiple Housing Final Report*, Hittman Associates, Inc., Columbia, Maryland, June 1974.

19. Dales L. Keyes, "Energy and Land Use: An Instrument of U.S. Conservation Policy?" *Energy Policy*, September 1976, p. 232.

20. U.S. Bureau of Labor Statistics, *Consumer Expenditure Survey Series: Diary Survey, July 1973-June 1974*, Report 448-3, Washington, D.C., 1976.

21. Margaret F. Fels and Michael J. Munson, "Energy Thrift in Urban Transportation: Options for the Future," in Robert H. Williams, ed., *The Energy Conservation Papers*, Ballinger Publishing Co., Cambridge, Mass., 1975.

22. James S. Roberts, *Energy, Land Use, and Growth Policy: Implications for Metropolitan Washington*, Metropolitan Washington Council of Governments, Washington, D.C., June 1975.

23. Irving Hoch, "City Size Effect, Trends and Policies," *Science*, Vol. 193, September 3, 1976, p. 857.

CHAPTER THIRTEEN

1. S. Greer, *The New Urbanization* (New York: St. Martin's Press, 1968).

2. V. Packard, *A Nation of Strangers* (New York: David McKay, 1972).

3. G. Suttles, *The Social Construction of Communities* (Chicago: University of Chicago Press, 1972).

4. D. Bell, "The Measurement of Knowledge and Technology," in *Indicators of Social Change*, ed. B. Sheldon and W.E. Moore (New York: The Russell Sage Foundation, 1968).

5. J. Friedmann, *Regional Development Policy* (Cambridge, Mass.: The MIT Press, 1966).

6. W. Thompson, "Internal and External Factors in the Development of Urban Economics," in *Issues in Urban Economics*, ed. H. Perloff and L. Wingo (Baltimore: Johns Hopkins Press, 1968), pp. 43-62.

7. For further elaboration of these statistics see B.J.L. Berry, *The Human Consequences of Urbanization* (Basingstoke, U.K.: Macmillan, 1973); Q. Gillard, *The Changing Shape of Metropolitan America* (Cambridge, Massachusetts: Ballinger, 1976); and D.C. Dahmann, "The Impact of Population Redistribution on the Urban Structure of the United States During the 1970s" (Washington, D.C.: National Academy of Sciences, forthcoming in 1977).

8. H. Tisdale, "The Process of Urbanization," *Social Forces* 20 (1942), pp. 311-16.

9. M. Webber, "Order in Diversity: Community without Propinquity," in *Cities and Space*, ed. L. Wingo (Baltimore: The Johns Hopkins Press, 1963), pp. 23-56.

10. J.J. Servan-Schreiber, *The American Challenge* (Paris: Denoel, 1967).

CHAPTER FOURTEEN

1. Metropolitan differentiation, in this discussion, refers to changes in the functions, reflected in economic base and population mix of various parts of the metropolitan area. These functions are related to stages in the life cycle of the

community. For discussions of structural features of metropolitan areas, see Edgar Hoover, and Raymond Vernon, *Anatomy of a Metropolis* (Garden City: Doubleday, 1959). Also see David Birch, *Patterns of Urban Change* (Lexington: Lexington Books, 1974).

2. For important works by Schnore in this area, see Leo F. Schnore, "The Growth of Metropolitan Suburbs," in *The Suburban Community*, William M. Dobriner (ed.) (New York: G.P. Putnam, 1958); and Leo F. Schnore, *Class and Race in Cities and Suburbs* (Chicago: Markam, 1972).

3. For a discussion of the conceptualizations over time, see E.W. Burgess, "The Growth of the City," in *The City*, R.E. Park et al. (ed.) (Chicago: University of Chicago Press, 1925); Chauncy Harris and Edward Ullman, "The Nature of Cities," *Annals*, Vol. 242 (1945), pp. 7-17; Amos H. Hawley, *Human Ecology* (New York: Ronald Press, 1950); Homer Hoyt, *The Structure and Growth of Residential Neighborhoods in American Cities* (Washington, D.C.: Federal Housing Administration, 1939); and Leslie Kish, "Differentiation in Metropolitan Areas," *American Sociological Review*, Vol. 19 (1954), pp. 388-398.

4. See George Sternlieb, "The City a Sandbox," *Public Interest*, 25 (Fall 1971), pp. 14-21; and William Baer, "On the Death of Cities," *Public Interest*, 45 (Fall 1976), pp. 3-19.

5. See generally, Gerald Manners, *The Office in Metropolis: An Opportunity for Shaping Metropolitan America*, Working Paper #22 (Cambridge: Joint Center for Urban Studies of M.I.T.-Harvard, 1973).

6. For a study of "high rise city" residents and their characteristics, see Kent Colton and Robert Earsy, *Boston's New High Rise Apartments: A Study of Residents and Their Preferences* (Boston Redevelopment Authority, 1973).

7. See Harland Douglass, *The Suburban Trend* (New York: The Century Company, 1925).

8. For up-to-date findings on the role of accessibility in location, see Michael Stegman, "Accessibility Models and Residential Location," *JAIP* (January 1969), pp. 20-22. (He argues that accessibility plays a smaller role in location than had been earlier estimated.)

9. For a disaggregated analysis of black suburban migration (1960-1970), see Phillip L. Clay, "The Process of Black Suburban Migration," Ph.D. Dissertation, MIT, 1975.

10. For a discussion of housing market trends in older suburban cities, see Solomon Suther and Sara Sutker (eds.), *Racial Transition in the Inner Suburbs: Studies of the St. Louis Area* (New York: Praeger, 1974).

11. There are two recent studies of neighborhood satisfaction of blacks in suburban cities. Both reported blacks show somewhat higher levels of satisfaction than similarly placed whites. See Francine Rabinovitz, *Black Borders: Minorities in Suburbs* (Lexington: D.C. Heath, forthcoming), Chapter 4. Also see Zehner and Chapin, *op. cit.*, p. 118.

12. For a discussion of the "Zone of Emergence" idea as it applied to original suburbs, see Robert Woods, *Zone of Emergence*, (Cambridge, Mass.: Harvard University Press, 1962) [a reprint of a book first published in the 1920's]. For a study of a recent application of the concept, see George Sternlieb and W. Patrick

Beaton, *The Zone of Emergence: A Case Study of Plainfield, New Jersey* (New Brunswick: TransAction Books, 1972).

13. See Alvin Mauer, "The Suburbs Also Are Feeling the Pinch—At a Different Level," *New York Times*, December 5, 1976, p. E-5.

CHAPTER FIFTEEN

1. Mel Scott, *American City Planning Since 1890*, Berkeley: University of California Press, 1971, p. 227.

2. Scott, p. 227.

3. For further details and specific data see H.J. Bryce, "Statement Before the House Subcommittee on Banking, Currency and Housing," 94th Congress, 2nd Session. September 27-October 1, 1976. *Rebirth of The American City/Part 2*, pp. 847-48.

4. Aaron Wildavsky, "If Planning Is Everything, Maybe It's Nothing," *Policy Sciences*, Vol. 4, June 1973, pp. 127-154.

5. U.S. Congress. Senate Committee On Agriculture and Forestry. *Agriculture, Rural Development, and the Use of Land*, "A Primer on Planning: Planning: Some Questions, Answers and Issues," by Dorn C. McGrath, Jr., U.S. Government Printing Office, Washington, D.C., 1974, p. 1.

CHAPTER SIXTEEN

1. Isard, Walter, *et al.*, *Methods of Regional Analysis, An Introduction to Regional Science*, New York: John Wiley and Sons, 1960, pp. 270-71.

2. These are the industries included: Agriculture, Forestry, Mining, Construction, Furniture, Primary Metals, Fabricated Metals, Machinery, Electrical Machinery, Motor Vehicles, Transportation Equipment, Other Durables, Food and Kindreds, Textiles, Apparel, Printing, Chemical, Other Nondurables, Railroad, Trucking, Other Transportation, Communications, Utilities, Wholesale Trade, Food Dairy, Eating, Other Retail, Finance, Business, Repair, Private Household, Personal Services, Entertainment, Education Government, Education Private, Welfare, Hospitals, Other Professional, and Public Administration.

3. George Sternlieb and James W. Hughes, 'The New Economic Geography of America," New Brunswick, N.J.: Rutgers University, Center for Urban Policy Research, January 1977.

4. Glenn Fuguitt and Calvin Beale, "Population Change in Non-Metropolitan Cities and Towns," Agricultural Economics Report no. 323, Economic Research Service, U.S. Department of Agriculture, February 1976.

EPILOGUE FOUR

1. Okun and Richardson's definition of a stagnant region is applicable here: "one in which there occurs, over time, relatively little or no increase in per capita income; a growing region, correspondingly, is one in which there is sustained secular improvement in per capita income." Bernard Okun and Richard W. Richardson, "Regional Income Inequality and Internal Population

Migration," in John Friedman and William Alonso (eds.), *Regional Development and Planning*, Cambridge, Mass.: MIT Press, 1965, p. 307.

2. Frederick B. Glantz, *The Intermetropolitan Migration of the Poor: An Empirical Analysis*, Working Paper 73-1, Boston: Federal Reserve Bank, 1973; and Robert Premus, "The Migration Decisions of the Underprivileged: An Application of the Friedman-Savage Hypothesis," paper presented at the Southern Economic Association Conference, Atlanta, November 1976.

3. Robert Reischauer, "The Federal Government's Role in Relieving Cities of the Fiscal Burdens of Concentrations of Low-Income Persons," *National Tax Journal*, September 1976, pp. 300-301.

4. For an extended discussion of the role of the city in development, see Eric E. Lampard, "The History of Cities in Economically Advanced Areas," in Friedman and Alonso (eds.), *Regional Development and Planning*, Cambridge, Mass.: MIT Press, 1965, pp. 321-342.

EPILOGUE NINE

1. Stanley H. Masters, *Black-White Income Differentials: Empirical Studies and Policy Implications,* Institute for Research on Poverty Monograph Series, New York: Academic Press, 1975.

Index

Abandonment rates, 177, 328, 331
Abzug bill, 260
Adams, Charles, 206
Administrative effectiveness, 68, 237-238, 252
Advisory Commission on Intergovernmental Relations, 64-65, 67
Advisory Committee on National Growth Policy Processes, 70
Affirmative action laws, 272
Age structure, 180, 290-291; in black suburbs, 87, 89, 91; and growth industries, 106; of households, 270-271
Agricultural Act of 1970, 55
Agriculture, 336, 344, 347, 356
Aid for Families with Dependent Children, 237
Alaska, 176, 357
Albany, N.Y., 121
Alcoa, 278
Alexandria, Va., 177
"All-Negro Towns," 74. See also Blacks, suburban
Allocative systems, 232, 245, 246, 248, 249-250
Alonso, W., 161, 162, 273, 296
Altadena, Calif., 80
Amenities, 219-222
American City Planning Since 1890 (Scott), 315
American Institute of Planners, 318
"America's Mayors and Councilmen," 316

Anderson, S.C., 30
Annexation, 115, 117, 137, 145, 168, 169, 175-176, 178-179, 185, 263, 330; and city growth, 19-24; and racial balance, 179, 390 n.12, 391 n.13
Anniston, Ala., 30
Antirecessionary programs, 230, 231
Appalachian Regional Commission, 356
Appalachian Regional Development Act of 1965, 52, 54, 56
Area Re-Development Administration, 53
Arizona, 96, 169
Arkansas, 198
Arlington, Va., 177
Aronson, J. Richard, 276
Arthur D. Little, Inc., 279
Aspen, Colo., 336
Astin, Alexander W., 272
Atlanta, 168, 169, 177, 303
Auld, D., 166
Austin, 173, 390 n.2
Australia, 165
Automobile industry, 97, 103, 112, 120
Automobile transportation, 108, 116, 177, 263, 275, 280, 281

Babcock, R., 165
Bahl, R.W., 156
Balanced Growth and Economic Planning Act, 69

397

398 Index

Baltimore, 262, 279, 373
Baton Rouge, 390 n.2
Bean, F.D., 156
Bedroom communities, 114, 115, 304
Bell, Daniel, 287
Berenson v. *Town of New Castle*, 64
Berry, Brian J.L., 77, 82, 156, 158
Bethlehem, Pa., 258
Birmingham, Ala., 168, 169, 175
Birth rate, 270, 271, 283, 290, 291
Blacks, 295, 352; and annexation, 179, 390 n.12, 391 n.13; housing and household characteristics, 306-311; occupational structure, 88-89; and population growth, 37-41; suburban, 73-92, 301-312; in Washington, D.C., 339, 340, 341; and whites compared, 82, 84, 92, 394 n.11
Bloomfield, N.J., 311
Boise, Idaho, 96
Bond programs, 60, 183, 332, 365-368
Boom towns, 176
Borrowing costs, 365-368
Borukhov, E., 164
Boston, 97-98, 259, 302n, 303, 373
Bowie, Md., 30
Bradford, D., 162, 276
Bridgeport, Conn., 174
Bronzeville (Chicago), 86
Brookings Institution, 249, 254
Brooklyn, Ill., 90-91
Buffalo, N.Y., 257, 373
Business Week, 71
Busing, 177, 235

California, 62, 169, 209, 315, 340
Camden, N.J., 169, 177, 183, 185
Cape Kennedy Space Center, 176
Capital, 60, 101, 104, 105, 111, 178, 180, 182, 206, 365; and growth transition theories, 296, 297, 298
Careerism, 286
Carson, Calif., 87
Carter, Jimmy, 7, 371
Categorical aid, 206, 208, 210
Cayton, Horace R., 86
CDBG. *See* Community Development Block Grants
Cedar Rapids, Iowa, 178
Ceiling provisions, 248
Central Administration Office and Auxiliary Employment, 127-128, 149
Central Business District, 174, 183, 316, 326; "economic city," 302-303

Century City (West Los Angeles), 278
Century Fox Corporation, 278
CETA. *See* Comprehensive Employment and Training Act
Charleston, S.C., 168, 182
Chester, Pa., 174, 183
Chicago, 112, 159, 373; black suburbs, 75, 80, 82, 86; Housing Authority, 62-63
Chinitz, B., 156
Christaller, W., 156
Cincinnati, 373
Cities, age of, 41, 169, 185
Cities, declining, 331-332; causes of, 176-177; and CDBG, 256-258; economic development policy of, 373-375; fiscal characteristics of, 169-172, 351-352; and planning, 320-330
Cities, growing: causes of, 175-177; fiscal response of, 179-181
Cities, neediest, 256-258
City boundaries, 117, 120, 176, 185, 262-263. *See also* Annexation
City of Hartford v. *Hills*, 63
City size, 14-16; benefits of, 280-281; defined, 113-116, 163, 164; and diversification/specialization, 155-158, 333-334; and efficiency, 158-161, 166, 334, 336; and fiscal characteristics, 169, 169-172; and innovation, 102-104; and municipal dependency, 194-196; as restraint on population growth, 107-111, 168-169; social and private costs of, 158-159, 161-166
Civil Rights Act of 1964, 63
Clark, C., 155-156, 158
Clemente, F., 156, 158
Cleveland, 257, 262, 303, 373; black suburbs, 75, 81-82, 87, 304
Cleveland Heights, Ohio, 304
Coastal Zone Management Act, 180
Collective bargaining, 236-237
Colorado, 58-59, 96
Colorado Springs, Colo., 96, 178
Columbus, Ga., 175, 178
Communications, 176, 269, 284, 298-299, 334, 348
Communities, types of, 285-287
Community Development Block Grants, 56, 196, 228, 230, 246-258 *passim*, 312, 330
Community Development Capability Study, 60
Commutation, 114, 168, 177, 268, 269, 274, 277, 279-280

Compensatory aid, 361-363
Competitiveness, intercity, 361
Comprehensive Employment and Training Act, 4, 196, 230
Compton, Calif., 304, 328
Conference of Mayors, 7, 61, 316
Congestion, 156, 160, 165-165, 269
Congressional Research Service, 68
Congressional Rural Caucus, 68
Connecticut, 60
Connolly, Harold X., 77, 78, 89
Consolidation, city-county, 108-109
Constitutional issues, 61-64
Construction Industry Association of Sonoma County v. *City of Petaluma*, 62
Consumer satisfaction, 345, 394 n.11
Consumption spending patterns, 97, 98
Cook, G., 166
Cosmopolitanism, 287
Cost accounting, 362
Cost of living, 161, 169, 280
Costs: and city size, 158-159, 161-166, 280; and density, 172-175
Council of State Governments, 58
Countercyclical aid, 230, 231
Counties, 32-37; financial aid to, 189, 190-194 *passim*, 250; and welfare costs, 234, 237, 259, 260
Courts, 61-64, 276-277
Creamer, Daniel B., 114
Credit market, 68, 182, 365
Crime, 91-92, 106, 108, 183-184, 356
Crowley, R.W., 156, 158
Cultural pluralism, 285
Cyprus, Calif., 30

Dacey, M.F., 156
Daley City, Calif., 91
Dallas, 303
Danbury, Conn., 336
Davidson County, Tenn., 109
Daytime/nighttime cities, 114, 115, 304
Dayton, Ohio, 169, 390 n.2
De-annexation, 178
Dearborn Heights, Mich., 304n
Death rate, 290
Debt services, 169, 175, 178, 181, 332, 352
Decentralization, 157, 247, 269, 362
Decline, indicators of, 43-47
Demobilization, 116-117
Demographic variables, 217, 227, 228; and locational decision, 268, 270-273; metropolitan/nonmetropolitan, 291-295; national, 290-291; and public service demands, 233-235
Density, 172-175, 176, 185, 299
Denver, 97n
Dependency rates, state and local, 190-194
Depressed areas legislation, 52
Des Moines, 174
Detroit, 165-166, 262, 303, 373; automobile industry, 97, 103, 112; black suburbs, 75, 80, 82, 83
Developers, 180
Development economics, 343-346
Developmental processes, 286-287
Diffusion mechanism, 288-289
Disamenities, 156, 160, 164; model, 297-298, 299
Disamenity premium, 297-298
Discretionary funds, 249, 256
Diseconomies, 107, 109, 111, 334
Disinvestment, 303, 311, 312
Disneyworld, 176
Distributional effects, 232
Distributive equity, 245, 246, 248
Diversification, 58, 102-104, 155-158, 289, 297, 333-336
Divorce rates, 291
Domestic service, 78, 89, 344
Downtown development, 316, 326
Drake, St. Clair, 86
Due process, 61
Duncan, O.D., 156, 163

East Chicago Heights, Ill., 84
East Cleveland, Ohio, 91, 304
East Orange, N.J., 91, 310-311
East Palo Alto, Calif., 88, 89
East St. Louis, Ill., 169, 185, 258
East Tennessee Development District, 378
Eastlake v. *Forest City Enterprises, Inc.*, 63
"Economic city," 302-303
Economic development, 59, 66, 158, 166, 179, 180, 182, 288-289, 343-346; anti-recessionary programs, 230, 231; economic stabilization, 354-357; local policy, 373-375; national policy, 69-70, 332; and planning, 319, 320, 324, 326; and three sector system, 216-223
Economic security, 86-89
EDA, 356
Educational attainment, 87, 89, 90, 309
Efficiency model, 296-297, 298

Eligibility standards, 248, 250, 258
Elizabeth, N.J., 311
Elmira, N.Y., 35
Eminent domain, 62
Employment, 98; and economic development, 343-346; private sector, 113-151, public sector, 169, 174-175, 181, 184, 236, 344, 345
Employment data, 127-128, 144
Employment programs, 68, 224, 230
Energy, 59, 98, 236, 274, 275, 279
Entitlement grants, 248, 249, 250
Environmental planning, 319, 322
Environmental quality, 59, 107-109, 180, 184
Equal opportunity, 245
Equal protection, 62, 63
Equalization provisions, 209, 243, 247, 356-357
Equity, concepts of, 245-246
Estonia, 106n
Euclid v. *Ambler Real Estate Co.*, 276
Europe, 66, 361, 371, 372
Exclusionary zoning, 37, 62-64, 85-86, 107, 165, 276-277
Expenditure obligations, 231
Externalities, 160, 161, 164-166, 289, 297, 298
Externalities zoning, 165
Exurbia, 304

Fair employment practice, 272
Fajans, M., 161
Familism, 286
Family size, 90-91, 270, 279, 308-309
Farley, Reynolds, 77
Federal aid, 180, 181, 189-211, 243, 312, 352, 360, 361; grants-in-aid, 228-232; targeting vs. spreading, 245-263
Federal urban policy, 7, 51-57; and economic development, 69-70, 319, 320, 324, 326; fiscal impact of, 206-211; and growth transition models, 297-298; and market, 360-363; and politics of planning, 369-372; and population growth, 64-71; and public sector, 213-243; and state-local government structure, 262-263
Federalism, fiscal, 190, 209-211, 260, 263
Fels, Margaret F., 279
Fertility, 90-91
FHA, 356, 361
Filtering-down strategies, 288-289, 375

Final investor demand, 367
Fire protection, 174, 180, 362
Firestine, R., 156
Fiscal equity, 68
Fiscal opportunity schedules, 224n
Fiscal zoning, 165
Floor provisions, 248
Florence-Graham, Calif., 88
Florida, 59, 169, 198, 295, 370
Flotation, costs of, 366
Food stamps, 246
Ford administration, 254
Formula grants, 229-230, 247-258, 357
Fort Wayne, Ind., 178
Fort Worth, Tex., 168
Fortune, 270
Fountain Valley, Calif., 30
Freeport, N.Y., 89
Friedman, John, 287
Fringe communities, 304

Gabler, L.R., 162
Ganz, Alexander, 138
Garden Cities, 371
Garn, Harvey, 296
Garrison, W., 156, 158
Gary, Ind., 169
Georgia, 177
Ghettos, 77, 82, 107, 374-375
Glenardon, Md., 84, 87, 88
Governors' Conference, 64
Grants-in-aid, 228-232, 247, 261-262, 356-357, 377
"Great Society," 370
Greenbelt Towns, 53
Greer, Scott, 284
Grimm, Pamela R., 378
Growth management, 107, 166, 185; legal issues, 61-64
Growth rates, 13-27, 96-99, 104-107, 111, 320-322
Growth transition theories, 295-298
GRS. *See* Revenue sharing

Hamilton, B., 165
Harlington, Tex., 30
Harrisburg, Pa., 174
Harrison, Bennett, 114, 148
Hartford, Conn., 175, 181, 390 n.2
Harvey, Ill., 91
Hawaii, 370
Health programs, 69, 209, 237, 361-362
Heartland-hinterland patterns, 288
Heating and cooling costs, 274, 275, 279

Hierarchical diffusion, 288-289
"High-rise cities," 303
Highland Park, Mich., 47, 328
Highways, 177, 217, 225, 269, 295, 316, 356, 361
Hills v. *Gautreaux*, 62
Hirsch, W., 163
Hittman Associates, 279
Hoboken, N.J., 30, 336
Hoch, I., 159-160, 161, 164, 280
Hollydale, Ohio, 84, 87, 88
Hoover, E., 156
Household characteristics, 270-271, 291, 308-309
Housing, 41, 104-105, 106, 172, 176, 352; black suburbs, 82, 83-86, 309-311; codes, 355; costs, 161, 169, 180, 306-308; and demographic change, 227, 228; discrimination, 62-63; and planning, 319-330 *passim*, 336; in "poor city," 303-304; rehabilitation, 243, 304; subsidies, 217, 225, 226; single/multiple unit, 275, 278, 279
Housing Act of 1954, 316
Housing-age formula, 252-253, 255, 258
Housing and Community Development Act of 1974, 56
Housing and New Community Development Act of 1970, 55
Howard, Ebenezer, 371
HUD. *See* United States Department of Housing and Urban Development
Hughes, James W., 336
Human resources planning, 322

Illinois, 96, 156, 209
Immigrants, overseas, 285, 292
Import substitution growth, 101-102
In-migration, 99-102, 106
Income, family, 272-273, 274, 341
Income, per capita, 41-43, 169, 171, 174, 175, 176, 179, 183, 184, 257; black suburbs, 81, 87, 89, 309; and efficiency model, 296-297; and growth industries, 97, 98, 101, 111
Income elasticity of demand, 97-98
Income maintenance programs, 222, 225, 226, 227, 231, 235, 260
Income tax, 168
Incubator industries, 160
Indexes of hardship and need, 206, 233-234, 252-258, 259
Indianapolis, 109n
Industrial filtering, 109-111, 288-289, 290
Industrial urbanization/counter-urbanization, 295-296

Industries, labor intensive, 160
Industries, market oriented, 157
Industry: and federal policy, 216, 217, 225, 227; growth, 96-99; incentives, 66, 182; location, 228, 231, 233, 238, 240, 268, 269-270, 274, 277; manufacturing and retailing employment, 113-151
Industry mix, 102-104, 155-158, 289, 297
Information systems, 299, 302
Infrastructure, 176, 178, 179, 180, 243, 252
Inglewood, Calif., 80
Innovation, 102-104, 287, 289
Institutional environment, 268, 302
Interest rates, 366
Irvington, N.J., 311
Isard, Walter, 335

Jamestown, N.Y., 336
Janss Corporation, 278
Jersey City, N.J., 173, 181
Job accessibility, 304, 394 n.8
Job banks, 360
Johnstown, Pa., 32

Kain, John F., 114, 115, 121, 128, 148
Kansas Development Credit Corporation, 60
Kelejian, Harry, 276
Kenner, La., 43
Keyes, Dale, 279
Keynesian economic theory, 99, 101
Kitsap County, Wash., 176
Kristol, Irving, 348

Labor force, 269, 287, 355; and growth transition theories, 296-298; and industrial filtering, 109-111, 288-289; productivity, 106, 159, 289, 296-298; women, 89, 271-272
Labor laws, 236, 355
Labor unions, 236, 297
Lancaster, Pa., 177, 183
Land dedication requirements, 180
Land prices, 105, 180, 269, 274
Land use planning, 101, 107, 165, 179, 180, 319-330 *passim*
Las Vegas, 175
Law enforcement, 106, 316
Law Enforcement Assistance Administration, 4
Levy, Frank, 245
Lichtenberg, R., 160

402 Index

Life cycle, 286
Life styles, 286, 287
Lillibridge, R.M., 156
Loans, 60, 105, 183
Local governments, 60, 61, 209, 254;
  dependency rates, 190-194 *passim*;
  service responsibilities, 67-68, 237-237; and state governments, 62-64, 262-263
Localism, 287, 299
Locational decision: 66, 108, 174, 214, 228, 238, 240, 268, 274, 332, 374; externalities, 164, 165, 166
Locational incentives, 214, 225-227, 231, 235, 238, 242-243
Los Angeles, 103, 270, 278; black suburbs, 75, 80, 81, 82, 83, 304, 305
Lösch, A., 156
Louisville, 169, 174

McGrath, Dorn C., Jr., 318
McKenzie, Roderick, 114, 116, 121, 127-138
Macon, Ga., 178
Maine, 295
Malt, R., 162
Manhattan, 177
Manpower training, 68, 224, 230
Marion County, Ind., 109n
Market adjustments, 360
Market equity, 245, 246
Market neutrality, 360-361
Market orientation, 157
Market supply and demand: and federal policy, 22
Markets, private, 360-361
Markham, Ill., 89
Marriage rates, 271, 291
Maryland, 180, 198, 339, 340, 341
Mass transit, 176-177
Massachusetts, 59, 168, 208, 209, 259, 357
Maywood, Ill., 91
Media, 8-9
Medicaid programs, 209, 237
Melbourne, Fla., 176
Meltsner, Arnold J., 245
Mentor, Ohio, 30
Mera, K., 158, 163
Metropolitan area authorities, 238
Metropolitan Community, The (McKenzie and Smith), 114
Metropolitan differentiation into separate "cities," 301-304, Chap. 14 n.1
Metropolitan/nonmetropolitan growth transition, 291-295; and planning, 319-320, 322, 330; theories of, 295-298
Miami, 75, 80, 83, 176, 178
Michigan, 209
Middle class, 183, 285. *See also* Out-migration
Migration, 276, 311, 356; Washington, D.C., 339-341. *See also* In-migration; Out-migration
Migration allowances, 67, 360
Military facilities, 76, 180
Milwaukee, 373
Mills, E., 156, 157, 158, 164, 165
Minimum wage, 236n
Mining and extraction industries, 176, 336
Minneapolis, 97n, 169, 175, 182-183, 303, 374
Minorities, 179, 257, 277. *See also* Blacks
Mississippi River delta area, 295
Missouri, 58
Mobility, 39, 276, 284-285, 286, 287, 297
Model Cities, 56, 249
Montana, 176
Montclair, N.J., 311
Montgomery County, Md., 341
Morrison, Peter, 67
Mortgages, 105, 356, 361
Motor freight, 157
Mount Laurel, N.J., 62, 64, 277
Multiplier effects, 99-102, 289
Municipal dependency, 189-211
Munson, Michael J., 279
Muth, Richard, 273

Nashua, N.H., 168
Nashville, 108-109, 174
Nathan, Richard P., 206
National Journal, 57
National League of Cities, 4, 61, 316
National League of Cities v. *Usery*, 236
Nation's Cities, 316
Neenan, W., 165-166
Neighborhoods, 286
Neutze, G.M., 164, 165
Nevada, 96
New Castle, N.Y., 64
New Castle, Pa., 47
New Hampshire, 168
New Jersey, 62, 276, 277, 310-311
New Orleans, 374
New Rochelle, N.Y., 278, 304
New York City, 7, 8, 160, 303, 374; bankruptcy, 367, 371; black sub-

urbs, 75, 80, 82, 305; mass transit, 176-177; welfare program, 237, 260
New York State, 64, 168, 208, 209, 276, 277, 340, 341, 357
Newark, N.J., 169, 173, 174, 177, 181, 182, 183, 185, 262, 390 n.2; black suburbs, 75, 311
Newport, R.I., 30-32
Newton, Mass., 304n
Nixon, Richard, 246, 370, 371
North Carolina, 295, 340
North Chicago, Ill., 43
Northern Los Angeles County, Calif., 278

Oakland, Calif., 169, 175, 374
Oates, W., 162
O'Brien, Thomas, 138
Office buildings, 270, 302-303
Offshore energy development, 180
Ohio, 209
Okun, Bernard, Epi.4 n.1
Opportunity equity, 245, 246
Oregon, 60
Orlando, Fla., 176, 390 n.2
Out-migration, 82, 177, 214, 225, 226, 227, 234, 235, 242, 276, 277, 331, 351

Packard, Vance, 284
Paraskevopoulos, C., 156, 158
Pasadena, Calif., 78, 80, 304
"Pass-through" financial aid, 192n, 228-229, 237
Pendleton, William W., 77
Pennsylvania, 64, 177, 209, 276, 277, 340, 341
Personal security, 89-92, 183-184, 269, 278
Petaluma, Calif., 52, 62, 276
Peterson, George E., 257
Pettigrew, Thomas A., 83, 84
Phares, D., 156
Philadelphia, 75, 262, 305, 374
Phoenix, 105
Piedmont area, 106n, 295
Pittsburgh, 257, 274, 374
Plainfield, N.J., 311
Planning, 315-330, 336, 370, 377-379; proposed legislation, 69-71
Planning questionnaire, 318-330
Police power, 61, 62
Police protection, 169, 174, 362
Political accountability, 68, 369-372
Political fragmentation, 108
Political participation, 179, 310

Pollution, 98, 108, 160, 164
Polynucleated metropolis, 267-268, 277-281, 299, 369-372
Pomona, Calif., 91, 304
Pontiac, Mich., 90-91, 92
"Poor city," 303-304
Population decline: metropolitan, 291-295, 373-374; national, 290-291
Population growth changes, 58-59, 95-96; and CDBG, 256-258; and city size, 107-111, 168-169; and manufacturing/retailing employment, 117-131, 144-151 *passim*; regional, 131-14, 167-168; and World War II, 115-117
Population redistribution, 158, 165
Post-industrial society, 95, 114, 287, 348
Poughkeepsie, N.Y., 43
Poverty, 107; in black suburbs, 83, 87, 88; and federal aid, 249, 259, 362; and in-migration, 227, 235; and planning, 322, 330; and welfare programs, 225, 226
Poverty index, 252, 253, 255, 257
Predictions and projections: industry, 102-103, 144, 150; population, 24-27
President's Report on National Growth and Development, 51, 58, 60-61
Pricing, 98, 164, 355
Prince Georges County, Md., 177, 341
Production/non-production worker census data, 127-128, 138, 149
Productivity, 67, 98, 344, 356; and city size, 158-161, 166, 334, 336; of labor, 106, 159, 289, 296-298; of public sector, 161, 162, 163-164; and technology, 176, 269, 345
Professional jobs, 105, 303
Project grants, 229-230, 247, 249, 250
Property taxes, 165, 178, 180-181, 182, 206, 312, 355; and fiscal advantage, 275-276
Property values, 226, 257, 306-308
Providence, R.I., 174, 175
Public facilities, 69, 176, 178, 179, 180, 217, 233, 243, 252, 362
Public service sector, 106, 176, 178, 180, 182, 276, 302, 303, 352; and city size, 161-164, 169, 180; costs, 161, 162, 163-164, 169, 172, 173, 174, 175, 184, 235-237, 361-362; curtailment, 331-332; demand, 172, 227, 233-235, 240, 281; employment, 169, 174-175, 181, 184, 236, 344, 345; and federal aid poli-

Public service sector (cont.)
  cy, 228-233 *passim*; local/state roles and responsibilities, 237-238, 252; productivity, 161, 162, 163-164; spillover of public goods, 165-166; and tax base, 224-228
Public Works and Economic Development Act of 1965, 54, 56
Public Works Assistance Act, 4
Puryear, D., 156, 158, 158, 165

Quante, Wolfgang, 270

Rabinovitz, Francine F., 81
Racial balance and annexation, 179, 390, n.12, 391 n.13
Racial discrimination and segregation, 62-63, 83, 303, 304, 375
Railroads, 157
Ramapo, N.Y., 52, 107
Ramsey, D., 166
Reading, Pa., 177
Recession, 230, 231
Recreational facilities, 316, 319, 336
Red tape, 378-379
Redevelopment, 176, 183, 184, 249, 302
"Redlining," 105
Regional Action Planning Commissions, 56
Regional Development Act of 1975, 56, 356
Regionalization, 206-208
Regions, 19, 32, 70, 71, 83, 96, 105, 112, 116, 117, 167-168, 185, 236, 259, 281, 304n, Epi.4 n.1; and annexation, 21-24, 263; and city size, 113, 115, 137; and diversification, 333-336; and federal aid policy, 57, 230, 249-250, 256, 262, 263, 357; and four stages of national development, 347, 348; and income per capita, 169, 288; and locational incentives, 214, 225-226; and manufacturing and retailing employment, 117-131 *passim*, 144-151 *passim*, 344; and planning, 228, 238, 243, 319, 324, 333; and population changes, 131-144, 293, 294-295; and productivity, 160, 289; and urban growth theory, 105, 112; and urban need, 252, 253, 256; and welfare programs, 243, 259
Regulatory policies, 235-236; 243
Reischauer, Robert, 352
Relocation assistance, 67, 360
Rents, 172
Research and development, 103, 289, 304
Resettlement Administration, 53
Residential location decision models, 273-274
Residential sector, 216, 225, 227, 228, 231, 238, 240, 268
Residential settlement patterns, 270-277, 279-280
Restoration, 182
Retailing system, 116, 127, 345
Retirement cities, 176
Revenue sharing, 3, 8, 56, 180, 206, 208, 233, 246, 312, 361, 377; and CDBG, 247, 248, 254, 255, 256; and grants-in-aid, 228, 229, 230; and municipal dependency, 194-196
Revenue subsidies, 232-233
Rhode Island, 59
Richardson, Richard W., Epi.4 n.1
Richmond, Calif., 88
Richmond, Va., 177, 178, 391 n.13
Riew, J., 163
Roberts, James S., 280
Rochester, N.Y., 106n, 181
Rural areas, 68-69, 107, 110, 176, 293; and black suburbs, 74, 78, 84; and federal aid, 248, 249; out-migration, 292, 295
Rural Development Act of 1972, 54-55

St. Louis, 257, 262-263, 303, 374; black suburbs, 75, 80, 82, 83
St. Paul, 169, 176, 303, 374
St. Petersburg, Fla., 176, 178
Sales tax, 181, 331, 355
Salt Lake City, 97n
San Francisco, 75, 138, 303, 374
San Jose, Calif., 173, 174, 175
Savannah, Ga., 168, 175, 177, 182
Scale economies, 107, 108, 109, 111, 157, 161-164, 166, 269, 277, 281, 296-297
Schettler, Clarence, 156
Schnore, Leo F., 77, 156
School desegregation, 177, 178-179, 225, 235, 356
School districts, 178-179, 234, 237
School taxes, 165
Schools, 180, 183-184, 234, 237-238
Schwartz, Eli, 276
Scott, Mel, 315
Scranton, Pa., 177
Seattle, 374

Servan-Schreiber, J.J., 299
Service industries, 98, 155-156, 157, 160, 184, 269, 277, 302, 303
Settlement patterns, 267-268, 271, 277, 279, 296, 299
Sewer facilities, 69, 180, 217, 233, 243, 362
Shaker Heights, Ohio, 87, 91
Shannon, John, 259-260, 262
Shapiro, Harvey, 162
Shopping centers, 304
Silver Spring, Md., 87, 91
Size of place preference, 92
Smith, Calvin, 114
Smith, David, 302n
Snohomish County, Wash., 156
Social costs, 280, 297, 331, 345
Social disorganization, 86, 106
Social environment, 284-285
Social space, 82, 84
Society, national, 283-387
Socioeconomic factors, 29-47, 285
Somerville, Mass., 174
South, the, 39, 47, 74, 294, 320, 330
South Carolina, 340
Southern Burlington County NAACP v. Township of Mount Laurel, 62
Southern Conference of Black Mayors, 4, 9
Space, horizontal/vertical, 269
Specialization, 155-158
Speculators, 105
Stafford, H.A., Jr., 156
State aid, 180, 181, 189-211 *passim*, 312
State capitals, 97
States, 57-61, 211, 236n, 263, 370; constitutional provisions, 62-64; and economic development, 354, 355-356; and federal grants, 228-229; and fiscal dependency, 190-194, 196-206 *passim*; and local governments, 60, 61, 70-71, 262-263; and schools, 237-238; and social services, 209, 237-238, 259-260
Sternlieb, George, 336
Sturgis, R.B., 156, 158
Subsidies, 360-361
Suburbs, 115, 116, 127, 138, 151, 174, 274, 394 n.11; black, 73-92, 302-312; demographic trends, 305-312; federal aid, 217, 238, 248, 249, 250, 256, 259; highways, 177, 225; housing, 217, 225-226, 274, 306-308, 309-311; industries, 269-270, 277; migration, 292, 299-300, 311; polynucleated metropolis, 267-268, 277; property taxes, 275-276, 312; service demand, 165-166, 304, 305, 311
Subways, 176-177
Suitland, Md., 87
Sundquist, James, 51-52, 158
Supplemental Security Income Program, 237
Suttles, Gerald, 285
Sveikauskas, L., 159, 165
Sydney, Australia, 165
Syracuse, N.Y., 181

Taeuber, Irene, 74
Takoma Park, Md., 87, 89, 91
Tax base sharing, 238
Tax expenditures, 232-233
Tax incentives and subsidies, 66, 182, 184, 217, 232-233, 237-238
Tax increment financing, 182-183
Tax rates, ad valorem, 275-276
Tax systems, 165, 168, 174, 179, 180-181, 182, 224-28, 240, 281, 326, 331, 352; and job opportunities, 374-375; and suburbs, 305, 311
Taylor, J., 156
Technology, 265, 296, 297, 345; communication, 269, 284, 298-299; transportation, 176-177, 269, 284, 298
Tennessee Valley Authority, 53
Texas, 178, 198, 263, 357
Textiles industry, 97, 336
Thompson, Warren, 121, 156
Thompson, Wilbur, 289
Tiebout, C., 163, 165
Time-space convergence vs. centrality, 298-300
Tisdale, Hope, 295
Titusville, Fla., 30
Tolley, G., 160, 161, 164
Township of Williston v. Chesterdale Farms, Inc., 64
Townships, 189-194 *passim*
Transfer payments, 224, 226-227, 246, 258-262, 331
Transportation, 68, 121, 127, 231, 243, 281, 372; and city size, 107, 108, 164, 176, 334; and decentralization, 157, 334, 348; and energy, 274, 275, 279-280, 281; and locational decision, 268, 269, 270, 273-275, 279-280; technology, 176-177, 269, 284, 298. *See also* Congestion; Highways
Trenton, N.J., 279

Trickle-down process, 288-289, 375
Trident submarine site, 176, 391 n.15
Trolley cars, 127
Trucking, 157
Tucson, Ariz., 96, 173
Tulsa, Okla., 159

Uhlman, Wes, 208
Ullman, E.L., 156
Underwriters, 366
Unemployment and price changes, 355
United States: four stages of national development, 347-349; national society, 283-287; population decline, 290-291
United States Bureau of Labor Statistics, 279, 379
United States Census Bureau data, 378-379
United States Congress, 64, 65-66, 68, 254, 255, 371
United States Constitution, 61, 63
United States Department of Housing and Urban Development, 62-63, 249, 258n
United States Office of Management and Budget, 317-318
United States Supreme Court, 62-64, 179, 236, 276
Universities, 43, 103, 278, 289
University City, Mo., 43, 89
University of California at Los Angeles, 278
University of Wisconsin Institute for Research on Poverty, 375
Upper Great Lakes area, 294-295
Urban renewal, 176, 183, 184, 249, 302
Urban Development Action Grants, 258n
Urban Development Bank, 262
Urban growth theory, 95-112
Urban-regional hierarchy, 287-290
Urban sprawl, 369-372
Utah, 96
Utica, N.Y., 175

Vacancy rates, 82, 84, 177, 328
Vanneman, Reeve D., 83
Varley, D.W., 156
Vermont, 59, 319
Vernon, R., 156
Veterans' housing program, 356
Vietnam, 138, 149-150
Village of Arlington Heights v. *Metropolitan Housing Development Corp.*, 63

Virginia, 178, 339, 340, 341
Visalia, Calif., 30
Voting power, 179

Wages; and city size, 159, 160, 161, 280; and growth transition models, 296-298; and productivity, 159, 160; and public employees, 169, 174-175, 181, 184, 236, 391 n.17, 344
Walzer, N., 163
Warrensville Heights, Ohio, 87, 89
Warth v. *Seldin*, 63
Washington, D.C., 121, 177, 279, 280; black suburbs, 75, 81, 82, 83, 87, 305; in-migration, 339-341
Washington University, 43
Waste disposal, 316
Water facilities, 69, 180, 217, 233, 243, 362
Water transport, 157
Weaver, Robert C., 81
Webber, Melvin, 298
Webster Groves, Mo., 35
Welfare programs, 209, 225, 226, 227, 351-352; and federal aid, 231, 243, 259, 260-262; local and state, 234, 237, 259-260; reforms, 235, 260-262; and regions, 243, 259
Wellston, Mo., 88
West Germany, 361
West Los Angeles, Calif., 278
Westlake Village (Northern Los Angeles County), 278
Westwood Village (Los Angeles), 278
White collar jobs, 302, 303
White House Conference on balanced national growth, 371
Whites: and blacks compared, 82, 84, 92, 394 n.11. *See also* Middle class; Out-migration
Wildavsky, Aaron, 245
Williamsport, Pa., 47
Willowbrook, Calif., 88
Wisconsin, 209
Wollongong, Australia, 165
Women, 89, 271-272, 291
Woodbury, Coleman, 115
Woodson, Carter, 74
World War I, 116, 120
World War II, 115-117, 120-121, 127, 150, 151
Wyandanch, N.Y., 84, 88
Wyoming, 176

Yonkers, 169, 173, 304
York, Pa., 33-35

Zero population growth, 283, 290-291, 295, 299
Zones of emergence, 311

Zoning, 165, 180, 355. *See also* Exclusionary zoning; Land use planning

JOINT CENTER FOR POLITICAL STUDIES

PRESIDENT	Eddie N. Williams
VICE PRESIDENT	Eleanor Farrar
DIRECTOR OF RESEARCH	Adam Herbert
DIRECTOR OF ADMINISTRATION	Alfred Lang
DIRECTOR OF DEVELOPMENT	Kathleen Vander Horst
FOCUS EDITOR	Oliver W. Cromwell

Board of Governors

Louis E. Martin, Chairman
Vice President and Editorial Director
Sengstacke Publications, Chicago

Honorable Edward W. Brooke
U.S. Senator from Massachusetts

James E. Cheek, President
Howard University
Washington, D.C.

Kenneth B. Clark, President
Clark, Phipps, Clarks & Harris
New York

Wendell Freeland
Esquire, Pittsburgh

Charles V. Hamilton
Wallace S. Sayre, Professor of Government
Columbia University

Samuel C. Jackson, Esquire
Washington, D.C.

Eddie N. Williams, President
Joint Center for
Political Studies

Public Policy Program
Advisory Board

Andrew Billingsley
Morgan State University
Baltimore, Maryland

Frank de Leeuw
Congressional Budget Office
Washington, D.C.

Harvey A. Garn
The Urban Institute
Washington, D.C.

Charles V. Hamilton
Department of Political Science
Columbia University
New York City, New York

Thomas A. Hart
Westinghouse Electric Corporation
Washington, D.C.

Matthew Holden
Public Service Commission of
 Wisconsin
Madison, Wisconsin

S.M. Miller
Department of Sociology
Boston University
Boston, Massachusetts

Eleanor Holmes Norton
Equal Employment Opportunity
 Commission
Washington, D.C.

Gilbert Steiner
Brookings Institution
Washington, D.C.

Charles Taylor
Wilberforce University
Wilberforce, Ohio

Ronald Walters
Political Science
 Department
Howard University
Washington, D.C.

Phillis A. Wallace
Sloane School of
 Management, MIT
Massachusetts Institute
 of Technology

About the Authors

William Alonso is the Director of the Center for Population Studies at Harvard University. Previously he had been Professor of City and Regional Planning at the University of California-Berkeley and at Harvard University. He is the author of *Location and Land Use*, and co-editor of *Regional Planning*. He has consulted on urban and regional development in this country and abroad.

Vera J. Banks is currently population analyst, Population Studies Group, Economic Research Service, U.S. Department of Agriculture. She is responsible for ongoing analysis of size, composition, growth trends, and other demographic characteristics of the U.S. farm population. She also participates in presentation of current data on the social and economic conditions of rural America.

Stephen M. Barro is senior economist at The Rand Corporation, Washington, D.C. Barro's current activities include directing a study of urban impacts of federal policies, sponsored by the Kettering Foundation. He emphasizes the effects of federal actions on fiscal conditions in the local public sector. Barro is also Deputy Director of Rand's Educational Policy Research Center on School Finance and Governance, where he is investigating the design of federal grant programs and collective bargaining in education.

Calvin L. Beale heads the Population Studies Group of the Economic Research Service in the U.S. Department of Agriculture. He is a demographer and geographer by training. His research has focused on the characteristics and location of rural people, migration between rural and urban areas, studies of ethnic minorities, and regional studies.

Norman Beckman is the director of the Bureau of Intergovernmental Personnel Programs, U.S. Civil Service Commission, which is responsible for strengthening management capabilities of state and local government through the Intergovernmental Personnel Act of 1970. Prior to that, he served six years as Deputy Director and Acting Director of the Congressional Research Service. Beckman is the author of numerous articles in the fields of urban development, public administration, and congressional information needs. He is a member of the editorial board of *Public Administration Review*.

Carolyn Shaw Bell holds the Katharine Coman Chair in Economics at Wellesley College. Chairwoman of the Federal Advisory Council on Unemployment Insurance, she has been particularly concerned with data problems in the fields of labor force and employment policy. Related publications include *The Economics of the Ghetto* (Bobbs-Merrill) and "Middle Class Action and the Ghetto Consumer," *Journal of Economic Issues*, 1973.

Brian J. Berry is Williams Professor of City and Regional Planning and Director of The Laboratory for Computer Graphics and Spatial Analysis in the Graduate School of Design at Harvard University. His most recent Ballinger Books include *The Changing Shape of Metropolitan America* and *The Social Burdens of Environmental Pollution*.

Herrington J. Bryce is Vice-President, Academy for Contemporary Problems, Washington, D.C. Formerly he was Director of Research, Joint Center for Political Studies, a senior research staff member at the Urban Institute, and a Brookings Institution Economic Policy Fellow. He was also on the faculties of Clark University and Massachusetts Institute of Technology. He is the editor of *Urban Governance and Minorities* (Praeger).

Benjamin Chinitz is professor of economics and director of the Center for Social Analysis at the Binghamton campus of the State University of New York. Chinitz was formerly Director of the Appalachian Regional Commission and Deputy Assistant Secretary of Economic Development. He is currently preparing a volume on regional policy in the 1980s.

About the Authors

Phillip L. Clay is an assistant professor of Urban Studies and Planning at the Massachusetts Institute of Technology. His teaching and research interests are housing, neighborhood development, and social policy. In addition to completing a book on black suburbanization, Clay is doing research on upgrading neighborhoods in central cities.

A.J. Cooper is mayor of Prichard, Alabama, and president of the Southern Conference of Black Mayors.

Gloria J. Cousar is special assistant to the director of research at the Joint Center for Political Studies. Her research efforts have been in the field of housing and economic development. She is a member of the Congressional Rural Caucus Advisory Team.

Doris Davis is mayor of Compton, California. Davis holds a Ph.D. in Public Administration.

Paul R. Dommel is on leave from an assistant professorship of political science at Holy Cross College, Worcester, Massachusetts. He is a senior fellow at the Brookings Institution and is a co-author of *Block Grants for Community Development*.

Stephanie B. Fain is a research assistant at the Joint Center for Political Studies.

Glenn V. Fuguitt is professor of rural sociology at the University of Wisconsin-Madison. His research activities have focused on population redistribution as it relates to nonmetropolitan areas of the United States, including the growth and decline of villages and small cities, migration between metropolitan and nonmetropolitan areas, and residential preferences. He has served as editor of the journal *Rural Sociology*, and is currently president of the International Rural Sociology Association.

Werner Z. Hirsch is professor of economics at the University of California, Los Angeles. He has served previously as Director of the Institute of Government and Public Affairs at UCLA, and Director of the Institute of Urban and Regional Studies at Washington University in St. Louis. Hirsch has held consultantships with the National Science Foundation, HUD, The Rand Corporation, Executive Offices of The President, OECD, and the Joint Economic Committee of Congress. He has published a variety of books and articles. Hirsch's efforts have been primarily in the area of Urban and Regional economic analysis and public sector economics.

About the Authors

Howard Lee is the former mayor of Chapel Hill, North Carolina and currently Secretary of the North Carolina Department of Natural and Economic Resources.

Ann C. Macaluso is currently at the Commission on Federal Paperwork. She directs five study groups which advise the executive and congressional branches on intergovernmental coordination, confidentiality and disclosure, the role of Congress, information management, and cost benefit analysis.

Thomas Muller is director of evaluation studies at the Land Use Center of the Urban Institute. His current research concentration is in two areas: examining causes for urban growth as well as decline, and assessing the economic effects of development at the local level from the regional and national perspective. His previous studies included assessment of education finance, economic effects of environmental legislation, and causes for expenditure differentials at the intrametropolitan level.

Selma J. Mushkin is director of the Public Services Laboratory and professor of economics at Georgetown University. She has been elected a member of the board of the National Academy of Public Administration, and of the Institute of Medicine of the National Academy of Sciences. In the past she has served as member of the staff of the Office of Management and Budget; as consultant to the Office of Education and to the Advisory Commission on Intergovernmental Relations; as an economist for the Public Health Service; and as director of the Division of Financial Studies of the Social Security Administration.

Richard P. Nathan is a senior fellow at the Brookings Institution. He is director of the Institution's monitoring study of the Community Development Block Grant program under a contract with the U.S. Department of Housing and Urban Development. The first report of the study was published by HUD in January 1977, entitled *Block Grants for Community Development*. The report was co-authored by Nathan, Paul R. Dommel, Sarah F. Liebschutz, and Milton D. Morris.

Ransford W. Palmer is professor of economics and director of graduate studies in the Department of Economics at Howard University. Palmer served as Chairman of the Economics Department from 1973 to 1976. His fields of teaching and research include public finance and economic development. His publications include *The Jamaican Economy* (Praeger, 1968) and a number of articles in professional journals. He is currently working on a manuscript entitled *The United States Economy and Caribbean Dependence.*

George E. Peterson is director of public finance programs at The Urban Institute. He is the author of the "Finance" chapter in *The Urban Predicament,* William Gorham and Nathan Glazer (eds.) (The Urban Institute, 1976), and author of the forthcoming *Federal Tax Policy and Urban Development* (The Urban Institute, 1977).

John Petersen is an economics consultant to the Municipal Finance Officers' Association. He was formerly director of the Center for Policy Research and Analysis at the National Governors' Conference, and director of public finance for the Securities Industry Association. Petersen's research efforts have been in the areas of public finance and capital markets.

David Puryear is assistant professor in the Department of Economics at Syracuse University and is affiliated with the Metropolitan Studies Program. He is currently project director for the Regional Financing Alternatives for Mass Transit study, sponsored by the Urban Mass Transportation Administration. His research and professional interests are in the fields of urban economics and public finance. Puryear was a consultant to the Joint Center for Political Studies on the National Science Foundation Project, Planning Needs of Small and Medium-Size Cities.

Jessie M. Rattley is vice mayor of Newport News, Virginia, and president of the National Black Caucus of Local Elected Officials.

Harold M. Rose is professor of geography and urban affairs at the University of Wisconsin-Milwaukee. His research interests have emphasized the evolution of black spatial residential patterns and patterns of black interregional migration. More recently he has begun to express an interest in behavioral environments with attention directed to violent environments. Rose is currently the president of the Association of American Geographers.

John P. Ross is senior academic resident in public finance with the Advisory Commission on Intergovernmental Relations, in the taxation and public finance section of the Commission staff. He is on leave from the Virginia Polytechnic Institute and State University, where he is an assistant professor in the division of environmental and urban systems. Ross is co-author of *Productivity in the Local Government Sector* as well as several articles and reports on general revenue sharing and local government needs.

Seymour Sacks is professor of economics at the Maxwell School, Syracuse University, Syracuse, New York. He has co-authored *City Schools/Suburban Schools: A History of Fiscal Conflict* (Syracuse University Press, 1972) and *Metropolitan America: Fiscal Patterns and Governmental Systems* (Free Press, 1967) with Alan K. Campbell.

John Shannon is an assistant director with the Advisory Commission on Intergovernmental Relations, in charge of the taxation and public finance section of the Commission Staff. Shannon has coordinated the preparation of over twenty reports, including one of the Advisory Commission's most recent publications, *General Revenue Sharing, An ACIR Re-Evaluation.*

James L. Sundquist, a senior fellow at the Brookings Institution in Washington, is the author of several books, two of which deal with national growth policy: *Making Federalism Work* (1969), and *Dispersing Population: What America Can Learn from Europe* (1975), both published by Brookings. In government service before joining Brookings, he worked on questions of growth policy as Deputy Under Secretary of Agriculture, as a member of the President's Appalachian Regional Commission, and as a Senate legislative assistant.

Wilbur R. Thompson has been a member of the Economics faculty of Wayne State University since 1950 and is currently teaching part-time both at Wayne State and at the Gannett Urban Journalism Center of Northwestern University. Thompson is the author of *A Preface to Urban Economics* (1965), and co-author of *An Econometric Model of Postwar State Industrial Development* (1959), as well as numerous articles on urban and regional economics in various professional journals.

Ralph R. Widner is president of the Academy for Contemporary Problems, a public policy research center, established by seven national organizations of state and local officials. He was formerly executive director of the Appalachian Regional Commission.